THE BEST OF
FOOD&WINE
1992 COLLECTION

THE BEST OF
FOOD&WINE
1992 COLLECTION

American Express
Publishing Corporation
New York

Cover: Baked Goat Cheese Salad with Garlic Coutons (p. 163)

THE BEST OF FOOD & WINE/1992 COLLECTION
Editor/Designer: Kate Slate
Assistant Editor: Martha Crow
Illustrations: Hong Chow

AMERICAN EXPRESS PUBLISHING CORPORATION
Editor in Chief/Food & Wine: Carole Lalli
Art Director/Food & Wine: Elizabeth Woodson
Marketing Director: Elizabeth Petrecca
Production Manager: Joanne Maio

Published by American Express Publishing Corporation
1120 Avenue of the Americas, New York, New York 10036

Manufactured in the United States of America

ISBN 0-916103-16-1

TABLE OF CONTENTS

FOREWORD

Recipes are the heart and soup of this magazine. We pride ourselves on putting those recipes into some intelligent context: the fascinating cultural background of a particular food style, the traditions connected to food, the regional specialties that define a place. In our journalistic way we try to keep up with our readers' lives—the realities of today's fast-paced, hard-pressed-for-time, two-job family and their health and fitness concerns. And some story ideas are inspired by what smart chefs are doing or by the once-exotic ingredients that manage to find their way into local supermarkets.

In the end, though, it all comes down to the recipes, the core information you expect from us every month. This explains why we think of our test kitchen as our nerve center. The challenge there is to bring every recipe as close to fail-safe as possible. We know there are forces beyond our control: the quality of the ingredients you will find, the vagaries of your ovens or even a printer's error that may slip by and foil our efforts. Short of that, we are confident that a published recipe in *Food & Wine* is one that is going to work as well in your kitchen as it did in ours.

This volume represents the work of all those writers, editors and recipe testers whose determined efforts resulted in this year's *The Best of Food & Wine*. It is the ninth such collection to have been compiled, and we send it along sure that it too will bring satisfaction, variety and pure pleasure to your table. That is no less than our readers deserve.

Carole Lalli

Carole Lalli
Editor in Chief

FOOD & WINE'S VINTAGE RATINGS
1980-1990

COMPILED BY ELIN McCOY & JOHN FREDERICK WALKER

	1980	1981	1982	1983	1984
Red Bordeaux	**5** Small-scale, lightweight, pleasant. Drink up.	**7½** Full, attractive wines. Drink now.	**9½** Rich, massive. Start sampling now.	**7½** Firm, powerful. Start drinking.	**6** Small-scale, firm. Start drinking.
Sauternes	**7** Attractive, small-scale. Start drinking.	**7** Well-balanced wines. Start drinking.	**6½** Variable. Best are big. Start drinking.	**9** Rich, classic wines. Start drinking.	**5½** Mixed quality. Few good. Drink now.
Red Burgundy	**6** Mostly light wines. Drink up.	**5½** Variable vintage. Thin. Drink up.	**7** Big, soft wines. Drink now.	**8** Variable. Some very good. Start drinking.	**5½** Variable, thin wines. Drink up.
White Burgundy	**5** Variable; the best are attractive. Drink up.	**7½** Attractive wines. Drink up.	**8** Big, rich wines. Drink now.	**7½** Good, rich wines. Drink up.	**7** Crisp wines. Some fine. Drink up.
Napa/Sonoma Cabernet Sauvignon	**8** Powerful, tannic. Drink now.	**8** Variable. Many attractive. Drink now.	**7½** Balanced, attractive. Drink now.	**7** Good, but not great. Drink up.	**8** Big, rich, powerful. Start drinking.
Napa/Sonoma Chardonnay	**8½** Balanced but fading. Drink up.	**7** Soft, ripe wines. Fading. Drink up.	**7½** Variable, light, fading. Drink up.	**7** Good moderate year. Drink up.	**7** Good full wines. Drink up.
Barolo & Barbaresco	**6** Uneven. Best are well-balanced, attractive. Drink now.	**6½** Firm, solid wines. Drink now.	**8½** Big, powerful wines. Start drinking.	**7** Lighter vintage. Drink up.	**5½** Light, variable. Drink up.
Chianti	**6** Uneven; small-scale, fading. Drink up.	**7** Good, firm wines. Drink up.	**7½** Attractive, early maturing. Drink up.	**7** Attractive, lighter. Drink up.	**5** Spotty. Avoid.
Germany	**5** Light & lean. Drink up.	**7** Well-balanced, attractive. Drink up.	**7** Soft, fruity. Drink up.	**9** Excellent year. Marvelous late-harvest wines. Drink now.	**6½** Lean & tart. Drink up.
Vintage Porto	**7** Light but good. Start sampling.	No vintage declared.	**7** Soft, well-balanced. Start drinking.	**8** Firm, solid wines. Sample in 2-6 years.	No vintage declared.

The following ratings and comments reflect a variety of opinions, including our own, on the quality and character of various categories of wines from recent vintages. The ratings—0 for the worst, 10 for the best—are averages, and better or worse wine than indicated can be found in each vintage. Assessments of the most current vintages are more predictive and hence less exact than those of older vintages.

Scores are based on a wine's quality at maturity. A lower-rated but mature wine will often be superior to a higher-rated but immature wine. When-to-drink advice is based on how such wines seemed to be developing in mid-1991, and presumes good storage. The earliest date suggested for consumption applies to the lesser wines of the vintage, which will mature faster than the finest examples of the year.

1985	1986	1987	1988	1989	1990
8½ Soft, delicious, elegant. Start sampling.	9 Powerful, tannic wines. Try in 4 years.	7 Flavorsome, but lightweight. Start drinking.	7½ Good, but somewhat tannic. Wait.	9 Variable. Some big fleshy wines. Wait.	8½ Promising, big, flavorsome.
7½ Soft, full, good. Sample now.	8½ Luscious & rich. Sample now.	5½ Light, lean; few good wines.	9 Superlative, rich, concentrated. Start sampling.	8½ Rich & powerful. Start sampling.	8½ Rich, ripe wines.
9½ Glorious, rich, round. Start drinking.	7 Variable; mostly light wines. Start drinking.	7½ Stylish wines. Start drinking.	9 Concentrated, fruity, classic. Start sampling.	8 Big fruity wines. Start sampling.	9 Promising; very rich and round.
8 Big but soft. Start drinking.	9 Crisp, balanced, classic. Start drinking.	7 Light, round, soft. Drink now.	7½ Good; some very fine. Start drinking.	8½ Attractive, fruity. Start sampling.	7½ Some good rich wines.
9½ Brilliant, firm & elegant. Start sampling.	8 Deep, rich & powerful. Start sampling.	8½ Dark, firm, balanced. Start sampling.	7½ Mixed vintage; some concentrated. Sample.	7½ Variable quality; start sampling.	8 Good, ripe vintage.
8 Lovely, balanced. Drink up.	9 Crisp, leaner style. Drink up.	8 Elegant & crisp. Drink now.	8½ Good, fruity. Start drinking.	7 Uneven quality. Some good. Start drinking.	8½ Excellent, balanced.
9 Splendid, rich. Wait 2 years.	8 Well-balanced & fruity. Start sampling.	7½ Round, fruity. Start drinking.	8½ Rich, full wines. Wait.	9 Big, powerful, promising wines. Wait.	8½ Very promising; ripe & full.
9½ Superb balance & flavor. Start drinking.	7½ Good quality. Start drinking.	7 Average quality. Drink now.	8½ Ripe, fruity, balanced. Sample now.	7 Fruity, pleasant wines.	8½ Excellent but early maturing.
8½ Excellent. Drink now.	6 Light, crisp wines. Drink now.	7 Mostly lean, some fine. Drink now.	9 Outstanding, full-flavored, fruity. Start sampling.	9 Full, rich & fruity. Start sampling.	9 Promising; ripe vintage.
9 Marvelous, deep & fruity. Wait 8 years.	No vintage declared.	No vintage declared.	No vintage declared.	No vintage declared.	———

APPETIZERS & FIRST COURSES

APPETIZERS & FIRST COURSES

CUMIN AND CAYENNE SPICED CASHEWS

Be sure to let these nuts cool completely and become crisp before putting them away. They can be stored for up to one week in an airtight container.

Makes About 3 Cups

1 egg white
1 pound salted roasted cashews
    (about 3 cups)
⅓ cup sugar
2 teaspoons cumin
2 teaspoons coarse (kosher) salt
1½ teaspoons cayenne pepper

1. Preheat the oven to 250°. In a medium bowl, whisk the egg white with 1 tablespoon of water until foamy. Add the cashews and toss to coat. Transfer the nuts to a strainer, shake and then let drain for at least 2 minutes.

2. Meanwhile, wipe out the bowl and add the sugar, cumin, salt and cayenne. Add the nuts and toss to coat.

3. On a large baking sheet with sides, spread the nuts out in a single layer. Bake for 40 minutes. Stir with a spatula and spread the nuts out again. Reduce the temperature to 200° and bake for 30 minutes longer, until dry.

4. Using a spatula, loosen the nuts from the baking sheet. Let them cool to room temperature on the sheet.

—*Kathy Casey*

• • •

CHEESE CRISPS

This recipe makes plenty to serve with drinks. If you'll be filling take-home bags too, make a triple batch.

Makes About 3½ Dozen

1 cup all-purpose flour
¼ teaspoon salt
¼ teaspoon crushed red pepper
1 stick (4 ounces) unsalted butter,
    softened
3 cups grated sharp Cheddar cheese
    (12 ounces)
1 tablespoon chopped fresh thyme
1 cup Rice Krispies

1. Preheat the oven to 350°. In a food processor, combine the flour, salt and crushed red pepper; pulse until blended. Add the butter, cheese and thyme and pulse just until a dough forms; bits of cheese should still be visible.

2. Transfer the dough to a large bowl and gently fold in the Rice Krispies. Working with a scant tablespoon at a time, roll the dough into balls. Place the balls about 2 inches apart on ungreased cookie sheets. Flatten slightly with your fingertips into 1½-inch rounds.

3. Bake the crisps for about 15 minutes, or until firm to the touch and just beginning to brown. Let cool on the sheets for 1 to 2 minutes, then transfer to wire racks to cool completely. Store in airtight containers for up to 1 day or freeze, well wrapped, for up to 1 month.

—*Elizabeth Woodson*

• • •

EGGPLANT BRUSCHETTA WITH PROSCIUTTO

12 First-Course Servings

1 large eggplant (1¼ pounds), peeled
1 tablespoon table salt
⅔ cup extra-virgin olive oil
Six ¾-inch slices from a round loaf of
    country bread
1 large garlic clove, halved
Sea salt
Freshly ground pepper
6 ounces very thinly sliced
    prosciutto, cut crosswise into
    ½-inch-wide strips
2 tablespoons finely chopped parsley

1. Trim and slice the eggplant into twelve ½-inch rounds. Place the rounds in a colander, sprinkling them with the table salt. Place a plate on top to weight them; set the colander over a bowl and set aside for 1 hour.

2. Prepare a medium charcoal fire or preheat the broiler. Remove the eggplant from the colander and blot off excess moisture and salt with paper towels. Brush both sides of the eggplant slices with some of the oil. Grill for 10 to 15 minutes, turning once, until brown and crusty on the outside and soft on the inside. Alternatively, broil the eggplant slices on a large baking sheet.

3. Cut the bread slices in half and brush very lightly on both sides with some of the remaining olive oil. Grill the bread, turning once, for about 2 minutes, until toasted. Alternatively, broil the bread. Rub each slice with the cut garlic clove and brush with olive oil.

4. Place a slice of eggplant on a slice of bread. Top with a little sea salt and pepper and the prosciutto. Sprinkle with the parsley.

—*David Rosengarten*

• • •

RED POTATOES WITH GORGONZOLA CREAM, BACON AND WALNUTS

12 Servings

¼ *cup walnut halves*
½ *cup sour cream*
¼ *cup Gorgonzola cheese, at room temperature (about 3 ounces)*
½ *teaspoon freshly ground black pepper*
⅛ *teaspoon hot pepper sauce*
6 *slices of bacon, cut into ¼-inch dice*
12 *small red potatoes (about 1¼ pounds)*
1 *tablespoon olive oil*
½ *teaspoon coarse (kosher) salt*
2 *tablespoons minced chives*

1. Preheat the oven to 400°. Place the walnuts on a baking sheet and roast for about 5 minutes, until fragrant and lightly toasted. Let cool, then chop coarsely and set aside.

2. In a small bowl, using a fork, combine the sour cream and Gorgonzola until well blended. Stir in ¼ teaspoon of the black pepper and all of the hot pepper sauce. (*The recipe can be made to this point up to 1 day ahead. Store the walnuts in an airtight container at room temperature. Cover and refrigerate the Gorgonzola cream until about 30 minutes before serving.*)

3. Heat a medium skillet over moderately high heat until hot. Add the ba-con and cook, stirring often, until crisp and brown, 4 to 5 minutes. Using a slotted spoon, transfer the bacon to paper towels to drain. Set aside.

4. In a roasting pan, toss the potatoes with the oil, salt and the remaining ¼ teaspoon black pepper until well coated. Bake for 25 to 30 minutes, until tender. Keep warm.

5. To serve, stir the reserved bacon and toasted walnuts into the Gorgonzola cream. Halve the potatoes lengthwise. If necessary, cut a small slice from the rounded (skin) side of the potato halves so that they can stand. Place the potato halves on a platter and dollop each one with a teaspoon of the filling. Sprinkle the chives on top and serve.

—*Kathy Casey*

• • •

AVOCADO AND ROASTED CORN GUACAMOLE WITH TOASTED CORN TORTILLAS

You can make a larger batch of the toasted tortillas and store them in an airtight container for future nibbling.

8 Servings

1 *cup fresh or thawed frozen corn kernels*
¼ *cup plus 3 tablespoons corn oil*
2 *large avocados, preferably Hass, cut into ½-inch dice*
1 *large tomato, cut into ¼-inch dice*
¼ *cup chopped fresh coriander (cilantro)*
2 *tablespoons minced red onion*
About 1 *teaspoon minced fresh or pickled jalapeño pepper*
1 *teaspoon minced garlic*
2 *tablespoons fresh lime juice*
1 *teaspoon cider vinegar*
1½ *teaspoons coarse (kosher) salt*
¼ *teaspoon cumin*
2 *packages (7 ounces each) 5-inch corn tortillas, quartered*
Table salt, for sprinkling

1. Preheat the oven to 450°. On a baking sheet, toss the corn with 1 tablespoon of the oil. Roast, tossing often, for 7 to 8 minutes, until golden. Let cool, then transfer to a medium bowl.

2. Fold in the avocado, tomato, coriander, onion, jalapeño and garlic. Stir in the lime juice, vinegar, coarse salt, cumin and 2 more tablespoons of the corn oil. Cover and refrigerate for up to 6 hours.

3. Meanwhile, in a large bowl, toss the tortilla pieces with the remaining ¼ cup oil. Arrange half of the tortillas in a single layer on 2 large baking sheets. Bake for 5 to 6 minutes, or until crisp. Remove from the oven, transfer to paper towels and season with table salt. Repeat with the remaining tortillas and more salt. Serve warm with the cold guacamole.

—*Kathy Casey*

• • •

MINI-SCALLION BISCUITS WITH SMOKED SALMON SPREAD

If there is any Smoked Salmon Spread left over, slather it on bagels.

12 Servings

1 *small red onion, quartered lengthwise and thinly sliced crosswise*

13

APPETIZERS & FIRST COURSES

¼ cup seasoned rice wine vinegar
2 cups all-purpose flour
2 teaspoons baking powder
1¼ teaspoons salt
¼ teaspoon dry mustard
¼ teaspoon freshly ground black pepper
⅛ teaspoon cayenne pepper
⅓ cup vegetable shortening
2 large scallions, minced
1 tablespoon chopped flat-leaf parsley
¾ cup plus 3 tablespoons milk
Smoked Salmon Spread (recipe follows)
3-inch chunk of a European seedless cucumber, unpeeled and thinly cut crosswise into 24 slices
24 small dill sprigs, for garnish

1. In a medium bowl, toss the sliced onion and vinegar. Cover and set aside to marinate at room temperature for at least 30 minutes and up to 3 hours.

2. Preheat the oven to 425°. In a large bowl, sift the flour, baking powder, salt, mustard, black pepper and cayenne. Using a pastry blender or 2 knives, cut in the shortening until the mixture resembles coarse crumbs. Stir in the scallions and parsley. Add the milk and, using a fork, stir together until a soft, moist dough forms.

3. Turn the dough out onto a lightly floured surface. With floured hands, pat the dough into a ¾-inch-thick, 8-by-10-inch rectangle. Sprinkle a little more flour on top. Using a 1½-inch round or fluted biscuit cutter, cut out 24 rounds of dough. Place the rounds with their sides touching on a baking sheet. Bake for about 20 minutes, until golden.

4. Transfer the baking sheet to a rack and let the biscuits cool for about 10 minutes. Split in half horizontally. Spread ½ teaspoon of the Smoked Salmon Spread on the bottom half of each biscuit. Layer a slice of cucumber and then another teaspoon of the Salmon Spread on top. Garnish each biscuit with some of the reserved pickled onion and a dill sprig. Arrange the biscuits on a serving platter, replace the top half of the biscuits slightly askew and serve immediately.

—Kathy Casey

• • •

SMOKED SALMON SPREAD

For this recipe, use inexpensive smoked salmon trimmings sold at deli counters.

Makes About 1¼ Cups

6 ounces cream cheese, at room temperature
6 ounces thinly sliced smoked salmon
1 teaspoon prepared white horseradish
2 teaspoons fresh lemon juice
1 teaspoon minced fresh dill

1. In a food processor, combine the cream cheese and half of the smoked salmon and process until smooth. Add the horseradish and lemon juice and process, scraping down as necessary, until smooth. Add the dill and process briefly until incorporated.

2. Transfer the spread to a small bowl. Finely chop the remaining salmon and stir it into the spread until distributed. (*The spread can be refrigerated, covered, for up to 2 days. Bring to room temperature before serving.*)

—Kathy Casey

• • •

WARM MEDITERRANEAN EGGPLANT DIP WITH HERBED PITA CRISPS

12 Servings

1 medium eggplant (about 14 ounces), trimmed and sliced crosswise ½ inch thick
3 tablespoons olive oil
2 teaspoons coarse (kosher) salt
1 medium yellow squash
1 medium zucchini
5 medium white mushrooms, cut into ¼-inch dice
½ of a medium red onion, finely chopped
1 tablespoon minced garlic
2 tablespoons dry red wine
2 teaspoons balsamic vinegar
1 jar (6 ounces) marinated artichoke hearts, chopped, liquid reserved
1 large tomato, cut into ¼-inch dice
¼ teaspoon crushed red pepper
⅛ teaspoon freshly ground black pepper
¼ cup tomato sauce, preferably homemade
¼ cup finely diced pimiento
1 tablespoon drained capers
1 tablespoon minced Calamata olives
2 tablespoons minced fresh basil
1 tablespoon minced flat-leaf parsley
Herbed Pita Crisps (recipe follows)

1. Preheat the oven to 450°. Spread the eggplant slices on a baking sheet and drizzle 1½ tablespoons of the oil on top. Season with 1 teaspoon of the salt. Bake for 25 minutes. Let cool slightly, then chop finely and set aside.

2. Meanwhile, using a sharp knife, cut a ¼-inch-thick lengthwise slice of the skin of the yellow squash. Place the squash cut-side down on a work surface and cut off the remaining skin in ¼-inch-thick lengthwise slices all around. Cut the skin slices into ¼-inch dice. Repeat with the zucchini. (Save the squash pulp for another use.) Set aside.

3. In a large, heavy, nonreactive saucepan, heat the remaining 1½ tablespoons olive oil over moderately high heat until shimmering, 1 to 2 minutes. Add the mushrooms, onion and diced yellow squash and zucchini. Cook, stirring occasionally, until the vegetables begin to brown lightly, about 4 minutes. Add the garlic and cook, stirring, for 1 minute.

4. Stir in the red wine, vinegar and artichoke liquid. Add the tomato, crushed red pepper, black pepper and the remaining 1 teaspoon salt. Cook, stirring, until the tomato softens and the mixture is thick, about 5 minutes.

5. Stir in the artichoke hearts, tomato sauce, pimiento, capers, olives, basil, parsley and the reserved eggplant. Reduce the heat to moderately low and cook until heated through, about 3 minutes. Serve warm with Herbed Pita Crisps. *(This dip can be made up to 2 days ahead; reheat before serving.)*

—*Kathy Casey*

• • •

HERBED PITA CRISPS

This recipe can easily be multiplied to yield larger batches. These triangles can be made in advance and stored in airtight containers.

Makes 40 Crisps

3 tablespoons olive oil
1 teaspoon basil
½ teaspoon coarse (kosher) salt
5 large whole wheat pita bread pockets (12-ounce bag), each cut into eighths

1. Preheat the oven to 450°. In a large bowl, combine the olive oil, basil and salt. Add the pita pieces and toss to coat well.

2. On 1 or 2 baking sheets, spread out the pita pieces in a single layer. Bake for 4 minutes. Using tongs, turn the pita pieces over and continue baking for 4 more minutes, until golden and crisp. *(The recipe can be made up to 2 days ahead. Let cool, then store in an airtight container. If necessary, recrisp in a 400° oven for 2 minutes.)*

—*Kathy Casey*

• • •

LEMONY HUMMUS

Makes About 2½ Cups

1 can (15 ounces) chickpeas with their liquid
¼ cup plus 3 tablespoons fresh lemon juice (about 3 lemons)
½ cup tahini* (sesame paste)
1 tablespoon vegetable oil
1 medium garlic clove, minced

2 tablespoons minced parsley
½ teaspoon cumin
⅛ teaspoon cayenne pepper
Salt
*Available at Middle Eastern markets and most supermarkets

Combine all the ingredients except the salt in a blender or food processor and puree until almost smooth. Season with salt to taste.

—*Linda Burum*

• • •

ANCHOIADE

Anchoïade is excellent with slivers of fennel, endive leaves, radishes, celery and carrot sticks, cauliflower florets and scallions. Or spread it on baguette halves and broil briefly. This pungent dip is inclined to separate, so stir it up as you eat it.

Makes About 1 Cup

1 cup extra-virgin olive oil
8 to 10 anchovy fillets, drained and coarsely chopped
3 garlic cloves, crushed through a press
3 tablespoons red wine vinegar
1 tablespoon fresh thyme blossoms or 1 teaspoon dried
Freshly ground pepper
1 tablespoon chopped fresh basil

15

In a small, heavy, nonreactive saucepan, warm the oil over low heat. Stir in the anchovies and mash them into the oil. Whisk in the garlic, vinegar and thyme. Do not let the mixture boil. Season with pepper to taste; stir in the basil.

—*Mireille Johnston*

• • •

SAUTEED CHEVRE ON A BED OF RED PEPPER MARMALADE

For this dish, you will need a small log-shaped chèvre, such as domestic or French Montrachet. I prefer the French, which is softer and melts more quickly than the American variety. Serve this first course with sliced toasted French bread.

8 Servings

1 cup fresh bread crumbs (from about 4 slices of white bread)
1 tablespoon olive oil
One 11-ounce log Montrachet goat cheese, sliced ½ inch thick and chilled
½ teaspoon freshly ground pepper
1 egg, beaten
Red Pepper Marmalade (p. 263)
8 small clusters of fresh basil

1. Spread the bread crumbs evenly on a baking sheet and let them air-dry for several hours. Alternatively, dry the crumbs in a preheated 250° oven for 5 minutes; set aside to let cool.

2. In a large nonstick skillet, heat the oil over moderately low heat until hot. Sprinkle the cheese slices with the pepper. Quickly dip each slice in the beaten egg and then in the bread crumbs. Fry the cheese, turning once, until golden brown, about 5 minutes per side. The cheese should be slightly melted inside and crisp on the outside. (*The cheese can be prepared to this point up to 3 hours ahead and kept at room temperature. Reheat in a 350° oven for 5 minutes before serving.*)

3. Arrange the Red Pepper Marmalade on 8 plates and place 1 slice of cheese on top. Garnish with the basil and serve immediately. Pass the remaining cheese separately.

—*Lydie Marshall*

• • •

CRUNCHY COCONUT SHRIMP WITH PINEAPPLE-JALAPENO SALSA

12 Servings

24 large shrimp
½ cup all-purpose flour
1 egg
¼ cup pineapple juice
¼ cup milk
1½ teaspoons salt
½ teaspoon baking powder
¼ teaspoon cayenne pepper
3½ cups vegetable oil
3½ cups (about 10½ ounces) unsweetened shredded coconut*
Pineapple-Jalapeño Salsa (p. 261)
*Available at health food stores

1. Shell the shrimp, leaving the tails intact. Place a shrimp on its side on a work surface and hold it down flat with one hand. Using a small sharp knife and beginning at the head end, slit the shrimp along the back to just above the tail, cutting about two-thirds of the way through. Scrape out the exposed vein. Open the shrimp and press flat. Repeat with the remaining shrimp and set aside.

2. In a blender, combine the flour, egg, pineapple juice, milk, salt, baking powder and cayenne and blend at medium speed. Transfer the batter to a medium bowl. Add the shrimp and set aside.

3. In a deep medium skillet, heat the oil over moderately high heat to 350° on a deep-fat thermometer.

4. Meanwhile, place the coconut in a bowl. One by one, remove the shrimp from the batter, shake off any excess and press into the coconut to adhere.

5. Working in batches of 6, fry the shrimp in the hot oil, turning once, until golden brown all over, about 2 minutes. Using tongs, transfer to paper towels to drain. Repeat with the remaining shrimp. Arrange the shrimp on a warmed platter and serve the Pineapple-Jalapeño Salsa alongside.

—*Kathy Casey*

• • •

Anchoïade (p. 15) with crudités.

Above, Dungeness Crab Cakes with Sherry Aioli (p. 24).
Right, Warm Shrimp Salad with Tarragon Dressing (p. 160)
and Provençal Eggplant Pizza (p. 26).

RICHMOND PEPPERED SHRIMP

These peppered shrimp are tradition-ally cooked in their shells for more shrimp flavor, but in this recipe I have removed them for easy eating. They may be eaten hot or cold; just remember to provide toothpicks and lots of napkins.

Makes About 48

12 medium scallions
2 tablespoons minced fresh ginger
2 garlic cloves, minced
2 tablespoons prepared horseradish
2 tablespoons sherry or Madeira
2 tablespoons dark soy sauce*
½ cup tomato sauce, preferably homemade
2 tablespoons dark brown sugar
3 tablespoons peanut oil
3 pounds large shrimp (about 48), shelled and deveined
½ teaspoon crushed red pepper
1 to 2 teaspoons freshly ground black pepper, to taste
2 tablespoons minced parsley
2 tablespoons minced fresh coriander (cilantro)
*Available at Asian markets

1. Thinly slice the scallions, sepa-rating the green and white portions; set the green aside for garnish. In a medium bowl, combine the sliced white portions with the ginger, garlic, horseradish, sherry, soy sauce, tomato sauce and brown sugar. Mix well and set aside.

2. In a wok or large skillet, heat the oil over moderately high heat until hot but not smoking. Add the shrimp and cook, stirring, until just pink, about 3 minutes.

3. Stir in the sauce mixture, crushed red pepper and black pepper. Cook, stir-ring frequently, until the shrimp are opaque and the sauce is heated through, 3 to 5 minutes. Transfer to a large serv-ing dish or platter and serve hot or at room temperature, garnished with the parsley, coriander and the reserved sliced scallion greens. *(The recipe can be pre-pared up to 1 day ahead and refrigerated, covered. Reheat, if desired, and garnish just before serving.)*

—Susan Costner

• • •

FISH TOSTADAS

Tostadas—toasted tortillas with top-pings—can be made with almost any leftovers for an instant, informal, out-of-hand meal. At Rosa Mexicano, they make such variations as tostadas topped with an escabeche of chicken; or mashed black beans along with crème fraîche, chiles and lettuce, or any leftover fish, as outlined in the recipe below.

♟ The tostadas are best matched by a crisp, herbaceous white, such as 1988 Viansa Sauvignon Blanc or 1988 Mc-Dowell Fumé Blanc from California.

Makes 6 Tostadas

½ cup vegetable oil
Six 6- to 8-inch corn tortillas
2 (packed) teaspoons chopped pickled jalapeño pepper plus 1 teaspoon of liquid from the jar
12 ounces cooked hake, grouper, red snapper or other lean whitefish
1 medium onion, finely chopped
1 medium tomato, seeded and diced
¼ cup olive oil
2 tablespoons fresh lemon juice
2 tablespoons chopped fresh coriander (cilantro), plus more for garnish
½ teaspoon salt
¼ teaspoon freshly ground black pepper
⅓ cup mascarpone cheese or crème fraîche
½ head of romaine lettuce, finely shredded
1 medium avocado, preferably Hass, cut into ½-inch dice

1. In a small skillet, heat the veg-etable oil over moderately high heat un-til hot, 2 to 3 minutes. One at a time, fry the tortillas, turning gently several times with tongs, until golden all over, about 2 minutes total. Drain on paper towels and let cool to room temperature.

2. Meanwhile, using a large knife, chop and mash the jalapeño until it be-comes a paste. Set aside.

3. Flake the fish into a large bowl. Add the onion and toss gently. One at a time, toss in the jalapeño paste, jalapeño juice, tomato, olive oil, lemon juice and coriander. Season with the salt and black pepper and set aside.

4. Spread each tortilla with a heaping teaspoon of mascarpone. Sprinkle the lettuce on top. Add the fish mixture next, spreading it out a little to the sides. Top with the avocado cubes and some more chopped coriander. Dollop the

Potato Ravioli with Sautéed Foie Gras and Cherry Sauce (p. 27).

remaining mascarpone in the middle of each tostada and serve.

—Josefina Howard, Rosa Mexicano, New York City

• • •

STEAMED CLAMS

2 Servings

½ cup dry white wine
3 medium shallots, minced
2 garlic cloves, thinly sliced
1 teaspoon coarsely ground pepper
2 sprigs of flat-leaf parsley plus 1 tablespoon, minced
4 tablespoons unsalted butter
2 dozen littleneck clams, well scrubbed
Lemon wedges, for serving

1. In a large nonreactive saucepan, combine the wine, shallots, garlic, pepper, parsley sprigs and 2 tablespoons of the butter. Bring to a boil over moderately high heat and add the clams. Cover and cook, stirring once or twice, until most of the clams have opened, 5 to 7 minutes.

2. Transfer the opened clams to 2 shallow bowls and cover to keep warm. Cook the remaining clams for 1 to 2 minutes longer. Add the open clams to the bowls; discard any that do not open.

3. Add the remaining 2 tablespoons butter to the liquid in the saucepan and boil over moderately high heat to reduce slightly, about 2 minutes. Strain the broth over the clams through a fine sieve. Sprinkle with the minced parsley and serve hot, with the lemon wedges on the side.

—Mark Peel, Campanile, Los Angeles

• • •

DEVILS ON HORSEBACK

These satisfying hors d'oeuvres are best when served freshly made. You can fry them while your guests are with you in the kitchen enjoying a glass of wine. Get a head start by making the cornmeal batter several hours ahead or the day before.

Makes 36

1½ cups all-purpose flour
½ cup yellow cornmeal
1½ teaspoons baking powder
2 eggs, lightly beaten
1¼ cups beer
18 thin slices of smoked bacon, halved crosswise (1¼ pounds)
1 quart peanut oil
3 dozen freshly shucked oysters
Lemon wedges, for serving

1. In a medium bowl, combine the flour, cornmeal and baking powder. Make a well in the center. Add the eggs and beer and whisk until smooth. Cover the batter and refrigerate for at least 2 hours or overnight.

2. In a large skillet, working in batches, cook the bacon over moderate heat, turning frequently, until the fat is rendered and the bacon just begins to brown but is still soft, about 4 minutes. Drain on paper towels and let cool.

3. In a deep fryer, wok or large skillet, heat the oil to 350° over moderately high heat, about 10 minutes. Meanwhile, wrap each oyster in a piece of bacon and secure with a toothpick.

4. Stir the batter. Working in batches, dip the oysters in the batter and then drop into the hot oil. Fry several at a time, turning, until golden brown and crisp, about 4 minutes. Drain them on paper towels. Serve immediately with the lemon wedges.

—Susan Costner

• • •

CORN-FRIED OYSTERS WITH TOMATO-TEQUILA SALSA AND CHIPOTLE CREAM

These oysters are spiked with a chile-hot salsa and served on the half shell.

4 Servings

4 large tomatoes (about 1¾ pounds total), seeded and cut into ¼-inch dice
3 serrano chiles*, seeded and minced
1 small red onion, finely diced
¼ cup tequila
1 teaspoon fresh lime juice
1 teaspoon finely chopped fresh coriander (cilantro)
⅛ teaspoon freshly ground black pepper
1¾ teaspoons salt
1 cup boiling water
2 dried chipotle chiles*
½ cup sour cream
3 tablespoons buttermilk
24 freshly shucked large oysters, concave shells reserved
About ¼ cup vegetable oil
½ cup cornmeal
*Available at Latin American markets

1. In a large bowl, mix the tomatoes with the serrano chiles, onion, tequila, lime juice, coriander, black pepper and 1½ teaspoons of the salt. Set the salsa aside for about 1 hour to allow the flavors to blend.

2. Meanwhile, in a small bowl, pour the boiling water over the chipotle chiles. Set aside until softened, about 20 minutes.

3. Drain the chipotle chiles. Halve lengthwise and discard the stems, cores and seeds. In a food processor, puree the chiles for 1 minute. Scrape the puree into a small bowl and mix in the sour cream until thoroughly blended. Stir in the buttermilk and the remaining ¼ teaspoon salt and set aside until needed.

4. Rinse out the oyster shells, dry well and place them on a serving platter or on individual plates. Place a rounded tablespoon of the reserved salsa in each shell and set aside.

5. In a large skillet, heat ¼ cup of the oil over high heat until it begins to shimmer, about 2 minutes. Meanwhile, place the cornmeal on a plate. Dredge 12 of the oysters in the cornmeal, shaking off any excess. Add them to the skillet and fry, turning once, until golden brown all over, about 4 minutes. Drain on paper towels. If necessary, add a little more oil to the pan and heat until shimmering. Dredge and fry the remaining 12 oysters.

6. Place the fried oysters on the salsa in each oyster shell and garnish with some of the reserved chipotle cream.

—Mark Militello, Mark's Place,
North Miami

• • •

THAI-SCENTED CHICKEN KEBABS

This recipe can also be prepared with large shrimp or pieces of pork tenderloin. The key to making delicious kebabs is long marination, so allow enough time.

Makes 24 Kebabs

1 can (14 ounces) unsweetened coconut milk*
½ cup fresh lime juice (from 4 limes)
2 tablespoons minced fresh ginger
2 medium garlic cloves, minced
2 tablespoons fish sauce (nuoc mam)*
2 tablespoons sugar
1½ tablespoons minced fresh lemon grass*
1½ tablespoons soy sauce
1 tablespoon Oriental sesame oil
½ teaspoon crushed red pepper
½ teaspoon salt
2 pounds skinless, boneless chicken breasts, cut into 48 one-inch pieces
12 medium scallions, white part only, halved crosswise
2 large red bell peppers—cored, seeded and cut into 24 triangles
1 tablespoon black sesame seeds*
½ cup fresh coriander (cilantro) leaves, chopped
*Available at Asian markets

1. Place 24 wooden skewers, 6 or 8 inches long, in a shallow pan. Cover with hot water and let soak for at least 1 hour.

2. In a small nonreactive saucepan, whisk the coconut milk with the lime juice, ginger, garlic, fish sauce, sugar, lemon grass, soy sauce, sesame oil, crushed red pepper and salt. Bring to a boil over moderately high heat and boil for 1 minute. Set aside to cool.

3. Assemble the kebabs: thread 1 piece of chicken, 1 piece of scallion and a second piece of chicken onto 1 end of a skewer. Pierce the tip of the skewer laterally through each red pepper triangle so that it looks like an arrowhead point. Repeat with the remaining skewers. Place the kebabs crosswise side by side in a 9-by-13-inch nonreactive baking dish so that the bare ends of the skewers rest on the edge of the dish. Pour the cooled marinade over the kebabs. Cover and refrigerate, turning once, for at least 12 hours and up to 24 hours.

4. Preheat the broiler. Arrange half of the kebabs on a broiler pan with the bare ends of the skewers toward the outside. Broil for 8 minutes, turning once, until the chicken is cooked through and the peppers are charred. Transfer the kebabs to a platter. Repeat with the remaining kebabs. Sprinkle the sesame seeds and coriander on top and serve warm.

—Kathy Casey

• • •

ROCK SHRIMP HASH CAKES
WITH MANGO

Allen Susser of Chef Allen's is famous for his tropical fruit and seafood combinations. This recipe calls for rock shrimp, which are abundant off the coast of Florida and available in most fish markets. These shrimp have an extremely hard shell, which makes shelling difficult; luckily, they are most often sold shelled.

5 Luncheon or 10 First-Course Servings

*1 large or 2 medium waxy potatoes
    (½ pound total)*
*½ pound shelled rock shrimp,
    deveined and cut into ½-inch
    pieces*
*1 plum tomato—peeled, seeded and
    finely diced*
*3 tablespoons snipped chives, plus
    more for garnish*
*1 tablespoon chopped fresh basil,
    plus sprigs for garnish*
1 tablespoon Cognac or other brandy
*2 teaspoons potato starch or
    cornstarch*
⅛ teaspoon cayenne pepper
3 egg whites, well beaten
1 large mango
Olive oil, for frying
1 garlic clove
Lime wedges, for serving

1. Preheat the oven to 400°. Wash and dry the potato. Prick it all over with a fork. Bake for 1 hour or until tender. Set aside to cool completely, then peel. Grate the potato on the large holes of a hand grater.

2. In a large bowl, combine the shrimp, tomato, chives, chopped basil, Cognac, potato starch and cayenne; mix well. Fold in the grated potato. Stir in the egg whites until evenly distributed. Let the mixture stand for 10 minutes.

3. Meanwhile, using a small sharp knife, peel the mango. Slice the fruit lengthwise parallel to the flat side of the pit on both sides, about ¼ inch thick. Halve each mango slice or cut into small dice. Set aside.

4. Pour ¼ inch of the olive oil into a large cast-iron skillet. Add the garlic clove and cook over high heat for 30 seconds; discard the garlic. Reduce the heat to moderately high and when the oil begins to shimmer, scoop a scant ¼ cup of the hash mixture into the skillet. Flatten slightly with the back of a spoon into a patty about 2½ inches in diameter. Form 4 more patties in the pan and fry, turning once with a spatula, until crisp, browned, and the shrimp turn bright pink, 2 to 3 minutes per side. (Be careful when turning because the patties are fragile.) Transfer the hash cakes to paper towels to drain. Using a slotted spoon, remove any hash particles from the oil. If necessary, add enough oil to reach a ¼-inch depth and heat over moderately high heat. Form and fry the remaining hash cakes.

5. To serve, top each cake with the reserved mango and some snipped chives. Garnish each plate with a lime wedge and a basil sprig.

—*Allen Susser, Chef Allen's, Miami*

• • •

DUNGENESS CRAB CAKES
WITH SHERRY AIOLI

Dungeness crabs, large crabs from the waters of the Pacific Northwest, have mild, sweet, tender meat. The crabs are available in markets across the country.

12 Servings

*1 pound Dungeness or lump
    crabmeat, picked over to remove
    any shell or cartilage*
1¾ cups dry bread crumbs
1 celery rib, finely diced
2 medium scallions, minced
½ of a small carrot, minced
2 teaspoons chopped flat-leaf parsley
2 eggs, lightly beaten
¼ cup mayonnaise
2 tablespoons sour cream
1½ teaspoons minced garlic
1½ teaspoons fresh lemon juice
1 teaspoon Worcestershire sauce
½ teaspoon sherry vinegar
½ teaspoon coarse (kosher) salt
¼ teaspoon dry mustard
⅛ teaspoon hot pepper sauce
*⅛ teaspoon freshly ground black
    pepper*
*3 cups peanut or vegetable oil, for
    frying*
Lemon wedges, for serving
Sherry Aioli (p. 264)

1. In a medium bowl, toss the crabmeat, ¼ cup of the bread crumbs, the celery, scallions, carrot and parsley. Stir in 2 tablespoons of the beaten eggs.

2. In a small bowl, whisk the mayonnaise, sour cream, garlic, lemon juice, Worcestershire sauce, vinegar, salt, mustard, hot pepper sauce and black pepper. Stir into the crabmeat mixture.

3. Place the remaining 1½ cups bread crumbs in a shallow bowl. In a separate bowl, beat 2 teaspoons of water into the remaining beaten eggs. Scoop up a heaping tablespoon of the crab mixture and form into a patty about ½ inch thick. Dip it into the beaten eggs, turn to coat and shake off any excess. Then dip it into the bread crumbs and turn to coat evenly. Place on a baking sheet lined with wax paper. Continue with the remaining crab mixture to form 24 small cakes. (*The crab cakes can be prepared to this point up to 2 hours ahead; cover and refrigerate.*)

4. In a deep medium skillet, heat the oil over moderately high heat until hot but not smoking (350° to 375° on a deep-fat thermometer). Six at a time, fry the crab cakes, turning once, until golden brown, about 4 minutes. Transfer to paper towels to drain briefly. Then transfer to a rack over a baking sheet; keep warm in a low oven while frying the remaining cakes.

5. Transfer them to a serving platter, garnish with lemon wedges and pass the Sherry Aioli alongside.

—*Kathy Casey*

• • •

FENNEL TART WITH ROSEMARY

The assertive flavors of fennel and rosemary, napped with extra-virgin olive oil, are mellowed by long, slow cooking. Studs of briny black olives set off the sweetness of the filling, and the whole wheat crust with rosemary adds a pleasing, earthy quality.

🍷 The fennel tart would be nicely contrasted by Champagne, such as Louis Roederer Brut Premier, or a fine, fruity West Coast sparkling wine, such as Domaine Ste. Michelle Brut or Domaine Chandon Blanc de Noirs.

10 to 12 Servings

1 cup unbleached all-purpose flour
½ cup whole wheat flour
3 tablespoons chopped fresh rosemary
¼ teaspoon table salt
6½ tablespoons cold unsalted butter, cut into pieces
¼ cup cold vegetable shortening, cut into small pieces
¼ cup ice water
3¾ pounds fennel bulbs with greens (about 7 small)
1 large onion, halved lengthwise
¼ cup extra-virgin olive oil
2 teaspoons coarse (kosher) salt
½ teaspoon freshly ground pepper
1½ teaspoons chopped flat-leaf parsley, for garnish
12 large imported black olives, such as Calamata or Gaeta, pitted and halved

1. Preheat the oven to 350°. In a food processor, combine the all-purpose and whole wheat flours with 1½ tablespoons of the rosemary and the table salt. Add 4½ tablespoons of the butter and the vegetable shortening; process until the mixture resembles coarse meal.

2. With the machine on, gradually add the ice water and process just until a dough forms. Flatten the dough into a 6-inch disk, cover tightly and refrigerate until chilled, or for up to 2 days.

3. On a lightly floured surface, roll the dough into a 13-inch circle, ¼ inch thick. Carefully lay the dough in an 11-by-1-inch fluted tart pan with a removable bottom and pat the dough into place. Trim the excess dough from the rim. Prick the bottom with the tines of a fork. Line the dough with aluminum foil and fill with pie weights or dried beans. Bake in the middle of the preheated oven for 10 minutes. Remove the foil and weights and bake the tart shell for 25 minutes, or until well browned. Transfer to a rack and let cool to room temperature.

4. Trim the tops of the fennel bulbs. Coarsely chop enough of the greens to yield ¼ cup; set aside. Halve the bulbs. Cut out the central cores and slice the fennel crosswise into ¼-inch strips; set aside in a large bowl.

5. Slice the onion halves lengthwise into ¼-inch strips and add to the fennel. Stir in 3 tablespoons each of the olive oil and reserved fennel greens, the remaining 1½ tablespoons rosemary and the coarse salt and pepper.

APPETIZERS & FIRST COURSES

6. In a large heavy saucepan, melt the remaining 2 tablespoons butter over moderate heat. Stir in the fennel and onion. Cover and cook, stirring occasionally, until the vegetables are very soft and jamlike, about 40 minutes.

7. Uncover, increase the heat to moderately high and cook until the mixture caramelizes, about 5 minutes. Season with salt and pepper to taste and let cool to room temperature. (*The filling can be prepared to this point up to 2 days ahead. Cover the filling and refrigerate. Let return to room temperature before proceeding.*)

8. Spread the fennel filling in the tart shell. Drizzle the remaining 1 tablespoon olive oil over the tart and sprinkle the parsley and the remaining 1 tablespoon fennel greens on top. Decoratively arrange the olive halves on the tart. Carefully remove the side of the pan and transfer the tart to a platter. Serve at room temperature.

—*Sheila Lukins*

• • •

PROVENCAL EGGPLANT PIZZA

If you can't find Japanese eggplants, choose the smallest eggplants you can find and peel them.

Makes Two 11-Inch Pizzas

About ¾ cup corn oil, for frying
¼ cup all-purpose flour, for dredging
1½ pounds Japanese eggplants, sliced into ½-inch rounds
Salt
1 pound fresh mozzarella cheese, shredded
2 cups shredded fresh basil leaves
2 tablespoons minced garlic
2 balls of Light Whole Wheat Bread Dough (recipe follows)
2 tablespoons olive oil

1. Pour ¼ inch of the corn oil into a large heavy skillet and heat over high heat until just smoking, about 4 minutes. Meanwhile, place the flour in a paper bag and dredge the eggplant slices. Shake off any excess flour. Working in 3 batches, fry the eggplant until golden brown on both sides, about 2 minutes. Add more corn oil to the skillet between batches if necessary. Drain the eggplant thoroughly on paper towels, patting to blot off excess oil. Season with salt.

2. In a medium bowl, toss the mozzarella with the basil, garlic and 2 teaspoons salt. (*The recipe can be prepared to this point up to 4 hours ahead.*)

3. Preheat the oven to 450°. Heavily flour a work surface and roll and stretch each ball of Light Whole Wheat Bread Dough into a 13-inch circle. Transfer the dough to 2 heavy black cookie sheets or pizza pans.

4. Spread the mozzarella mixture over each piece of dough to within 1 inch of the rims. Arrange the fried eggplant rounds on the cheese and drizzle 2½ teaspoons of the olive oil over each pizza. Fold in the dough rims to just cover the edge of the filling and brush the rims with the remaining 1 teaspoon olive oil. Bake the pizzas for about 20 minutes, until the cheese is melted and the crusts are golden brown.

—*Lydie Marshall*

• • •

LIGHT WHOLE WHEAT BREAD DOUGH

This makes more than you will need for the pizzas. Freeze the third ball of dough for later, or bake it in a small loaf pan. You will need to prepare the starter, which gives a good flavor to this bread, at least two days before making the dough.

Makes Enough for Two Pizzas and One Small Loaf

1 envelope (¼ ounce) plus 1 teaspoon active dry yeast
1½ teaspoons sugar
About 4½ cups all-purpose flour
½ cup whole wheat flour
2 teaspoons coarse (kosher) salt

1. In a medium bowl, sprinkle 1 teaspoon of the yeast over ½ cup of warm water. Mix in ½ teaspoon of the sugar and set aside until foamy, about 10 minutes. With a wooden spoon, gradually mix in 1½ cups of the all-purpose flour. When the starter can no longer be mixed with the spoon, turn it out onto a lightly floured work surface and knead until the flour is thoroughly incorporated. Place the starter in a clean bowl, cover with plastic wrap, and set aside in a warm place for 2 days.

2. In a large bowl, sprinkle the envelope of yeast over 1½ cups of warm water. Stir in the remaining 1 teaspoon sugar and set aside until foamy, about 10 minutes. Gradually stir in 1 cup of the all-purpose flour and all of the whole wheat flour. Stir in the starter and the coarse salt. Gradually stir in as much of the remaining 2 cups all-purpose flour as necessary to make a sticky dough.

3. Turn the dough out onto a floured work surface and knead, adding more flour if necessary, until smooth and still a bit sticky, about 10 minutes. Transfer the dough to a large, lightly oiled mixing bowl. Cover with plastic wrap and set aside in a warm place until doubled in bulk, about 1 hour.

4. Punch down the dough and cut it into 3 even pieces. Knead each piece on a lightly floured surface and shape into a ball. Place the balls on a lightly oiled cookie sheet, cover with plastic wrap and refrigerate. (*The dough can be prepared up to 3 days before baking.*)

—*Lydie Marshall*

• • •

VIETNAMESE RAVIOLI WITH CHILE-LIME SAUCE

Because chile seeds are very hot, the number added to the mortar in Step 3 will depend on your heat tolerance.

4 First-Course Servings

¼ *pound ground pork*
½ *small onion, minced*
Salt and freshly ground black pepper
½ *cup vegetable oil*
4 *large shallots, very thinly sliced*
1 *dried red Chinese chile*
2 *teaspoons distilled white vinegar*
1½ *teaspoons sugar*
1 *garlic clove, minced*
2½ *tablespoons fresh lime juice*
1½ *tablespoons fish sauce (nuoc mam)**
32 *gyoza skins or wonton wrappers**
1 *egg, beaten*
½ *cup thin, halved cucumber slices (from ¼ European cucumber)*
**Available at Asian markets*

1. In a small skillet, cook the pork and onion over moderate heat, mashing the pork into small even pieces with a wooden spoon until the pork is cooked through and the onion is translucent, about 5 minutes. Season with salt and black pepper. Transfer the mixture to a shallow dish and set aside to cool.

2. In a medium saucepan, heat the oil over high heat. Add the shallots, stir once and cook until brown and crisp, about 4 minutes. Turn off the heat and, using a slotted spoon, transfer the shallots to paper towels to drain.

3. In a mortar, pound the chile with the seeds (see headnote) to a coarse powder. Alternatively, using a large knife, finely chop the chile to a coarse powder; transfer to a small bowl.

4. In a small nonreactive saucepan, heat the vinegar over high heat until hot, about 30 seconds. Pour the hot vinegar over the chile powder and let steep for 3 minutes. Add the sugar and garlic and pound to a paste with the pestle or a wooden spoon.

5. Stir in the lime juice, fish sauce and ¼ cup of water. Mix well and set aside at room temperature for 20 minutes to let the flavors develop.

6. Working with 4 at a time, spread the *gyoza* skins flat on a work surface. Using your fingertips, moisten the perimeter of each skin with some of the beaten egg. Put a scant tablespoon of the reserved pork filling neatly in the center. Cover with another *gyoza* skin and press down to expel any trapped air and to seal the edges. Cover with a damp kitchen towel until ready to cook. Repeat with the remaining skins and filling.

7. Bring a large saucepan of salted water to a boil over high heat. Drop in the ravioli 2 at a time, stirring gently with a wooden spoon to prevent them from sticking to each other, until they have all been added. Boil over high heat, stirring occasionally, until translucent and tender, about 5 minutes. Transfer gently to a colander to drain, tossing a few times to remove all the water.

8. To assemble, stir the reserved chile-lime sauce and put about 2 tablespoons on a serving platter. To prevent the hot ravioli from sticking, transfer 4 at a time to the platter, drizzling more sauce over each addition. Sprinkle any remaining sauce on top. Scatter the reserved fried shallots and the cucumber slices over the ravioli and serve at once.

—*Marcia Kiesel*

• • •

POTATO RAVIOLI WITH SAUTEED FOIE GRAS AND CHERRY SAUCE

At Olives restaurant in Boston's Charlestown, the chef-owner, Todd English, forms these ravioli into crescents. If you want to take a shortcut here, use 24 *gyoza* skins, available at Asian markets, in place of homemade pasta.

6 Servings

2 *red bliss, California white or other waxy potatoes (6 ounces)*
½ *teaspoon salt*
½ *cup sour cream*
½ *teaspoon freshly ground pepper*
½ *cup dried sour cherries* (about 2½ ounces)*
Boiling water
Pasta Dough (recipe follows)

3 tablespoons unsalted butter
½ cup finely chopped onion or
    shallots
½ cup balsamic vinegar
¼ cup dry red wine
1 tablespoon sugar
¼ cup veal or poultry demiglace (see
    Note, p. 103)
1 egg, lightly beaten
½ cup instant blending flour
1½ pounds chilled fresh duck foie
    gras, sliced crosswise ½ inch thick
    (see Note, p. 103)
*Available at specialty food shops

1. Place the potatoes in a small saucepan and add enough water to cover them by 1 inch. Add ¼ teaspoon of the salt and bring to a boil over high heat. Reduce the heat to moderately high and boil the potatoes until fork tender, about 20 minutes. Drain and place in a bowl. Using a potato masher, mash the potatoes coarsely with their skins. Stir in the sour cream, pepper and the remaining ¼ teaspoon salt. Set aside.

2. Place the dried cherries in a heat-proof bowl and cover with boiling water. Set aside to plump for 30 minutes.

3. Meanwhile, cut the Pasta Dough into 4 pieces. Flatten 1 section of the dough with the heel of your hand and roll it through a pasta machine set on the widest notch. Continue rolling the dough through the machine at progressively narrower settings until you reach the thinnest. The dough should be about 25 inches long. Lay the dough on a kitchen towel and cover to prevent it from drying out. Repeat with the remaining 3 pieces of Pasta Dough.

4. In a medium nonreactive skillet, melt 1 tablespoon of the butter. Add the onion and cook over moderately low heat until very soft but not brown, about 5 minutes. Add the vinegar and wine, increase the heat to moderately high and bring to a rapid boil. Add the sugar and cook, stirring occasionally, until the liquid reduces by half, about 2 minutes. Remove from the heat.

5. Drain the plumped cherries and add them to the skillet along with the demiglace. Bring to a boil and simmer until the sauce reduces slightly and is syrupy, about 2 minutes longer. Season with salt and pepper to taste and set aside.

6. Place 1 strip of the pasta dough on a work surface and, using a 4-inch round cutter, stamp out 6 rounds. Repeat with the remaining strips to make a total of 24 rounds. Scoop 1 tablespoon of the potato filling into the center of 12 rounds. Brush the edges with the beaten egg and top with the remaining 12 rounds. Press around the edges with a fork to seal.

7. Bring a large pot of lightly salted water to a boil. Meanwhile, place the instant blending flour on a plate and season with salt and pepper. Quickly dip all the foie gras slices in the flour.

8. Heat a large heavy skillet over high heat until almost smoking. One by one, add the foie gras slices to the hot pan without crowding and cook until crisp and browned, about 30 seconds per side. Drain on paper towels and keep warm while you cook the rest.

9. Working in 2 batches, cook the ravioli in the boiling water until they float to the surface and are al dente, 4 to 5 minutes; drain well on paper towels.

10. While the ravioli cook, bring the cherry sauce back to a boil. Remove from the heat and swirl in the remaining 2 tablespoons butter.

11. To serve, place 2 ravioli on one side of each warmed plate. Lay several slices of the foie gras on the other side and spoon about 1½ tablespoons of the cherry sauce over the ravioli. Serve hot.

—*Todd English, Olives,
Charlestown, Massachusetts*

• • •

PASTA DOUGH

Makes About ¾ Pound

2 cups unbleached all-purpose flour
¼ teaspoon salt
3 eggs
2 teaspoons olive oil

In a food processor, combine the flour and salt and process briefly to blend. In a small bowl, lightly beat the eggs with the oil. With the motor running, add the beaten eggs to the flour and process until the dough just begins to form a ball. Transfer the dough to a work surface and knead until smooth and elastic, 1 to 2 minutes. Shape the dough into a disk, cover with a towel and let rest for 15 minutes before rolling out.

—*Todd English, Olives,
Charlestown, Massachusetts*

• • •

SOUPS & STEWS

SOUPS & STEWS

FRESH TOMATO SOUP

This uncooked soup is a great starter, especially if you can get excellent tomatoes. Serve it with buttered and lightly toasted, thinly sliced French bread.

8 Servings

4 pounds juicy, ripe tomatoes, coarsely chopped
2 tablespoons fresh lemon juice
Salt
¼ cup fresh ricotta cheese
¼ cup plain yogurt
Small mint sprigs, for garnish

1. In a food processor, puree half the tomatoes until smooth. Strain the puree into a large bowl, pressing on the solids with a rubber spatula to extract the pulp and juices. Repeat with the remaining tomatoes. Discard the skins and seeds. Season the soup with the lemon juice and salt to taste. Cover and refrigerate for several hours or up to 1 day.

2. In a food processor, combine the ricotta and yogurt and puree until smooth. Season with salt to taste. To serve, stir the soup and pour into 8 bowls. Garnish with 1 tablespoon of the ricotta mixture and a mint sprig.

—*Lydie Marshall*

• • •

MUSHROOM-BARLEY SOUP

The inspiration for this soup came from my sister-in-law Linda. Mine is a meatless version.

8 to 10 Servings

2 tablespoons vegetable oil
2 medium onions, coarsely chopped
2 large celery ribs, cut into small dice
¾ cup pearl barley
½ ounce imported dried mushrooms, rinsed and coarsely chopped
½ large head of escarole, coarsely chopped (4 cups packed)
1 can (16 ounces) Italian plum tomatoes, drained and coarsely chopped, juice reserved
2 large carrots, sliced ¼ inch thick
½ pound fresh white mushrooms, sliced ¼ inch thick
Salt and freshly ground pepper

1. In a large nonreactive saucepan, heat the oil over moderate heat. Add the onions and cook, stirring occasionally, until softened and lightly browned, about 10 minutes. Add the celery and cook until slightly softened, about 3 minutes.

2. Stir in 2 quarts of water. Add the barley, dried mushrooms, escarole and the tomatoes with their juice. Increase the heat to high and bring to a boil. Reduce the heat to moderately low, cover and simmer gently until the barley is tender and the broth is flavorful, about 1 hour and 15 minutes.

3. Add the carrots and simmer, covered, for 15 minutes. Add the fresh mushrooms and continue to simmer, covered, for 30 minutes. Season with

the salt and pepper to taste. Serve immediately. (*The soup can be made up to 2 days ahead. Let cool, cover and refrigerate. Reheat slowly before serving.*)

—*Susan Shapiro Jaslove*

• • •

SIMPLE STEW OF LIMA BEANS, CORN AND TOMATOES

Frozen baby lima beans are simply frozen fresh beans with no preservatives or added salt.

4 to 6 Servings

1 package (10 ounces) frozen baby lima beans
¼ of a medium onion
1 parsley sprig plus 2 tablespoons chopped
1 small bay leaf
4 whole black peppercorns
Salt
1¾ cups fresh corn kernels (from 4 to 6 ears) or 1 box (10 ounces) frozen corn
2 tablespoons unsalted butter
6 medium scallions, white and tender green, thinly sliced
1 tablespoon minced basil
½ teaspoon chopped fresh mint
1 large tomato—peeled, seeded and coarsely chopped
½ teaspoon freshly ground pepper
3 tablespoons sour cream
3 tablespoons chopped fresh coriander (cilantro)

1. In a medium saucepan, combine the lima beans, onion, parsley sprig, bay leaf, peppercorns and a pinch of salt. Add 2 cups of water and bring to a boil over high heat. Reduce the heat to moderate and simmer until the beans are tender, about 15 minutes. Drain the beans in a colander set over a bowl and reserve the broth. Discard the bay leaf, parsley, onion and peppercorns.

2. If using fresh corn, boil the kernels in lightly salted boiling water until tender, 3 to 5 minutes. Drain and rinse briefly; set aside.

3. In a large saucepan, melt the butter over moderate heat. Add the scallions and cook, stirring occasionally, until softened, about 2 minutes. Add the lima beans, chopped parsley, basil, mint, fresh or frozen corn, reserved bean broth and ½ teaspoon of salt. Bring to a simmer and cook for 3 minutes.

4. Add the tomato and cook until the tomato is soft and the broth just coats the vegetables, about 5 minutes. Remove from the heat. Stir in the ground pepper, sour cream and coriander. Season with salt to taste and serve warm.

—*Deborah Madison*

• • •

FLAGEOLET AND LEEK SOUP

Pale green, gray-green and shale white, flageolets are the Champagne, the ne plus ultra, of dried beans. Their appearance is as delicate as their taste. If you like, serve this soup with croutons fried in butter or light olive oil.

4 Servings

1½ cups dried flageolet beans (10½ ounces), picked over
2 medium leeks—greens coarsely chopped, whites quartered lengthwise and thinly sliced crosswise
1 large carrot, coarsely chopped
1 small onion, chopped
1 celery rib, chopped
5 parsley sprigs
10 whole black peppercorns
2 bay leaves
1½ teaspoons salt
2 tablespoons unsalted butter
3 tablespoons minced parsley or chervil
½ cup milk or cream
¼ teaspoon freshly ground pepper

1. In a large saucepan, soak the beans in plenty of cold water for at least 6 hours or overnight. Pour off the water, re-cover the beans with fresh water and bring to a boil. Boil the beans vigorously for 5 minutes. Drain the beans in a colander and rinse well to remove any scum.

2. In a stockpot, combine the leek greens, carrot, onion, celery, parsley sprigs, peppercorns, 1 of the bay leaves and 1 teaspoon of the salt. Add 10 cups of water and bring to a boil over high heat. Reduce the heat to moderately low and simmer for 25 minutes. Strain the broth and reserve. Discard the solids.

3. In a large saucepan, melt the butter over moderately high heat. Add the leek whites, the remaining bay leaf, 2 tablespoons of the minced parsley and ½ cup of water. Simmer for 5 minutes. Add the beans and the reserved vegetable broth and bring to a boil over high heat. Reduce the heat to moderately low, cover partially and simmer

very gently until the beans are almost tender, about 1¼ hours.

4. Add the remaining ½ teaspoon salt and continue cooking until the beans are very tender, about 10 minutes longer. If the liquid evaporates, add enough boiling water to keep the beans amply covered.

5. Remove 1 cup of beans and broth from the pot and puree in a blender or food processor until smooth. Gently stir the puree back into the beans in the pot. Stir in the milk. Reheat the soup and season with salt to taste. Stir in the pepper and the remaining 1 tablespoon minced parsley just before serving.

—*Deborah Madison*

• • •

SANTA FE FARMERS' MARKET STEW

This stew was inspired by the bustling Santa Fe farmers' market one day last fall. The green chiles were in, as well as pinto beans and dried red chiles; and squash, tomatoes, peppers and onions were everywhere. With some cooked greens, a tomato salad and tortillas or corn bread, this stew makes a fine meal. ♟ Beer might be an obvious choice, but if choosing wine, a big red with forthright flavors would be a good match for this hearty, thick, chili-style stew. An Australian Shiraz, such as 1986 Taltarni, or a California Petite Sirah, such as 1986 Louis M. Martini Reserve, come to mind.

4 Servings

1 cup dried anasazi or pinto beans (7 ounces), picked over

SOUPS & STEWS

3 medium tomatoes (about 1½ pounds)

5 large, unpeeled garlic cloves

1 tablespoon sunflower oil

1 small onion, finely chopped

1 medium zucchini or yellow summer squash, cut into ⅓-inch dice

1 green bell pepper, cut into ¼-inch dice

2 to 3 teaspoons pure ground red chile, such as New Mexican

1 can (16 ounces) white or yellow hominy, rinsed and drained

1 teaspoon salt

½ cup chopped fresh coriander (cilantro)

1 cup sour cream, for serving

1½ cups shredded sharp Cheddar cheese (4 ounces), for serving

1. In a large saucepan, soak the beans in plenty of cold water for at least 6 hours or overnight. Pour off the water, re-cover the beans with fresh water and bring to a boil. Boil the beans vigorously for 5 minutes. Drain the beans in a colander and rinse well to remove any scum.

2. Return the beans to the saucepan, add 8 cups of water and bring to a boil over high heat. Reduce the heat to moderately low and simmer until the beans are tender, about 1¼ hours. Drain the beans, reserving the broth.

3. Heat a heavy, medium, nonreactive skillet over moderate heat. Place the tomatoes in the skillet and roast, turning frequently, for about 20 minutes; the skins will brown lightly and the tomatoes will soften partially. Peel the tomatoes and transfer them to a blender.

4. In the same pan, roast the garlic cloves, turning frequently, until browned and the garlic is soft, 12 to 15 minutes.

Peel the garlic cloves and add them to the blender. Puree until smooth.

5. In a medium casserole, warm the oil over moderately high heat. Add the onion, zucchini and bell pepper and cook for 3 minutes. Stir in the ground chile and 1 cup of the reserved bean broth. Bring to a rapid simmer and cook until the liquid is reduced by half, about 5 minutes.

6. Stir in the beans, hominy, salt, tomato-and-garlic puree and 1 cup of the bean broth. Bring to a boil over moderately high heat. Reduce the heat to moderately low and cook for 20 minutes. Season with salt to taste. Stir in the coriander and serve the stew in bowls. Pass the sour cream and Cheddar cheese separately.

—*Deborah Madison*

• • •

THREE-MUSHROOM SOUP WITH PORT AND TARRAGON

6 Servings

1 cup dried porcini mushrooms (1 ounce), rinsed in cold water

About 8 cups chicken stock or canned low-sodium broth

4 tablespoons unsalted butter

1 medium shallot, minced

½ pound fresh shiitake mushrooms, stems discarded, caps sliced into ¼-inch strips

½ pound white button mushrooms, sliced lengthwise ¼ inch thick

¼ cup all-purpose flour

¼ cup vintage or tawny port

½ teaspoon tarragon

Salt and freshly ground pepper

6 tablespoons crème fraîche, for serving

3 tablespoons snipped chives, for garnish

1. In a large nonreactive saucepan, combine the dried porcini mushrooms and chicken stock and bring to a boil over high heat. Reduce the heat to moderate and simmer, partially covered, for 40 minutes. Pour the broth through a cheesecloth-lined strainer. Rinse the mushrooms in the strainer to remove any grit. Cut off any tough stems. Coarsely chop the mushrooms; set the mushrooms and broth aside.

2. Wipe out the saucepan. Add the butter and melt over moderate heat. Add the shallot and cook, stirring, until softened, about 1 minute.

3. Add the sliced shiitake and white button mushrooms and increase the heat to moderately high. Cook, stirring frequently, until the mushrooms have exuded most of their liquid, 5 to 7 minutes.

4. Reduce the heat to moderately low and sprinkle the mushrooms with the flour. Cook for 1 minute, stirring constantly and scraping the bottom of the saucepan with a wooden spoon. Gradually whisk in the reserved mushroom broth and the port. Add the reserved porcini and the tarragon and bring to a boil over high heat. Reduce the heat to moderate and simmer, partially covered, for 20 minutes. Season with salt and pepper to taste. (*The recipe can be prepared to this point up to 2 days ahead. Reheat over moderately low heat, stirring frequently, before serving.*) Serve the soup piping hot, garnished with the crème fraîche and a sprinkling of chives.

—*Rick Rodgers*

• • •

GRILLED CORN SOUP WITH CILANTRO AND ANCHO CHILE CREAMS

This colorful soup from Stephan Pyles is a fine-tuned blend of southwestern flavors. The Cilantro Cream and Ancho Chile Cream are swirled in at the end, not only for flavor but for a striking presentation.

8 Servings

8 ears of corn, shucked but with the last, inner layer of husk left on
4 cups chicken stock or canned low-sodium broth
2 medium carrots, chopped
1 large celery rib, chopped
2 small onions, chopped
4 medium garlic cloves
2 serrano chiles, seeded and minced
2 cups heavy cream
Salt
Cilantro Cream (at right)
Ancho Chile Cream (at right)

1. Prepare a slow charcoal fire or preheat the oven to 375°. Arrange half of the corn on the grill and cook on one side for 5 minutes; turn the corn and grill until browned and flecked with black spots, about 5 minutes more. Alternatively, arrange all the corn on a large heavy baking sheet and roast for 7 minutes. Turn and continue roasting until the leaves are dry and falling off, about 7 minutes more. Set aside to cool, then remove and discard the remaining leaves and silk from the corn.

2. In a large saucepan, combine the chicken stock, carrots, celery, onions, garlic and serrano chiles and bring to a boil over moderate heat. Reduce the heat to low and simmer until the vegetables soften slightly, about 5 minutes.

3. Meanwhile, using a small knife, cut the kernels from the ears. Add the kernels to the stock and simmer for 10 minutes.

4. In a blender, puree the contents of the saucepan in two batches until smooth. Strain the soup back into the saucepan. (*The soup can be prepared to this point and refrigerated, covered, overnight.*)

5. Bring the soup to a simmer over moderate heat. Stir in the heavy cream and season to taste with salt. Reduce the heat to low and simmer for 5 minutes. Ladle the soup into warmed, shallow soup bowls. For each serving swirl in about 1 tablespoon each of the Cilantro and Ancho Chile Creams. Serve hot.

—Stephan Pyles,
Routh Street Cafe, Dallas

• • •

CILANTRO CREAM

Makes About ⅔ Cup

5 large spinach leaves, stemmed
1 cup (loosely packed) fresh coriander (cilantro) leaves
3 tablespoons half-and-half or milk
2 tablespoons sour cream or crème fraîche

1. In a small saucepan, bring 2 cups of water to a boil over high heat. Add the spinach and cook, stirring, until soft, about 1 minute. Drain and plunge into cold water. Squeeze the spinach dry by wringing it in a clean kitchen towel.

2. In a blender, puree the fresh coriander, spinach and half-and-half. Blend until smooth. Strain through a fine sieve into a bowl. Add the sour cream.

—Stephan Pyles,
Routh Street Cafe, Dallas

• • •

ANCHO CHILE CREAM

Ancho chiles are dried, ripened poblano chiles and are available at Spanish markets or specialty food stores.

Makes About ⅔ Cup

1 small ancho chile—halved, stemmed and seeded
3 tablespoons half-and-half or milk
2 tablespoons sour cream or crème fraîche

1. Heat a small skillet over high heat until quite hot, then add the ancho chile and toast until fragrant, about 30 seconds per side. Transfer the chile to a small bowl and add hot water to cover. Set aside for 10 minutes to soften.

2. Pat the chile dry and place in a blender with the half-and-half; puree until smooth. Strain the mixture through a fine sieve into a bowl; whisk in the sour cream.

—Stephan Pyles,
Routh Street Cafe, Dallas

• • •

SOUPS & STEWS

PRESSURE-COOKER CURRIED SWEET POTATO SOUP

This soup has a strong kick of fresh ginger to it.

Makes About 6 Cups

2 tablespoons unsalted butter
2 medium onions, coarsely chopped
2 celery ribs, finely chopped
1 tablespoon minced fresh ginger
1½ pounds sweet potatoes—peeled, halved lengthwise and sliced crosswise ¼ inch thick
1 tablespoon mild curry powder
Dash of cayenne pepper (optional)
4 cups Pressure-Cooker Chicken Stock (p. 269) or canned low-sodium broth
Salt and freshly ground pepper
Plain yogurt, for serving

1. In a 6-quart pressure cooker, melt the butter over moderately high heat. Add the onions, celery and ginger and cook, stirring frequently, until softened, about 2 minutes.

2. Add the sweet potatoes, curry powder, cayenne, stock and a pinch of salt. Lock the lid in place and bring to high (15 pounds) pressure over high heat. Cook for 4 minutes. Quick-release the pressure according to the manufacturer's instructions, or set the pot under cold running water until all pressure is released. Remove the lid, tilting it away from you to allow excess steam to escape.

3. In a food processor, puree the soup in one or two batches. Season to taste

with salt and pepper and serve hot, garnished with a dollop of yogurt.

—*Lorna Sass*

• • •

PARSNIP VICHYSSOISE

This rich, thick soup is the result of taking a little creative license with the classic vichyssoise. Parsnips provide a sweet contrast to the potatoes, leeks and garlic, and the flavors are brightened with a dash of lemon juice. I think this soup is best when served just warmed through.

12 Servings

2 large leeks, white parts only, halved lengthwise and sliced crosswise ½ inch thick
2½ pounds parsnips, peeled and cut into 2-inch chunks
3 medium boiling potatoes (¾ pound), peeled and cut into 2-inch chunks
8 large garlic cloves, lightly crushed
1 large onion, halved and thinly sliced
2 tablespoons light brown sugar
1 teaspoon ground cardamom
6 cups chicken stock or canned low-sodium broth
1 stick (4 ounces) unsalted butter, cut into small pieces
¼ cup fresh lemon juice
3 cups milk
2 cups heavy cream
Salt and freshly ground pepper
12 whole chives plus 2 tablespoons snipped, for garnish

1. Preheat the oven to 350°. In a large shallow roasting pan, combine the leeks, parsnips, potatoes, garlic and

onion. Sprinkle with the sugar and cardamom and stir to combine. Pour 2 cups of the stock over the vegetables and dot with the butter. Cover tightly with aluminum foil and bake for 2 hours, until the vegetables are very tender, stirring the vegetables occasionally.

2. Transfer the vegetables and any liquid to a large nonreactive saucepan. Add the remaining 4 cups stock and the lemon juice and bring to a boil over high heat. Reduce the heat to moderately low, cover and simmer for 20 minutes.

3. Working in small batches, transfer the vegetables and liquid to a blender or a food processor and puree until just smooth. (*The soup can be prepared to this point up to 2 days ahead. Let cool, cover and refrigerate. It may be necessary to thin the soup with a little stock or water before reheating.*)

4. To finish the soup, add the milk and cream and cook over moderately low heat, stirring occasionally, until warmed through. Do not boil. Season with salt and pepper to taste. Serve in a tureen or in shallow bowls garnished with the whole chives and a sprinkling of the snipped.

—*Sheila Lukins*

• • •

SPICY GRILLED SHRIMP SOUP WITH CILANTRO

This light, sea-bright summer soup is served cool but offers a hot spicy kick; adjust the number of chiles called for in the recipe according to your threshold.

6 Servings

36 large shrimp in their shells (about 1½ pounds)
Salt and freshly ground black pepper
½ cup plus 1 tablespoon extra-virgin olive oil
1 large red bell pepper, finely diced
½ of a medium green bell pepper, finely diced
4 to 5 fresh chiles, such as serrano, seeded and minced
½ pound plum tomatoes, finely diced
½ cup finely chopped fresh coriander (cilantro)
2 garlic cloves, minced
⅓ cup fresh lime juice (about 3 limes)

1. Preheat the broiler. Remove all but the last segment of shell on the tail end of each shrimp. Reserve the shells. Using a small sharp knife, butterfly the shrimp by slicing lengthwise down the middle—leaving the tails intact—without cutting all the way through; spread the shrimp flat. Devein the shrimp, season well with salt and black pepper and moisten with 1 teaspoon of the olive oil.

2. Transfer the shrimp to a baking sheet and broil 5 inches from the heat, turning once, just until pink and loosely curled, 1 minute per side. Transfer to a medium bowl and toss with 1 teaspoon of the olive oil; set aside.

3. In a heavy medium saucepan, heat 1 teaspoon of the olive oil over moderately high heat. Add the shrimp shells and cook, stirring, until lightly browned, about 3 minutes. Add 4 cups of water, bring to a boil and cook until the liquid reduces by half, about 10 minutes. Strain the shrimp stock into a measuring cup. If you have more than 2 cups, boil again to reduce the liquid. Refrigerate to cool.

4. In a large bowl, combine the red and green bell peppers with the chiles, tomatoes, coriander and garlic. Stir in the lime juice, then stir in the remaining ½ cup olive oil in a steady stream. Slowly pour in the cooled shrimp stock, stirring. Season to taste with salt and black pepper.

5. In each of 6 wide, shallow bowls, arrange 6 shrimp in a circle with their tails resting against each other in the center. Stir the soup well and ladle it all around the shrimp. Serve cool.

—David Rosengarten

• • •

LOBSTER-CORN BISQUE

Reduced lobster stock is the base for this slightly sweet, flavorful soup, which gets its creaminess from pureed fresh corn.

Makes About 8 Cups

Salt
Two 1½-pounds lobsters
1 cup dry white wine
1 large sweet onion (such as Vidalia, Maui or Walla Walla), cut into 1-inch chunks
2 medium carrots, scrubbed but not peeled and cut into 1-inch chunks
1 large celery rib, cut into 1-inch chunks
10 whole black peppercorns
½ teaspoon thyme
6 cups fresh corn kernels (from 8 to 9 ears) or 3 packages (10 ounces each) frozen corn kernels, thawed
¼ teaspoon freshly ground black pepper
1 large tomato—peeled, seeded and cut into ¼-inch dice

½ cup (lightly packed) basil leaves, finely shredded
Homemade croutons (see Note)

1. In a large nonreactive pot or flameproof casserole, combine 1½ teaspoons of salt and 6 quarts of water. Bring to a boil over moderately high heat. Plunge the lobsters headfirst into the water, cover and cook for 17 minutes. Using tongs, transfer the lobsters to a plate and set aside to cool for 15 minutes. Reserve the cooking liquid.

2. Giving a twist and a pull, break off the tails and claws from the lobsters and set aside on a plate. Remove the tiny legs from the lobsters and, with cooking shears, snip into 1-inch segments; add to the cooking liquid. Remove the shell from the bodies; discard the head sac and green tomalley. Add the body shells to the cooking liquid.

3. Add the wine, onion, carrots, celery, peppercorns and thyme to the lobster cooking liquid and bring to a boil over high heat. Boil until the liquid is reduced to 1 quart, about 1½ hours. Strain through a sieve into a large measuring cup; discard the solids. (If you have more than 1 quart, return the stock to the pot and boil to reduce further.)

4. In a blender, combine 3 cups of the corn with ½ cup of the reduced lobster stock. Blend at high speed until fairly smooth, about 1 minute. Strain through a sieve into a large saucepan; discard the solids. Repeat with the remaining 3 cups corn and ½ cup more of the stock. Stir the remaining 3 cups stock into the saucepan and set aside. (*The recipe can be prepared to this point up to 1 day ahead. Cover the bisque and the claws and tails separately and refrigerate overnight.*)

SOUPS & STEWS

5. Place 1 of the lobster tails belly-up on a work surface and use sharp kitchen shears to cut down through the thin underside shell to expose the meat. Remove the tail meat and set aside. Repeat with the remaining tails. Using a lobster cracker or a nutcracker, crack the claws and knuckles and extract the meat. Discard all the shells. Cut all the meat into ½-inch pieces and transfer to a medium bowl.

6. Warm the bisque over moderate heat, stirring occasionally, until hot, about 10 minutes. Stir in the lobster meat and the ground pepper. Pour the bisque into soup bowls and sprinkle the tomato and basil on top. Garnish with croutons and serve.

NOTE: *To make croutons, preheat the oven to 375°. Trim the crusts from 8 slices of firm commercial white bread. Cut the bread into ⅓-inch cubes. Place on a baking sheet and bake for 10 minutes, until golden. Set aside to cool.*

—Tracey Seaman

• • •

FISHERMAN'S SOUP

This traditional, intensely flavored broth utilizes fish trimmings. Ask your fishmonger for the trimmings from lean fish (seek out any combination of rockfish, scorpion fish, whiting, porgy or mullet). For a richer version, add two cups of sautéed cod, halibut, squid or bass for the last 10 minutes of cooking.

To serve, rub the toasted bread with garlic, then sprinkle the Parmesan on top. Or spread a bit of the *rouille* on the bread and float it in the soup.

☙ A crisp, lean white—a white Bordeaux, such as a 1989 Château Carbonnieux or even a Chilean Sauvignon Blanc, such as a 1989 Santa Rita— would be a refreshing backdrop to the broth and *rouille*.

6 Servings

18 slices (¼-inch-thick) of French
  bread
One 3-inch strip of orange zest
3 tablespoons olive oil
2 large leeks, white parts only,
  halved lengthwise and thickly
  sliced crosswise
1 small onion, coarsely chopped
8 garlic cloves—4 sliced, 4 halved
2 tablespoons vegetable oil
2 pounds fresh, cleaned, lean fish
  heads, tails and bones, cut into 3-
  inch pieces
2 teaspoons salt
¼ cup peeled, seeded and chopped
  tomato (fresh or canned)
3 bay leaves
2 teaspoons thyme
1 teaspoon fennel seeds
¾ teaspoon saffron threads, softened
  in 1 teaspoon warm water
Freshly ground pepper
Freshly grated Parmesan, Swiss or
  hard sheep's milk cheese
Rouille (p. 263)

1. Preheat the oven to 300°. Spread the bread and zest on a baking sheet. Bake until dried but not browned, about 10 minutes.

2. In a large heavy skillet or saucepan, heat the olive oil over moderately high heat. Add the leeks, onion and sliced garlic and cook, stirring frequently with a wooden spoon, until slightly softened, about 5 minutes. Transfer to a bowl.

3. Add the vegetable oil and fish trimmings to the pan and cook over moderately high heat, stirring occasionally, for 5 minutes. Season with 1 teaspoon of the salt and return the leeks, onion and garlic to the pan. Add the tomato, bay leaves, thyme, fennel seeds and reserved orange zest. Stir to blend. Add 6 cups of cold water and bring to a boil over high heat. Reduce the heat to moderately low, cover and simmer, stirring occasionally, for 1 hour.

4. Pour the soup into a fine sieve set over a clean saucepan, pressing gently with the back of a wooden spoon, without crushing, to extract the juices. Set the broth aside. Scrape the pulp into a double layer of cheesecloth and set aside in a colander to cool slightly.

5. Working over the bowl of broth, twist the cheesecloth with your hands to extract as much liquid as possible. Open the cheesecloth and pour a cup of the broth over the mixture inside. Then twist the cheesecloth once more to extract all the liquid.

6. Stir the saffron and its liquid into the broth. Reheat the broth over low heat for about 5 minutes. Stir in the remaining 1 teaspoon salt and season with pepper to taste. Using a spoon, skim any oil from the surface. Serve the soup with the oven-dried bread, halved garlic cloves, grated cheese and Rouille.

—Mireille Johnston

• • •

Veal Stew with Lemon Zest and Mint (p. 48).

Above, Beef and Pasta in
Broth (p. 43). Right, Lobster-
Corn Bisque (p. 35).

Kentucky Chicken, Mushroom and Rice Chowder (p. 46).

MUSSEL-LEEK SOUP WITH ROASTED RED PEPPER AND THYME

6 Servings

4 pounds mussels, scrubbed and
*   debearded*
1 cup dry white wine
3 tablespoons olive oil
3 large leeks, white parts only,
*   halved lengthwise and very thinly*
*   sliced crosswise*
1 tablespoon plus 1 teaspoon fresh
*   thyme leaves, finely chopped*
¼ teaspoon freshly ground black
*   pepper*
1 pound red potatoes, peeled and cut
*   into ½-inch dice*
1 medium red bell pepper
1 cup milk
½ cup heavy cream
2 tablespoons minced parsley
Salt

1. Place half of the mussels in a large casserole. Add ½ cup of the wine, cover and cook over high heat just until the mussels open, 4 to 5 minutes. Drain in a colander set over a large bowl to save the broth. Repeat with the remaining mussels and ½ cup wine.

2. Remove the mussels from their shells, discarding any that did not open. Set aside 6 mussel shells for garnish. Discard any remaining bits of beard from the mussels and rinse them individually in the reserved broth to remove any grit. Strain the mussel broth through a fine

Three-Mushroom Soup with Port and Tarragon (p. 32).

TREE-TRIMMING PARTY

Serves 8

Mulled Cider

Cheese Straws

Grandpa's Hearty Chicken Soup
(p. 41)

Grilled Ham and Swiss Sandwiches

Assorted Pickles

🍷 *Fruity Pinot Noir, such as 1988*
Beaulieu Vineyards Los Carneros
Reserve or 1988 Robert Sinskey

Heavenly Puff Angels (p. 233)

Lacy Ginger Snowflakes (p. 234)

Chocolate-Dipped Snowballs (p. 230)

Coffee

strainer lined with cheesecloth, leaving behind the sandy broth at the bottom. Set the strained broth aside.

3. Rinse and dry the casserole. Add the olive oil and leeks and cook over high heat, stirring constantly, until the leeks soften slightly, about 3 minutes. Cover, reduce the heat to moderate and cook the leeks until soft, about 5 minutes longer. Stir in 1 tablespoon of the thyme and cook, stirring, for 1 minute. Add the black pepper, potatoes and the reserved mussel broth and cook over moderately high heat until the potatoes are tender, 20 to 25 minutes.

4. Meanwhile, roast the bell pepper directly over a gas flame or under a broiler as close to the heat as possible, turning frequently, until charred all over. Transfer the pepper to a paper bag, fold

over the top and set aside for 10 minutes. When cool, peel the pepper and discard the core, seeds and ribs. Cut the pepper into ¼-inch dice.

5. Crush about half of the potatoes against the side of the casserole with the back of a wooden spoon. Stir in the milk and cream and simmer for 5 minutes. Return the reserved mussels to the pot and cook until warmed through, about 3 minutes. Stir in the parsley, roasted pepper and the remaining 1 teaspoon thyme. Season with salt to taste. Ladle the soup into shallow bowls and garnish each serving with a mussel shell.

—Ann Chantal Altman

• • •

GRANDPA'S HEARTY CHICKEN SOUP

The secret to this traditional chicken soup, adapted from my father-in-law's recipe, is long, slow simmering. A pullet (young hen) is used instead of a fowl or stewing chicken because its meat is moist and tender. Chicken backs and wings are added for additional flavor. The pullet and stock are made the first day, and the soup is finished the next day. The stock can be used as a base for countless combinations of ingredients. Kreplach (meat or cheese-filled noodle dumplings) or matzo balls (traditional for Passover but good anytime) would be right at home in this soup.

8 to 10 Servings

1 pullet or chicken (3½ to 4 pounds)
1 pound chicken backs or wings
2 large onions, halved
5 large carrots, halved crosswise

4 large celery ribs with leaves,
  halved crosswise, plus additional
  leaves from the bunch
3 small rutabagas or 3 medium white
  turnips (about 1½ pounds), peeled
  and halved
1 cup (packed) fresh dill sprigs
2 cups fine egg noodles (3 ounces)
¼ cup finely chopped parsley
Salt and freshly ground pepper

1. In a large heavy stockpot, combine the pullet, chicken backs, onions, carrots, celery and its leaves, rutabagas and dill. Add about 3½ quarts of cold water to just cover the chicken and vegetables. Bring to a boil over high heat. Immediately reduce the heat to low so that the liquid barely simmers. Simmer, partially covered, skimming as necessary, until the pullet is cooked through, about 1 hour.

2. Transfer the pullet to a plate; let cool slightly. Test the carrots, celery and rutabagas for doneness with a fork; the rutabagas may need about 10 minutes more but the carrots and celery will probably be done. When the vegetables are just tender, transfer 4 carrot halves, 4 celery halves and 2 rutabaga halves to a plate to cool. Let the rest of the vegetables continue to simmer, partially covered, in the stock.

3. Pull most of the meat from the pullet and cut it into strips about 1 inch long. Cut the cooled carrots and celery into ½-inch chunks and the rutabagas into ½-inch dice. Cover the chicken and vegetables and refrigerate overnight.

4. Return the chicken bones and skin to the stockpot and continue simmering, partially covered, for at least 3 more hours. For a very full-bodied soup, simmer the stock for a total of 6 hours.

Strain the stock through a fine strainer into a large saucepan; discard the solids. Let the stock cool completely, then cover and refrigerate overnight.

5. The next day, in a medium saucepan of boiling salted water, cook the noodles until al dente, about 6 minutes. Drain, rinse under cold running water and set aside.

6. Skim the fat from the surface of the stock and discard. Reheat the stock over moderately high heat until it is liquefied. Add the noodles and the reserved chicken and vegetables. Cook until heated through, about 15 minutes. Stir in the parsley and season with salt and pepper to taste. Serve hot in large soup bowls. *(The soup can be made up to 3 days ahead. Let cool, cover and refrigerate. Reheat slowly before serving.)*

—Susan Shapiro Jaslove

• • •

ROBUST SOUP FOR AN ICY EVENING

Serves 6

Lentil Soup with Ham (p. 42)

*Hot Pepper Skillet Corn Bread
(p. 198)*

Warm Escarole Salad (p. 148)

♟ *California Zinfandel*

Italian Biscotti

Tangerines or Clementines

Espresso

—Stephanie Lyness

LENTIL SOUP WITH HAM

♟ The saltiness of the ham suggests a fruity wine for contrast, and the lentils would best be complemented by a red. A light California Zinfandel, such as 1988 J. Pedroncelli or 1988 Ridge Lytton Springs, would be fine.

4 Servings

1 tablespoon olive oil
1 medium onion, chopped
2 medium celery ribs, thinly sliced
3 medium carrots, sliced into thin
  rounds
2 garlic cloves, crushed through a
  press
2 teaspoons thyme
1 bay leaf
½ cup dry red wine
1 can (16 ounces) Italian plum
  tomatoes with their juice
1 cup lentils, rinsed and picked over
6 cups canned low-sodium chicken
  broth
1 thick slice baked or boiled ham
  (about ½ pound), cut into ½-inch
  dice
Salt and freshly ground pepper

1. In a medium nonreactive flameproof casserole, heat the oil over moderate heat. Add the onion, celery, carrots, garlic, thyme and bay leaf. Cover and cook until the onion is translucent, about 5 minutes.

2. Add the wine and bring to a boil over high heat. Add the tomatoes with their juice, breaking them up with the back of a spoon. Add the lentils and broth, and return to a boil. Reduce the heat to moderately low, cover partially and simmer, stirring occasionally, until the lentils are tender, about 35 minutes. Add the ham and cook for 5 minutes. Season to taste with salt and pepper and serve hot.

—*Stephanie Lyness*

• • •

BEEF AND PASTA IN BROTH

I also make this dish with pork or veal and substitute chicken or veal stock if I have it.

6 Servings

2 tablespoons olive oil
1½ pounds trimmed beef tenderloin, sliced ¼ inch thick and then cut into 2-inch strips
1 pound mushrooms, coarsely chopped
2 tablespoons unsalted butter
1 large onion, chopped
2 medium carrots, coarsely chopped
2 medium garlic cloves, minced
½ teaspoon freshly ground pepper
1 tablespoon all-purpose flour
4 cups beef stock or canned broth
1½ cups small, dried pasta shells or tubetti (8 ounces)
Salt
6 tablespoons minced fresh chives, for garnish

1. In a medium flameproof casserole, heat the oil over high heat for about 1 minute. Add half of the beef strips and cook, stirring, until well seared, about 4 minutes. Using tongs, transfer the strips to a platter. Repeat with the remaining meat.

2. Add the mushrooms to the casserole and cook, stirring often, until browned and dry, about 7 minutes. Re-

duce the heat to moderately low and stir in the butter until melted. Add the onion and carrots and cook, stirring, until the onion is golden, about 10 minutes. Stir in the garlic and pepper and cook for 3 minutes. Add the flour and cook, stirring, until pasty, about 1 minute.

3. Gradually stir in the stock and 4 cups of water and bring to a boil over moderately high heat. Reduce the heat to moderate and boil gently for 5 minutes. Using a slotted spoon, skim the fat from the surface. Stir in the pasta, increase the heat to moderately high and return the broth to a boil. Cook, stirring occasionally, until the pasta is tender, 8 to 10 minutes.

4. Stir in the reserved beef strips; season to taste with salt and more pepper. Ladle the soup into shallow bowls and sprinkle the chives on top.

—*Lee Bailey*

• • •

GREAT LAKES CORN CHOWDER

6 Servings

6 medium ears of corn
6 strips of bacon, cut into ½-inch pieces
1 small onion, finely chopped
1 small green bell pepper, finely chopped
1 jalapeño pepper—seeded, deveined and chopped
1 small celery rib, finely chopped
3 medium tomatoes—peeled, seeded and finely chopped
2 medium boiling potatoes (about 1 pound), peeled and cubed
1 teaspoon salt

⅛ teaspoon ground allspice
Pinch of sugar
1 small bay leaf
2 cups half-and-half or light cream, at room temperature
1 cup milk
Freshly ground black pepper
Chopped parsley, for garnish

1. Working over a bowl, cut the corn kernels from the cobs at about half their depth. Then, using the back of the knife, scrape the cobs over the bowl to release all the "milk"; set aside.

2. In a large nonreactive saucepan, fry the bacon over moderately high heat, stirring occasionally, until crisp, about 10 minutes. Transfer the bacon to paper towels to drain. Crumble and reserve.

3. Discard all but 3 tablespoons of the bacon drippings from the pan. Add the onion and cook over moderate heat until golden, 4 to 5 minutes. Add the green bell pepper, jalapeño and celery and cook until slightly softened, about 2 minutes. Add the tomatoes, potatoes, salt, allspice, sugar, bay leaf and the reserved corn kernels with their "milk" and stir well. Cook over moderate heat until the mixture begins to sizzle.

4. Reduce the heat to low. Cover and cook, stirring occasionally, until the potatoes are tender, 35 to 45 minutes. Stir in the cream and milk and bring just to a boil. Remove from the heat and season with black pepper to taste. Ladle the chowder into bowls and garnish with the reserved crumbled bacon and the parsley.

—*Phillip Stephen Schulz*

• • •

SOUPS & STEWS

NEW JERSEY TOMATO AND SWEET POTATO CHOWDER

Named for the home of the world's tastiest tomatoes, this chowder is one for which ripe, fresh tomatoes are a must. If they're not available in your part of the country right now, save this recipe for the appropriate season.

4 Servings

2 tablespoons unsalted butter
1 medium onion, chopped
1 large celery rib, minced
2 medium sweet potatoes (1 pound), peeled and diced
1⅔ cups beef stock or canned broth
4 large ripe tomatoes (2 pounds)— peeled, seeded and chopped
Pinch of sugar
½ teaspoon salt
¼ teaspoon freshly ground pepper
⅛ teaspoon cinnamon
Pinch of freshly grated nutmeg
3 tablespoons chopped parsley, for garnish

1. In a large nonreactive saucepan, melt the butter over moderately low heat. Add the onion and cook until slightly softened, about 5 minutes. Stir in the celery and sweet potatoes and cook for 5 minutes longer.

2. Add the beef stock, tomatoes and sugar and bring to a boil over moderately high heat. Reduce the heat to moderately low, cover and cook until the sweet potatoes are tender, about 30 minutes.

3. Transfer 1 cup of the chowder to a blender or food processor and puree until smooth. Return the puree to the chowder and add the salt, pepper, cin-

namon and nutmeg. Cook for 5 minutes to blend the flavors. Season with additional salt and pepper to taste. Ladle the chowder into bowls, garnish with the parsley and serve immediately.

—*Phillip Stephen Schulz*

• • •

ROASTED GARLIC AND LEEK CHOWDER

The garlic cloves in this chowder can be roasted unpeeled in a 350° oven for 25 minutes, then peeled and mashed. Or cook as specified below. Either way, the garlic loses much of its sting as the chowder cooks, but it's still strong enough to produce a redolent soup.

❦ This pungent soup would find its complement in a fruity but textured red, such as a light Bordeaux. Try 1988 Barton & Guestier Merlot or 1986 Château St-Georges St-Emilion.

3 to 4 Servings

1 tablespoon unsalted butter
6 large garlic cloves, peeled
⅓ cup diced salt pork (1 ounce)
3 medium leeks, white and tender green, chopped
2 medium carrots, diced
1 celery rib with leaves, finely chopped
4 cups chicken stock or canned broth
2 medium baking potatoes (about 1 pound), peeled and cut into ½-inch dice
1 teaspoon chopped fresh sage
Salt and freshly ground pepper
1 tablespoon chopped parsley

1. In a small skillet, melt the butter over very low heat. Add the garlic cloves, cover and cook, turning once, until tender, about 25 minutes; the garlic will be golden, but should not burn. Using a fork, mash the garlic to a paste.

2. Meanwhile, blanch the salt pork in a small saucepan of boiling water for 3 minutes. Drain well.

3. In a large heavy saucepan, fry the salt pork over moderate heat until golden, about 4 minutes. Discard all but 1 tablespoon of the fat, but leave the salt pork in the pan. Add the leeks and cook, stirring constantly, for 1 minute. Stir in the garlic paste and cook for 1 minute longer. Stir in the carrots and celery. Reduce the heat to moderate, cover and cook, stirring occasionally, until the vegetables have softened, about 10 minutes.

4. Stir in the chicken stock and bring to a boil over moderately high heat. Add the potatoes and return to a boil. Reduce the heat to moderate and simmer until the potatoes are tender, about 15 minutes.

5. Transfer 1 cup of the chowder to a blender or food processor and puree until smooth. Return the puree to the chowder and stir in the sage. Season with salt and pepper to taste. Ladle the chowder into bowls and garnish with the parsley.

—*Phillip Stephen Schulz*

• • •

PORTSMOUTH FISH CHOWDER

I had my first taste of genuine East Coast chowder at a small waterfront seafood restaurant that overlooked the Piscataqua River in Portsmouth, New Hampshire. It was a rich, golden soup that I have never forgotten. This is my version.

6 Servings

2 tablespoons unsalted butter
1 medium onion, finely chopped
1 garlic clove, minced
½ of a red bell pepper, finely chopped
1 medium carrot, diced
2 medium baking potatoes (about 1 pound), peeled and cut into ¾-inch cubes
2 cups bottled clam juice

DOWN-EAST LUNCH

Serves 6

Hard Cider

Vermont Cheddar Cheese

Water Crackers

Mixed Green Salad

Portsmouth Fish Chowder (p. 45)

Warm Crusty Bread

♙ *Medium-bodied Chardonnay, such as 1988 Ste. Chapelle or 1988 St. Andrew's*

Cranberry Pie (p. 207)

---

1 cup chicken stock or canned broth
2 teaspoons all-purpose flour
2½ cups heavy cream
1 pound whitefish fillets, such as cod, flounder or petrale sole, cut into 1-inch pieces
½ pound bay scallops
Dash of hot pepper sauce
Salt and freshly ground black pepper
2 egg yolks
Chopped parsley, for garnish

1. In a large heavy saucepan, melt 1 tablespoon of the butter over moderately low heat. Add the onion and cook for 1 minute. Add the garlic and cook for 4 minutes longer. Add the bell pepper, carrot and potatoes and stir to coat with the onion mixture. Add the clam juice, chicken stock and 1 cup of water and bring to a boil over moderately high heat. Reduce the heat to moderately low, cover and cook until the potatoes are tender, about 20 minutes.

2. In a small bowl, mix the remaining 1 tablespoon butter with the flour until blended and smooth. Whisk the flour paste into the chowder along with 2 cups of the cream and bring to a boil over moderate heat. Reduce the heat to moderately low and cook for 2 minutes. Add the fish and scallops and cook for 4 minutes longer. Add the hot pepper sauce and season with salt and black pepper to taste. Reduce the heat to low.

3. In a small bowl, whisk the egg yolks with the remaining ½ cup cream. Whisk in ¼ cup of the hot chowder. Gradually stir this mixture into the chowder and cook for 2 minutes; do not let the soup boil. Serve hot, sprinkled with parsley.

—*Phillip Stephen Schulz*

• • •

NEW ENGLAND CLAM CHOWDER

When it comes to clam chowder, I must admit that I like mine creamy and thick. On the East Coast, large hard-shell quahogs, often called chowder clams, are preferred for their rich sea flavor. Soft-shell clams, or steamers, that are larger than two and a half inches can be used as well, but they have a milder, sweeter taste. On the West Coast, mahogany, surf and piddock clams and geoducks are all good chowder clams.

♙ A crisp, light white would provide a refreshing contrast to the richness of this soup. Try a California Sauvignon Blanc, such as 1989 Callaway, or Fumé Blanc, such as a 1988 J. Pedroncelli.

6 to 8 Servings

2½ dozen large clams or quahogs, well scrubbed
1 teaspoon baking powder
½ cup diced salt pork (2 ounces)
4 parsley sprigs plus chopped parsley, for garnish
1 bay leaf
2 onions—1 small, quartered, 1 large, finely chopped
2 tablespoons unsalted butter, softened
1 large garlic clove, minced
1 celery rib, finely chopped
½ of a medium green bell pepper, minced
2 medium baking potatoes (about 1 pound), peeled and cut into ¼-inch dice
2 cups milk
2 cups heavy cream
2 tablespoons all-purpose flour
Dash of hot pepper sauce

Dash of Worcestershire sauce
¼ teaspoon chopped fresh thyme or a
  pinch of dried
Salt and freshly ground black pepper

1. Place the clams in a large pot and cover with cold water. Stir in the baking powder and let stand for 30 minutes. Drain and rinse the clams under cold running water.

2. Meanwhile, in a small pan of boiling water, blanch the salt pork for 3 minutes; drain well and set aside.

3. Return the clams to the pot and add the parsley sprigs, bay leaf, quartered onion and 1 cup of water. Cover and bring to a boil over high heat. Reduce the heat to moderately high and cook until the clams begin to open, about 3 minutes. Continue to cook, uncovering the pot as necessary to remove the clams as soon as their shells separate just enough to pry them open with a knife; do not overcook. Discard any clams that do not open.

4. When cool enough to handle, remove the clams from their shells over the pot to catch all the juices. Coarsely chop the clams. Place the chopped clams in a bowl, cover and set aside. Strain the broth and reserve.

5. In a large heavy saucepan or dutch oven, cook the salt pork over moderate heat until golden, about 6 minutes. Discard all but 1 tablespoon of the fat from the pan and add 1 tablespoon of the butter. Add the chopped onion and cook for 1 minute. Add the garlic, celery and green pepper and cook until the vegetables are soft but not browned, about 5 minutes. Add the potatoes and the reserved clam broth and bring to a boil. Reduce the heat to moderately low, cover and cook until the potatoes are tender, about 15 minutes.

6. Meanwhile, in a medium saucepan, scald the milk and cream, about 5 minutes.

7. In a small bowl, mix the remaining 1 tablespoon butter with the flour until smooth. Whisk this paste into the chowder, 1 teaspoon at a time, and cook until no raw flour taste remains, about 2 minutes. Add the hot milk and cream and the hot pepper sauce, Worcestershire sauce, thyme and salt and black pepper to taste. Stir in the reserved clams and cook until heated through, about 1 minute. Ladle the chowder into bowls and garnish with the chopped parsley.

—*Phillip Stephen Schulz*

• • •

KENTUCKY CHICKEN, MUSHROOM AND RICE CHOWDER

♟ Look for an off-dry white, such as Chenin Blanc, to act as a simple foil for the medley of hearty flavors in this soup. From California, 1989 Hacienda or 1989 Villa Mt. Eden would work well.

6 Servings

1 chicken (2½ to 3 pounds)
1 onion, unpeeled and halved
1 large carrot, thickly sliced
1 large celery rib, coarsely chopped
1 parsnip, thickly sliced
4 parsley sprigs plus chopped parsley,
  for garnish
8 whole black peppercorns
6 cups chicken stock or canned broth
6 ounces mushrooms, sliced (2½
  cups)
1 tablespoon plus 1 teaspoon fresh
  lemon juice

2 tablespoons unsalted butter plus 1
  teaspoon, softened
3 medium leeks, white and tender
  green, thinly sliced
1 garlic clove, minced
¼ cup chopped red bell pepper
½ cup uncooked rice
1 teaspoon all-purpose flour
1 cup heavy cream, at room
  temperature
Pinch of freshly grated nutmeg
Salt and freshly ground black pepper

1. Place the chicken in a saucepan just large enough to hold it. Add the onion, carrot, celery, parsnip, parsley sprigs, peppercorns, chicken stock and 2 cups of water. Bring to a boil over high heat. Reduce the heat to moderate, cover and simmer until the chicken is tender, about 50 minutes.

2. Transfer the chicken to a plate and let cool slightly. Remove the meat from the bones and set aside.

3. Return the skin and bones to the saucepan and cook over moderate heat until the stock has reduced to 6 cups, about 15 minutes. Strain the stock and discard the solids.

4. Shred enough of the chicken to yield 1 cup; reserve the remaining chicken for another use.

5. Toss the mushrooms with 1 tablespoon of the lemon juice and set aside for 10 minutes.

6. In a large saucepan, melt 2 tablespoons of the butter over moderately high heat. Add the mushrooms and cook, stirring frequently, until the mushrooms release their liquid and are lightly browned, about 5 minutes. Reduce the heat to moderately low and stir in the leeks, garlic and red bell pepper. Cook, stirring occasionally, until the vegetables are slightly softened, about 5 minutes. Stir in the reserved chicken stock and the rice and bring to a boil. Reduce the heat to low, cover and cook until the rice is tender, about 20 minutes.

7. In a small bowl, mix the flour with the remaining 1 teaspoon butter until blended; set aside.

8. Scoop ½ cup of the chowder into a blender. Add the cream and blend until smooth. Return the puree to the chowder and whisk in the flour mixture. Bring to a boil over moderate heat. Reduce the heat to low and simmer gently for 10 minutes. Stir in the shredded chicken, nutmeg and the remaining 1 teaspoon lemon juice. Season with salt and black pepper to taste and simmer for 3 minutes longer. Ladle the chowder into bowls and sprinkle with the chopped parsley.

—*Phillip Stephen Schulz*

• • •

MOROCCAN VEGETABLE STEW

Serve the stew over a mound of Whole Wheat Couscous (p. 138).

4 Servings

2 tablespoons vegetable oil
1 medium onion, thinly sliced
1 medium red bell pepper, cut into ¼-inch strips and halved crosswise
1 teaspoon cinnamon
2 teaspoons cumin
¼ teaspoon cayenne pepper
4 canned plum tomatoes plus ½ cup juice (from a 14-ounce can)
2 tablespoons fresh lime juice
¼ teaspoon saffron threads

FAST MOROCCAN FEAST

Serves 4

Moroccan Vegetable Stew (p. 47)

Whole Wheat Couscous (p. 138)

Warm Pita Bread

Dried Dates

Almond-Oat Cookies (p. 231)

Mint Tea

—*Susan Shapiro Jaslove*

---

4 small red potatoes, sliced ¼ inch thick
2 cups broccoli florets (from 1 large stalk)
1 can (19 ounces) chickpeas, drained and rinsed
1 teaspoon salt

1. In a large, heavy, nonreactive pot or flameproof casserole, heat the oil over moderate heat. Add the onion, red bell pepper, cinnamon, cumin and cayenne and cook, stirring occasionally, until the vegetables are soft, about 5 minutes.

2. Add the tomatoes and ½ cup of juice; break up the tomatoes with a large spoon. Add the lime juice, saffron, potatoes and ½ cup of water and bring to a boil. Cover, reduce the heat to moderately low and simmer, stirring occasionally, until the potatoes are almost tender, about 20 minutes.

3. Stir in the broccoli florets and chickpeas. Increase the heat to moderately high and bring to a boil. Reduce the heat to moderately low, cover and simmer until the potatoes are very ten-

der and the broccoli is just tender, 10 to 15 minutes. Season with the salt and serve hot.

—*Susan Shapiro Jaslove*

• • •

CHICKPEA STEW WITH GREENS AND SPICES

Chickpeas are probably the best of the canned beans. They are generally firm, and once the salty liquid is washed away, they taste quite good. Since chickpeas take several hours to cook, the canned variety can come in very handy.

Served with rice or couscous, this stew makes a good meatless meal—or serve it as a side dish with chicken or lamb. It is even better the next day, so it's a good dish to make ahead.

---

4 Main-Course or 6 Side-Dish Servings

1½ pounds swiss chard, tough ribs removed—or a mixture of greens, such as chard, spinach, kale, tatsoi, mustard and arugula—torn into large pieces (8 to 10 cups total)
1 can (16 ounces) chickpeas, drained and rinsed
6 medium garlic cloves, coarsely chopped
1 teaspoon coarse (kosher) salt
2 teaspoons sweet paprika
1½ teaspoons cumin
½ teaspoon turmeric
1 teaspoon whole black peppercorns
3 tablespoons plus 1 teaspoon extra-virgin olive oil
¼ cup chopped fresh coriander (cilantro)
2 tablespoons minced parsley
1 medium onion, chopped

1 green bell pepper or Anaheim
chile, cut into ½-inch dice
1 small dried red chile
2 large tomatoes—peeled, seeded and
chopped, juice reserved—or 2
cups drained canned Italian plum
tomatoes, coarsely chopped

1. Place the greens in a steamer, cover and steam over boiling water until wilted, about 5 minutes. When the greens are cool enough to handle, coarsely chop them and set aside.

2. Place the chickpeas in a medium bowl and add water to cover. Rub the beans between your hands to loosen the skins. Discard the skins.

3. In a mortar, pound the garlic with the salt until it begins to break down. Add the paprika, cumin, turmeric and peppercorns and pound until the peppercorns are well broken up. Add 1 teaspoon of the olive oil to moisten the mixture. Add 2 tablespoons of the coriander and the parsley and continue to pound for a few minutes until a rough paste forms.

4. In a large nonreactive skillet, heat the remaining 3 tablespoons olive oil over moderate heat. Add the onion and green pepper and crumble in the dried chile. Cook, stirring occasionally, for 4 minutes. Stir in the garlic paste, chickpeas and ½ cup of water. Bring to a simmer and cook until the onion is soft, about 5 minutes.

5. Stir in the tomatoes and their juice, the greens and ½ cup of water. Cook over moderately low heat for 20 minutes. Stir in the remaining 2 tablespoons coriander and serve hot.

—*Deborah Madison*

• • •

This stew—inspired by ingredients of the Pacific Northwest—is mild, rich, full of satisfying flavor, yet very quick to make. A tip on the oysters—if you don't have freshly shucked, buy the smallest possible top-quality jarred oysters. If you can only find medium or even large ones, don't worry. Cut them into bite-size pieces before adding to the stew.

6 Servings

1 large head of cauliflower (about 2
pounds), separated into florets
2½ cups milk
1 cup heavy cream
Salt and freshly ground white pepper
¼ teaspoon turmeric plus more for
garnish
24 oysters and ¼ cup of their liquor
(see Note)
1 tablespoon each of chopped fresh
chives and chervil, for garnish

1. Pour 1 inch of water into a large heavy saucepan or medium flameproof casserole and add the cauliflower florets. Cover and steam over high heat until tender, about 10 minutes.

2. Transfer the cauliflower to a food processor and puree with ½ cup of the milk until very smooth. Transfer the puree to the casserole and whisk in the remaining 2 cups milk and the cream until smooth. Cook over moderate heat, whisking occasionally, until very hot, about 3 minutes; don't let it boil or it may curdle. Season with salt and pepper to taste; whisk in ¼ teaspoon of the turmeric.

3. Add the oysters and their liquor and cook, stirring frequently, until just heated through, about 3 minutes. Do not boil or the oysters will become tough and chewy. Serve the stew in warmed bowls, garnished with the chives, chervil and a sprinkling of turmeric.

NOTE: *If you shuck your own oysters, rinse the oysters in their liquor. Set them aside, then strain the liquor through cheesecloth to remove any grit.*

—*Susan Hermann Loomis*

• • •

VEAL STEW WITH LEMON ZEST AND MINT

Rice is an excellent accompaniment to this slightly tangy stew.

6 Servings

2½ pounds trimmed boneless veal
shoulder, cut into 2-inch pieces
1 teaspoon salt
½ teaspoon freshly ground pepper
¼ cup all-purpose flour
2 tablespoons unsalted butter
3 tablespoons olive oil
2½ cups chicken stock or canned
low-sodium broth
2 teaspoons finely grated lemon zest
¼ cup fresh lemon juice
1 bay leaf
1 pound carrots, sliced 1 inch thick
on the diagonal
1 pound white pearl onions
½ cup heavy cream
½ cup chopped fresh mint

1. Season the veal with the salt and pepper. Dredge the meat in the flour, shaking off the excess. In a large heavy skillet, melt the butter in 2 tablespoons of the olive oil over moderately high heat until foaming. Add half of the veal to the skillet and cook undisturbed for 5 minutes. Continue cooking, turning as necessary, until the pieces are well browned all over, 5 to 7 minutes longer. Transfer the browned veal to a large heavy casserole. Add the remaining 1 tablespoon oil to the skillet and repeat with the remaining veal.

2. Discard the fat from the skillet. Pour in 1 cup of the chicken stock and scrape the bottom of the pan with a wooden spoon to release all the browned bits. Pour this liquid into the casserole and add the lemon zest, lemon juice, bay leaf and the remaining 1½ cups chicken stock. Bring to a simmer over moderately high heat. Reduce the heat to low, cover and simmer for 1¼ hours.

3. Meanwhile, bring a medium saucepan of salted water to a boil over high heat. Add the carrots and cook until tender, about 8 minutes. Remove with a slotted spoon and set aside in a large bowl. Add the pearl onions to the saucepan and boil for 2 minutes. Drain and let cool. Peel the skins, trim the root ends and set the onions aside in a small bowl.

4. After 1¼ hours, add the cream and onions to the veal. Cook over moderate heat until the meat is tender, 20 to 30 minutes longer. (*The recipe can be prepared to this point up to 3 days ahead. Let cool, cover and refrigerate. Reheat before proceeding.*)

5. Using a slotted spoon, transfer the meat and onions to the bowl with the carrots. Discard the bay leaf. Cook the sauce over moderately high heat until it reduces by half, about 10 minutes. Return the meat, onions and carrots to

the casserole and cook, stirring occasionally, until warmed through, about 5 minutes. Stir in the mint just before serving.

—*Ann Chantal Altman*

• • •

VEAL STEW WITH SPRING VEGETABLES AND HERBS

🍷 This stew is a natural partner for a distinctive Sauvignon (Fumé) Blanc, such as 1988 Beaulieu Vineyard or 1988 Robert Mondavi Fumé Blanc Reserve.

4 Servings

½ *pint pearl onions (about 20)*
3 *medium carrots, halved lengthwise and cut into 1-inch pieces*
½ *pound white turnips, peeled and cut into ½-inch wedges*
1 *cup fresh or thawed frozen peas*
½ *pound fresh spinach, large stems removed*
2½ *tablespoons unsalted butter, softened*
1 *tablespoon olive oil*
Four 1-pound veal shanks
Salt and freshly ground pepper, to taste
1 *large leek, halved lengthwise and thinly sliced crosswise*
1 *large shallot, thinly sliced*
1 *cup dry white wine, preferably Sauvignon Blanc*
2 *sprigs of fresh thyme plus ½ teaspoon chopped leaves or ½ teaspoon dried thyme*
2½ *tablespoons all-purpose flour*
½ *cup heavy or light cream*
¼ *pound white mushrooms, thinly sliced*
1 *tablespoon grainy mustard*

HEARTY SPRING DINNER

Serves 6

Braised Artichokes with Spinach (p. 166)

Veal Stew with Lemon Zest and Mint (p. 48)

Basmati Rice

Steamed Asparagus

Fresh Rhubarb Tart (p. 213)

—*Ann Chantal Altman*

2 *tablespoons finely chopped chives*
2 *tablespoons coarsely chopped chervil or parsley*

1. Bring a small saucepan of water to a boil. Add the pearl onions and blanch for 2 minutes to loosen the skins. Drain, rinse and pop the onions out of the skins. Using a sharp knife, trim a thin sliver off the root end. Set aside.

2. Pour 1 inch of water into a large saucepan and insert a steamer basket. Bring the water to a boil over high heat. Add the carrots to the basket in an even layer, cover and steam until tender, about 7 minutes. Transfer the carrots to a medium bowl.

3. Add the pearl onions to the steamer. Cover and steam until tender, about 5 minutes; add to the carrots.

4. Steam the turnips, covered, until tender, about 6 minutes. Add to the carrots and onions. If necessary, add more water to the pan.

5. If using fresh peas, steam them, covered, until tender, about 3 minutes

and add to the bowl of vegetables.

6. Finally, steam the spinach, covered, until just wilted, about 1½ minutes. Remove the steamer basket with the spinach and let cool slightly in the sink. Gently squeeze as much water as you can from the spinach, leaving the leaves intact if possible. Carefully pull the leaves to restore their shape and add them to the vegetables.

7. In a flameproof casserole or dutch oven, melt 1 tablespoon of the butter in the oil over high heat. Season the veal shanks with salt and pepper. Place in the casserole and cook until lightly browned, about 3 minutes per side.

8. Transfer the shanks to a large platter and reduce the heat to low. Add the leek and shallot to the casserole, cover and cook, stirring occasionally, until wilted, about 2 minutes. Add the wine, increase the heat to high and boil, scraping the brown bits from the bottom of the pan, until the liquid reduces by one-third, about 4 minutes.

9. Add 4 cups of water, the thyme and the veal shanks with any accumulated juices from the platter. Bring to a simmer, reduce the heat to low, cover and cook until the veal is very tender when pierced with a fork, about 1½ hours. Do not let the liquid boil vigorously—it should remain at a simmer.

10. Transfer the veal shanks to a platter and let cool slightly. Skim any fat from the surface of the stew. Bring the liquid to a boil over high heat, and boil, skimming occasionally, until it reduces by one-third, about 5 minutes.

11. Meanwhile, in a small bowl, combine 1 tablespoon of the butter with the flour. Gradually whisk the butter-flour mixture into the boiling liquid and cook, whisking, until slightly thickened, 2 to 3 minutes. Reduce the heat to mod-

erate and whisk in the cream. Set aside.

12. Remove the meat from the bones and discard the gristle and fat. Cut the meat into 1-inch pieces and add to the liquid. *(The recipe can be prepared to this point up to 1 day ahead. Let the stew cool. Cover and refrigerate the veal and the vegetables separately.)* Reheat the stew over low heat if necessary. Add all of the cooked vegetables and the thawed peas and cook until heated through.

13. Meanwhile, in a small skillet, melt the remaining ½ tablespoon of butter over moderate heat. Add the mushrooms and cook, stirring frequently, until softened, about 2 minutes. Remove from the heat and stir in the mustard. Add to the stew and season with salt and pepper to taste. Just before serving, stir in the chives and chervil.

—*Marcia Kiesel*

• • •

SPICY BLACK-EYED PEA AND PORK STEW

Allow time to soak the black-eyed peas overnight.

4 Servings

1¼ cups dried black-eyed peas (8 ounces), picked over
3 slices bacon
2 pounds meaty, country-style pork ribs, lean pork shoulder or fresh ham
¼ teaspoon freshly ground black pepper
⅛ teaspoon ground cinnamon
1 teaspoon salt
2 dried ancho chiles
1 medium onion, chopped
6 garlic cloves, chopped
1 cinnamon stick
1 small dried red chile
1 teaspoon tomato paste

1. In a large bowl, cover the black-eyed peas with 4 inches of water. Let soak overnight at room temperature.

2. In a medium saucepan, cook the bacon over moderate heat until the fat is rendered and the bacon is crisp, about 6 minutes. Remove the bacon and reserve for another use.

3. Season the pork ribs or whole piece of pork all over with the black pepper, ground cinnamon and ¼ teaspoon of the salt. Heat the bacon fat over moderately high heat. Working in batches, if using ribs, brown the pork well, turning once, about 4 minutes per side; transfer to a plate.

4. Meanwhile, place a small skillet over high heat to warm for about 30 seconds. Add the ancho chiles and toast, turning once, until blistered and puffed, about 30 seconds per side. Pull off and discard the stems and seeds and chop the chiles coarsely.

5. Drain the fat from the saucepan. Drain the black-eyed peas and add to the pan. Add the onion, garlic, ancho chile, cinnamon stick, dried red chile, pork and 4 cups of cold water. Bring to a boil over high heat. Reduce the heat to low and simmer, skimming and stirring occasionally, until the peas are tender, about 1 hour.

6. Transfer the pork to a platter. If not using ribs, cut the pork into thick slices. Stir the tomato paste into the peas and season with the remaining ¾ teaspoon salt or more to taste. Spoon the peas around the pork and serve.

—*Marcia Kiesel*

• • •

FISH & SHELLFISH

CORN-CRUSTED CATFISH WITH TOMATO-TEQUILA BUTTER

Drying fresh corn kernels and grinding them for cornmeal gives a concentrated sweetness to the breading for catfish fillets, says chef Kevin Rathbun, though you could substitute regular cornmeal. ♟ A fruity-tart California white, such as 1989 Pine Ridge or 1989 Villa Mt. Eden Chenin Blanc, would provide a refreshing contrast to the lively flavors of this spicy dish.

6 Servings

5 medium ears of corn, husked, (about 2 cups) or 1 package (10 ounces) frozen corn kernels
½ cup all-purpose flour
½ teaspoon cayenne pepper
1 tablespoon freshly ground black pepper
2 teaspoons salt
1 cup buttermilk
Six 5-ounce catfish fillets
⅓ cup dry red wine
2 shallots, finely chopped
1 pound plum tomatoes—peeled, seeded and chopped
2 serrano chiles, seeded and minced
1 tablespoon fresh lime juice
1½ sticks (6 ounces) cold unsalted butter, cut into ½-inch pieces
3 tablespoons chopped fresh coriander (cilantro)
2 tablespoons chopped basil
2 tablespoons Monte Tecá (tequila liqueur) or tequila
¼ cup olive oil
Black-Eyed Pea and Mint Marigold Salad (p. 159)

NORTH-OF-THE-BORDER SUPPER

Serves 6

Tequila Sunrises

Guacamole with Blue Corn Tortilla Chips

Corn-Crusted Catfish with Tomato-Tequila Butter (p. 52)

Black-Eyed Pea and Mint Marigold Salad (p. 159)

Brown Rice

Corn Chili (p. 168)

♟ Fruity white, such as 1989 Pine Ridge or 1989 Villa Mt. Eden Chenin Blanc

Flan with Fresh Strawberries

Cinnamon Cookies

Coffee

1. Preheat the oven to 275°. Using a sharp knife, slice the corn kernels off the cobs. Spread the fresh or thawed frozen kernels in a baking pan and bake for about 2 hours, stirring occasionally, until the kernels are completely dry. Let the corn cool, then grind to a coarse powder in a spice mill or coffee grinder.

2. In a medium bowl, toss the ground corn with the flour, cayenne, 1 teaspoon of the black pepper and 1 teaspoon of the salt. Set aside.

3. In a large bowl, combine the buttermilk and the remaining 1 teaspoon salt. Add the catfish fillets and let marinate for 20 minutes.

4. Meanwhile, in a medium nonreactive saucepan, combine the wine, shallots, tomatoes and serrano chiles. Simmer over high heat until almost all of the liquid has evaporated, about 5 minutes. Transfer the mixture to a blender or food processor and puree until smooth.

5. Return the puree to the saucepan and stir in the lime juice. Bring just to a boil over high heat. Off the heat, whisk in all the butter, a few pieces at a time, until the sauce is creamy and smooth. Add the coriander, basil, Monte Tecá and the remaining 2 teaspoons black pepper. Season with salt to taste. Set aside in a warm place.

6. Remove the catfish from the buttermilk, letting excess liquid drip off. One at a time, dip the fillets into the reserved ground corn flour, pressing lightly to adhere.

7. In a large skillet, heat the olive oil over moderately high heat until almost smoking. Add as many fillets as will fit comfortably in the pan and fry until golden brown and crisp on one side, about 4 minutes. Reduce the heat to moderate and turn the fillets. Cook on the other side until crisp and cooked through, about 4 minutes longer. Transfer the fillets to paper towels to drain while you fry the remaining catfish.

8. To serve, gently reheat the tomato-tequila butter over low heat, if necessary, whisking constantly. Pour the sauce onto 6 plates and place the catfish fillets on top. Serve with the Black-Eyed Pea and Mint Marigold Salad alongside.

—*Kevin Rathbun, Baby Routh, Dallas*

• • •

ROAST COD WITH SAKE AND CHINESE BLACK BEANS

Chef Edward Brown restores humble cod to its rightful place at the gastronomic pinnacle with a fragrant, Asian-inspired black bean sauce. Cod from New York's historic Fulton Fish Market, "so fresh it's still twitching," is what he prefers, but another firm-textured white-meat fish could be substituted.

4 Servings

1 cup instant couscous
4 tablespoons unsalted butter
1½ teaspoons salt
2 teaspoons Chinese fermented black
    beans*
1 large garlic clove, smashed
1 small shallot, finely chopped
1 teaspoon finely grated fresh ginger
1 cup plus 4 teaspoons sake
Freshly ground pepper
3 cups vegetable oil, for frying
1½ cups all-purpose flour
2 tablespoons paprika
2 medium onions, sliced paper thin
Four 6- to 7-ounce cod fillets, about
    ¾ inch thick
¼ cup chopped chives, for garnish
*Available at Asian markets

1. In a medium saucepan, bring 2 cups of water to a boil over high heat. Gradually stir in the couscous. Add 1 tablespoon of the butter and ½ teaspoon of the salt. Boil for 2 minutes, stirring occasionally. Remove from heat, cover tightly and set aside in a warm place.

2. In a small nonreactive saucepan, melt 1 tablespoon of the butter over low heat. Stir in the black beans, garlic, shallot and ginger and cook until the shallot is translucent, about 2 minutes. Increase the heat to high, add 1 cup of the sake and boil until reduced by one-third, about 10 minutes. Remove from the heat and whisk in the remaining 2 tablespoons butter until creamy. Season to taste with salt and pepper and set aside.

3. Preheat the oven to 375°. In a large saucepan, heat the oil over moderately high heat to 400°.

4. Meanwhile, working over a large bowl, sift the flour with the remaining 1 teaspoon salt and the paprika. Add the onion rings and toss to coat thoroughly. Transfer the onions to a large strainer and shake well to remove excess flour. Deep-fry the onions in small batches until golden brown and crisp, 4 to 5 minutes. Drain on paper towels and sprinkle lightly with salt while still warm.

5. Place the cod on an oiled baking sheet and sprinkle with salt and pepper. Spoon 1 teaspoon of the sake over each fillet and cover with foil. Bake the fish for about 8 minutes, until the flesh just flakes with a fork and the interior is just opaque. Remove from the oven and pour any accumulated cooking juices into the sauce. Gently rewarm the sauce, whisking, over low heat.

5. Spoon the couscous into the center of 4 warmed plates. Set the cod on the couscous and spoon the sauce around the couscous and the fish. Top with onion rings and garnish each serving with 1 tablespoon of the chopped chives.

—Edward Brown, Tropica,
New York City

• • •

DOVER SOLE AND SHRIMP TIMBALES WITH RED PEPPER PUREE

Serve these timbales with thinly sliced cucumber and yellow bell peppers or with cooked fava beans and radish sprouts.

♟ This delicate preparation could be overwhelmed by a heavy white. Try a light, crisp Italian white, such as 1989 Castello d'Albola Chardonnay or 1989 Barone Fini Pinot Grigio, to best complement this elegant dish.

2 Servings

2 very large red bell peppers
12 medium shrimp—shelled, halved
    lengthwise and deveined
3 small shallots, sliced
1 small garlic clove, crushed and
    peeled
½ cup sake
Pinch of crushed red pepper
Two 5-ounce sole fillets, halved
    lengthwise

1. Peel the peppers with a vegetable peeler. Halve the peppers lengthwise and remove the cores. With a small sharp knife, remove the membranes and any seeds. Lay the pepper halves on a

work surface. Using a 2½-inch round biscuit or cookie cutter, stamp out a disk from each pepper half; reserve the scraps.

2. In a medium saucepan, bring 2 cups of water to a boil over moderately high heat. Add the pepper disks and simmer until tender, about 20 minutes. Carefully transfer the pepper disks to paper towels to drain; let cool.

3. In the same saucepan of simmering water, blanch the shrimp just until opaque, about 30 seconds. Drain and set aside to cool.

4. In a small nonreactive saucepan, combine the pepper scraps, shallots, garlic, sake and crushed red pepper. Bring to a boil over high heat. Reduce the heat to moderate, cover and cook until the vegetables are very soft, about 15 minutes. Remove from the heat and let cool. Pour the mixture into a food processor and puree until smooth. Strain the sauce through a fine sieve and set aside.

5. In a wok, bring 4 cups of water to a boil over moderately high heat. Meanwhile, place a softened pepper disk in the bottom of four ½-cup ramekins, peeled-side down. Line the side of each ramekin with half of a sole fillet. Place 6 shrimp halves in the center of each ramekin and press lightly to pack.

6. Place a bamboo steamer in the wok and arrange the ramekins in the steamer. Cover and steam the timbales until the sole is opaque and the shrimp is piping hot, about 7 minutes.

7. Remove the ramekins from the steamer. When cool enough to handle, cover each ramekin with a small dish and tilt to drain off any liquid. Unmold 2 ramekins onto each plate and spoon the red pepper sauce around them. Serve warm or at room temperature.

—*Seppi Renggli*

• • •

SAUTEED HALIBUT WITH WARM CREAMY VINAIGRETTE

Based on classic techniques that chef Don Pintabona learned while working in France, this warm vinaigrette is made with a dense preserve of garlic and shallots in olive oil. The addition of fresh herbs gives it a lively finish that marries well with the clear, sweet flavor of the halibut.

4 Servings

⅓ *cup minced shallots*
1½ *cups good-quality dry white wine*
2 *garlic cloves, minced*
7 *tablespoons extra-virgin olive oil*
1 *fresh thyme sprig*
¾ *teaspoon tomato paste*
2 *tablespoons fresh lemon juice*
2 *tablespoons red wine vinegar*
1 *teaspoon soy sauce*
4 *tablespoons cold unsalted butter, cut into 1-inch pieces*
Salt and freshly ground pepper
Four 6-ounce halibut steaks, about ¾ inch thick
2 *tablespoons chopped chives*
2 *plum tomatoes—peeled, seeded and cut into ¼-inch dice*

1. In a blender or small food processor, combine 2 tablespoons of the shallots with 2 tablespoons of the wine and puree until blended. Transfer this shallot juice to a small bowl and set aside. *(The shallot juice can be prepared up to 5 hours ahead.)*

2. In a medium nonreactive saucepan, combine the remaining shallots, garlic and 6 tablespoons of the olive oil and cook over low heat, stirring, until softened, about 7 minutes. Add the thyme sprig and the remaining wine, increase the heat to high and boil until reduced to ½ cup, about 15 minutes.

3. Discard the thyme sprig. Stir in the tomato paste, lemon juice, reserved shallot juice, vinegar and soy sauce and bring to a boil, whisking constantly. Remove from the heat and whisk in the cold butter, a little at a time, until creamy and smooth. Season with salt and pepper to taste and set aside.

4. Sprinkle the halibut steaks on both sides with salt and pepper. In a large skillet, heat the remaining 1 tablespoon olive oil over high heat. When the oil begins to smoke, add the halibut steaks to the pan and cook until well browned on one side, about 4 minutes. Turn over and cook the other side until the fish is firm to a light touch and just opaque throughout, about 3 minutes longer.

5. Meanwhile, gently reheat the vinaigrette sauce over low heat, whisking constantly. Stir in the chives and tomatoes. Spoon the sauce onto 4 dinner plates and set the halibut steaks on top. Serve immediately.

—*Don Pintabona, TriBeCa Grill, New York City*

• • •

MONKFISH AND SHRIMP SAUTE WITH CHICORY AND ORANGES

6 Servings

1½ teaspoons fresh lemon juice
¼ cup plus 3 tablespoons olive oil
½ teaspoon freshly ground pepper
1½ pounds monkfish, peeled thoroughly of all gray skin and sliced ½ inch thick
1 pound large shrimp, shelled and deveined
4 navel oranges
2 shallots, finely chopped
1 head of chicory (about 1 pound), large stems removed, leaves chopped
2 tablespoons shredded basil leaves
Salt and freshly ground pepper

1. In a medium bowl, whisk the lemon juice with ¼ cup of the olive oil and the pepper. Add the monkfish and shrimp and toss to coat. Let stand for 5 to 15 minutes.

2. Finely grate enough of the oranges to yield 1 tablespoon of zest; set aside. Using a sharp knife, peel and section all the oranges, making sure to remove all of the bitter white pith; set aside.

3. Heat a large, high-sided nonreactive skillet over high heat until very hot. Add the monkfish and shrimp in their marinade and sauté, stirring frequently, until opaque, 3 to 4 minutes. Transfer to a medium bowl and cover with foil. Wash and dry the skillet.

4. Add 2 tablespoons of the olive oil to the skillet and heat over high heat until beginning to smoke. Add the shallots and sauté until translucent, 1 to 1½ minutes. Stir in the reserved orange zest and half the chicory and sauté until wilted. Add the remaining chicory and reduce the heat to moderately high. Cover and cook, stirring occasionally, until tender, 3 to 4 minutes. Pour any juices from the seafood into the pan as the chicory cooks.

5. Meanwhile, in a medium skillet, heat the remaining 1 tablespoon oil over moderate heat. Add the orange sections and basil and toss until hot, about 1 minute.

6. Add the seafood to the chicory and toss gently to combine and heat through. Season with salt and pepper to taste. To serve, mound the seafood and chicory in the center of a large platter and surround with the oranges.

—*Bob Chambers*

• • •

BAKED MONKFISH FOR SIX

Serves 6

Baked Monkfish with Dill Beurre Blanc (p. 55)

Lemon Rice

Shredded Zucchini (p. 186)

🍷 *Italian Pinot Grigio*

Strawberries with Chocolate Cream (p. 236)

—*Lee Bailey*

BAKED MONKFISH WITH DILL BEURRE BLANC

A classic butter sauce flavored with dill accompanies this fish.

🍷 The buttery sauce points to a mild white, such as a 1988 Lungarotti Pinot Grigio from Italy or a 1988 Trimbach Pinot Blanc from France.

6 Servings

2 pounds monkfish, in 1 or 2 equal pieces
2 teaspoons soy sauce
Freshly ground black pepper
3 medium shallots, minced
⅓ cup dry white wine
⅓ cup white wine vinegar
2 sticks (8 ounces) cold unsalted butter, cut into tablespoons
¼ cup minced fresh dill
½ teaspoon salt
¼ teaspoon ground white pepper

1. Preheat the oven to 400°. Using a sharp knife, remove any skin from the monkfish and trim off all of the dark flesh. Place the fish in a 9-by-13-inch roasting pan and rub the soy sauce all over. Season generously with black pepper and bake for 22 to 25 minutes, until the flesh is firm when pressed and just starts to separate. Transfer the fish to a serving platter and cover loosely with foil.

2. Meanwhile, in a small nonreactive saucepan, combine the shallots, wine and vinegar and bring to a boil over moderately high heat. Boil until almost all the liquid has evaporated, about 7 minutes.

FISH & SHELLFISH

3. Shortly before serving, return the shallot mixture to moderately high heat and cook until it begins to sizzle. Whisk in the butter, one tablespoon at a time, until incorporated. Stir in the dill, salt and white pepper. Set the sauce aside in a warm place away from direct heat.

4. To serve, cut the fish into thick slices and arrange on 6 plates. If desired, pour the fish juices on top. Serve with the dill sauce alongside.

—Lee Bailey

• • •

PAN-FRIED SALMON STEAKS

These fish steaks are best made in a well seasoned cast-iron skillet large enough to hold them comfortably with enough space between them for easy turning. Preheating the skillet until it is very hot ensures that the salmon will have a nice crusty surface. The empty skillet may begin to smoke a bit. Once the steaks have been placed in the skillet, don't move them until they are ready to be turned. There are several tests for doneness. The flesh should be opaque and should separate slightly from the central bone. When the steaks are pressed lightly, you should be able to feel the natural separations of the flesh flaking from the pressure.

4 Servings

Four 8-ounce center-cut salmon steaks, 1 inch thick
½ teaspoon salt
1 teaspoon freshly ground pepper
2 teaspoons olive oil
Lemon wedges, for serving

1. Season the salmon steaks on both sides with the salt and pepper.

2. Heat a 12-inch cast-iron skillet over moderately high heat until very hot all over, about 4 minutes. Add the oil and tilt the pan to coat it evenly.

3. Add the steaks to the pan without touching and fry, turning once, until browned and slightly crusty, about 5 minutes per side. Serve with lemon wedges.

—Susan Shaprio Jaslove

• • •

GRILLED SALMON WITH TAWNY PORT-TARRAGON SAUCE

The sauce for this rich, flavorful dish is made with tawny port, which has some sweetness. An aged port that has dried out a bit, like a 20-year-old, is best.

4 Servings

Four 8-ounce salmon steaks, 1 inch thick
Salt and freshly ground pepper
⅓ cup dry tawny port
¼ cup (tightly packed) fresh tarragon
1 large shallot, minced
¼ cup beef stock or canned broth
1 stick (4 ounces) cold unsalted butter, cut into tablespoons
1 teaspoon hazelnut oil

1. Light a grill or preheat the broiler. Season the salmon steaks well with salt and pepper and set aside.

2. Meanwhile, prepare the sauce. In a small nonreactive saucepan, combine the port, tarragon, shallot and beef stock. Bring to a boil over high heat, skimming off any foam that rises to the sur-

face. Boil until the liquid is reduced to 2 tablespoons, about 5 minutes. Remove from the heat and whisk in the cold butter, 1 tablespoon at a time, until the sauce is smooth and thickened. Strain the sauce through a fine-mesh sieve into a clean saucepan and set aside.

3. Rub the salmon steaks with the hazelnut oil and grill over moderately hot heat, turning once, until crusty brown on the outside and rosy-pink inside, about 10 minutes total. Alternatively, broil the steaks 5 inches from the heat for about 5 minutes per side.

4. Reheat the sauce in the saucepan, stirring constantly, over very low heat. Do not boil.

5. Transfer the salmon steaks to heated plates and pour the sauce on top.

—*David Rosengarten*

• • •

SAUTEED SALMON STEAKS WITH FENNEL, CUCUMBER AND LIME

Save the feathery fennel tops to garnish the salmon, and chop some extra to toss with buttered noodles or rice.

4 Servings

1 pound fennel bulbs, cored and very thinly sliced crosswise, tops reserved
Four 8-ounce salmon steaks, ¾ inch thick
1 teaspoon freshly ground pepper
1 teaspoon salt
¼ cup olive oil
4 tablespoons unsalted butter
3 scallions, thinly sliced
1 European cucumber—peeled, halved lengthwise, seeded and sliced ⅛ inch thick
¼ cup fish stock or bottled clam juice
¼ cup dry white wine
Juice of 1 lime

1. Preheat the oven to 200°. Place a heatproof platter in the oven to warm.

2. Mince enough of the fennel tops to yield 1 tablespoon. Rub the salmon steaks with the pepper and minced fennel tops and sprinkle with the salt.

3. In a large, high-sided nonreactive skillet, heat 2 tablespoons of the olive oil over high heat until it begins to smoke.

Add 2 of the salmon steaks and sauté for 2 minutes on each side. Transfer the steaks to the platter and repeat with another tablespoon of the oil and the remaining salmon. Place the salmon in the oven.

4. Pour the oil from the skillet. Add 1 tablespoon of the butter and the remaining 1 tablespoon oil. When the fat bubbles vigorously, add the scallions and sauté for 30 seconds. Add the sliced fennel and cucumber and sauté until lightly browned, about 3 minutes.

5. Add the fish stock and wine and deglaze the pan, scraping up any browned bits from the bottom. Cook until most of the liquid has evaporated, about 2 minutes. Stir in the remaining 3 tablespoons butter and half of the lime juice. Season with salt and pepper to taste.

6. Remove the salmon from the oven and sprinkle the remaining lime juice on top. Arrange the vegetables around the fish and serve immediately.

—*Bob Chambers*

• • •

BROILED SALMON WITH DILL

Salmon is a glorious fish that makes a good meal at any time of the year. It is best prepared very simply so as not to disguise its flavor; here, it's seasoned with just a touch of olive oil, dill and white wine. The thick center-cut fillets benefit from being quickly seared under the broiler.

4 Servings

2 tablespoons olive oil
½ teaspoon salt
¼ teaspoon freshly ground pepper

Four 6- to 8-ounce center-cut skinless salmon fillets, ¾ to 1 inch thick
2 tablespoons dry white wine
2 tablespoons minced fresh dill

1. Preheat the broiler. In a nonreactive baking dish large enough to hold the salmon in a single layer, combine the oil, salt and pepper. Add the salmon fillets and turn to coat thoroughly.

2. Broil the salmon in the baking dish about 2 inches from the heat for 6 minutes, or until almost cooked through. Sprinkle the wine on top and broil, without turning, for about 2 minutes, or until the salmon is just opaque at the center.

3. Transfer the fillets to plates and spoon a little of the pan juices on top. Garnish with the dill and serve.

—*Stephanie Lyness*

• • •

SALMON WITH SESAME OIL AND SOY SAUCE

At L'Arpège in Paris, chef Alain Passard serves this salmon raw but warmed up. For those apprehensive about eating raw fish, follow the microwave adaptation below in which the salmon is just cooked through.

🍷 Capers and raisins spark this salmon dish and indicate a fruity, lively young 1988 California Chardonnay, such as Meridian or Christophe.

2 Servings

2 teaspoons Oriental sesame oil
Two 5-ounce salmon fillets, ½ inch thick
1 tablespoon soy sauce

2 teaspoons drained capers
2 tablespoons golden raisins
¼ teaspoon freshly ground pepper

Spread 2 microwaveable plates with 1 teaspoon each of sesame oil. Place a salmon fillet in the center of each plate and sprinkle the soy sauce, capers, raisins and pepper on top. Cover tightly with microwave plastic wrap. Cook, one plate at a time, on High, or full, power for 50 seconds, or until just cooked through. Serve immediately.

—*Barbara Kafka*

• • •

SALMON WITH ROASTED HAZELNUT AND ORANGE BUTTER

Chef Wayne Ludvigsen uses king salmon for this dish, but he suggests coho or sockeye as good Pacific Coast alternatives or Atlantic salmon on the East Coast.

❦ This wonderfully rich salmon dish calls for an equally rich white, but one with enough bite to provide contrast—try a fleshy California Chardonnay, such as 1989 Sanford.

8 Servings

3 tablespoons hazelnuts
½ cup (packed) thinly sliced fresh
    sorrel leaves
2 tablespoons fresh orange juice
1 stick (4 ounces) unsalted butter, at
    room temperature

¼ teaspoon salt
¼ teaspoon freshly ground white
    pepper
1 stick (4 ounces) salted butter
2 garlic cloves, finely chopped
Pinch of rosemary
Pinch of oregano
Pinch of thyme
Pinch of freshly ground black pepper
Eight 8-ounce salmon fillets, skinned

1. Preheat the oven to 350°. Place the hazelnuts in a pie pan and roast until fragrant and lightly browned, about 12 minutes. Rub the warm nuts in a dish towel to remove most of the skins. Chop coarsely and let cool completely.

2. In a food processor, puree the sorrel. Add the hazelnuts and process to a pesto-like consistency. Add the orange juice and process to combine. Add the unsalted butter, salt and white pepper and process until blended.

3. Place a 12-inch-long sheet of wax paper on a work surface. Using a rubber spatula, scrape the hazelnut butter onto the paper and form it into a 6-by-1-inch log. Roll up tightly, twist the ends and refrigerate until firm, at least 3 hours. (*The hazelnut butter can be refrigerated for up to 2 days or frozen for up to 2 weeks and allowed to soften at room temperature for 2 to 3 hours before using.*)

4. Preheat the broiler. In a saucepan, melt the salted butter over low heat. Add the garlic, rosemary, oregano, thyme and black pepper and cook until the garlic is soft, about 5 minutes.

5. Place the salmon fillets on a large broiling pan or heavy baking sheet and broil 5 inches from the heat for 1 minute. Using a pastry brush, baste the salmon generously with the garlic-herb butter and broil for 1 minute longer. Rotate the pan and generously baste the

fish again with the garlic-herb butter. Broil and baste again after 1 minute. Continue broiling for 1 to 2 minutes longer, until the fish is crusty on top and just opaque in the center. The salmon is done when the flesh is easily separated with a fork and the thickest part is no longer translucent. Alternatively, grill the salmon fillets over a hot mesquite or hardwood fire 5 inches from the heat for 4 to 5 minutes. Baste constantly and turn the fillets 90 degrees after 2 minutes to make crisscross grill marks.

6. Serve the salmon topped with a ½-inch slice of the hazelnut butter.

—*Wayne Ludvigsen,
Ray's Boathouse, Seattle*

• • •

SALMON WITH SWEET-AND-SOUR ONIONS

Joyce Goldstein says that this dish is based on a classic Venetian recipe for fillet of sole, but the treatment is delicious with salmon as well. Traditionally the fish is sautéed, covered with the onion marinade and served at room temperature—sort of an Italian escabeche. However, she finds that most Americans prefer fish served hot, so she serves the sweet-and-sour onion mixture as a sauce over baked salmon.

4 Servings

¼ cup raisins
¼ cup pine nuts
¼ cup plus 2 teaspoons mild olive oil
2 large Spanish onions (about 2
    pounds), halved lengthwise and
    thinly sliced crosswise
¼ cup red wine vinegar

1 tablespoon finely grated orange zest
2 teaspoons finely grated lemon zest
Salt and freshly ground pepper
Four 6-ounce salmon steaks, ¾ inch
thick

1. Preheat the oven to 400°. In a small bowl, cover the raisins with ½ cup hot water and set aside to plump. Spread the pine nuts in a pie pan and toast in the oven for 3 to 4 minutes, stirring occasionally, until lightly browned. Set aside.

2. In a large nonreactive skillet, heat ¼ cup of the oil over moderate heat until hot, about 1 minute. Add the onions, cover partially and cook, stirring occasionally, until tender and translucent, about 15 minutes.

3. Drain the raisins and add them to the onions with the vinegar and the grated orange and lemon zests. Cook to reduce the vinegar slightly, about 1 minute. Season with salt and pepper to taste. (*The recipe can be prepared to this point up to 1 day ahead. Cover and refrigerate. Reheat before proceeding.*)

4. Season the salmon steaks on both sides with 1 teaspoon salt and ½ teaspoon pepper. In a large heavy skillet, heat the remaining 2 teaspoons olive oil over high heat. Add the salmon steaks to the pan and cook until well browned on one side, about 3 minutes. Turn and cook the steaks for about 3 minutes longer. The salmon is done when the flesh separates easily with a fork and the thickest part is no longer translucent. Transfer the salmon steaks to plates and spoon the hot onion mixture on top. Garnish with the toasted pine nuts.

—*Joyce Goldstein, Square One,*
San Francisco

• • •

UPSCALE DINNER PARTY

Serves 8

Cumin and Cayenne Spiced Cashews
(p. 12)

🍷 Cocktails

Baked Goat Cheese Salad with Garlic
Croutons (p. 163)

Salmon with Roasted Hazelnut and
Orange Butter (p. 58)

Orzo

Haricots Verts

🍷 1988 Clos du Bois Flintwood
Chardonnay

Caramelized Baked Apples with
Cinnamon Ice Cream (p. 243)

Café Filtre

Truffles

PAN-FRIED SALMON WITH TORTILLA SALAD AND SPICY GINGER DRESSING

Robert Del Grande uses Norwegian salmon for this south-of-the-border style salmon dish.

4 Servings

2 tablespoons grainy mustard
1 tablespoon sherry vinegar
3 tablespoons red wine vinegar
2 garlic cloves, finely chopped
1 tablespoon finely chopped shallot

2 serrano chiles—stemmed, seeded
(optional) and finely chopped
2 tablespoons finely chopped fresh
basil
1 tablespoon minced fresh ginger
¾ cup walnut oil
1 tablespoon Oriental sesame oil
1 tablespoon honey
2 teaspoons Worcestershire sauce
½ teaspoon coarse (kosher) salt
½ teaspoon coarsely ground black
pepper
Four 8-inch corn tortillas
Peanut oil for frying, plus 2
teaspoons
Four 6-ounce salmon fillets, skinned
1 medium carrot, cut into 2-by-⅛-
inch strips
1 red bell pepper—stemmed, seeded
and cut into ⅛-inch strips
2 poblano chiles—stemmed, seeded
and cut into ⅛-inch strips
1 leek, white portion only, cut into
2-by-⅛-inch strips
2 bunches of watercress, large stems
removed

1. In a medium bowl, combine the mustard, sherry vinegar, red wine vinegar, garlic, shallot, serrano chiles, basil, ginger, walnut oil, sesame oil, honey, Worcestershire sauce, coarse salt and black pepper. Whisk well and set aside for at least 30 minutes to allow the flavors to develop. (*The dressing can be prepared up to 1 week ahead and refrigerated.*)

2. Cut the tortillas into ⅓-inch strips. In a large skillet, heat ⅛ inch of peanut oil over moderately high heat until very hot, about 3 minutes. Fry the tortilla strips in batches until crisp and lightly browned, about 1 minute. Transfer to paper towels to drain thoroughly. (*The tortilla strips can be fried up to 1 hour ahead.*)

FISH & SHELLFISH

3. In a large skillet, heat the 2 teaspoons of peanut oil over high heat until almost smoking. Reduce the heat to moderate and add the salmon fillets and cook, turning once, until lightly browned and the center of the fillets just begins to turn opaque, about 3 minutes per side.

4. Just before serving, in a large bowl, combine the carrot, bell pepper, poblano chiles and leek with the fried tortilla strips. Add ½ cup of the reserved dressing and toss gently to coat without breaking the tortilla strips. Arrange a ring of watercress around 4 plates and spread the tortilla salad inside the rings.

5. To serve, transfer the salmon fillets to the tortilla salad, spoon the remaining spicy ginger dressing over the salmon and watercress and serve immediately.

—*Robert Del Grande,*
Cafe Annie, Houston

• • •

SEARED GRAVLAX WITH DILL-CREAMED POTATOES

Gravlax becomes a little salty when cooked, so creamed potatoes are the ideal foil. Make the gravlax a day in advance.

4 Servings

Gravlax (recipe follows)
1½ pounds Idaho potatoes (3 large)
2 tablespoons unsalted butter
2 tablespoons all-purpose flour
2 cups milk, warmed
¼ cup heavy cream
½ teaspoon salt
½ teaspoon freshly ground pepper
½ cup chopped fresh dill

1. Scrape the dill and seasonings off the gravlax and pat the fish dry. Using a long sharp knife, slice the salmon at a 45-degree angle into 8 very wide slices, about ¼ inch thick. Cut off any skin from the slices and cut out the little triangle of gray flesh at the bottom of each slice. Cover tightly with plastic wrap and refrigerate for up to 6 hours.

2. In a large saucepan, cover the potatoes with water and bring to a boil over moderately high heat. Boil until tender, about 20 minutes. Drain well. When the potatoes are cool enough to handle, peel and slice crosswise ¼ inch thick. Set aside.

3. In a medium saucepan, melt the butter over moderately high heat. Add the flour and cook, stirring, for 30 seconds. Gradually whisk in the milk and bring to a boil. Reduce the heat to low and cook, whisking, until thickened and smooth, about 5 minutes. Stir in the cream, salt and pepper. Gently fold the potatoes and dill into the sauce. Cover and keep warm. (*The potatoes can be prepared up to 3 hours ahead and kept covered at room temperature. Rewarm over moderate heat before proceeding.*)

4. Just before serving, heat a large cast-iron skillet over high heat until very hot, 3 to 4 minutes. Add the gravlax slices and sear until browned, about 15 seconds. With a spatula, turn the slices over and sear the other side, about 15 seconds longer. The salmon should be crusty and glazed. Serve 2 slices per person with some of the creamed potatoes.

—*Christer Larsson, Aquavit,*
New York City

• • •

GRAVLAX

Makes About 1 Pound

2 tablespoons coarse (kosher) salt
2 tablespoons sugar
1½ teaspoons crushed white peppercorns
1 pound center-cut salmon fillet
1 large bunch of dill

In a small bowl, combine the salt, sugar and peppercorns. Rub a handful of this mixture over both sides of the salmon. Set the salmon in a nonreactive dish, skin-side down, and sprinkle the rest of the mixture on top. Spread the dill over the salmon and cover the dish with plastic wrap. Let stand at room temperature for 6 hours, then refrigerate for 24 hours.

—*Christer Larsson, Aquavit,*
New York City

• • •

SALMON CROQUETTES WITH SALSA MAYONNAISE

Run your fingers along the salmon fillet to check for bones before cutting the fish.

♟ The rich, salty taste of this dish, enhanced by a spicy mayonnaise dressing, would be nicely set off by a California Chardonnay with broad, deep flavors. Either 1988 Sonoma-Cutrer or 1988 Viansa would work particularly well.

6 Servings

5 tablespoons unsalted butter
3 large celery ribs, finely chopped
4 to 5 shallots, minced

FIFTIES-STYLE DINNER

Serves 6

Salmon Croquettes with Salsa Mayonnaise (p. 60)

Roasted Red Potatoes (p. 176)

Mixed Green Salad

🍷 *California Chardonnay*

Chocolate Custard with Pecans (p. 256)

Coffee

—*Lee Bailey*

1½ *pounds skinless salmon fillet, cut into 1-inch cubes*
1 *egg, lightly beaten*
2 *tablespoons Dijon mustard*
1 *tablespoon Worcestershire sauce*
1 *teaspoon salt*
¼ *teaspoon freshly ground black pepper*
Dash of hot pepper sauce
1 *cup (packed) fine fresh bread crumbs*
½ *cup flour*
3 *tablespoons canola oil*
Salsa Mayonnaise (p. 264)

1. In a medium skillet, melt 2 tablespoons of the butter over moderate heat. Add the celery and shallots and cook, stirring occasionally, until softened, about 5 minutes. Transfer to a large bowl.

2. Place the salmon in a food processor and pulse 8 times to chop coarsely. Add the salmon to the celery and shallots.

3. Stir in the egg, mustard, Worcestershire sauce, salt, black pepper and hot pepper sauce until well blended. Stir in the bread crumbs. The mixture should just hold together.

4. Place the flour on a work surface. With a ⅓-cup measure and floured hands, scoop up and form the salmon mixture into 12 oval patties about ¾ inch thick. Lightly flour the patties and set aside on a sheet of wax paper until ready to fry. (*The patties can be made to this point up to 2 hours ahead; cover and refrigerate. Let the patties stand at room temperature for 30 minutes before frying.*)

5. In a large heavy skillet, melt 1½ tablespoons of the butter in 1½ tablespoons of the oil over moderately high heat until the foam subsides. Working in 2 batches, fry half of the salmon patties, turning once, until brown and crisp on both sides, about 4 minutes. Using a spatula, transfer the croquettes to paper towels to drain, then transfer to a rack set over a baking sheet and keep warm in a low oven. Wipe out the skillet and then repeat with the remaining 1½ tablespoons each of butter and oil and the remaining salmon patties. Serve warm with the Salsa Mayonnaise.

—*Lee Bailey*

• • •

SALMON IN PHYLLO PASTRY WITH MUSHROOMS AND WILD RICE

🍷 This dish is designed for bubbles, especially a brut rosé Champagne or top-class sparkling rose, such as NV Billecart Salmon or 1987 Iron Horse Brut Rosé.

4 Servings

½ *cup uncooked wild rice, or brown basmati rice*
2 *sticks (8 ounces) unsalted butter*
½ *pound fresh shiitake mushrooms, stems removed, caps cut into ¼-inch dice*
3 *large shallots, minced*
1 *teaspoon fresh lemon juice*
1 *tablespoon chopped fresh dill*
¾ *teaspoon salt*
⅛ *teaspoon freshly ground pepper*
8 *sheets of phyllo dough*
Four 6-ounce salmon fillets
¼ *cup dry white wine or Champagne*
2 *tablespoons white wine vinegar*

1. In a small saucepan, bring 1½ cups of water to a boil. Add the rice, cover and cook over low heat until tender but still a bit chewy, 30 to 45 minutes. Add up to ¼ cup more water if needed. Drain the rice and set aside.

2. In a large skillet, melt 2 tablespoons of the butter over high heat. When the foam subsides, add the mushrooms and two-thirds of the shallots. Cook, stirring frequently, until the shallots are soft and the mushrooms are lightly browned, about 5 minutes.

3. Transfer to a medium bowl and toss with 1 tablespoon butter. Stir well to coat and then add the cooked rice, lemon juice, 2 teaspoons of the dill, ½

FISH & SHELLFISH

teaspoon of the salt and the pepper. Set aside.

4. Cut 1 stick plus 2 tablespoons of the butter into 1-inch pieces and refrigerate them.

5. In a small saucepan, melt the remaining 3 tablespoons butter over low heat. Cut the sheets of phyllo in half crosswise to 12-by-8-inch rectangles. Place one piece of phyllo on a work surface; keep the rest covered with a damp towel as you work. Brush the sheet lightly with the melted butter. Place another sheet of phyllo on top, butter it and repeat until you have 4 stacked sheets of buttered phyllo. Place a piece of salmon diagonally in the center. Top with ½ cup of the rice mixture.

6. To form the package, bring the corners of the phyllo dough up over the salmon to meet in the center. Gather the pastry and fold the corner tips back slightly. Separate the layers of phyllo to make a petal effect on top. Repeat with the remaining phyllo, melted butter, salmon and rice. Place the salmon packages on a baking sheet and refrigerate for at least 20 minutes and up to 4 hours.

7. Preheat the oven to 350°. Bake the salmon packages in the upper third of the oven for about 25 minutes, until the phyllo is brown and crisp on top and an instant-reading thermometer inserted into the fish registers 140°.

8. Meanwhile, in a small nonreactive saucepan, combine the wine, vinegar and the remaining shallots and boil over high heat until reduced to 1 tablespoon, about 7 minutes. Remove from the heat and whisk in the chilled butter pieces, several at a time, adding more when the butter is nearly melted. Continue whisking until all the butter has been added and the sauce is thick. Strain the sauce through a fine sieve into an-

other saucepan and add the remaining 1 teaspoon dill, ¼ teaspoon salt, and a pinch of pepper. Set aside. Just before serving, whisk the sauce over moderate heat until just warm.

9. To serve, place each salmon package on a warmed dinner plate. Cut the packages in half, open slightly. Pour the sauce between the package halves and around the salmon.

—*Marcia Kiesel*

• • •

FRESH SALMON CAKES

Fish often becomes the focus of the Hanukkah meal. Instead of the lox and smoked whitefish I grew up eating, I like to offer these fresh fish cakes. If you won't be serving them straight from the pan, keep them warm in a 200° oven on a rack set over a baking sheet.

❢ These cakes would be overpowered by a rich white but complemented by a fruity, balanced one from California, such as 1988 Chateau St. Jean Fumé Blanc or 1988 Kenwood Sauvignon Blanc.

8 Servings

1 large onion, finely chopped
1½ pounds skinless salmon fillet, ½ inch thick
2 large celery ribs, finely chopped
3 tablespoons finely chopped parsley
1½ teaspoons salt
1 teaspoon freshly ground pepper
1 cup plus 6 tablespoons dry bread crumbs
3 egg whites
About 1 cup vegetable oil, for frying
1 lemon, cut into 8 wedges, for serving

1. Pour 1½ inches of water into a deep skillet that's at least 10 inches in diameter. Add half of the onion and bring the water to a boil over high heat. Add the salmon, making sure it is completely immersed, and return to a boil. Reduce the heat to moderate and simmer, uncovered, until the fish is opaque throughout, about 7 minutes. Transfer the salmon to a plate and let cool. (*The recipe can be prepared to this point up to 1 day ahead. When the fish has cooled completely, cover and refrigerate.*)

2. Break the fish into ½-inch pieces, discarding any bones, and place in a large bowl. Add the remaining onion and the celery, parsley, salt and pepper and mix gently. Stir in 6 tablespoons of the bread crumbs.

3. In a nonreactive bowl, lightly beat the egg whites until frothy. Gently fold the whites into the salmon mixture. To form the patties, measure out scant ¼ cups of the salmon mixture and press firmly into 2½-inch rounds about ½ inch thick.

4. In a large heavy skillet, heat ¼ inch of vegetable oil over high heat until it begins to shimmer, 3 to 5 minutes. Meanwhile, spread the remaining 1 cup bread crumbs on a plate. Working in batches, gently but thoroughly coat both sides of the salmon cakes with the crumbs. Add them to the skillet and fry until well browned, about 2½ minutes per side. Reduce the heat to moderately high if they are browning too quickly or beginning to burn.

5. Transfer the cakes to paper towels to drain, then cover and keep warm while you coat and fry the rest. Serve 2 salmon cakes per person, garnished with a lemon wedge.

—*Susan Shapiro Jaslove*

• • •

MICROWAVE CHINESE CABBAGE STUFFED WITH SALMON IN CHIVE-BUTTER SAUCE

Although this unusual dish from Pierre Romeyer (whose restaurant near Brussels bears his name) requires a bit of work, the mix of flavors is delicious.

6 Servings

1 large baking potato
2 cups Microwave Fish Stock
   (p. 270)
1 large Chinese cabbage (about 2
   pounds), large leaves separated
1½ pounds salmon fillet, cut into 6
   slices
6 slices of smoked bacon
3 large tomatoes—peeled, seeded and
   finely chopped (about 3 cups)
18 fresh tarragon leaves or 1
   teaspoon dried, crumbled
Coarse (kosher) salt and freshly
   ground pepper
2 sticks plus 6 tablespoons (11
   ounces) cold unsalted butter, cut
   into pieces
1 bunch of chives, minced (about ½
   cup)

1. Peel the potato and cut six ¼-inch lengthwise slices from the center. In a 9-by-13-inch glass dish, arrange the potato slices in a single layer. Pour the Fish Stock over the potatoes. Cover tightly with microwave plastic wrap and cook on High, or full, power for 7 minutes, or until the potatoes are almost cooked through. Prick the plastic to release the steam.

2. Spread 6 very large cabbage leaves in a large microwaveable container.

Cover and cook on High for 2 minutes, or until wilted. Rinse the leaves with cold water and dry thoroughly with paper towels.

3. Lay 1 cabbage leaf, rib-side down, on a work surface. Place a salmon slice in the center. Top with a slice of the bacon, ½ cup of the tomatoes and 3 tarragon leaves. Season with coarse salt and pepper to taste.

4. Fold the top and bottom of the cabbage leaf into the center, then fold in the sides to enclose. Place the salmon package, seam-side down, on top of a potato slice. Repeat with the remaining ingredients to form 5 more packages. Spoon some stock in the dish over the packages. Cover with microwave plastic wrap and cook on High for 15 minutes.

5. Prick the plastic to release the steam. Transfer 1½ cups of the cooking liquid to a small saucepan; cover the cabbage bundles to keep them warm. Bring the stock to a boil over high heat and boil until it has reduced to ½ cup, about 10 minutes. Reduce the heat to low and whisk in the cold butter, a few pieces at a time. Add the chives and season the sauce with salt and pepper to taste.

6. To serve, spoon some of the sauce on each dinner plate. Place a potato slice with a cabbage bundle on top in the center of each plate and spoon additional sauce over the cabbage. Pass any remaining sauce separately.

—*Barbara Kafka*

• • •

SALMON ROUELLES WITH FENNEL JULIENNE

The fennel oil for this elegant salmon dish is prepared the day before in order to allow the flavors to develop.

4 Servings

1 tablespoon whole black
   peppercorns
2 tablespoons fennel seeds
½ cup extra-virgin olive oil
1 garlic clove, crushed
1 medium fennel bulb—trimmed,
   cored and cut lengthwise into thin
   strips, trimmings reserved
1 whole center-cut salmon fillet (1½
   pounds), skinned
½ cup finely shredded fresh basil
1 tomato—peeled, seeded and cut
   into ¼-inch dice
2 tablespoons fresh lemon juice
Salt and freshly ground pepper

1. Crush the black peppercorns in a mortar or with the bottom of a heavy skillet. Place in a medium saucepan. Crush the fennel seeds and add to the peppercorns. Add the olive oil, garlic and some of the fennel trimmings. Warm the mixture over moderate heat until just hot, 2 to 3 minutes. Let cool, transfer to a lidded glass jar and set aside at room temperature overnight.

2. Set the salmon fillet on a work surface. Run your hand over the fillet to locate any stray bones and remove them with tweezers. Slice the salmon crosswise into ¾-inch strips. Lay one of the strips, cut-side up, in a semicircle.

Use another strip to complete the circle, arranging the slices so that the thin portions overlap the thick portions. Fit a third strip of salmon in the center, folding it as necessary to fill the circle. Tie the rouelle with cotton string. Repeat with the remaining salmon strips to make 4 rouelles. Stuff about 1 teaspoon of the shredded basil between the slices in each assembled rouelle. (*The rouelles can be assembled up to 1 day ahead and refrigerated, covered.*)

3. Strain the fennel oil into a medium bowl. Add the fennel strips, diced tomato, lemon juice, ½ teaspoon salt and ¼ teaspoon pepper.

4. Heat a large heavy skillet over high heat until hot, 2 to 3 minutes. Season the rouelles lightly on both sides with salt and pepper. Add 2 teaspoons of the fennel oil to the skillet and when it begins to smoke, add the salmon rouelles. Cook until crusty and brown, about 3 minutes. Turn and cook until the other side is browned and the interior barely cooked through, about 1 minute longer. Transfer the rouelles to serving plates. Using a slotted spoon, remove the fennel and tomato from the oil and scatter on top. Sprinkle with the remaining basil and pour 1 to 2 tablespoons of the fennel oil over each. Serve immediately.

—*Le Bernardin, New York City*

• • •

RED SNAPPER BAKED IN COARSE SALT

At Port Alma, one of the best fish restaurants in Paris, chef Paul Canal knows his fish, and there is no better way to prepare a fresh whole fish than baking it in an envelope of sea salt, which cooks it gently and evenly.

Begin with the freshest of fish; pay careful attention to its weight, the oven temperature and the size of the baking dish. A two-pound fish should bake perfectly in 30 minutes, a three-pound fish in 40.

Traditionally this dish is prepared with no seasoning other than the salt, not even pepper, to allow the pure flavor of the fish to dominate. And contrary to what one might expect, the fish does not end up tasting particularly salty, for the salt serves not so much as a seasoning but more as a harness, sealing in juices and flavor. Try this with rockfish, striped bass or even a small salmon.

4 Servings

One cleaned 3-pound red snapper—gills removed, scales and head left on, tail and fins trimmed
7 to 8 cups coarse (kosher) salt
Extra-virgin olive oil, for serving
Fresh lemon wedges, for serving

1. Preheat the oven to 450°. Rinse the fish thoroughly inside and out until there is no trace of blood. Pat dry.

2. In a baking dish just large enough to hold the fish comfortably, spread 1 cup of the salt in an even layer. Place the fish on top of the salt and pour the remaining 6 to 7 cups of salt over and around the fish to cover it completely from head to tail.

3. Bake the fish in the middle of the oven for 40 minutes, or until an instant-reading thermometer inserted in the thickest part registers 130°.

4. Place the baking dish on a sheet pan or piece of newspaper. Using a brush, remove as much salt as possible from the top of the fish so that it won't get on the flesh when you remove the skin. (This is a rather awkward procedure, and it helps to have two pairs of hands, one pair to hold the baking dish and another to carefully brush off the salt.)

5. Using the blade of a sharp knife or a fork, gently scrape the skin from the top fillet of the fish and discard. Using two large spoons or two forks, gently remove the top fillet in neat pieces and transfer to 2 warmed dinner plates. With the spoons, carefully lift out the bones and discard. Remove the bottom fillet in pieces, scraping off any excess salt, and transfer, skin-side up, to 2 more warmed dinner plates; gently scrape off the skin and discard. Serve immediately with a cruet of olive oil and a bowl of lemon wedges.

—*Patricia Wells*

• • •

BAKED YELLOWTAIL SNAPPER WITH BALSAMIC VINEGAR

❦ The delicacy of the snapper points to a medium-bodied, crisp, dry white, such as a 1987 Robert Mondavi Fumé Blanc Reserve from California to underscore the accent of balsamic vinegar.

3 to 4 Servings

1 whole yellowtail or red snapper, cleaned (about 3 pounds)
2 tablespoons all-purpose flour
2 tablespoons olive oil
2 tablespoons balsamic vinegar
2 tablespoons dry white wine
1 medium garlic clove, smashed
1 tablespoon fresh rosemary, plus sprigs for garnish
1½ teaspoons fresh thyme, plus sprigs for garnish
1 teaspoon salt
½ teaspoon freshly ground pepper
1 bottle (8 ounces) clam juice
2 tablespoons fresh lemon juice
Lemon slices, for garnish

1. Preheat the oven to 350°. Using a small sharp knife, make 2 diagonal slashes, about ½ inch deep, on both sides of the fish. Dust the fish with the flour and shake off any excess.

2. In a large, nonreactive roasting pan, heat the oil over moderate heat. Add the fish and cook for 1 minute on each side. Transfer to a large platter and set aside. Wipe the oil from the pan.

3. Reduce the heat to low and add the vinegar, wine, garlic, rosemary, thyme, salt, pepper and half of the clam juice. Cook, stirring, for 1 minute.

4. Return the fish to the pan and bake for 15 minutes. Add the remaining clam juice and the lemon juice and bake for 12 minutes longer or until the fish is opaque and flakes with a fork. Transfer the fish to a serving platter. Strain the pan juices through a sieve and pour them over the fish. Garnish with the rosemary and thyme sprigs and the lemon slices.

—Sandrino Benitez and Filippo Il Grande, Il Tulipano, Miami

• • •

ENGLISH COUNTRY HOUSE DINNER PARTY

Serves 4

Pimm's Cup

Assorted Olives

Roasted Garlic and Leek Chowder (p. 44)

Toast Points

Vermouth-Poached Sole with Vegetables (p. 65)

New Potatoes with Parsley

Buttered Asparagus Spears

❦ *Crisp light white, such as 1989 Torres Viña Sol or 1989 Mastroberardino Fiano di Avellino*

Field Salad with Walnut Oil Vinaigrette and Goat Cheese

Coconut Cream Custard (p. 255)

Café Filtre

VERMOUTH-POACHED SOLE WITH VEGETABLES

Chef Christopher Gross uses sparkling fresh Atlantic sole, caught off the Breton coast and shipped by air overnight, for this utterly simple presentation. Any lean, white-fleshed fish with a firm texture and delicate flavor could be substituted, but it should be the freshest fish you can find.

4 Servings

1 tablespoon olive oil
1 medium carrot, thinly sliced
4 medium shallots, thinly sliced crosswise to form small rounds
Eight 4-ounce sole fillets
½ cup dry vermouth
3 tablespoons fresh lemon juice
Coarse (kosher) salt and freshly ground pepper
⅓ cup heavy cream
4 tablespoons cold unsalted butter, cut into ½-inch pieces
2 teaspoons chopped fresh chervil

1. Coat the bottom of a very large nonreactive skillet with the olive oil. Scatter the carrot and shallot slices in the pan and lay the sole fillets in one layer on top. Pour in the vermouth and lemon juice and sprinkle with coarse salt and pepper. Bring to a simmer over high heat, then reduce the heat to low. Press a round of wax paper over the fish and cover with a lid. Cook until the fish is just opaque throughout, about 5 minutes. With a spatula, carefully transfer the sole fillets to a warm platter. Cover with foil and set aside in a warm place.

2. Increase the heat to moderate and bring the liquid in the skillet to a simmer. Stir in the cream and simmer until reduced slightly, about 2 minutes. Remove from the heat and whisk in the cold butter, piece by piece. Season to taste with coarse salt and pepper and stir in the chervil. Transfer the sole to warmed plates and spoon the sauce and vegetables on top.

—*Christopher Gross,*
Christopher's, Phoenix

• • •

GRILLED SWORDFISH WITH GREEN MANGO SLAW

Using underripe fruits as vegetables is a tropical tradition. Chris Schlesinger reaches back into his childhood for an old-fashioned southern slaw, then reinterprets it with green mangoes from the Caribbean. Green papaya could be used instead, and tuna steaks can take the place of swordfish.

4 Servings

½ cup (packed) fresh coriander (cilantro) leaves
1 large garlic clove, minced
¼ cup coarsely chopped pecans (1 ounce)
¼ cup olive oil
Salt and freshly ground pepper
Four 8-ounce swordfish steaks, 1 inch thick
Green Mango Slaw (p. 156)

1. In a food processor or blender, combine the coriander, garlic and pecans and process, scraping down the sides of the bowl once, until a rough paste forms. With the machine on, slowly pour in 3

tablespoons of the oil to make a smooth paste. Scrape the coriander pesto into a bowl and season with salt and pepper to taste. Cover and refrigerate. (*The pesto can be made up to 1 day ahead.*)

2. Light a grill or preheat the broiler. Rub both sides of the swordfish steaks with the remaining 1 tablespoon oil and sprinkle lightly with salt and pepper. When you can hold your hand 5 inches above the grill for 3 to 4 seconds, but no longer, the fire is ready. Grill the fish for 4 to 5 minutes on each side until the surface is lightly browned and the flesh flakes easily with a fork and is almost opaque. Alternatively, broil the fish until done.

3. Transfer the fish to plates and top each with a generous tablespoon of the coriander pesto. Spoon the Green Mango Slaw alongside.

—*Chris Schlesinger, East Coast Grill,*
Cambridge, Massachusetts

• • •

GRILLED TUNA WITH ROSEMARY AND THYME

4 Servings

3 tablespoons olive oil
1 tablespoon fresh rosemary, plus sprigs for garnish
2 teaspoons fresh thyme
Four 6- to 8-ounce tuna steaks, ¾ to 1 inch thick
Freshly ground pepper
½ teaspoon salt
Lemon quarters, for serving

1. Light a grill or preheat the broiler. On a large plate, combine the olive oil, rosemary and thyme. Add the tuna and season with pepper to taste; turn to coat with oil. Marinate for up to 30 minutes, turning a few times.

2. Season both sides of the tuna steaks with the salt. Grill about 4 inches from the heat for about 4 minutes on each side or until just pink in the center. Transfer the tuna to plates and serve garnished with lemon wedges and rosemary sprigs.

—*Stephanie Lyness*

• • •

TUNA IN A YUCATAN-STYLE MARINADE

The style of cooking that became known as California cuisine was successfully transplanted to New York by Jonathan Waxman at Jams. Its nouvelle cuisine foundation is evident in the butter sauce served with the grilled tuna, but his use of big-flavored ethnic ingredients—jalapeños, saffron, cumin, coriander and ginger—is pure California style.

4 Servings

1 large red onion, thinly sliced (2 cups)
1 cup plus 2 tablespoons extra-virgin olive oil
10 medium garlic cloves, peeled
3 jalapeño peppers, stemmed and quartered
Pinch of saffron threads
Pinch of cumin
½ teaspoon ground coriander
½ cup fresh orange juice
2 tablespoons fresh lemon juice

1 cup sake

1 cup (loosely packed) opal or purple
   basil leaves*

Four 6-ounce tuna steaks, ¾ inch
   thick

1½ pounds fresh spinach, stemmed

1 stick (4 ounces) plus 2 tablespoons
   cold unsalted butter, cut into
   tablespoons

¾ teaspoon salt

¾ teaspoon freshly ground black
   pepper

4 small shallots, minced (¼ cup)

¼ cup Champagne vinegar

2½ tablespoons minced fresh ginger

*Available at green markets and
   specialty produce stores

1. In a medium nonreactive saucepan, combine the onion with ½ cup of the olive oil and cook over moderately low heat, stirring, until softened, about 10 minutes. Add the garlic, jalapeños, saffron, cumin, coriander, orange juice, lemon juice and ¼ cup of the sake. Increase the heat to moderately high and cook, stirring, until the garlic is soft and the liquid is syrupy and

has reduced to 1½ cups, about 10 minutes. Set aside to cool slightly.

2. Reserve 4 of the nicest basil leaves for garnish. In a food processor, combine the remaining basil leaves with the onion mixture. Process until smooth, scraping the sides down. With the motor running, slowly add ½ cup of the oil in a stream and process until the mixture is well blended. Pour half of this marinade into an 8-inch square nonreactive baking dish. Place the fish on top and cover with the rest of the marinade. Set aside uncovered for at least 30 minutes and up to 3 to 4 hours.

3. Set aside 8 large, unblemished spinach leaves for garnish. In a large skillet, melt 2 tablespoons of the butter in the remaining 2 tablespoons of oil over moderately high heat. Add the remaining spinach, several handfuls at a time, and cook, turning, until just wilted, about 5 minutes. Season with ¼ teaspoon each of the salt and pepper. Remove from the heat and set aside.

4. Preheat the broiler. In a medium nonreactive saucepan, combine the shallots, Champagne vinegar, ginger and the remaining ¾ cup sake. Boil over high heat until all the liquid has evaporated, about 5 minutes. Reduce the heat to low and whisk in the remaining stick of butter, 1 piece at a time, adding the next piece only after the previous piece is nearly incorporated. Season with ¼ teaspoon each of the salt and pepper. Set aside in a warm place but don't let the sauce get too hot or it will separate.

5. Transfer the tuna to a broiler pan, leaving a generous coating of the marinade on top. Sprinkle with the remaining ¼ teaspoon each salt and black pepper. Broil about 7 inches from the heat, without turning, until the mari-

nade is bubbling and slightly browned, about 7 minutes.

6. To serve, reheat the spinach, if necessary, then place a thin layer on 4 serving plates. Place a tuna steak on top and spoon about 2 tablespoons of sauce over each. Serve the remaining sauce on the side. Garnish with the reserved spinach leaves and basil leaves.

—Jonathan Waxman

• • •

SEAFOOD POUCHES

This aromatic dish is baked at the same time as the corn. If scrod isn't available, you can use cod or halibut instead.

4 Servings

4 scrod fillets (5 ounces each)

2 medium shallots, thinly sliced

1 medium tomato, cut into 8 thin
   slices

2 teaspoons basil

8 medium mushrooms, thinly sliced

4 tablespoons unsalted butter

32 mussels (about 1¾ pounds),
   scrubbed and debearded

1 teaspoon salt

½ teaspoon freshly ground pepper

½ cup dry white wine

Lemon wedges, for serving

1. Preheat the oven to 475°. Tear off four 2-foot-long sheets of heavy-duty aluminum foil. Place a scrod fillet in the center of each. Top each with one-fourth of the shallots, tomato slices, basil, mushrooms, butter, mussels, salt and pepper.

2. Bring the corners of the foil up towards the center and sprinkle 2 tablespoons of wine into each pouch.

**HERBED TUNA ON THE
GRILL**

Serves 4

Grilled Bread Salad with Tomatoes,
Fennel and Goat Cheese (p. 157)

Grilled Tuna with Rosemary and
Thyme (p. 66)

Fresh Raspberries with Cream and
Chocolate (p. 236)

—Stephanie Lyness

FISH & SHELLFISH

Bring the 2 long ends of the foil together and roll down tightly over the ingredients. Roll up the short ends to form the pouches.

3. Place 2 pouches on each of 2 large baking sheets and bake for 10 minutes. Switch the sheets around and bake for 15 minutes longer. Empty the pouches into shallow soup bowls and serve hot with lemon wedges.

—*Jim Fobel*

• • •

SCALLOPS IN SAFFRON BROTH WITH CORIANDER PESTO CROUTONS

The surprising use of coriander with a touch of jalapeño is a twist on a classic pesto and balances what chef Greg Higgin calls "a Provençal seasoning profile" in this light and simple presentation.

4 Servings

1 lemon
½ teaspoon saffron threads
2 cups bottled clam juice diluted with 2 cups water
½ cup amontillado sherry or well-aged fino sherry
½ cup extra-virgin olive oil
12 garlic cloves, peeled
1 large jalapeño pepper, halved lengthwise and seeded
½ cup coarsely chopped fresh coriander (cilantro) leaves, plus additional leaves for garnish
1 tablespoon freshly grated Parmesan cheese
2 anchovy fillets, drained

Salt and freshly ground black pepper
2 medium leeks, white and tender green, cut into thin julienne strips
6 tomatoes, preferably Roma (about 1 pound)—peeled, seeded and cut into ½-inch dice
1 baguette, preferably sourdough, sliced ¼ inch thick
1¼ pounds sea scallops
About ¼ cup all-purpose flour, for dredging

1. Using a swivel-bladed peeler, remove the lemon zest in large strips, leaving behind the bitter white pith. Using a sharp knife, slice the zest lengthwise into very thin slivers. Set aside. Squeeze the juice from the lemon and set aside.

2. In a medium nonreactive saucepan, crumble the saffron into the diluted clam juice. Add the lemon juice, slivered lemon zest and sherry. Cover partially and cook over low heat to infuse the saffron, about 10 minutes. Transfer this broth to a large bowl and set aside. (*The broth can be made 1 day ahead and refrigerated, covered.*)

3. In a small skillet, warm ¼ cup of the olive oil over low heat. Add the garlic cloves and jalapeño, cover and cook, shaking the pan occasionally, until the garlic is golden brown and tender, about 5 minutes. In a food processor, combine the garlic, jalapeño and oil with the chopped coriander, Parmesan and anchovies and pulse until a paste forms, scraping down the sides of the bowl as necessary. With the machine on, slowly pour in 2 tablespoons of the olive oil and process until incorporated. Season the pesto to taste with salt and pepper.

4. In a medium nonreactive saucepan, warm 1 tablespoon of the olive oil over low heat. Add the leeks and cook, stirring occasionally, until tender, about

SEASIDE DINNER

Serves 6

Sautéed Sea Scallops with Toasted Almonds (p. 69)

Green Chile Spoon Bread (p. 198)

Boston Lettuce with Stuffed Endive Spears (p. 153)

🍷 *1987 Zind Humbrecht Riesling*

Dried Sour Cherries and Pineapple in Port (p. 237)

—*Lee Bailey*

5 minutes. Add the tomatoes and the reserved broth. Increase the heat to moderate and bring to a simmer. Season with salt and pepper to taste. Cover and set aside over low heat to keep warm.

5. Preheat the broiler. Arrange the baguette slices on a baking sheet and broil 5 inches from the heat, turning once, for about 30 seconds each side until lightly browned on both sides. Let cool slightly, then spread a thin layer of the coriander pesto on each slice. Broil the croutons for about 30 seconds, until the pesto is glazed and bubbly.

6. Place the scallops in a large strainer or sieve and sprinkle the flour evenly over them. Shake to coat the scallops and remove all excess flour.

7. In a large skillet, heat the remaining 1 tablespoon olive oil over high heat until smoking. Add the scallops in a single layer and cook undisturbed until browned and crusty on the bottom, about 1 minute. Using tongs, turn the scallops and cook until browned, crusty and firm to a light touch, about 1 minute longer. The scallops are done when there is just a trace of translucency left in the center.

8. Transfer the scallops to 4 large, shallow bowls and pour over the hot saffron broth. Garnish with the coriander leaves and serve with the croutons on the side.

—*Greg Higgins, The Heathman Hotel, Portland, Oregon*

• • •

SAUTEED SEA SCALLOPS WITH TOASTED ALMONDS

❡ These sweet, briny scallops point to a fragrant, crisp white that will enhance but not overpower them, such as 1987 Zind Humbrecht Riesling from Alsace.

6 Servings

½ cup sliced almonds (about 1½ ounces)
3 medium shallots, minced
2 garlic cloves, minced
1 cup dry white wine
6 tablespoons unsalted butter, cut into bits
⅓ cup minced parsley
¼ teaspoon salt
½ teaspoon freshly ground pepper
1½ pounds sea scallops

1. In a medium skillet, toast the almonds over moderate heat, tossing occasionally, until golden, about 5 minutes. Set aside to cool.

2. In a small nonreactive saucepan, combine the shallots, garlic and wine and bring to a boil over high heat. Boil until the wine has reduced to ½ cup, about 5 minutes. Reduce the heat to low and whisk in 4 tablespoons of the

butter until incorporated. Stir in the parsley, salt and pepper and set aside in a warm spot.

3. Heat a large heavy skillet over high heat. Add the remaining 2 tablespoons butter, and when it begins to sizzle, add the scallops. Sauté, stirring, until the scallops are translucent, about 4 minutes. Transfer the scallops to a serving dish and pour the sauce on top. Garnish with the toasted almonds and serve immediately.

—*Lee Bailey*

• • •

SAUTEED SHRIMP WITH GARLIC AND HERBS

It is very easy to toughen shrimp by overcooking. Here, the shrimp are slit down the back and partially butterflied to insure even cooking. This cutting method also gives the finished shrimp an attractive shape. As with most sautés, it is important to have all your ingredients measured out before you begin. Tongs make easy work of turning the shrimp. Use a pan large enough to hold the shrimp in a single layer. Serve this zesty dish over pasta or with rice.

4 Servings

2 dozen large shrimp (about 1¾ pounds), shelled
¼ cup plus 1 tablespoon olive oil
3 garlic cloves, minced
½ teaspoon oregano
3 medium scallions, white and green parts thinly sliced separately
2½ tablespoons fresh lemon juice
2 tablespoons dry white wine
¼ teaspoon salt

½ to ¾ teaspoon freshly ground pepper, to taste
2 tablespoons unsalted butter in one piece
1 tablespoon minced flat-leaf parsley

1. Place a shrimp flat on a work surface with the tail nearest you. Hold the shrimp flat with one hand. Using a sharp paring knife and beginning at the head end, slit two-thirds of the way down the shrimp toward the tail, cutting about halfway through. Scrape out the exposed vein. Repeat with the remaining shrimp.

2. In a large nonreactive skillet, combine ¼ cup of the oil with the garlic, oregano and scallion whites. Cook over moderate heat, stirring occasionally, until the oil is simmering gently, about 5 minutes. Do not let the garlic brown.

3. Arrange the shrimp in the pan in rows, cut-sides down, tails up. Increase the heat to high. When the shrimp begin to sizzle, cook for 30 seconds. Turn the shrimp with tongs and cook for 30 seconds on each of the other 2 sides. Then cook, stirring frequently, until opaque throughout, about 1 minute longer. Add the lemon juice and wine and simmer until the sauce thickens, about 1½ minutes. Sprinkle the salt, pepper and 1 tablespoon of water over the shrimp and cook, stirring, for 30 seconds.

4. Add the remaining 1 tablespoon oil to the pan, then swirl in the butter until incorporated. Stir in the sliced scallion greens and the parsley until evenly distributed. Arrange the shrimp on warmed plates and spoon the sauce on top.

—*Tracey Seaman*

• • •

FISH & SHELLFISH

MICROWAVE MEDALLIONS OF SHRIMP AND VEGETABLES

At Troisgros in Roanne, this dish is made with circular layers of crayfish, but my simplified shrimp version is as good.

4 Servings

1 pound medium shrimp (about 24) in their shells
Microwave Court Bouillon (p. 270)
1 large carrot, very thinly sliced
1 small zucchini, sliced into very thin rounds
1 small onion, very thinly sliced
½ cup dry white wine
Pinch of saffron threads
3 tablespoons unsalted butter
¼ teaspoon fresh lemon juice
⅛ teaspoon coarse (kosher) salt

1. In a microwaveable 5-quart casserole, combine the shrimp and Court Bouillon. Cover tightly with microwave plastic wrap. Cook on High, or full, power for 7 minutes, interrupting the cooking twice to stir. Prick the plastic to let the steam escape, then uncover. Using a slotted spoon, transfer the shrimp to a plate. When cool enough to handle, shell and devein the shrimp.

2. Add the carrot to the casserole. Cover and cook on High for 5 minutes. Using a slotted spoon, transfer to the plate with the shrimp. Add the zucchini slices to the casserole. Cover and cook for 2 minutes. Using a slotted spoon, transfer to the plate. Add the onion to the casserole. Cover and cook for 2 minutes. Using a slotted spoon, transfer to the plate.

3. Pour out all but ½ cup of the broth from the casserole and reserve for an-

other use. Add the wine and saffron and cook, uncovered, on High for 12 minutes. Whisk in the butter, lemon juice and salt. *(The recipe can be prepared to this point up to 6 hours ahead. Let cool, then cover and refrigerate. Let come to room temperature before proceeding.)*

4. Arrange the vegetables on 4 dinner plates and garnish with the shrimp. Spoon some of the wine sauce on top. Cover and cook each serving on High for 55 seconds and serve immediately.

—*Barbara Kafka*

• • •

SHRIMP WITH ORANGE-PISTACHIO COUSCOUS AND CHUNKY MINTED YOGURT SAUCE

Chef Eddie Matney of Eddie's Grill in Phoenix says that this marinade also works very nicely with chicken, fish and veal.

6 Servings

18 jumbo shrimp, in their shells
½ cup extra-virgin olive oil
½ cup strained fresh orange juice
3 tablespoons strained fresh lemon juice
1½ tablespoons strained fresh lime juice
1½ teaspoons soy sauce
1½ teaspoons Dijon mustard
2 garlic cloves, minced
Freshly ground pepper and salt
Orange Pistachio Couscous (p. 138)
Chunky Minted Yogurt Sauce (p. 263)

1. Using scissors, snip each shrimp shell down the back to expose the dark vein. Scrape out the veins, leaving the shells attached.

2. In a deep nonreactive bowl, whisk the oil with the orange, lemon and lime juices, soy sauce, mustard, garlic and 1 teaspoon pepper. Add the shrimp and toss well. Cover and refrigerate for 1 hour. Soak twelve 8-inch bamboo skewers in water for 20 minutes.

3. Light the grill. Thread 3 of the shrimp onto 2 parallel skewers. Repeat with the remaining shrimp and skewers. Set the skewered shrimp on a rack set over a platter for 5 minutes to drain.

4. When the coals are medium-hot, grill the shrimp on an oiled rack for 3 to 4 minutes on each side, or until opaque throughout. Alternatively, broil the shrimp for 2½ minutes on each side, until firm and opaque throughout. Salt the shrimp lightly and remove the skewers. Serve 3 shrimp on each plate, with the couscous and yogurt sauce.

—*Linda Burum*

• • •

SHRIMP SAUTE WITH TARRAGON, TOMATOES AND MUSTARD

If you split the shrimp lengthwise, they will cook evenly and form a nice curlicue shape. In this recipe, clam broth is used in place of fish stock; since brands vary, it's important to taste the broth to see how salty it is before you add any salt to the dish.

6 First-Course Servings

4 tablespoons unsalted butter
¼ cup minced shallots

2 pounds medium shrimp—shelled,
  halved lengthwise and deveined
1 bottle (8 ounces) clam juice
½ cup dry white wine
1½ pounds plum tomatoes—peeled,
  seeded and cut into ¼-inch dice
1 tablespoon Dijon mustard
2 teaspoons finely chopped fresh
  tarragon, plus 6 sprigs for garnish
½ teaspoon freshly ground pepper
2 tablespoons crème fraîche
2 medium Belgian endives, trimmed
  to 4 inches and broken into
  individual spears

1. In a heavy 12-inch nonreactive skillet, melt the butter over moderately high heat. Add the shallots and cook, stirring, until softened, about 2 minutes. Add the shrimp to the pan; increase the heat to high and cook, stirring frequently, until the shrimp are opaque throughout and curled, about 5 minutes. Transfer the shrimp to a bowl.

2. Add the clam broth and wine to the skillet and boil until the liquid reduces to ½ cup, about 8 minutes. Add the tomatoes and continue to cook for 4 minutes longer. Stir in the mustard, tarragon, pepper and crème fraîche and boil over high heat for 2 minutes. Return the shrimp to the pan and cook until warmed through, about 3 minutes.

3. Mound the shrimp in the center of each plate. Garnish each serving with 3 or 4 endive spears and a tarragon sprig.
—Ann Chantal Altman

• • •

SHRIMP AND GARBANZO BEANS IN RAGOUT

Chiles, mint and cilantro, says chef Amaryll Schwertner of Sol y Luna in San Francisco, are all references to Central American cuisine, but the combination of shrimp and garbanzos could easily recall Italy as well. For variety, substitute fresh scallops or baby calamari for the shrimp.

6 Servings

½ cup plus 3 tablespoons extra-virgin
  olive oil
2 pounds large fresh shrimp, shelled
  and deveined, shells reserved
4 medium tomatoes—1 halved, 3
  peeled, seeded and chopped
1 small yellow onion, halved, plus 1
  large yellow onion, minced
1 bay leaf
5 whole white peppercorns
Pinch of crushed red pepper
1 tablespoon plus a few drops fresh
  lemon juice
2 tablespoons finely grated orange
  zest
Pinch of freshly ground white pepper
Pinch of coarse (kosher) salt
Pinch of ground ginger
2 large garlic cloves, minced
¼ teaspoon crushed whole dried
  chiles
3 fresh mint sprigs, minced, plus ½
  cup mint leaves
3 tablespoons cider vinegar
2 cans (19 ounces each) garbanzo
  beans, drained and rinsed

Salt and freshly ground black pepper
½ cup flat-leaf parsley leaves
½ cup fresh coriander (cilantro)
  leaves

1. In a large nonreactive saucepan, heat 1 tablespoon of the olive oil over high heat. Add the shrimp shells and cook, stirring, until pink and aromatic, about 3 minutes. Add the tomato and onion halves and continue to cook until the onion begins to brown, about 4 minutes.

2. Add enough water to the pan to cover the shrimp shells (about 5 cups). Stir in the bay leaf, white peppercorns and crushed red pepper and bring to a boil over high heat. Reduce the heat to moderately low and simmer until the broth is very fragrant, about 30 minutes. Strain the stock through a fine sieve and into another large saucepan and return to a boil over high heat. Boil until the stock has reduced to 2 cups, about 15 minutes. Set aside.

3. Meanwhile, in a large bowl, whisk 3 tablespoons of the olive oil with 1 tablespoon of the lemon juice, 1 tablespoon of the orange zest and the ground white pepper, coarse salt and ginger. Add the shrimp and toss to coat thoroughly. Cover and let marinate in the refrigerator for at least 1 hour and up to 4 hours.

4. In a large nonreactive saucepan, heat ¼ cup of the olive oil. Add the minced onion and the garlic and cook over moderately low heat, stirring, until the onion is translucent, about 10 minutes. Stir in the crushed chiles, minced mint and the remaining 1 tablespoon orange zest. Increase the heat to high, add the chopped tomatoes, reserved shrimp stock and 2 tablespoons of the cider vinegar and bring to a boil. Re-

duce the heat to moderate and simmer until the sauce reduces to 3½ cups, about 20 minutes.

5. Add the garbanzo beans to the sauce and continue simmering until the beans have absorbed its flavor, about 10 minutes. Stir in the remaining 1 tablespoon cider vinegar and 1 tablespoon of the olive oil. Season with salt and black pepper to taste. Remove from the heat, cover and set aside. (*The recipe can be prepared to this point 1 day ahead. Let cool, then cover and refrigerate.*)

6. In a large skillet, heat 2 teaspoons of the olive oil over moderately high heat until almost smoking. Drain the shrimp and add half to the pan. Cook, turning once, until pink, about 1 minute per side. As the shrimp are cooked, transfer them to the bean ragout. Repeat with the remaining shrimp, adding up to 1 more teaspoon of oil to the pan if necessary. Keep warm.

7. In a bowl, toss the ½ cup mint, parsley and coriander. Add the remaining 1 tablespoon olive oil, a few drops of lemon juice, salt and black pepper to taste. Ladle the ragout into 6 shallow serving bowls and garnish each serving with some of the herb "salad." Serve immediately.

—*Amaryll Schwertner, Sol y Luna,*
San Francisco

• • •

DEEP-FRIED CALAMARI WITH SESAME DIPPING SAUCE

Of all the coatings used to deep-fry squid, I prefer flour. It produces a light yet crunchy result. Since its one drawback is that the final color is relatively pale, a little bit of baking soda is added to the flour to help it brown.

This is the kind of dish best served to friends who don't mind standing around the kitchen nibbling while you cook. It's pointless to try making an elegant presentation out of it or even bringing it into the dining room. The squid must be bone-dry before frying, or you and your kitchen will be spattered with oil. If you own a covered electric deep-fat fryer, such as the one made by DeLonghi, use it; it reduces the mess. Otherwise, use a pot and deep-frying thermometer.

4 Servings

2 pounds cleaned squid (bodies and
*   tentacles)*
1 quart vegetable oil, for frying
3 cups all-purpose flour
1 tablespoon baking soda
1 teaspoon salt
1 teaspoon freshly ground pepper
Lemon wedges, for serving
Sesame Dipping Sauce (p. 262)

1. Using a sharp knife, cut the squid bodies crosswise into ¼-inch rings. Slice the tentacles in half lengthwise if they are large. Rinse the squid several times, drain well and spread evenly on a kitchen towel. Cover with another clean towel and roll up the towels together.

Set aside to dry thoroughly. (*The squid can be prepared to this point up to 4 hours ahead and refrigerated.*)

2. In a deep-fat fryer, preferably with a basket, heat the oil to 375°. Alternatively, heat the oil in a large saucepan or skillet. Meanwhile, in a large bowl, combine the flour with the baking soda, salt and pepper. Have a strainer handy.

3. When the oil is hot, transfer about one-quarter of the squid to the flour mixture and toss until coated. Shake off any excess flour, place the squid in the strainer and shake above the bowl of flour to release any more excess flour.

4. Transfer the squid to the frying basket and carefully lower it into the hot oil. Fry until golden, 2 to 3 minutes; do not overcook. Remove the frying basket from the oil and let drain briefly over the fryer, then transfer the squid to paper towels to drain thoroughly. Alternatively, fry the squid in the saucepan or skillet and use a slotted spoon to transfer it to paper towels.

5. Serve the squid immediately with lemon wedges and the Sesame Dipping Sauce. Repeat the procedure with the remaining squid.

—*Mark Bittman*

• • •

Scallops in Saffron Broth (p. 68).

When I should be her lover
forever and a day,
And she my faithful sweetheart
the golden hair was gray.

Far left, Dover Sole and Shrimp
Timbales with Red Pepper
Puree (p. 53). Above, Parmesan-
Crusted Soft-Shell Crab
Sandwiches (p. 78). Near left,
Pan-Fried Salmon Steaks (p. 56).

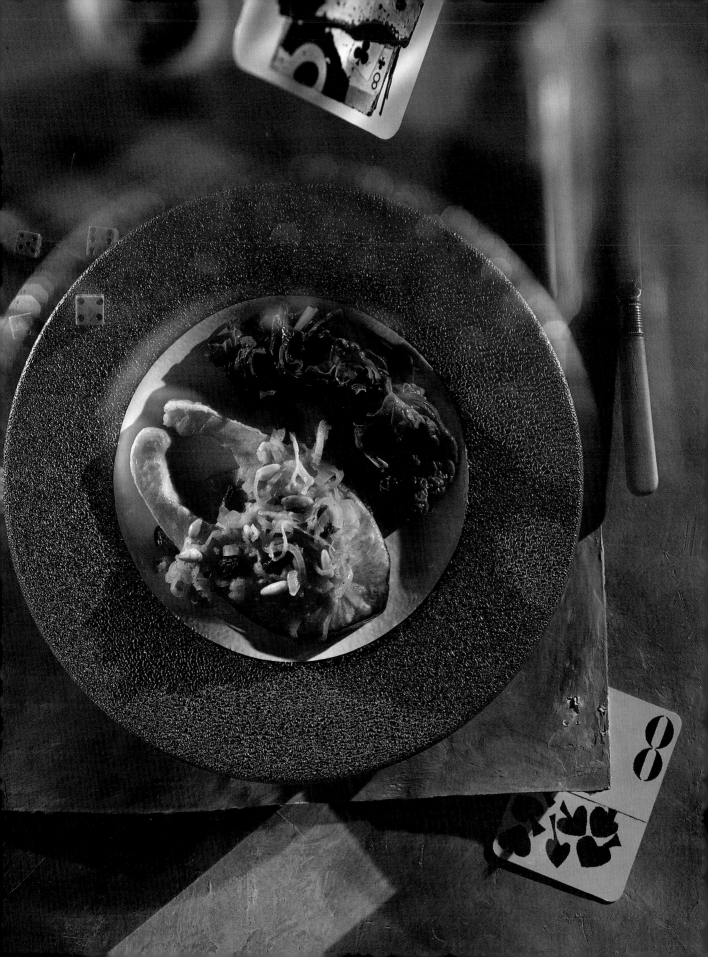

STIR-FRIED SQUID WITH BASIL AND GARLIC

This dish is amazingly quick and easy to make. Be sure to cut the squid into fairly uniform pieces to ensure even cooking. There is some, but not too much, crushed red pepper in the dish. I sometimes make it with about five whole dried red chiles, which are removed before serving. Either method is fine. The goal is to let some heat come through without overwhelming the basil and garlic. For a more prominent basil flavor, marinate the squid and basil in Step 1 up to an hour ahead.

You can also serve the squid as a hot hors d'oeuvre. Use a slotted spoon to transfer it from the wok to a plate or bowl and pass with toothpicks. But I like it best poured with its juices over cooked white rice. Serve a colorful vegetable alongside.

4 Servings

1½ pounds cleaned squid, bodies cut into ½-inch rings or diamonds, and tentacles halved lengthwise if large
½ cup (packed) basil leaves, coarsely chopped
2 tablespoons peanut oil
1 tablespoon minced garlic
⅛ to ¼ teaspoon crushed red pepper
1 teaspoon salt

1. In a large bowl, combine the squid and basil.

Salmon with Sweet-and-Sour Onions (p. 58).

2. Heat a wok or a large heavy skillet over high heat until smoking, 4 to 5 minutes. Reduce the heat to moderate, add the oil and swirl the pan to coat. Add the garlic and stir-fry until it begins to brown, about 15 seconds. Increase the heat to high and add the squid-basil mixture and crushed red pepper. Stir-fry until the squid becomes opaque, about 1 minute. Continue cooking, stirring often, until tender, 2 to 3 minutes longer. Stir in the salt and serve.

—*Mark Bittman*

• • •

OVEN-BRAISED SQUID WITH GARLIC

A straightforward dish for squid lovers, this stew exudes an enticing, heady aroma. Serve over rice, with buttered orzo or with lots of crusty bread to sop up the sauce.

♟ A crisp white with enough acidity to cut across the garlicky flavor is just what's needed here for cooking and for drinking. A tart, flavorful Sauvignon Blanc, such as 1989 Beringer or 1989 Matanzas Creek, would make an ideal match.

4 Servings

2 tablespoons olive oil
8 garlic cloves
2 pounds cleaned squid, bodies cut crosswise into ½-inch rings and tentacles halved lengthwise if large
1 tablespoon all-purpose flour
1 teaspoon paprika
1 teaspoon freshly ground pepper
½ cup chopped parsley
1 cup dry white wine

1. Preheat the oven to 350°. In a medium nonreactive flameproof casserole, warm the oil over moderately low heat. Add the garlic and cook gently, stirring occasionally, until just beginning to color, about 5 minutes. Add the squid and stir to coat for 1 minute.

2. Stir in the flour, paprika, pepper and all but 2 tablespoons of the parsley. Stir in the wine. Increase the heat to moderately high and bring to a boil. Stir once more, cover and bake in the oven for 1 hour, until the squid is tender and the garlic is soft enough to spread.

3. Uncover the casserole and place over moderate heat. Simmer until the sauce thickens slightly, 5 to 10 minutes. Stir in the reserved 2 tablespoons parsley and serve hot.

—*Mark Bittman*

• • •

SOFT-SHELL CRABS PROVENCAL

Any small pasta tossed with butter and chopped parsley would be lovely with this summery dish.

♟ The mild herbaceousness of a crisp, well-balanced California Sauvignon Blanc, such as 1989 Bergfeld or 1989 Sterling, would underscore the sweet flavor of the sautéed crab and harmonize with the accents of bell pepper and tomato.

4 Servings

¼ cup plus 2 tablespoons olive oil
1 medium red onion, thinly sliced
1 tablespoon minced garlic
1 red bell pepper, sliced lengthwise into ⅛-inch strips
1 yellow bell pepper, sliced

lengthwise into ⅛-inch strips
1 green bell pepper, sliced lengthwise
   into ⅛-inch strips
2 small zucchini, cut into 3-by-¼-
   inch sticks
1 pint cherry tomatoes, halved
1 teaspoon salt
¾ teaspoon freshly ground black
   pepper
8 cleaned soft-shell crabs
1 cup all-purpose flour
1 tablespoon herbes de Provence
2 tablespoons unsalted butter
½ cup shredded fresh basil

1. In a large nonreactive skillet, heat 2 tablespoons of the olive oil over moderately high heat. Add the onion and cook, stirring, until translucent, about 3 minutes. Add the garlic and cook for 1 minute. Stir in the bell pepper strips and the zucchini sticks and cook until softened slightly, 4 to 5 minutes. Add the tomatoes and ½ teaspoon each of the salt and black pepper. Toss to combine. Set aside, partially covered. (*The recipe can be prepared to this point up to 4 hours ahead.*)

2. Preheat the oven to 250°. Dry the crabs between 2 layers of paper towels. On a plate, toss the flour with the herbes de Provence and the remaining ½ teaspoon salt and ¼ teaspoon black pepper. Dredge the crabs in the seasoned flour.

3. In a large nonstick skillet, melt 1 tablespoon of the butter in 2 tablespoons of the olive oil over moderately high heat. Add 4 of the crabs and sauté, turning once, until red and crisp, about 3 minutes per side. Transfer to a heatproof platter and place in the oven to keep

warm. Repeat with the remaining 1 tablespoon butter, 2 tablespoons olive oil and 4 crabs.

4. Reheat the vegetables and stir in the basil. Spoon the vegetables onto 4 warmed plates and arrange 2 crabs on top of each.

—*Bob Chambers and Carl Parisi*

• • •

PARMESAN-CRUSTED SOFT-SHELL CRAB SANDWICHES

Makes 8 Sandwiches

2 cups all-purpose flour
1 cup freshly grated Parmesan
   cheese (4 ounces)
½ teaspoon salt
¼ to ½ teaspoon freshly ground
   pepper
2 eggs, lightly beaten
¼ teaspoon hot pepper sauce
1 cup mayonnaise
Juice of 1 lemon
Finely grated zest of 1 lemon
½ teaspoon minced garlic
½ teaspoon thyme
1 tablespoon extra-virgin olive oil
1 cup peanut oil, for frying
8 cleaned soft-shell crabs
8 round hard rolls, halved
2 ripe medium tomatoes, thinly sliced
2 bunches of arugula, large stems
   removed

1. In a medium bowl, combine 1 cup of the flour with the Parmesan cheese, salt and pepper. Make a well in the center and add the eggs and ¾ cup of water. Beat the eggs and water together and gradually incorporate the flour mixture to form a smooth batter. Add ⅛

teaspoon of the hot sauce and set aside to rest for 30 minutes.

2. In another bowl, combine the mayonnaise, lemon juice, lemon zest, garlic, thyme, olive oil and the remaining ⅛ teaspoon hot sauce. Whisk to blend and set aside for at least 30 minutes. (*The recipe can be prepared to this point up to 1 day ahead. Refrigerate the batter and mayonnaise. If the batter becomes very thick, thin it out with a little water.*)

3. Preheat the oven to 250°. In a large skillet, heat the peanut oil over moderately high heat to 350°. Dredge the crabs in the remaining 1 cup flour and shake off the excess.

4. Dip 4 of the crabs in the batter, let some of the batter drip off, and then fry them in the skillet, turning once, until golden brown, 2 to 3 minutes per side. Drain on paper towels, place on a heatproof platter and keep warm in the oven. Repeat with the 4 remaining crabs.

5. Scoop out some of the bread from

LUNCH BY THE POOL

Serves 8

Iced Tea

Tempura Onion Rings (p. 176)

*Parmesan-Crusted Soft-Shell Crab
Sandwiches (p. 78)*

Creamy Garlic Coleslaw (p. 156)

🍷 *California Chardonnay, such as
1988 Domaine Michel or 1989
Rodney Strong*

Strawberry Shortcake

Cappuccino

the center of the rolls to hollow them slightly. Spread 2 heaping teaspoons of the mayonnaise on the cut side of each half. Assemble the sandwiches by placing 2 or 3 slices of tomato and 4 or 5 arugula leaves on the bottom half of each roll. Set the fried crabs on top and close the sandwiches. Serve hot.

—*Bob Chambers and Carl Parisi*

• • •

SOFT-SHELL CRABS WITH CREAMY TOMATO SAUCE

Couscous and grilled eggplant would make delicious accompaniments.

4 Servings

½ *cup olive oil*
6 *garlic cloves, thinly sliced*
6 *large shallots, thinly sliced*
½ *teaspoon cumin seeds*
¼ *teaspoon celery seeds*
¼ *teaspoon crushed red pepper*
1 *teaspoon salt*
1 *teaspoon freshly ground black pepper*
½ *teaspoon sugar*
1 *can (35 ounces) Italian plum tomatoes, drained and chopped*
1 *cup crème fraîche*
1 *cup all-purpose flour*
8 *cleaned soft-shell crabs*

1. In a large nonreactive skillet, heat ¼ cup of the olive oil over moderate heat for 2 minutes. Add the garlic and shallots and cook, stirring frequently, until the shallots are translucent and the garlic begins to brown, 5 to 6 minutes. Stir in the cumin and celery seeds, red pepper and ½ teaspoon each of the salt and black pepper. Cook for 1 minute

longer. Stir in the sugar and tomatoes and bring to a boil. Reduce the heat to moderately low and simmer the sauce for 15 minutes. Add the crème fraîche and simmer for 6 minutes longer. Cover and keep warm. (*The sauce can be made up to 1 day ahead. Cover and refrigerate. Reheat before serving.*)

2. Preheat the oven to 250°. On a plate, toss the flour with the remaining ½ teaspoon each of salt and black pepper. Pat the crabs dry with paper towels and dredge them in the seasoned flour.

3. In a large skillet, preferably nonstick, heat 2 tablespoons of the olive oil over moderately high heat. Add 4 of the crabs and cook, turning once, until red and crisp, about 3 minutes per side. Transfer the crabs to a heatproof platter and place in the oven to keep warm. Repeat with the remaining 2 tablespoons olive oil and 4 crabs. Spoon the tomato sauce onto 4 warmed plates and arrange 2 crabs on the sauce on each plate.

—*Bob Chambers and Carl Parisi*

• • •

SOFT-SHELL CRABS WITH LEMON AND CAPERS

4 Servings

2 *lemons*
1 *cup all-purpose flour*
1 *teaspoon freshly ground pepper*
¼ *cup olive oil*
8 *cleaned soft-shell crabs*
3 *tablespoons unsalted butter*
5 *medium shallots, chopped*
½ *cup dry white wine*
2 *tablespoons drained capers*

1. Using a small sharp knife, peel 1 of

the lemons, removing all of the bitter white pith. Working over a bowl, cut in between the membranes to release the sections. Squeeze the juice from the remaining lemon into the bowl of sections and set aside.

2. Preheat the oven to 250°. On a large plate, combine the flour with the pepper. In a large nonreactive nonstick skillet, heat 2 tablespoons of the olive oil over moderately high heat. Pat the crabs dry with paper towels and dredge them in the flour. Add 4 of the crabs to the skillet and cook, turning once, until red and crisp, about 3 minutes per side. Transfer them to a heatproof platter and place in the oven to keep warm. Repeat with the remaining 2 tablespoons olive oil and 4 crabs.

3. Add the butter and shallots to the skillet and cook over moderately high heat, stirring frequently, until softened, 3 to 4 minutes. Increase the heat to high, add the wine and simmer until reduced by half, about 2 minutes. Add the reserved lemon sections and juice and the capers and stir well. Place 2 crabs on each plate and spoon the sauce on top.

—*Bob Chambers and Carl Parisi*

• • •

SOFT-SHELL CRABS WITH BLACK BEAN SAUCE

♥ The assertive flavors of the black beans, soy, garlic, ginger and sesame oil would work well with a light red—a Beaujolais, such as 1989 Georges Duboeuf, or California Pinot Noir, such as 1988 Mirassou Monterey or 1988 Bouchaine.

4 Servings

3 tablespoons Chinese fermented
    black beans*
5 tablespoons cornstarch
1 teaspoon fresh lemon juice
3 tablespoons soy sauce
1 tablespoon sesame seeds
5 tablespoons peanut oil
2 garlic cloves, minced
1-inch piece of fresh ginger, peeled
    and cut into small, thin
    matchsticks
¾ cup chicken stock or canned low-
    sodium broth
2 tablespoons dry sherry
¼ teaspoon chili oil*
8 cleaned soft-shell crabs
2 bunches of watercress, large stems
    removed
½ teaspoon Oriental sesame oil
½ cup thinly sliced scallions
*Available at Chinese markets

1. In a small bowl, soak the black beans in ½ cup of water for 15 minutes. Meanwhile, in another bowl, combine the cornstarch with the lemon juice, 1 teaspoon of the soy sauce and ¼ cup of water. Whisk to blend and set aside.

2. In a small dry skillet, toast the sesame seeds over moderate heat, stirring frequently, until fragrant and lightly browned, about 1½ minutes. Set aside.

3. In a medium skillet, heat 1 tablespoon of the peanut oil over moderately high heat. Add the garlic and ginger and stir-fry for 30 seconds. Drain the black beans and add them to the skillet along with the stock and sherry. Bring to a boil and cook for 30 seconds. Stir in 1½ teaspoons of the reserved cornstarch mixture and the chili oil. Remove from the heat, cover and set aside.

4. Preheat the oven to 250°. In a large skillet, preferably nonstick, heat 2 tablespoons of the peanut oil over moderately high heat. Working with 1 at a time, dip 4 of the crabs into the cornstarch mixture and then add them to the skillet. Cook, turning once, until browned and crisp, about 3 minutes per side. Transfer the crabs to a heatproof platter and place in the oven to keep warm. Repeat with another tablespoon of the peanut oil and the remaining 4 crabs.

5. Heat the remaining 1 tablespoon peanut oil in the skillet. When hot, add the watercress and sauté, tossing constantly, until wilted, about 1 minute. Add the remaining 2 tablespoons plus 2 teaspoons soy sauce and the sesame oil and toss well.

6. Reheat the black bean sauce and stir in the scallions. Mound the watercress on 4 warmed plates and arrange the crabs on top. Spoon the sauce over the crabs and sprinkle with the toasted sesame seeds.

—Bob Chambers and Carl Parisi

• • •

SPICED CRABS WITH FENNEL AND PEPPER SLAW

❧ The mélange of sweet and spicy flavors in this dish would be neatly bridged by a tart, fruity white, such as 1990 Callaway White Riesling, or balanced by the light sweetness of 1990 Fetzer Johannisberg Riesling.

4 Servings

1 teaspoon paprika
1 teaspoon thyme
1 teaspoon oregano
½ teaspoon ground coriander
½ teaspoon celery seeds
½ teaspoon salt
¼ teaspoon cayenne pepper
⅓ cup all-purpose flour
⅓ cup cornmeal
¼ cup vegetable oil
8 cleaned soft-shell crabs
1 egg, beaten with 2 tablespoons of
    water
Fennel and Bell Pepper Slaw
    (p. 156)

1. In a mortar or in a spice mill, combine the paprika, thyme, oregano, coriander, celery seeds, salt and cayenne. Grind to a fine powder. On a plate, toss the ground seasonings with the flour and cornmeal.

2. Preheat the oven to 250°. In a large skillet, preferably nonstick, heat 2 tablespoons of the vegetable oil over moderately high heat. Dip 4 of the crabs into the beaten egg and shake off any excess. Dredge them in the seasoned flour and cornmeal and fry, turning once, until browned and crisp, about 3 minutes per side. Transfer the crabs to a heatproof platter and place in the oven to keep warm. Repeat with the remaining 2 tablespoons oil and 4 crabs.

3. To serve, mound some of the Fennel and Bell Pepper Slaw on 4 plates and place 2 crabs alongside. Pass the remaining slaw separately.

—Bob Chambers and Carl Parisi

• • •

SOFT-SHELL CRABS WITH PINEAPPLE-PAPAYA SALSA

4 Servings

1 small ripe pineapple—peeled,
   cored and cut into ½-inch dice
¾ teaspoon salt
1 firm, ripe papaya—peeled, seeded
   and cut into ½-inch dice
1 small onion, chopped
½ jalapeño pepper, seeded and
   minced
Juice of 1 lime
1 cup chopped fresh coriander
   (cilantro)
¼ teaspoon freshly ground black
   pepper
⅔ cup fine dry bread crumbs
½ teaspoon dry mustard
½ teaspoon ground allspice
½ teaspoon ground cardamom
¼ teaspoon cayenne pepper
1 egg
Dash of hot pepper sauce
¼ cup vegetable oil
8 cleaned soft-shell crabs

1. Place the pineapple in a colander, sprinkle ½ teaspoon of the salt on top and toss well. Set aside for 15 minutes to drain. Press the pineapple gently against the side of the colander to extract any additional juices. In a nonreactive bowl, toss the pineapple with the papaya, onion, jalapeño, lime juice, coriander and black pepper. Set aside to macerate at room temperature for at least 1 hour and up to 3 hours.

2. Preheat the oven to 250°. On a plate, toss the bread crumbs with the mustard, allspice, cardamom, cayenne and the remaining ¼ teaspoon salt. In a shallow bowl, beat the egg with the hot pepper sauce and 2 tablespoons of water.

3. In a large skillet, preferably nonstick, heat 2 tablespoons of the oil over moderately high heat. Dip 4 of the crabs in the beaten egg and then dredge in the seasoned crumbs. Fry the crabs, turning once, until browned and crisp, about 3 minutes per side. Transfer the crabs to a heatproof platter and place in the oven to keep warm. Repeat with the remaining 2 tablespoons oil and 4 crabs. Serve the crabs hot, with the cooling salsa alongside.

—*Bob Chambers and Carl Parisi*

• • •

GRILLED LOBSTER DINNER

Given that this dish is made with lobster, clams and corn, you need only add a salad to make a meal. This recipe is specifically designed for outdoor grilling. If you have a gas grill, put the flame on a medium setting; if you are using a charcoal grill, wait until the coals are just red-hot.

🍷 This simple mixed grill has sweet undertones and would be neatly matched by a round-textured California Chardonnay, such as 1989 Rodney Strong or 1989 Covey Run.

2 Servings

4 medium ears of fresh corn,
   unhusked
1 stick (4 ounces) unsalted butter
2 large garlic cloves, smashed
2 teaspoons minced fresh oregano
⅛ teaspoon cayenne pepper
Salt
One 2½- to 3-pound lobster, halved
   lengthwise, claws and knuckles
   removed but not cracked
1 tablespoon olive oil
1 dozen littleneck clams, scrubbed
Lemon wedges, for serving

1. Light a grill (see headnote). Meanwhile, fill a large bowl halfway with cool water. Add the corn with their husks intact and let soak for 20 minutes.

2. In a small saucepan, combine the butter and garlic and melt over very low heat. Stir in the oregano, cayenne and ½ teaspoon salt. Cover and set aside.

3. Using the blunt edge of a knife, crack the lobster claws and knuckles in 2 spots on 1 side without crushing the meat inside.

4. Brush the shell of the lobster body and the uncracked side of the claws and knuckles with the olive oil. Place the lobster pieces cracked-side up on a platter and brush with some of the reserved herb butter. (Have tongs, a small cup of water and a clean brush handy.)

5. Drain the ears of corn and place in the center of the grill. Cover and grill for 5 minutes. Add the lobster pieces, cracked-side up, cover and grill, occasionally brushing with herb butter, for 15 minutes.

6. Brush the ears of corn thoroughly with water and rotate them slightly to blacken evenly. Add the clams to the hottest spot on the grill. Cover and grill for about 5 minutes, until the clams open. Leave any unopened clams on the grill while you transfer the opened clams, corn and lobster to a large platter. Using tongs, check the lobster meat for doneness by pulling up the tail meat and checking the underside; it should be firm and a dark orange color; return to the grill if necessary. Remove the remaining clams from the grill and discard any that have not opened.

FISH & SHELLFISH

7. Brush the clams and lobster tails with more herb butter. Peel off and discard the corn husks and silk; brush the corn with some of the herb butter. Garnish the platter with lemon wedges and serve; pass the remaining herb butter for dipping.

—*Tracey Seaman*

• • •

LOBSTER WITH CORAL SAUCE

❦ This dish calls for an elegant enveloping Chardonnay, such as 1988 Mazzocco "Sonoma County," 1988 Rosemount "Show Reserve" or 1989 Sonoma-Cutrer "Russian River Ranches."

4 Servings

Four 1¼-pound lobsters
1 tablespoon vegetable oil
1 small onion, chopped
1 tablespoon tomato paste
1 bay leaf
2 fresh thyme sprigs or ¼ teaspoon dried
½ cup dry white wine, preferably Chardonnay
2 teaspoons unsalted butter
1 shallot, minced
1 teaspoon Indian curry paste* or powder
½ cup heavy cream
Salt and freshly ground pepper
2 tablespoons finely chopped chives
*Available at Indian or Asian markets or specialty stores

1. Bring a large pot of water to a rolling boil over high heat. Plunge the lobsters in head first; return to a boil and boil for 6 minutes. Using tongs, transfer the lobsters to a large bowl and let cool slightly. Reserve 2 cups of the cooking water.

2. Break off the claws of the lobsters and with a nut cracker or the back of a heavy knife, crack the lobster claws and knuckles. Remove the meat, leaving the pieces as whole as possible. Set the meat aside in a medium bowl. Separate the heads from the tails by twisting off the heads. Scrape the light green tomalley from the tails into a small bowl. Crack the underside of the tail shells and remove the meat in one piece. Slice the tails in half lengthwise and add to the lobster meat in the bowl. Cover and refrigerate the lobster meat and tomalley.

3. Discard the lobster claw and tail shells. Break the head portions of the shells into small pieces. In a large saucepan, heat the oil over high heat. Add the shell pieces and cook, stirring, until they begin to brown, about 5 minutes. Add the onion and cook, stirring, until golden and fragrant, about 3 minutes. Add the tomato paste and cook, stirring, for 1 minute.

4. Stir in the bay leaf, thyme, wine and the reserved 2 cups of lobster cooking liquid. Bring to a boil, scraping the bottom of the pan. Reduce the heat to moderately low and simmer for 20 minutes. Strain the stock through a fine sieve; discard the solids. (*The recipe can be prepared to this point up to 1 day ahead. Let the stock cool; cover and refrigerate.*)

5. In a large saucepan, melt the butter over low heat. Add the shallot and cook, stirring, until softened, about 1 minute. Add the curry paste and cook, stirring, until fragrant, about 1 minute. Increase the heat to moderately high and stir in 1½ cups of the lobster stock and cream. Bring to a boil; cook until the sauce has thickened and coats the back of a spoon, about 10 minutes. Re-duce the heat to low and whisk in the reserved tomalley. Season the sauce with salt and pepper to taste and stir in the lobster meat. Simmer gently to warm the lobster. Spoon onto warmed plates and sprinkle with chives.

—*Marcia Kiesel*

• • •

LOBSTER AMERICAINE

Serve this dish over white rice, preferably an aromatic variety such as jasmine. Use a spoon, a fork and fingers to eat it and have large napkins on hand.

❦ Look for a crisp, herbaceous white, such as 1989 Comte Lafond Sancerre, or 1989 Caymus California Sauvignon Blanc.

4 Servings

Four 1¼-pound lobsters, cut into pieces, juices and tomalley reserved
¼ cup olive oil
⅓ cup Cognac or other brandy
1 small carrot, minced
1 small onion, minced
3 medium shallots, minced
1 small garlic clove, minced
¾ cup dry white wine
⅓ cup canned low-sodium chicken broth
3 medium tomatoes, chopped
¼ cup tomato paste
1 small apple, coarsely chopped
1 parsley sprig
2 pinches of cayenne pepper
6 tablespoons unsalted butter, softened
Salt
2 tablespoons chopped fresh tarragon

LOBSTER DINNER

Serves 4

🍷 *Rich, young Chardonnay throughout the meal, such as Sonoma-Cutrer "Russian River Ranches"*

Avocado with Lemon-Perfumed Mayonnaise

Lobster with Coral Sauce (p. 82)

Steamed New Potatoes

Banana and Papaya Tart

1. Using a large sharp knife, cut the lobster tails crosswise into 4 pieces.

2. In a large skillet, heat 2 tablespoons of the oil over moderately high heat. Divide all the lobster pieces into 3 batches. Add 1 batch to the skillet and cook until the undersides of the shells have reddened, about 1 minute. Turn the pieces over and cook until the other side has reddened, about 1 minute longer. Using tongs, transfer to a platter. Repeat with a second batch of lobster pieces, adding up to 1 more tablespoon of the oil if necessary. Add the remaining batch of lobster pieces to the skillet and cook in the same manner just until reddened on both sides. Add the Cognac and ignite it with a match. Stir until the flames subside, about 2 minutes. Transfer the lobster and the liquid to the platter with the rest of the lobsters and set aside.

3. Heat the remaining 1 tablespoon olive oil in the skillet over moderate heat. Add the carrot, onion, shallots and garlic and cook until softened, about 5 minutes.

4. In a large nonreactive saucepan, combine the white wine, chicken broth, tomatoes, tomato paste, apple, parsley and cayenne. Add the carrot and onion mixture and the reserved lobster and its liquid and bring to a boil over high heat. Reduce the heat to moderate, cover and simmer until the lobster is firm but tender, 10 to 15 minutes. Transfer the lobster claws, knuckles, tails and any other meaty pieces you like to a plate and set aside. Discard the remaining lobster pieces.

5. Increase the heat to high and boil the sauce until it has reduced by half, about 20 minutes. Strain the sauce into a large measuring cup, then return it to the saucepan. (If you have more than 2 cups, boil again to reduce further.) Keep warm over moderately low heat.

6. Measure out ¼ cup of the reserved tomalley and lobster juice; discard the rest. In a small bowl, using a wooden spoon, mash the butter into the tomalley; it may be slightly lumpy. Set aside.

7. A spoonful at a time, stir in the butter-tomalley paste until combined, removing the pan from the heat if the sauce boils up. Season to taste with salt and stir the tarragon into the sauce. Return the reserved lobster and reduce the heat to low. Cover and cook just until the lobster is heated through, about 2 minutes. Serve at once.

—*David E. Outerbridge*

• • •

ASIAN-STYLE LOBSTER STIR-FRY

You can make this dish hotter by adding seeds from the jalapeño pepper. Serve with steamed rice to sop up all the sauce.

---

2 Servings

---

1 stalk of fresh lemon grass, green top trimmed off to a 6-inch base
1 teaspoon tomato paste
1 tablespoon vegetable oil
3 garlic cloves, minced
2 teaspoons minced fresh ginger
1 medium onion, halved and thinly sliced
1 jalapeño pepper, seeded and minced
2 medium tomatoes, seeded and diced
1 teaspoon sugar
Two 1½-pound lobsters, cut into pieces, tomalley reserved
1 large scallion, thinly sliced
2 tablespoons shredded fresh basil
1 tablespoon fresh lime juice
¼ teaspoon freshly ground black pepper
Salt

1. Lightly crush the lemon grass stalk and cut it into 1-inch lengths. Place in a small nonreactive saucepan with ¾ cup of water and bring to a simmer over moderate heat. Reduce the heat to low, cover and simmer for 3 minutes. Stir in the tomato paste, cover and set aside.

2. Heat a wok over high heat for 1 minute. Add the oil. Add the garlic and ginger and stir-fry for 5 seconds. Add the onion and jalapeño and stir-fry until the onion wilts, about 1½ minutes. Stir in the tomatoes and sugar.

3. Add the reserved lemon grass and its broth. Add the lobster pieces and stir well to evenly distribute them in the cooking liquid. Cover and cook, stirring every 3 minutes and rearranging the pieces to make sure they cook evenly, until the lobster meat in the tails is white, plump and just beginning to shrink from the shell, about 8 minutes.

4. Transfer the tails to a large serving bowl. Add the remaining lobster pieces to the bowl as they are done. Stir the scallion, basil, lime juice, black pepper and reserved tomalley, if desired, into the sauce in the wok. Season to taste with salt. Pour the sauce over the lobster and serve at once.

—*Marcia Kiesel*

• • •

LOBSTER BAKED POTATOES

At Mark's Restaurant, chef Philippe Boulot deep-fries the baked potato skins before filling them. Refrigerate any leftover lobster oil and use it to baste fish steaks before broiling.

❦ The creamy richness of this dish would be nicely set off by a round, equally rich white, such as an Australian Chardonnay. A 1987 Brown Brothers King Valley Family Reserve or 1989 Tyrrell's Hunter Valley would be splendid.

4 Servings

Four 1¼-pound lobsters
1 cup light extra-virgin olive oil
4 very large russet baking potatoes
   (½ to ¾ pound each), scrubbed
   and dried
⅔ cup light cream or half-and-half
1 tablespoon minced fresh tarragon
¾ teaspoon salt
¼ teaspoon freshly ground white
   pepper
3 tablespoons richly flavored extra-
   virgin olive oil
About 1 tablespoon aged sherry
   vinegar
½ pound arugula or other bitter
   salad greens, large stems removed

1. In a large wide pot or stockpot, bring 2 inches of salted water to a rolling boil over high heat. Drop the lobsters headfirst into the water. Cover and cook until the lobsters have turned bright red, about 8 minutes. Tip the lobsters into the sink and run cold water over them to stop the cooking.

2. Shell the lobsters, keeping the claw and tail meat intact; reserve. Pick the meat out of the "arms" and bodies and reserve. With a large sharp knife, chop the legs into 1-inch pieces. Crush the body innards. Set aside 2 cups of leg pieces and body innards; discard the rest.

3. In a heavy medium saucepan, warm the light olive oil over moderate heat. When the oil is hot, add the reserved chopped legs and body pieces. Reduce the heat to very low and let steep for 1 hour. (Do not let the oil get too hot. If it begins to sizzle, remove from the heat.) Strain the lobster oil through a fine sieve into a small saucepan, pressing on the lobster shells to extract all the oil. Keep warm over

very low heat. (*The recipe can be prepared to this point up to 1 day ahead. Cover and refrigerate the lobster meat and the lobster oil separately.*)

4. Meanwhile, preheat the oven to 450°. Bake the potatoes on the middle rack for 1 hour, or until fork tender.

5. Cut about 1 inch from the wide end of each lobster tail. Chop coarsely with the reserved arm and body meat and set aside. Leave the rest of the tails intact for garnish. In a small saucepan, warm the cream over moderate heat. Rewarm the lobster oil if necessary.

6. As soon as the potatoes are done, cut a thin lengthwise slice from each potato and scoop the flesh into a bowl. Using a fork, rapidly beat in ½ cup of the warm lobster oil. With a wooden spoon, stir in the cream. Beat in the tarragon, salt and pepper, then stir in the reserved chopped lobster. Fill the potato skins with the lobster-studded mashed potatoes and place on a baking sheet.

7. Preheat the broiler. In a small bowl, whisk the 3 tablespoons of richly flavored olive oil with the vinegar. Place 2½ tablespoons of the dressing in a medium bowl; reserve the remainder. Add the arugula to the bowl and toss until well coated.

8. Drizzle a little of the remaining lobster oil over the top of each stuffed potato and broil as close to the heat as possible for 1 to 2 minutes, or until lightly browned and crusty.

9. Place each potato in the center of a large plate. Arrange a lobster claw on either side of the potatoes and a tail on the end. Place the greens on the plates and drizzle the reserved dressing over the lobster. Serve immediately.

—*Philippe Boulot, Mark's Restaurant,
New York City*

• • •

POULTRY

POULTRY

ROAST CHICKEN

For superior flavor and texture, it is worth tracking down a free-range or a kosher chicken. The secret to a perfectly cooked bird with moist tender meat and a crisp skin is a hot oven and frequent basting. The chicken is done when the drumsticks bend easily and the juices run clear, not pink, when the thigh is pierced.

To flavor a roast chicken simply, either add one head of whole unpeeled garlic cloves to the oil in the pan or stuff a quartered orange into the cavity along with a quartered small onion.

♟ This simple preparation is the perfect foil for a straightforward white, such as 1988 Ste. Chapelle Canyon Chardonnay from Idaho, or an elegant red, such as 1988 Robert Mondavi Reserve Pinot Noir from California.

3 to 4 Servings

One 3½-pound free-range or kosher roasting chicken
Coarse (kosher) salt
Freshly ground pepper
¼ cup olive oil

1. Preheat the oven to 450°. Rinse the chicken inside and out and pat it dry. Generously season the cavity with salt and pepper.

2. Spread 2 tablespoons of the oil in a small roasting pan. Set the chicken in the pan and season generously with salt and pepper. Rub the remaining 2 tablespoons oil over the bird. Roast the chicken in the middle of the oven for 25 minutes; do not open the oven door.

3. Remove the chicken from the oven and baste well. Return the chicken to the oven, reduce the temperature to 400° and roast for 20 minutes longer, basting after each 10-minute interval. Reduce the temperature to 350° and roast for 15 minutes longer, basting once after 8 minutes.

4. Remove the chicken from the oven and let rest for 5 minutes before carving.

—*Bob Chambers*

• • •

ROAST CHICKEN WITH FIG-GIBLET SAUCE

♟ A big and rich Pinot Noir is the right match for this richly sauced chicken. Full-flavored bottlings, such as 1986 Chalone or 1985 Edna Valley from California or 1988 Elk Cove "Wind Hill" from Oregon would do beautifully.

4 Servings

One 5-pound roasting chicken
½ lemon, cut in half
2 tablespoons unsalted butter, softened
Salt and freshly ground pepper
½ cup dry red wine, preferably Pinot Noir
8 large garlic cloves, unpeeled
2 large or 3 small dried figs, preferably Calimyrna
1 teaspoon chopped fresh tarragon
2 teaspoons chopped fresh chives

1. Preheat the oven to 400°. Place the chicken in a roasting pan just large enough to accommodate it. Place the lemon quarters in the cavity of the bird. Rub 1 tablespoon of the butter all over the chicken and sprinkle lightly with salt and pepper. Pour the wine into the roasting pan and add ½ cup of water. Scatter the garlic cloves and figs around the chicken and roast in the middle of the oven for 30 minutes to brown the bird.

2. In a small bowl, combine the remaining 1 tablespoon butter with the tarragon and chives. Season with a pinch of salt and pepper. Cover and refrigerate.

3. After 30 minutes, reduce the oven temperature to 350° and baste the chicken. Roast for 10 minutes longer and then add ½ cup of water to the pan. Continue to roast, basting occasionally and turning the figs to keep them moist, until a thermometer inserted in the inner thigh registers 160°, about 50 minutes longer. Pour the juices from inside the chicken into the roasting pan and transfer the chicken to a warm platter.

HEARTY DINNER

Serves 4

♟ *Rich Pinot Noir throughout the meal, such as 1988 Maison Jaffelin Volnay*

Wild Mushroom Crostini

Roast Chicken with Fig-Giblet Sauce (p. 86)

Crisp Polenta Squares

Chocolate-Dipped Hazelnut Biscotti

Remove the figs and garlic and set aside on a plate. Pour all of the pan juices into a measuring cup and with a small ladle, skim the fat from the surface.

4. Set a small, coarse strainer over a small nonreactive saucepan. Put the garlic cloves in the strainer and pour over the degreased pan juices. With a rubber spatula, push the cooked garlic through the strainer into the juices, scraping the garlic from the underside of the strainer into the juice. Discard the garlic skins.

5. To carve the chicken, cut off the legs and cut the drumsticks from the thighs at the joint using a sharp knife. Cut off the wings. Slice the breast meat off the bone. Pour any accumulated juices into the sauce. Arrange the chicken on a warmed platter and cover loosely with foil.

6. Cut the figs into ¼-inch dice and add them to the sauce. Heat the sauce over moderate heat until hot. Remove from the heat and whisk in the chilled herb butter, bit by bit, until the sauce is smooth and thickened slightly. Season with salt and pepper to taste and serve separately in a sauceboat.

—*Marcia Kiesel*

• • •

HOT AND SOUR CHICKEN WITH RED AND GREEN PEPPERS

Although you can serve this spicy chicken dish with rice, it's best with the noodle pancake on page 136.

4 Servings

3 tablespoons rice wine vinegar
2 tablespoons soy sauce
1 tablespoon sugar
2 teaspoons cornstarch
¾ teaspoon crushed red pepper
1 teaspoon Oriental sesame oil
1 pound skinless, boneless chicken breast halves, sliced crosswise into ¼-inch strips
2 tablespoons peanut oil
1 tablespoon minced fresh ginger
1 large onion, sliced lengthwise into ¼-inch strips
1 large red bell pepper, sliced lengthwise into ¼-inch strips
1 large green bell pepper, sliced lengthwise into ¼-inch strips
⅓ cup chicken stock or low-sodium canned broth
½ teaspoon salt
¼ teaspoon freshly ground black pepper

1. In a medium bowl, whisk the rice vinegar, soy sauce, sugar, cornstarch and crushed red pepper. Whisk in the sesame oil. Add the chicken and toss to coat. Let marinate at room temperature for about 2 minutes.

2. Meanwhile, heat a large cast-iron skillet or wok over high heat. Add the peanut oil, then add the ginger and onion and stir-fry until the onion is slightly softened, about 1 minute. Add

the red and green bell peppers and stir-fry until slightly softened, about 1 minute. Add the chicken and its marinade and the chicken stock and stir-fry until the chicken is just cooked through, about 3 minutes. Season with the salt and black pepper and serve hot.

—*Jim Fobel*

• • •

THAI-STYLE GRILLED CHICKEN

This Asian-influenced dish is from Philipe La Mancusa, the chef at Embarko in San Francisco. He serves the chicken with fried plantains, rice and Singha beer from Thailand. The chicken must marinate for one to two days before grilling.

8 Servings

5 tablespoons Thai or Vietnamese fish sauce (nam pla or nuoc mam)*
¼ cup light brown sugar
¼ cup canned unsweetened coconut milk*
2½ tablespoons fresh lime juice
2 tablespoons five-spice powder*
2 tablespoons soy sauce
1 tablespoon crushed dried Asian chiles (about 8 small)*
1 tablespoon plus 1 teaspoon curry powder
Two 3-pound chickens—quartered, rinsed and patted dry
8 leaves of butter lettuce
2 medium tomatoes, quartered
2 medium cucumbers, sliced ¼ inch thick
½ of a red onion, sliced and separated into strips

POULTRY

Amerasian Dipping Sauce (p. 262)
*Available at Asian markets

1. In a small bowl, mix the fish sauce, brown sugar, coconut milk, lime juice, five-spice powder, soy sauce, crushed chiles and curry powder. Set aside for at least 2 hours.

2. Stir the marinade well. Place the chicken in a glass baking dish and coat thoroughly with the marinade. Transfer the chicken to 2 large, heavy Ziploc plastic bags. Pour in any extra marinade. Press out any air and zip the bags to close. Set aside to marinate at room temperature for 2 hours, then refrigerate for at least 24 hours or up to 2 days, turning the bags occasionally.

3. Light the grill. Cut the chicken wings off at the second joint or fasten the wing tips to the rib cages with metal skewers. The fire is ready when you can hold your hand 7 inches above the coals for at least 4 seconds. Grill the chicken, bony sides down, for 1½ minutes, then turn and grill for 1½ minutes to seal in the juices. Turn the chicken again and grill for about 6 minutes, until the surface meat is firm. Turn and grill for 6 minutes longer. If the fire is too hot, the skin will char, so watch carefully and turn the chicken if necessary. Grill the chicken, turning occasionally, for 17 to 25 minutes longer. It is done as soon as the meat is white throughout and the juices run clear when the meat is deeply pierced.

4. Alternatively, preheat the broiler. Broil the chicken for about 35 minutes, beginning skin-side up and turning every 10 minutes.

5. Serve the chicken on plates or a platter, garnished with the lettuce, tomatoes, cucumbers and red onion. Serve

each person ¼ cup of the Amerasian Dipping Sauce in small dishes.

—*Linda Burum*

• • •

SESAME CHICKEN ON A BUN

Skinless chicken breasts take so little time to cook that they can be featured in many different ways on busy weeknights.

4 Servings

¼ cup dry bread crumbs
2 tablespoons unhulled sesame seeds
¼ teaspoon salt
Pinch of cayenne pepper
4 skinless, boneless chicken breast halves (1¼ pounds total), slightly flattened
2 tablespoons vegetable oil
4 whole wheat hamburger buns
1 small bunch of watercress, large stems removed
1 tomato, sliced ¼ inch thick
¼ cup Lemon-Sesame Sauce (p. 262)
1 tablespoon Oriental sesame oil

1. In a medium plastic bag, combine the bread crumbs, sesame seeds, salt and cayenne; shake until blended. Rinse the chicken breasts and shake off any excess water. One at a time, add them to the bag and shake to coat.

2. In a large heavy skillet, heat the oil over moderately high heat. Add the chicken and fry until golden brown, about 5 minutes. Turn the chicken and fry until golden and cooked through, about 5 minutes longer.

3. Meanwhile, place an opened bun on each dinner plate. Divide and arrange the watercress and tomato slices on the top half of each bun. Spread a heap-

ing tablespoon of the Lemon-Sesame Sauce on the bottom half of the bun.

4. Place the chicken breasts on the sauced half; drizzle some sesame oil on top and serve.

—*Susan Shapiro Jaslove*

• • •

CHICKEN WITH MUSHROOMS AND CHIVES

This is a very simple, homestyle sauté. None of the chicken is wasted. Those parts that are not sautéed are used to make a quick stock that forms the basis of the sauce. The intensity of the sauce depends on browning the bones very well in the oven.

6 Servings

Two 3½-pound chickens
1 medium onion, cut into 1-inch pieces
1½ teaspoons salt
½ teaspoon freshly ground pepper
2 tablespoons olive oil
1 pound cremini or portobello mushrooms, stems removed, caps sliced ¼ inch thick
2 medium garlic cloves, minced
2 tablespoons crème fraîche
1 small bunch of chives, chopped

1. Preheat the oven to 425°. Remove the innards from the chickens; reserve the livers and giblets for another use. Place the necks in a 13-by-9-inch roasting pan and set aside. Cut off the wings and cut each one into 3 pieces at the joints. Add to the necks. Remove the legs from the chicken, then separate them into thighs and drumsticks and reserve on a tray. Beginning at the top of

FANCY FAMILY FEAST

Serves 6

Mussel-Leek Soup with Roasted Red Pepper and Thyme (p. 41)

Chicken with Mushrooms and Chives (p. 88)

Buttered Egg Noodles

Strawberries with Cream

Pistachio Madeleines (p. 229)

—Ann Chantal Altman

the breast bone, cut against the ribs with a sharp knife to remove each breast half. Add the breast meat to the legs. Cover and refrigerate the chicken for at least 1 hour.

2. Meanwhile, cut the carcasses into 2-inch pieces and add to the roasting pan. Add the onion and toss well. Roast the bones for about 1 hour, turning them every 15 minutes, until well browned all over.

3. Transfer the contents of the roasting pan to a large saucepan and add 6 cups of water. Bring to a boil over moderately high heat. Pour off the fat from the roasting pan. Set the pan over moderate heat, add 2 cups of water and bring to a boil, scraping up the browned bits from the bottom of the pan with a spoon. Pour this liquid into the saucepan and boil gently until the broth is aromatic and has reduced by half, about 1 hour.

4. Strain the broth into a bowl, discarding the solids. Return the broth to the saucepan and boil over moderately high heat until reduced to 1 cup, about

45 minutes longer. Set aside. *(The recipe can be prepared to this point up to 1 day ahead. Cover and refrigerate overnight. Remove the chicken from the refrigerator about 1 hour before proceeding.)*

5. Season the chicken with the salt and pepper. Heat the oil in a large heavy skillet over moderately high heat. Add the drumsticks and thighs, skin-side down, and cook, turning once, until well browned on both sides, about 15 minutes. Transfer to a plate. Add the breast halves to the pan, skin-side down, and cook, turning once, until browned on both sides, about 10 minutes. Add the breasts to the legs.

6. Discard all but 2 tablespoons of fat from the skillet. Add the mushrooms and cook over moderately high heat, stirring, until softened, about 4 minutes. Add the garlic and cook, stirring, until fragrant, about 1 minute longer. Return all of the chicken to the pan, cover and cook over low heat until the breast halves are done, about 15 minutes. Remove the breasts to a platter. Continue cooking the drumsticks and thighs until the juices run clear when the meat is pierced, about 15 minutes longer. Transfer to the platter. Drain the mushrooms in a sieve to remove excess fat; set aside.

7. Skim the fat from the reserved chicken broth. Pour the broth into the skillet and simmer over moderately high heat until the liquid reduces to ¾ cup, 3 to 4 minutes. Stir in the reserved mushrooms and the crème fraîche. Return the chicken to the pan, cover and reheat thoroughly, turning occasionally, about 3 minutes. Stir in the chives and serve hot.

—Ann Chantal Altman

• • •

GRILLED GRATINEED CHICKEN

This is the dish to order at Chez Maître Paul, a small, newly refurbished Left Bank restaurant in Paris that specializes in the foods of the Jura. It combines many of the region's specialties, including farm chicken, fresh cream and the nutty cow's-milk cheese known as Comté. Serve this with plenty of boiled white or brown rice.

4 to 6 Servings

One 3-pound roasting chicken, preferably free-range
½ cup fresh lemon juice
3 tablespoons peanut oil
2 pounds mushrooms, sliced ¼ inch thick
Salt
2 tablespoons unsalted butter
2 tablespoons instant-blending flour
2 cups chicken stock or canned low-sodium broth, heated
1 cup Crème Fraîche (p. 267) or heavy cream, at room temperature
Freshly ground pepper
⅛ teaspoon freshly grated nutmeg
2 cups freshly grated imported Comté or Gruyère cheese

1. Place the chicken on a work surface, breast down. With poultry shears or a sharp knife, split the bird lengthwise along one side of the backbone. Turn the bird over, spread open and press down with the heel of your hand to flatten it completely. The bird should be as flat as possible to ensure even cooking. Tuck the wing tips under the wings.

2. Place the chicken in a roasting pan and pour 5 tablespoons of the lemon juice and the oil on top. Marinate, covered, at room temperature for about 2 hours, turning the chicken once or twice.

3. Meanwhile, in a large nonreactive saucepan, combine the mushrooms with the remaining 3 tablespoons lemon juice, a pinch of salt and 1 cup of water. Bring to a boil over high heat. Reduce the heat to moderate, cover and cook until the mushrooms are tender and most of the liquid has been absorbed, about 25 minutes. Remove from the heat and set aside.

4. In a medium nonreactive saucepan, melt the butter over moderately low heat. Add the flour and cook, stirring with a wooden spoon, until the mixture separates slightly and takes on a granular look, 2 to 3 minutes. Do not let the flour brown. Add the hot chicken stock all at once, whisking to blend. Increase the heat to moderate and bring to a boil, whisking constantly. Reduce the heat to moderately low and cook at a slow simmer, whisking occasionally, until the stock reduces to a scant cup, about 40 minutes. Remove from the heat and let cool slightly; stir in the crème fraîche. Season with salt and pepper to taste and add the nutmeg. (*The sauce can be prepared up to 1 hour ahead. Keep warm in a double boiler, covered, over low heat.*)

5. Preheat the broiler. Remove the chicken from the marinade and sprinkle generously with salt and pepper. Broil the chicken 5 inches from the heat, breast-side up, basting occasionally for about 10 minutes, until the skin is browned. Turn the chicken and broil, basting occasionally, for about 15 minutes longer. The chicken is done when the juices run clear when the thighs are pierced. Quarter and set it aside.

6. Preheat the oven to 475°. In a shallow baking dish just slightly larger

than the chicken, spread the mushrooms and their liquid in an even layer. Place the quartered chicken on top of the mushrooms and pour the cream sauce over it. Sprinkle with the grated cheese. Bake in the middle of the oven for about 15 minutes, until the cheese has melted and is lightly browned. Serve immediately from the baking dish.

—*Patricia Wells*

• • •

MIDDLE EASTERN LEMON CHICKEN BURRITOS

A flour tortilla pinch-hits for the customary pita in this southwestern presentation of an otherwise very Middle Eastern dish from Michael Fennelly, formerly at Santa Cafe in Santa Fe. Keep accompaniments simple: rice cooked in chicken broth and a simple salad are ideal.

🍷 An off-dry fruity white, such as 1990 Dry Creek Chenin Blanc from California or 1988 Marc Brédif Vouvray from France, would stand up best to the contrasting flavors.

---

4 Servings

¼ cup plus 2½ tablespoons olive oil
2 tablespoons fresh lemon juice
4 medium garlic cloves, minced
1 teaspoon minced fresh rosemary
½ teaspoon crushed red pepper
½ teaspoon freshly ground black pepper
6 to 10 dashes of hot pepper sauce, to taste
Salt
4 boneless chicken breast halves (about 1¼ pounds), trimmed of excess fat

2 Anaheim or poblano chiles, cut into ¼-inch dice
½ of a medium red onion, thinly sliced
3 tablespoons chopped sweet pickles
Four 8-inch flour tortillas, warmed
Tahini-Garlic Mayonnaise (p. 264)
1 large beefsteak tomato, seeded and cut into ¼-inch dice

1. In a medium glass baking dish, mix ¼ cup of the oil with the lemon juice, garlic, rosemary, red pepper, black pepper, hot pepper suace and ½ teaspoon salt. Add the chicken breasts to the marinade and turn to coat completely. Let marinate in the refrigerator, skin-side up, for at least 2 hours. Turn and marinate for at least 30 minutes longer.

2. Light the grill. When the coals are medium-hot, grill the chicken, skin-side down, for 1½ minutes; turn and grill for 1½ minutes. Continue to grill, turning frequently, for 10 to 12 minutes longer, until the meat is firm and the juices run clear. Alternatively, preheat the broiler. Broil the chicken, skin-side up, for 5 minutes. Turn and broil for about 5 minutes longer, until done. Slice the chicken breasts crosswise into ½-inch strips.

3. Meanwhile, heat the remaining 2½ tablespoons oil in a medium skillet. Add the chiles and onion and cook over moderately high heat until softened and colored slightly, about 5 minutes. Stir in the pickles and cook for 30 seconds longer. Remove from the heat.

4. To assemble the burritos, spread each warm tortilla with 1 heaping tablespoon of the Tahini-Garlic Mayonnaise. Arrange the chicken strips in the center and top with the onion-chile mixture and the diced tomato. Roll up the tortillas and spear with a toothpick. Serve warm.

—Linda Burum

• • •

CHICKEN, SAUSAGE AND GRITS HASH WITH WILD MUSHROOMS

If you're making the hash with leftovers, you will need three cups of cooked chicken meat. But there is also a method for starting from scratch. Do not use instant or quick-cooking grits in this recipe, for the results will be less than satisfactory.

♈ For an exciting contrast to this new-style hash, try a big, oaky California Chardonnay. Look for rich examples, like 1988 Cuvaison or 1989 Cambria "Katherine's Vineyard."

6 Servings

6 medium chicken thighs (about 2½ pounds)
Salt and freshly ground pepper
3¼ cups canned chicken broth
¾ cup enriched white hominy grits
½ pound sage-seasoned breakfast sausage, removed from casings if in links
2 tablespoons unsalted butter
1 large onion, chopped
½ teaspoon thyme
½ pound white mushrooms, thinly sliced
½ pound assorted wild mushrooms, such as chanterelles, morels, cèpes (porcini) or shiitakes, thinly sliced
2 tablespoons vegetable oil

1. Preheat the oven to 375°. Place the chicken thighs in a roasting pan. Season with salt and pepper and bake for about 40 minutes, until the juices run clear when a thigh is pierced with a knife. Set aside to cool.

2. Meanwhile, lightly grease a small baking sheet with oil or vegetable cooking spray and set aside. In a medium saucepan, bring the chicken broth to a boil over high heat. Gradually pour in the grits in a steady stream, stirring constantly. Reduce the heat to low and simmer, stirring occasionally, for 15 minutes. Let cool slightly, then scrape the grits onto the prepared baking sheet and, using a rubber spatula, spread evenly to a ½-inch thickness. Set aside to cool completely, about 30 minutes. (*The recipe can be prepared to this point up to 1 day ahead; cover and refrigerate the chicken and grits separately.*)

3. While the grits cool, cook the sausage meat in a large skillet over moderately high heat, stirring occasionally with a wooden spoon or spatula to break up the clumps, until well browned and crusty in spots, about 10 minutes. Using a slotted spoon, transfer the meat to a large bowl.

4. Reduce the heat to moderate and melt 1 tablespoon of the butter in the skillet. Add the onion and cook, stirring often, until soft and browned, about 8 minutes. Stir in the thyme, white mushrooms and wild mushrooms. Increase the heat to moderately high and cook, stirring occasionally, until the mushrooms are soft, browned and dry, 10 to 12 minutes. Transfer to the bowl with the sausage.

5. Using a small knife, cut the cooled grits into ¾-inch cubes. Using a spatula, transfer the grits to the bowl with the sausage and mushrooms.

ELEGANT BRUNCH FOR SIX

Serves 6

Chicken, Sausage and Grits Hash with Wild Mushrooms (p. 91)

Slow-Baked Tomatoes (p. 184)

♈ *California Chardonnay*

Coconut-Macadamia Pudding (p. 254)

—Lee Bailey

6. Remove and discard the skin from the cooled chicken. Pull the meat from the bones and shred into ¾- to 1-inch pieces. Add the chicken to the bowl of mushrooms and grits and season with ½ teaspoon pepper and ¼ teaspoon salt. Toss gently.

7. Heat a large heavy skillet over moderately high heat until hot but not smoking. Add the oil and the remaining 1 tablespoon butter. When the butter is melted, spoon in the hash, distributing it evenly in the pan and pressing down lightly with the back of a spoon or spatula to pack it in. Cook the hash, without disturbing it, for 10 minutes. Remove the skillet from the heat and let rest for 3 minutes.

8. Preheat the broiler. Place the skillet under the broiler as close to the heat as possible for about 3 minutes, rotating the pan as necessary, until the top of the hash is browned. Serve at once directly from the skillet.

—Lee Bailey

• • •

BAKED EGGS AND CHICKEN HASH

The chicken for the hash is poached and the resulting stock is used to make the gravy. The stock will be easier to degrease if refrigerated overnight. The potatoes can be cooked ahead as well.

8 Servings

3 large baking potatoes (about 1½ pounds), scrubbed

One 3½-pound chicken, gizzard and neck reserved

2 onions—1 medium, cut into 1-inch chunks, and 1 large, chopped

2 large celery ribs with leaves, cut into 1-inch chunks

2 medium carrots, cut into 1-inch chunks

1 large garlic clove, lightly crushed

1 large bay leaf

½ teaspoon thyme

3 parsley sprigs plus 2 tablespoons minced

1 teaspoon whole black peppercorns

2 teaspoons salt

7 tablespoons unsalted butter

2 tablespoons vegetable oil

1 teaspoon freshly ground pepper

8 eggs

2 tablespoons all-purpose flour

¼ cup heavy cream

1. Preheat the oven to 400°. Pierce the potatoes in several places with a fork and bake for 1 hour. Set aside to cool. Then peel the potatoes, wrap them in foil and refrigerate .

2. Meanwhile, remove any excess fat from the cavity of the chicken and discard. Rinse the chicken thoroughly inside and out with cool water and place in a small flameproof casserole. Rinse the gizzard and neck and add to the pot.

3. Add the medium onion, celery, carrots, garlic, bay leaf, thyme, parsley sprigs, peppercorns and 1 teaspoon of the salt to the casserole. Pour in 6 cups of water and bring to a boil over high heat. Reduce the heat to moderately low, cover and simmer for 1 hour. Transfer the chicken to a platter and set aside to cool to room temperature.

4. Increase the heat to moderately high and boil the stock for 35 minutes. Strain the stock into a large measuring cup, pressing on the solids with a spoon to extract any liquid. If you have more than 1¾ cups, boil again to reduce; if you have less, add enough water to compensate. Let the stock cool to room temperature, then cover and refrigerate.

5. Remove the skin from the cooled chicken and discard. Pull the meat from the bones, tearing it into bite-size pieces, and place in a medium bowl. Cover and refrigerate. *(The recipe can be prepared to this point up to 1 day ahead.)*

6. In a 10-inch ovenproof skillet, preferably cast iron, melt 2 tablespoons of the butter over moderate heat. Add the chopped onion and cook until softened, about 5 minutes. Using a slotted spoon, transfer the onion to a medium bowl and set aside.

7. Increase the heat to moderately high and add 1 tablespoon of the butter. When the butter begins to foam, add the chicken. Cook, turning once, until the meat is browned and crisp in spots, about 10 minutes. Add the chicken to the onions in the bowl and mix.

8. Preheat the oven to 350°. Cut the potatoes into ½-inch dice. Add 1 tablespoon of the oil and 1 tablespoon of the butter to the skillet and increase the heat to high. When the butter has melted, add half of the potatoes. Cook, stirring only occasionally, until golden and crisp, about 10 minutes. Season with ½ teaspoon each of the salt and pepper and add to the chicken and onion in the bowl. Repeat with 1 more tablespoon of the butter and the remaining 1 tablespoon oil, potatoes, ½ teaspoon salt and ½ teaspoon pepper. Return all the chicken and potato mixture to the skillet and smooth the surface with the back of a spoon.

9. Using a spoon, make 8 indentations about 2½ inches wide and ½ inch deep in the hash. One at a time, crack the eggs into the indentations. Cover loosely with foil and bake for about 25 minutes, until the eggs are cooked through.

10. Meanwhile, skim the congealed fat from the surface of the stock. In a medium skillet, melt the remaining 2 tablespoons butter over moderately high heat. Whisk in the flour and cook, whisking constantly until thick and pasty, 2 to 3 minutes. Gradually whisk in the stock and cook, whisking frequently, for 5 minutes. Add the cream and bring to a boil. Reduce the heat to very low, stir in the minced parsley and keep the sauce warm until the eggs are cooked. (If the sauce gets too thick, stir in water by the tablespoon.) Serve the hash hot from the oven and pass the gravy on the side.

—*Tracey Seaman*

• • •

Green Beans with Walnuts and Lemon (p. 175), Poussins with Wild Rice (p. 99) and Scalloped Potatoes with Bacon and Cheese (p. 178).

Above, Roasted Poussins with Carrots and
Parsnips (p. 100) and Mom's Fried Dressing (p. 199).
Right, Thai-Style Grilled Chicken (p. 87) with
Amerasian Dipping Sauce (p. 262).

CHICKEN BIRYANI

This Indo-Persian dish is perhaps one of the world's most elegant rice dishes. Partially cooked rice and spicy meat chunks are layered, and saffron-infused milk is poured over the top. The pot is then sealed and the dish bakes slowly in the oven. If you want the biryani to remain tricolored—white, saffron and brown—do not mix the rice until ready to serve. In a warm place, a covered pot of biryani will keep its heat for a good hour.

6 Servings

*2 teaspoons lightly packed saffron
    threads*
3 tablespoons hot milk
3 cups basmati rice, picked over
3 tablespoons salt
*2-inch piece of fresh ginger, peeled
    and coarsely chopped*
5 garlic cloves
*2 cups plain yogurt, preferably whole
    milk*
½ cup coarsely chopped fresh mint
*½ cup coarsely chopped fresh
    coriander (cilantro)*
*1 to 2 fresh green chiles, thinly
    sliced*
½ cup vegetable oil
*3 medium onions—2 halved
    lengthwise and thinly sliced, 1
    finely chopped*
¼ cup slivered almonds
¼ cup golden raisins

Chicken Biryani (p. 97).

4 cinnamon sticks
12 cardamom pods
10 whole cloves
2 bay leaves
*1 teaspoon black cumin seeds or ½
    teaspoon regular cumin seeds*
6 chicken drumsticks, skin removed
6 chicken thighs, skin removed
2 tablespoons fresh lemon juice
1 teaspoon ground cumin
½ teaspoon cayenne pepper
*½ teaspoon freshly ground black
    pepper*
3 hard-cooked eggs, quartered

1. Set a small cast-iron skillet over moderate heat. When hot, add the saffron and stir until the threads turn a few shades darker, about 1 minute. Pour the hot milk into a small cup and crumble in the saffron threads. Set aside for 3 hours.

2. Meanwhile, place the rice in a large bowl and wash in several changes of cold water. Add enough water to the bowl to cover the rice by 2 inches. Add 1 teaspoon of the salt, mix and set aside to soak for at least 3 hours.

3. In a blender, combine the ginger, garlic and 1 tablespoon water. Blend on low speed, scraping down the sides a few times, until a fine paste forms.

4. In a bowl, beat the yogurt lightly until smooth. Stir in the mint, coriander and chiles.

5. In a large, straight-sided skillet, heat the oil over moderately high heat. Add the sliced onions and fry, stirring once or twice, until deep reddish-brown and crisp, about 5 minutes. Using a slotted spoon, transfer the onions to paper towels to drain. Reduce the heat to moderate. Add the almonds to the skillet and fry, stirring, until golden, about 30 seconds. Transfer to paper towels to drain. Add the raisins to the skillet; they

will plump up immediately. Quickly transfer them to paper towels to drain.

6. Add 2 cinnamon sticks, 6 cardamom pods, 5 cloves and 1 bay leaf to the skillet. Stir once and add the cumin seeds. Stir once and add the chopped onion. Increase the heat to moderately high and fry until the onion is browned at the edges, about 1 minute. Add the ginger-garlic paste and stir-fry for 1 minute. Add the chicken pieces and fry for 1 minute. Add half of the yogurt mixture, half of the fried almonds and raisins, 1½ teaspoons of the salt and the lemon juice, ground cumin and cayenne.

7. Stir ¼ cup water into the skillet and bring to a simmer. Reduce the heat to low. Cover and simmer gently for 10 minutes, then uncover and add half of the fried onions. Increase the heat to moderate and cook, stirring frequently, until the sauce is dark and thickened and the chicken is just tender, about 5 minutes. Add the black pepper and season the sauce with salt to taste. Transfer the chicken and sauce to a large casserole. *(The recipe can be prepared to this point up to 6 hours ahead.)*

8. Preheat the oven to 375°. Stir ½ teaspoon of the salt and 2 teaspoons of the reserved saffron milk into the remaining yogurt. Spread this mixture over the chicken.

9. In a large pot, bring 10 cups of water to a rolling boil. Add the remaining 2 tablespoons salt, 2 cinnamon sticks, 6 cardamom pods, 5 cloves and 1 bay leaf. Drain the rice and slowly pour it into the pot. When the water returns to a rapid boil, cook the rice until just barely tender, 7 to 8 minutes; drain quickly, leaving in the spices.

10. Pour the rice over the chicken in a heap, making a small mound. Working quickly, use a chopstick or a long spoon to make a well in the center of the rice all the way down to the bottom of the pot. Drizzle the remaining saffron milk on the sides of the mound. Lay a clean, dampened dish cloth over the rice and cover the casserole tightly, first with a piece of foil and then with a lid. Bake for 35 minutes.

11. To serve, have a large, warmed platter ready. Stir the rice gently with a slotted spoon to mix and spoon the biryani onto the platter. Garnish with the remaining fried onions, almonds, raisins and the hard-cooked eggs.

—*Madhur Jaffrey*

• • •

HAINANESE CHICKEN RICE

In this traditional rice dish (*gai fan*) from Singapore, the separate elements—rice, chicken and soup are presented as a single course, to be eaten together according to the eater's whim. If made the day before, the stock will be easier to degrease.

6 Servings

Chicken, Rice and Soup:
One 4- to 4½-pound chicken, giblets reserved
3 tablespoons Chinese rice wine,* 2 tablespoons gin or ¼ cup white wine
2 teaspoons salt
5 small onions (1¼ pounds), quartered
3 ounces fresh ginger (about a 2-by-1½-inch piece), peeled and coarsely chopped
2 garlic cloves
18 fresh coriander (cilantro) sprigs
2 tablespoons peanut oil
6 medium shallots, finely chopped
2 small fresh red chiles, minced
1 large tomato, cut into ½-inch dice
1 medium cucumber—halved, seeded and cut into ¼-inch dice
2 cups uncooked rice

Ginger-Garlic Sauce:
3 tablespoons peanut oil
1 tablespoon plus 1 teaspoon grated fresh ginger
2 medium garlic cloves, minced

Chile-Soy Sauce:
2 small fresh red chiles, minced
1 large scallion, thinly sliced
1 tablespoon light (thin) soy sauce*

1 teaspoon Oriental sesame oil
½ teaspoon Chinese rice wine* or gin
2½ tablespoons chicken stock or canned low-sodium broth
*Available at Asian markets

1. Trim off any excess fat from the chicken and discard. Rinse the bird thoroughly inside and out and pat dry with paper towels. Rub the chicken with the rice wine and sprinkle the salt on the skin and inside the cavity. Set aside on a platter for 45 minutes.

2. In a medium oval flameproof casserole or dutch oven, combine the onions, ginger, garlic, 12 coriander sprigs, the reserved giblets and 10 cups of water. Cover, leaving a slight opening, and bring to a boil over high heat. Reduce the heat to low and simmer for 45 minutes.

3. Place the chicken in the casserole breast-side up. Increase the heat to moderate and bring to a boil. Cover, again leaving a slight opening, reduce the heat to low and simmer for 30 minutes. Turn the chicken over and simmer for 15 minutes longer. Turn the chicken breast-side up again and simmer for 15 minutes longer. Remove the casserole from the heat and let sit, covered, for 15 minutes. Transfer the chicken to a platter to cool, then cover and refrigerate overnight. Strain the stock and measure out 8 cups (if you have less than that, add enough water to compensate). Let cool, then cover and refrigerate overnight.

4. Skim and discard the fat from the stock; set the stock aside. Remove the skin from the chicken and discard. Slice the meat into bite-size pieces and transfer to a serving platter. Garnish with the remaining 6 coriander sprigs and set aside at room temperature.

5. In a large saucepan, heat the peanut oil over high heat until hot, about 1 minute. Add the shallots and cook, stirring constantly, until they begin to brown, about 3 minutes. Stir in the chiles and the tomato. Add all but 2 cups of the reserved stock and bring to a boil over high heat. Reduce the heat to moderately low, cover, leaving a slight opening, and simmer for 20 minutes. Add the cucumber, return to a boil and remove from the heat. Keep the soup tightly covered.

6. Meanwhile, in a medium saucepan, combine the rice and enough water to cover. Rub the rice between your hands a few times. Drain well in a colander. Repeat this procedure 2 more times. Return the rice to the saucepan and add the remaining 2 cups of stock. Bring to a boil over high heat, stir, then cook until bubbles begin to form on the surface, about 3 minutes. Reduce the heat to low, cover and cook for 6 minutes. Stir, cover and cook until tender, 3 to 5 minutes longer. Transfer the rice to a warm serving bowl.

7. Meanwhile, in separate serving bowls, whisk together all the ingredients for the Ginger-Garlic Sauce and the Chile-Soy Sauce. *(The sauces can be made up to 1 day ahead. Cover and refrigerate; let return to room temperature before using.)*

8. To serve, place the chicken, the rice and the dipping sauces on the table for people to help themselves. Pour the soup into 6 soup bowls and serve.

—*Eileen Yin-Fei Lo*

• • •

HARVEST DINNER PARTY

Serves 4

Kirs Royales

Spiced Almonds

Flageolet and Leek Soup
(p. 31)

🍷 *Light red Bordeaux, such as 1988 Barton & Guestier Merlot or 1986 Château St-Georges St-Emilion*

Poussins with Wild Rice (p. 99)

Carrot and Turnip Puree

Crescent Rolls (p. 193)

🍷 *Full-bodied California Chardonnay, such as 1988 Pine Ridge or 1989 McDowell*

Salad of Winter Greens (p. 154)

Poached Pears with Caramel Ice Cream (p. 237)

Café Filtre

POUSSINS WITH WILD RICE

This recipe is representative of the Midwest harvest. Because poussins are not always available, Cornish game hens can be used as a somewhat larger substitute. When properly cooked, the wild rice in this dish is still somewhat chewy. 🍷 The moist birds and nutty rice would be complemented by a full-bodied, round California Chardonnay, such as 1988 Pine Ridge or 1989 McDowell.

4 Servings

1½ *cups wild rice*
4 *cups chicken stock, canned low-sodium broth or water*
Salt
1 *tablespoon goose fat or butter*
1 *large shallot, minced*
10 *ounces mushrooms, finely chopped (about 2 cups)*
1 *teaspoon finely grated lemon zest*
½ *teaspoon coriander seeds, crushed*
2 *tablespoons plus 1 teaspoon fresh lemon juice*
Freshly ground pepper
½ *cup hazelnuts (3 ounces)*
4 *poussins (1 to 1½ pounds each) or Cornish game hens (1¼ to 1½ pounds each)*
1 *tablespoon extra-virgin olive oil*
2 *tablespoons minced flat-leaf parsley*

1. In a large saucepan, combine the wild rice and stock and bring to a boil over high heat. Reduce the heat to moderately low and cook, covered, until most of the water is absorbed and about two-thirds of the rice kernels have burst and are somewhat chewy but not hard, 35 to 50 minutes (the cooking time varies dramatically, depending on the age and quality of the rice). Check the rice occasionally as it cooks and add more water if necessary. If you prefer more tender rice, cook for 5 to 10 minutes longer, but do not overcook the rice or it will become mushy. Season to taste with salt.

2. While the rice is cooking, melt the goose fat in a large skillet over moderate heat. Add the shallot and cook, stirring constantly, until translucent, about 2 minutes. Add the mushrooms and cook, stirring occasionally, until they have released all their liquid and it has evaporated, about 6 minutes. Add the lemon zest, coriander seeds and 1 tablespoon of the lemon juice.

3. Stir in the cooked rice and season to taste with salt and pepper. Partially cover and keep warm. (*The rice can be made up to 1 day ahead; cover and refrigerate. Reheat in a 325° oven.*)

4. Preheat the oven to 450°. On a baking sheet, toast the hazelnuts for about 5 minutes, until golden. Let cool, then rub them together in a kitchen towel to remove the skins. Coarsely chop the nuts; set aside. Leave the oven on.

5. Thoroughly rinse the poussins inside and out until the water runs clear. Pat dry thoroughly. Season the cavities of the birds with salt and pepper and 1 tablespoon of the lemon juice. Truss the birds, then rub them all over with the olive oil.

6. Place the birds breast-side up in a roasting pan with space between them. Roast in the upper part of the oven, basting every 10 to 15 minutes, for about 30 minutes. Reduce the heat to 350° and continue roasting until the skin is golden, the thigh juices run clear when pierced with a sharp knife and an instant-reading thermometer inserted into the thickest part of a thigh reads 160°, about 15 minutes longer for smaller birds and 20 minutes for larger birds. Transfer the birds to a platter and set aside. Cover with foil to keep warm.

7. Place the roasting pan with the pan juices over two burners and heat over moderately high heat until beginning to smoke, about 30 seconds. Pour in ½ cup of water and scrape the bottom of the pan with a wooden spoon to loosen the browned bits. Add the remaining 1 teaspoon lemon juice and boil until brown and syrupy, about 2 minutes. Sea-

son to taste with salt and pepper and transfer to a gravy boat.

8. Just before serving, stir the reserved hazelnuts into the wild rice. Spoon the rice onto 4 warmed dinner plates and sprinkle the parsley on top. Place the birds on top of the rice. Pass the pan juices separately and serve at once.

—*Susan Hermann Loomis*

• • •

ROASTED POUSSINS WITH CARROTS AND PARSNIPS

If you have a hard time finding poussins (baby chickens), Cornish game hens can be used instead.

▼ With this roasted chicken dish, serve a light Pinot Noir, such as 1988 Domaine Dujac Morey St-Denis from Burgundy, 1989 Saintsbury Garnet from California or 1988 Bethel Heights from Oregon.

8 Servings

3 pounds small carrots, trimmed, or large carrots, cut into 5-by-1-inch sticks
3 pounds small parsnips, trimmed, or large parsnips, cut into 5-by-1-inch sticks
¼ cup olive oil
Salt and freshly ground pepper
8 poussins (about 1 pound each), rinsed and patted dry
2 lemons, quartered
8 sage leaves
16 garlic cloves, crushed and peeled

1. Preheat the oven to 450°. Toss the carrots and parsnips with 2 tablespoons of the oil and place in a single

layer in a large shallow roasting pan or 2 smaller ones that will fit on one oven shelf. Season with salt and pepper. Roast for 15 minutes, shaking the pan every 5 minutes.

2. Meanwhile, loosen the breast skins of the poussins with your fingers. Cut 1 thin slice from each lemon quarter, top with 1 sage leaf and place under the breast skin of each bird. Season the cavities with salt and pepper and place 2 garlic cloves and 1 lemon quarter in each. Using kitchen string, tie the legs of each poussin together to give the birds a nice shape. Brush them with the remaining 2 tablespoons olive oil.

3. Set the poussins on top of the vegetables and roast for 20 minutes. Reduce the temperature to 350° and continue roasting, basting the birds and vegetables with the pan juices every 10 minutes, for about 25 minutes longer. The poussins are done when the skin is golden and the juices run clear when the thighs are pierced. Transfer the birds and vegetables to plates or a large platter and remove the trussing strings. Degrease the pan juices and spoon them on top.

—*Elizabeth Woodson*

• • •

SAUTEED POUSSINS WITH CARROTS AND DILL

Either brown or wild rice or a simple pilaf would be a nice complement to this dish.

6 Servings

3 poussins (1 to 1¼ pounds each)
1 teaspoon salt
1 teaspoon freshly ground pepper

¼ cup olive oil
1 medium onion, chopped
1 pound carrots, halved lengthwise and sliced ¼ inch thick
2 celery ribs, sliced ¼ inch thick on the diagonal
1 cup chicken stock or canned low-sodium broth
½ cup dry white wine
½ cup chopped fresh dill

1. Using kitchen shears, cut along both sides of the poussins' backbones and remove. Quarter the birds and pat dry. Sprinkle both sides with the salt and pepper.

2. In a very large, high-sided nonreactive skillet, heat 2 tablespoons of the olive oil over high heat until it begins to smoke. Add the leg quarters, skin side up, and sauté until browned, about 3 minutes. Turn the pieces and sauté for 3 minutes longer. Transfer to a large plate and cover loosely with foil to keep warm. Repeat with the breast quarters.

3. Pour the fat from the skillet; wipe out the pan if there's any dark sediment on the bottom. Add the remaining 2 tablespoons olive oil and heat over high heat until just beginning to smoke. Add the onion and sauté for 1 minute. Add the carrots and celery and sauté until beginning to brown, about 5 minutes.

4. Deglaze the pan with the chicken stock and wine, scraping up any browned bits from the bottom. Bring to a boil and stir in the dill. Place the chicken legs on top of the vegetables and arrange the breast quarters over the legs. Reduce the heat to moderate, cover and simmer until the meat is cooked through, about 20 minutes. Transfer the poussins to a warmed serving platter and spoon the vegetables alongside.

—Bob Chambers

• • •

ARMADILLO TURKEY

Here is Floridian Robert Barnum's unusual turkey recipe. Use the leftover pineapple for another use, such as a winter citrus fruit salad. We suggest using pineapple juice in a carton or bottle to avoid the unpleasant metallic taste of the canned variety.

Cooking time will vary slightly: a fresh, unfrozen bird will take less time to roast than a frozen one.

🍷 The use of pineapple with the mild turkey suggests a fruity, light red, such as California Gamay Beaujolais. Try a 1989 Monterey Vineyard or 1988 Beaulieu Vineyard.

10 to 12 Servings

1 turkey (about 15 pounds)
1 lime, halved
1 small onion, quartered
Freshly ground pepper
1½ cups unsweetened pineapple juice
1 large pineapple (about 2 pounds)
3 tablespoons unsalted butter
Salt

1. Preheat the oven to 325°. Thoroughly rinse the turkey inside and out and pat it dry. Squeeze the lime into the cavity of the turkey and leave the lime halves inside. Place the onion in the cavity. Sprinkle pepper all over the turkey, inside and out. Truss the bird and place it on a rack in a nonreactive roasting pan large enough to hold it with plenty of room to spare.

2. Pour ½ cup of the pineapple juice over the turkey and roast in the lower part of the oven for 30 minutes. Pour another ½ cup of the juice on top and roast for another 30 minutes.

3. Meanwhile, using a large stainless steel knife and cutting from top to bottom, remove the skin from the pineapple in 4 equal pieces, leaving ¼ inch of pineapple on the skin. Set the skins aside (reserve the rest of the pineapple for another use).

4. Pour the remaining ½ cup pineapple juice over the turkey and cover the turkey breast with the 4 pieces of pineapple skin. Secure the pineapple skins in place with small metal skewers. Continue to roast the turkey, basting it over the pineapple skin every 30 minutes, for 2½ to 3 hours longer, until deep golden brown and an instant-reading thermometer inserted into the thickest part of a thigh reads 170° to 180°.

5. Remove the roasting pan from the oven and prop the turkey up with the legs slightly higher than the breast to let the juices run back into the breast meat. Let rest for at least 30 and up to 45 minutes.

6. To serve, place the turkey on a heated platter. Pour the pan juices into a small saucepan, scraping up any browned—but not burned—bits from the bottom of the roasting pan. Skim off all the fat from the surface and bring the juices to a boil over high heat. Cook for 1 minute. Remove from the heat and let cool slightly, about 2 minutes. Whisk in the butter and season with salt and pepper. Strain the gravy through a coarse sieve into a sauceboat. Remove the skewers and discard the pineapple skins before carving the turkey.

—*Susan Hermann Loomis*

• • •

SAUTEED DUCK BREASTS WITH PRUNES, MADEIRA AND CORIANDER SEEDS

4 Servings

8 pitted prunes, cut crosswise in thirds
1 cup Malmsey Madeira (see Note)
2 teaspoons coriander seeds
4 boneless duck breasts (about 7 ounces each)
Salt and freshly ground pepper
5 tablespoons cold unsalted butter
½ cup beef broth

1. In a small bowl, cover the prunes with the Madeira; let soak for at least 8 hours or overnight.

2. Heat a heavy skillet over high heat for two minutes, then add the coriander seeds. Cook, tossing, until golden brown, about 1 minute. On a work surface, crush the seeds slightly with the back of a heavy knife. Set aside.

3. Lightly sprinkle both sides of the duck breasts with salt and pepper. In a heavy sauté pan or cast-iron skillet, melt 3 tablespoons of the butter over moderately high heat. When the foam subsides, add the duck breasts, skin-sides down. Cook until the skin is dark brown and crisp, about 8 minutes. Turn and cook until medium-rare on the inside, about 7 minutes more. Transfer the cooked duck to a platter and keep warm while preparing the sauce.

4. Increase the heat to high. Pour off all the butter from the pan and add the soaked prunes and Madeira. Boil rapidly until reduced to ½ cup, about 2 minutes. Add the beef broth and reduce to ¼ cup, about 2 to 3 minutes longer. Turn off the heat; after 1 minute, whisk in the remaining 2 tablespoons of cold butter to thicken the sauce. Set aside.

5. Cut each breast crosswise into 4 thick slices and arrange them in the center of a dinner plate. Top with the sauce and prunes, sprinkle the toasted coriander seeds over all and serve immediately.

NOTE: *Malmsey is a rich, luscious Madeira traditionally made from the Malvoisie grape.*

—*David Rosengarten*

• • •

OUTDOOR SUMMER DINNER

Serves 8

Sautéed Chèvre on a Bed of Red Pepper Marmalade (p. 16)

Broiled Marinated Guinea Hens (p. 103)

Haricots Verts with Persillade (p. 175)

Espresso Mousse (p. 253)

—*Lydie Marshall*

CRISP POTATO PANCAKES WITH SAUTEED FOIE GRAS

Serve this dish with braised leeks to balance the rich foie gras.

❦ Foie gras is a brilliant match with Bordeaux's classic sweet wine, Sauternes. The wine echoes the richness and unctuousness of the foie gras. Choose a lighter, less honeyed example for this match, such as 1986 Château Nairac. A satisfying alternative would be a dry Sauvignon Blanc-Sémillon blend, such as 1988 Vichon Chevrignon from California.

6 Servings

1¼ pounds medium red bliss or other waxy potatoes
2 eggs, beaten
1 teaspoon salt
1 teaspoon freshly ground pepper
About ½ cup duck fat (see Note) or vegetable oil
½ cup instant blending flour

1½ pounds chilled fresh duck foie
    gras, sliced crosswise ½ inch
    thick (see Note)
¼ cup duck or veal demiglace (see
    Note)
1 cup Sauternes
1 small fresh black truffle, peeled
    and cut into very thin
    matchsticks, or 1 can truffle
    peelings with juice

1. Peel the potatoes and grate them on the large holes of a box grater set over a strainer. Press firmly on the potatoes to squeeze out the moisture. Pat the potatoes dry and place in a medium bowl. Add the eggs and ½ teaspoon each of the salt and pepper and mix well.

2. Preheat the oven to 300°. In a small skillet, heat 2 tablespoons of the duck fat over high heat until sizzling. Add ⅓ cup of the potato mixture to the pan and spread with the back of a fork to make a 5-inch pancake about ½ inch thick. Fry, turning once, until well browned, about 2 minutes per side. Adjust the heat as necessary. Transfer the pancake to a rack set over a baking sheet and place in the oven to keep warm. Repeat with the remaining potato mixture to make a total of 6 pancakes, adding more duck fat as necessary.

3. Spread the flour on a plate and season with the remaining ½ teaspoon each of salt and pepper. Place a large, heavy, nonreactive skillet over high heat until very hot, 1 to 2 minutes. Quickly dip the foie gras slices in the seasoned flour to coat thoroughly. One by one, add the floured slices to the hot pan without crowding and cook until browned and crisp, about 30 seconds per side. Transfer to paper towels to

drain and set aside in a warm place while you cook the remaining foie gras.

4. Pour off any fat from the pan. Add the demiglace, Sauternes and truffle juice if using. Bring to a boil over high heat, scraping the bottom of the pan, and boil until the liquid reduces to ⅓ cup, about 5 minutes. Remove from the heat and stir in the truffle matchsticks. Season with salt and pepper to taste.

5. To serve, place each potato pancake on a warmed plate, top with the sautéed foie gras and drizzle with the sauce.

NOTE: *Duck fat, fresh foie gras and demiglace are available from D'Artagnan (800-327-8246), a company that specializes in fresh and prepared game meats, game birds and foie gras.*

—Ariane Daguin, D'Artagnan

• • •

BROILED MARINATED GUINEA HENS

You can prepare this dish with either guinea hens or chicken, but the guinea hens have more flavor. The birds can either be broiled indoors or grilled outside. The main difference is that broiling yields a simple sauce because the marinade drips into the pan and can be rescued.

8 Servings

Three 2½-pound guinea hens
¼ cup fresh lemon juice
3 tablespoons fruity extra-virgin olive
    oil
1 tablespoon minced garlic
1½ teaspoons minced fresh rosemary
Salt

1. Remove the whole legs from the guinea hens and set aside. Split the breasts in half. With a sharp knife, and using the breastbones as your guide, bone the breasts, leaving the wings attached. Cut off the first 2 joints from the wings. You should have 6 whole legs and 6 boneless breast halves with the first wing joints attached. (Save the carcasses and the wing joints for stock.)

2. In a nonreactive pan large enough to hold the hens in one layer, combine the lemon juice, oil, garlic, rosemary and 1 teaspoon salt. Add the hen pieces and turn to coat. Let marinate for several hours at room temperature or overnight in the refrigerator. (Let return to room temperature before cooking.)

3. Preheat the broiler. Remove the hen pieces from the marinade and arrange them, skin-side up, on a rack set over a broiler pan. Broil, basting occasionally with the marinade, until golden brown, about 15 minutes. Turn the pieces and continue to broil, basting occasionally, until the breasts are cooked through, about 10 minutes longer. Transfer the breasts to a serving platter, skin-side up. Continue broiling the legs until the juices run clear when a thigh is pierced, about 5 minutes more. Transfer the legs to the platter.

4. Pour the juices into a small nonreactive saucepan along with any leftover marinade. Bring the juices to a boil when ready to eat. Serve the birds warm or at room temperature, with the juices passed separately.

—Lydie Marshall

• • •

103

POULTRY

ROAST PHEASANT WITH WILD RICE SAUCE AND GLAZED PEARL ONIONS

Always a champion of native ingredients, Larry Forgione makes innovative use of wild rice and pecans to flavor the sauce for a luscious roast pheasant.

4 Servings

3 tablespoons uncooked wild rice
Two 2½-pound pheasants, necks reserved
3 tablespoons olive oil
½ teaspoon salt
½ teaspoon freshly ground pepper
1 medium onion, sliced
1 garlic clove, crushed
3 cups chicken stock or canned low-sodium broth
¼ cup chopped pecans (1½ ounces)
1 cup heavy cream
1 teaspoon cornstarch
1 medium scallion, thinly sliced
48 tiny pearl onions, trimmed and peeled
4 tablespoons unsalted butter
¼ cup sugar

1. Preheat the oven to 375°. In a small saucepan, combine the rice with ¾ cup of water. Bring just to a boil over high heat. Reduce the heat to low, cover and simmer gently until the rice has popped and is tender, 35 to 40 minutes. Remove from the heat, uncover and set aside.

2. Meanwhile, remove the wings from the pheasants. Cut them into 3 pieces at the joints; cut each of the necks into 3 pieces and set aside.

3. Tie the legs of the pheasants together with cotton string. Rub the birds with 1 tablespoon of the olive oil, then sprinkle on both sides with ¼ teaspoon each of the salt and pepper. Set aside.

4. Pour the remaining 2 tablespoons olive oil into a large roasting pan. Heat the pan in the oven for about 5 minutes; remove and tilt to coat with the oil.

5. Lay the pheasants in the pan on their sides and roast in the oven for 15 minutes. Turn and roast for 15 minutes more. Transfer the birds to a large platter and pour any grease out of the pan. Return the birds to the roasting pans, breast-side up, and add the wing and neck pieces, onion and garlic. Return to the oven and roast, stirring the vegetables occasionally, for about 30 minutes or until the juices run clear when the thighs are pierced with a fork. Transfer the birds to a cutting board and cover with foil. Leave the oven on.

6. Add the chicken stock to the roasting pan and scrape up any brown bits from the bottom of the pan with a wooden spoon. Pour the contents of the roasting pan into a medium saucepan. Bring to a boil over moderately high heat and cook until reduced to 1 cup, about 20 minutes.

7. Meanwhile, toast the pecans on a small baking sheet in the oven until fragrant and lightly browned, about 3 minutes.

8. In a small bowl, whisk together the cream and cornstarch. Whisk the cream into the reduced stock and bring to a boil over moderately high heat. Reduce the heat to moderately low and simmer, skimming, until the sauce is thick enough to lightly coat the back of a spoon, about 10 minutes. Strain the sauce through a fine strainer into a small saucepan. Add the cooked wild rice, the toasted pecans and the scallion. Bring to a simmer over moderate heat and cook for 2 minutes. Season with the remaining ¼ teaspoon each of salt and pepper; keep warm.

9. Meanwhile, in a large skillet, combine the pearl onions with the butter, sugar and 1½ cups of water and bring to a boil over high heat and cook until the water has evaporated and the sugar and butter begin to caramelize, 20 to 25 minutes. Reduce the heat to low and cook until well browned, about 2 minutes longer. Keep warm over low heat.

10. Using a sharp knife, remove the legs from the pheasants. Cut the tough drumsticks from the thighs and discard. Remove the bones from the thighs. Cut each of the breasts off the bone in one piece.

11. To serve, place 1 breast and 1 thigh on each plate. Surround with some of the onions and ladle about 3 tablespoons of sauce over the meat. Pass the remaining sauce separately .

—*Larry Forgione, An American Place, New York City*

• • •

MEAT

MEAT

PAN-BROILED VEAL CHOPS

6 Servings

Six 12-ounce rib veal chops, 1½
*   inches thick*
2 tablespoons olive oil
¼ cup dry white wine
1 medium onion, chopped
1 large celery rib, chopped
1 medium carrot, chopped
1 large bay leaf
2 medium garlic cloves, lightly
*   crushed*
1 teaspoon tomato paste
1 teaspoon salt
¾ teaspoon freshly ground pepper
2 tablespoons unsalted butter

1. Bone the chops and set the meat and bone on separate plates.

2. In a large heavy skillet, preferably cast iron, heat 1 tablespoon of the oil over high heat. When the oil is hot, add the veal bones and cook, turning occasionally, until dark brown, about 12 minutes. Transfer with tongs to a plate.

3. Pour off any grease in the pan. Add the wine and deglaze the pan by scraping up any brown bits from the bottom with a wooden spoon. Return the browned bones to the pan and add the onion, celery, carrot, bay leaf, garlic, tomato paste, salt and pepper. Add 6 cups of water and bring to a boil. Reduce the heat to low and simmer gently for 1 hour.

4. Remove the bones and discard. Pour the stock through a fine-mesh sieve into a medium saucepan. Let sit for 1 hour. Skim off the fat. *(The recipe can be prepared to this point up to 1 day ahead. Cover and refrigerate; skim off the fat.)* Bring to a boil over high heat. Boil until reduced to 1 cup, about 30 minutes.

5. Heat a large heavy skillet, preferably cast iron, over high heat and add the remaining 1 tablespoon oil. When the oil is hot, add the veal and cook about 3 minutes on each side, or until lightly browned. Reduce the heat to moderate and cook for 4 minutes on each side until medium pink inside. Transfer to a platter, cover to keep warm and let sit for about 5 minutes.

6. Place the reduced stock in the skillet over high heat. Boil for 4 minutes until reduced to ½ cup and then remove from the heat. Pour in any exuded juices from the cooked meat. Whisk in the butter until incorporated.

7. Serve the veal chops on individual dinner plates over a pool of the sauce.

—*Lee Bailey*

• • •

EARLY FALL
DINNER PARTY

Serves 6

Pan-Broiled Veal Chops (p. 106)

Pear and Apple Chutney (p. 261)

Tomato-Watercress Salad (p. 154)

🍷 *1987 Trefethen Chardonnay*

Four-Layer Strawberry Torte (p. 220)

—*Lee Bailey*

VEAL PICCATA WITH LEMON
AND CAPERS

Veal scallops cut from the leg are lean, delicate and expensive. Ask the butcher to pound the veal very thin for you. If you would rather do it yourself, order a piece of veal cut from the leg. Thinly slice it across the grain. Then gently pound each slice from the center to the sides without tearing the meat. Season the slices just before you add them to the pan. In order to brown properly, they must be cooked quickly in small batches in very hot butter and oil.

Although the veal is usually dredged in flour before cooking, we omitted this step because we found that the flour left a bitter residue in the pan. The sauce is quick and easy. Homemade chicken stock could be used in place of the wine to loosen the browned bits from the bottom of the pan in the step known as deglazing.

4 Servings

4½ tablespoons unsalted butter—2
*   at room temperature, 2½ chilled*
*   and cut into pieces*
2 tablespoons olive oil
1 pound veal scaloppine, pounded
*   very thin*
Salt and freshly ground pepper
¼ cup dry white wine
2 tablespoons fresh lemon juice
2 teaspoons drained capers
2 teaspoons chopped parsley
Lemon slices, for serving

1. In a large nonreactive skillet, melt 1 tablespoon of the room-temperature butter in 1 tablespoon of the oil over high heat until very hot, about 3 minutes. Lightly season a few slices of the veal with salt and pepper and add just enough to fit comfortably in the pan. Cook until just browned, about 30 seconds per side. Transfer the veal to a large platter. Season and cook the remaining veal in batches, adding the remaining oil and 1 tablespoon room-temperature butter to the skillet as necessary.

2. When all the veal has been browned, pour the wine into the pan and stir to deglaze, scraping up the browned bits from the bottom. Cook until the wine has reduced by half, about 2 minutes. Add the lemon juice and cook for 30 seconds longer. Remove from the heat and stir in the 2½ tablespoons chilled butter to make a smooth sauce. Add the capers and season with salt and pepper to taste. Add any accumulated juices from the meat, then pour the sauce over the veal. Sprinkle the parsley on top, garnish with lemon slices and serve at once.

—*Marcia Kiesel*

• • •

SAUTEED VEAL WITH SHIITAKE MUSHROOMS

This rich, creamy sauté is delicious with steamed carrots and buttered white or wild rice or peppered pasta.

♈ The delicate veal and earthy perfume of mushrooms could easily be matched with a light red, such as 1988 Barton & Guestier Merlot.

6 to 8 Servings

1 tablespoon unsalted butter
¼ cup plus 2 tablespoons olive oil
½ pound shallots, finely chopped

2 garlic cloves, crushed through a press
1½ pounds fresh shiitake mushrooms, stemmed, caps sliced ¼ inch thick
2 teaspoons salt
1½ teaspoons freshly ground pepper
1 cup dry white wine
2 tablespoons all-purpose flour
2 pounds veal scaloppine, pounded ¼ inch thick
1 cup heavy cream
1 package (10 ounces) frozen baby peas, thawed

1. In a large, high-sided nonreactive skillet, melt the butter in 2 tablespoons of the olive oil over moderately high heat. When the fat is very hot, add the shallots and sauté until beginning to brown, 3 to 4 minutes. Add the garlic and sauté for 1 minute longer.

2. Add the mushrooms and sprinkle with 1 teaspoon of the salt and ½ teaspoon of the pepper. Cover and cook, stirring frequently, until the mushrooms exude their juices, about 3 minutes. Uncover and increase the heat to high. Sauté until the pan is dry and the mushrooms begin to brown, 5 to 6 minutes.

3. Stir in ½ cup of the wine and deglaze the pan, scraping up any browned bits from the bottom with a wooden spoon. Transfer the mushrooms to a bowl, cover with foil and set aside. Rinse the skillet and dry well.

4. In a medium bowl, toss the flour with the remaining 1 teaspoon each of salt and pepper. Pat the veal dry with paper towels. Slice the meat into ½-inch strips and toss to coat in the seasoned flour.

5. Return the skillet to high heat and add 2 tablespoons of the olive oil. When the oil begins to smoke, add half

of the veal strips and sauté until browned on all sides, about 1½ minutes; transfer to a warmed plate. Repeat with the remaining 2 tablespoons olive oil and veal. Cover the meat loosely with foil.

6. Deglaze the skillet with the remaining ½ cup wine, scraping up any browned bits from the bottom. Add the cream and bring to a boil. Add the reserved mushrooms and cook until the sauce lightly coats the back of the spoon, 3 to 4 minutes. Add the peas and stir, then return the veal to the skillet and rewarm until heated through. Serve hot.

—*Bob Chambers*

• • •

BEEF POT ROAST

Rump is the cut of choice for this comforting old favorite. It has lots of flavor, which is enhanced by initially searing the meat all over. Rump is tough and needs to be tenderized by long, slow cooking in a covered pot. The small amount of fat that is rendered is removed after cooking, and the softened onions and meat juices are pureed together to make a rich, satisfying and fat-free gravy. This version was inspired by my dear mother-in-law, Clara, who made the best pot roast I've ever tasted. It is really better the next day, so plan ahead. It's good served with carrots, turnips, potatoes or green beans and potato pancakes or noodles.

8 Servings

1 teaspoon olive oil
3½ pounds trimmed and tied lean beef rump, at room temperature
1 large onion (about 12 ounces), chopped

MEAT

2 bay leaves
1¼ teaspoons salt
½ teaspoon freshly ground pepper
1 tablespoon chopped flat-leaf parsley

1. Preheat the oven to 325°. Heat a heavy medium casserole or ovenproof saucepan over moderately high heat until very hot, about 4 minutes. Add the oil. Place the meat in the center of the pot and cook, without turning, until the bottom is well browned, about 4 minutes. Using tongs, turn the meat on its side and cook until browned, 3 to 4 minutes longer. Repeat until the meat has been seared on all sides. Remove the pan from the heat.

2. Push the meat to the side and add the onion. Stir well to coat the onion with the browned bits in the bottom of the pot. Stir in the bay leaves and set the meat on top of the onion mixture. Cover the pot with a tight-fitting lid or foil and roast in the middle of the oven for 30 minutes. Reduce the temperature to 300° and cook for 1½ hours longer, until the meat is fork-tender. Remove from the oven. Turn the meat over in the pot, cover and let cool to room temperature, then refrigerate overnight.

3. Remove the meat from the pot. Carefully remove and discard the layer of solidified fat from the surface of the onion mixture. Discard the bay leaves.

4. Transfer the onion mixture to a blender and add the salt and pepper. Blend until smooth. Pour the gravy into a large skillet. Rinse the blender with 2 to 3 tablespoons of water and add to the gravy.

5. Slice the cold meat across the grain a scant ¼ inch thick. Add the slices to the gravy in the skillet, overlapping them slightly. Cook over moderate heat, basting the meat with the gravy, until heated through, about 15 minutes. Sprinkle with the parsley before serving.

—*Diana Sturgis*

• • •

BOILED BEEF STEWED WITH POTATOES

In Italian cooking, leftover food always goes into making new dishes called *rifatti*. Since there is a lot of boiled beef left over from making homemade broth—or left over from the classic dish *bollito misto*, a mixture of boiled meats—the meat is then used to make a traditional boiled beef dish, or *lesso rifatto*.

♟ Try a flavorsome red, such as 1985 Santa Rita Cabernet Sauvignon Medalla Real from Chile or 1985 Olarra Añares Rioja Tinto from Spain.

6 Servings

¼ cup olive oil
3 ounces pancetta or prosciutto, cut into ¼-inch dice
Leaves from 30 flat-leaf parsley sprigs, half coarsely chopped
1 teaspoon tarragon
2 imported bay leaves
2 pounds all-purpose or new potatoes
2 pounds leftover boiled beef, cut into 1-inch cubes
½ teaspoon salt
½ teaspoon freshly ground pepper
2 tablespoons red wine vinegar

1. In a large heavy stockpot or dutch oven, warm the oil over moderate heat. Add the pancetta and cook until some of the fat is rendered, about 2 minutes. Add the unchopped parsley leaves, tarragon, bay leaves and 2 cups of warm water. Cook until the water has reduced to 1½ cups, about 15 minutes.

2. Meanwhile, peel the potatoes. Cut them into 1-inch cubes and place in cold water to prevent them from discoloring. When the water in the stockpot has reduced, drain the potatoes and add them to the pot. Reduce the heat to moderately low, cover and cook until the potatoes are just tender, about 20 minutes.

3. Add the boiled beef, season with the salt and pepper and mix well. Cook, covered, until the meat is heated through, about 5 minutes. Add more warm water if the mixture seems too dry. Stir in the vinegar and transfer the stew to a serving platter. Discard the bay leaves. Sprinkle the chopped parsley on top.

—*Giuliano Bugialli*

• • •

ROPA VIEJA

This is Havana Clipper's version of shredded beef, or "old clothes," a traditional dish. As with most Cuban food, it is not hot-spicy, but you can add hot pepper sauce if you wish. Turn it into a complete meal by serving it with rice and black beans. The stock that results from cooking the skirt steak can be strained and refrigerated. The next day, skim off the fat that collects on the top and use the stock to cook the beans or as a base for soups and sauces.

♟ This spicy, sweet dish would contrast nicely with a refreshingly cold, dry California rosé—such as 1989 Saintsbury Vin Gris or Pinot Noir—or, alternatively, with a crisp lager beer, such as Carlsberg or Harp.

---

6 Servings

---

3 pounds skirt steak
3 large onions (about 2¼ pounds)—
   1 halved, 2 thinly sliced
1 medium head of garlic, halved
   horizontally, plus 4 large garlic
   cloves, finely chopped
2 large celery ribs, halved crosswise
1 tablespoon salt
¼ cup olive oil
2 large green bell peppers, cut into
   thin lengthwise strips
3 large tomatoes (about 1½ pounds),
   cut into small dice
½ cup dry white wine
¼ cup cumin
4 bay leaves

1. Place the skirt steak in a large stockpot and add water to cover by 2 to 3 inches. Add the halved onion and head of garlic, the celery and the salt and bring to a boil over high heat. Cover, reduce the heat to moderate and boil until the meat is tender, about 1¾ hours. Transfer the meat to a plate, cover and refrigerate until cool. (*The recipe can he prepared to this point up to 1 day ahead.*) Shred the cooled meat with your fingers and set aside.

2. In a large nonreactive flameproof casserole, heat the olive oil. Add the chopped garlic and cook over high heat until lightly browned, about 1 minute. Reduce the heat to moderate and stir in the sliced onions and bell peppers. Cook, stirring occasionally, until softened, about 10 minutes.

3. Stir in the tomatoes, wine, cumin, bay leaves and a pinch of salt. Increase the heat to moderately high and cook, stirring occasionally, until the tomatoes are almost completely broken down, about 25 minutes. Stir in the shredded meat and cook until heated through, about 5 minutes. Remove from the heat and season to taste with salt.

—*Havana Clipper, Miami*

• • •

UNA COMIDA LATINA

Serves 6

Rum and Tonic

Corn-Fried Oysters with Tomato-Tequila Salsa and Chipotle Cream (p. 22)

Ropa Vieja (p. 108)

Rice Pilaf

Buttered Green Beans

♟ *Dry California Rosé, such as 1989 Simi Rosé of Cabernet Sauvignon*

Pineapple-Mango Bisque (p. 245)

Café Cubano

OLIVE-STUFFED SKIRT STEAKS WITH BLACK BEAN SAUCE

Try to find skirt steaks of even thickness for this full-flavored, Mexican-style treat. Allow enough time to marinate the steaks. If you have an outdoor grill, you can use it for the initial cooking of the steaks (Step 9). You can then finish them up in the broiler.

---

4 Servings

---

1 large garlic clove, minced
2 teaspoons sweet Hungarian
   paprika
3 tablespoons olive oil
1½ teaspoons salt
Four 8-ounce skirt steaks, about 4 by
   2 inches, trimmed of excess fat
1 cup dried black turtle beans
2 tablespoons cumin seeds
1 small onion, finely chopped
1 small green bell pepper, finely
   chopped
½ teaspoon freshly ground black
   pepper
½ cup finely chopped parsley, plus
   more for garnish
16 small oil-cured black olives, such
   as Gaeta, halved and pitted
½ teaspoon oregano
1 cup (lightly packed) shredded
   romaine lettuce
¼ pound Monterey Jack cheese, cut
   into 24 thin slices

1. In a small bowl, mix the garlic with the paprika. Blend in 2 tablespoons of the olive oil to form a smooth paste. Stir in ½ teaspoon of the salt. Spread the paste evenly over the skirt steaks, making sure that all sides are coated.

109

Place the steaks in a shallow pan and set aside to marinate at room temperature for 2 hours, or for 8 hours in the refrigerator.

2. In a large saucepan, cover the black beans with 1½ cups of water and bring to a boil over high heat. Boil for 3 minutes. Cover the pot and remove from the heat. Let stand for 1 hour.

3. In a small dry skillet, toast the cumin seeds over high heat until fragrant, about 30 seconds. Transfer to a spice grinder and pulverize, or grind in a mortar with a pestle.

4. In a large skillet, heat the remaining 1 tablespoon oil. Add the onion and bell pepper and cook over moderate heat, stirring once or twice, until just starting to brown, about 3 minutes. Reduce the heat to low, stir in the cumin and cook until fragrant, about 1 minute.

5. Add the onion-pepper mixture to the black beans and stir well. Add 5 cups of water and bring to a boil over high heat. Reduce the heat to low and simmer, partially covered, until the beans are tender, about 1½ hours.

6. Pour the beans into a colander set over a bowl. Measure the bean liquid; if you have less than 1½ cups, add enough water to compensate.

7. Set aside 3 tablespoons of the beans. In a food processor, combine the remaining beans with 1 cup of the bean liquid and process until smooth. Transfer the puree to a coarse strainer set over a small saucepan and, using a wooden spoon or a spatula, push the puree through. Stir in the remaining ½ cup bean liquid and the 3 tablespoons reserved beans. Season the sauce with the remaining 1 teaspoon salt and the black pepper. *(The sauce can be made up to 1 day ahead; cover and refrigerate.)*

8. Make a lengthwise incision in the side of each skirt steak, without cutting all the way through, to form a deep pocket. Keep the pockets closed.

9. Preheat the broiler. Place the steaks on a broiling pan and broil 3 inches from the heat for 3 minutes per side.

10. Transfer the steaks to a work surface. Layer the inside of the pocket of each steak with 2 tablespoons of the parsley, 4 olives, a pinch of oregano and ¼ cup of the shredded lettuce. Press together the seam of the pocket to enclose the stuffing.

11. Place 6 overlapping slices of cheese on each steak. Return the steaks to the pan and broil for about 30 seconds, or until the cheese has melted. Transfer the steaks to heated plates.

12. Reheat the black bean sauce. Pour the sauce on the plate along both sides of each steak. Sprinkle some chopped parsley on top.

—*David Rosengarten*

• • •

MICROWAVE-POACHED BEEF WITH BANYULS SAUCE

Joseph Lampreia, chef of the ultra-fashionable Maison Blanche in Paris, serves the broth as a first course and the meat and sauce as the second course. Here, each piece of meat is placed in a large soup dish along with some broth, vegetables and sauce.

---

4 Servings

---

2 leeks, white and light green portion only, quartered lengthwise
1 celery rib—peeled, halved lengthwise and crosswise
2 carrots, halved lengthwise and crosswise
1 turnip, peeled and cut into wedges
Bouquet garni: 1 bay leaf, stems from 1 bunch of parsley and ½ teaspoon thyme tied in cheesecloth
3 garlic cloves, unpeeled
Microwave Beef Broth (p. 270)
1½ pounds trimmed fillet of beef, cut crosswise into 4 medallions and tied with string
1 teaspoon drained green peppercorns, rinsed
2 tablespoons crème fraîche
1 tablespoon dry Banyuls wine or 1 tablespoon plus 1 teaspoon dry sherry
½ teaspoon coarse (kosher) salt

1. Arrange the leeks and celery in the center of a 5-quart microwaveable casserole and surround with the carrots and turnips. Add the bouquet garni, garlic and 2½ cups of the Beef Broth. Cover with microwave plastic wrap and cook on High, or full, power for 9 minutes.

2. Place each of the beef medallions in a corner of the casserole on top of the vegetables. (The meat should not be covered with broth.) Cover and reheat on High for 5½ minutes, or until the beef is just rare inside. Prick the plastic to release the steam. Remove the garlic. *(The recipe can be prepared to this point up to 3 hours ahead. Let cool, then cover and refrigerate. Cover and reheat on High for 3 minutes before serving.)*

3. In a mortar, crush the green peppercorns. Squeeze the cooked garlic flesh into the mortar and mash with the peppercorns. Add the crème fraîche, wine and salt and stir until smooth.

4. With a slotted spoon, arrange the vegetables and meat in 4 large soup dishes. Add the remaining broth, about 1½ cups, to the casserole. Cover and cook on High for 4 minutes. Pour the broth over the meat and vegetables. Spoon a dollop of the sauce on each medallion and serve.

—*Barbara Kafka*

• • •

ROAST TENDERLOIN OF BEEF WITH MUSTARD SAUCE

The sauce has a very mild mustard flavor, so if you like a strong mustard taste, feel free to add more.

♀ Mustard and soy sauce sharpen the tastes here, indicating a red with pointed flavor as the best complement. A rich Italian 1982 Barolo, such as those from Renato Ratti or Cordero di Montezemolo would be ideal.

6 Servings

2 teaspoons soy sauce
2½ pounds beef tenderloin
1 teaspoon freshly ground pepper
1 tablespoon olive oil
1 medium garlic clove, minced
3 medium shallots, minced
⅓ cup dry red wine
1½ tablespoons Dijon mustard
1 cup canned low-sodium beef broth
¼ cup plus 1 tablespoon heavy cream
2 tablespoons unsalted butter

1. Rub the soy sauce all over the beef and let sit for 30 minutes. Season with the pepper.

A RICH LITTLE REPAST

Serves 6

Roast Tenderloin of Beef with Mustard Sauce (p. 111)

Garlic Mashed Potatoes (p. 180)

♀ *Barolo*

Green Salad

Meringue Cake with Chocolate Bourbon Sauce (p. 221)

Coffee

—*Lee Bailey*

---

2. Meanwhile, preheat the oven to 450°. In a large, heavy, ovenproof skillet, heat the oil over high heat. Add the beef and cook until well browned all over, about 6 minutes.

3. Transfer the pan to the oven and roast the tenderloin for about 20 minutes, turning once, until the internal temperature reads 120° on a meat thermometer for rare. Transfer the meat to a cutting board, cover loosely with aluminum foil and let sit for 10 minutes.

4. Meanwhile, pour off any fat from the skillet. Add the garlic and shallots and cook over moderately low heat, stirring, until lightly browned, about 2 minutes. Pour in the wine, increase the heat to high and simmer for 1 minute. Stir in the mustard, broth and cream and bring to a boil. Reduce the heat to moderate and simmer until the sauce has reduced to 1 cup and is thick enough to lightly coat the back of a spoon, about 6 minutes. Reduce the heat to low and stir in the butter until incorporated.

5. Using a sharp knife, cut the meat into 12 slices. Arrange the meat on plates or a platter, spoon the mustard sauce on top and serve hot.

—*Lee Bailey*

• • •

SAUTEED BEEF MEDALLIONS WITH OLIVES AND SUN-DRIED TOMATOES

Serve the beef with a creamy risotto or buttered orzo and a simple green vegetable, such as wilted spinach.

♀ With its Mediterranean accents of olives and sun-dried tomatoes, this beef dish calls for a solid, savory red, such as 1986 Vieux Télégraphe Châteauneuf-du-Pape from the Rhône or 1987 Foppiano Petite Sirah from California.

6 Servings

2 pounds trimmed fillet of beef, cut crosswise into ¾-inch medallions
2 teaspoons coarsely ground pepper
1 can (14 ounces) Italian plum tomatoes
3 tablespoons olive oil
1 medium red onion, very thinly sliced
3 garlic cloves, crushed through a press
½ cup brandy
½ cup sun-dried tomatoes in oil, cut into ¼-inch strips (3 ounces)
⅔ cup Calamata or other brine-cured black olives, pitted and sliced

MEAT

SIMPLE WINTER'S MEAL

Serves 6

Broiled Marinated Flank Steak
(p. 112)

Corn-Kernel Pancakes (p. 199)

🍷 *Full-bodied red wine*

Baked Banana-Pear Crumble
(p. 244)

Coffee

—*Lee Bailey*

½ *teaspoon sugar*
Salt
⅔ *cup chopped flat-leaf parsley*

1. Rub both sides of the beef medallions with the pepper and set aside for at least 15 minutes or up to 1 hour. Meanwhile, in a food processor, pulse the tomatoes with their juice until coarsely chopped; set aside.

2. In a large, high-sided nonreactive skillet, heat 1 tablespoon of the olive oil over high heat until smoking. Add half of the beef medallions and sauté for 1½ minutes on each side. Transfer the medallions to a warmed platter and cover loosely with foil. Repeat with another tablespoon of oil and the remaining meat.

3. Add the remaining 1 tablespoon oil to the skillet, and when it begins to smoke, add the onion and sauté until beginning to brown, about 1½ minutes. Add the garlic and sauté for 30 seconds longer.

4. Add the brandy and deglaze the pan, scraping up any browned bits from the bottom with a wooden spoon. Add the sun-dried tomatoes, olives, sugar and the reserved chopped tomatoes and bring to a boil. Reduce the heat to moderate and simmer, stirring occasionally, until thickened, about 4 minutes.

5. Add any accumulated meat juices to the sauce and season with salt and pepper to taste. Stir in the parsley. Spoon the sauce around the meat and serve hot.

—*Bob Chambers*

• • •

BROILED MARINATED FLANK STEAK

🍷 This richly sauced dish requires a big red to match, such as 1985 Travaglini Gattinara from Italy or 1986 Penfolds Bin 389 Cabernet/Shiraz from Australia.

6 Servings

2½ *pounds flank steak, trimmed of*
all fat
1 *can (14 ounces) crushed tomatoes*
¾ *cup canned beef broth diluted with*
¾ cup water
¾ *cup dry red wine*
1 *large onion, halved and thinly*
sliced
1 *large garlic clove, thinly sliced*
1 *tablespoon Worcestershire sauce*
1 *teaspoon thyme*
1 *bay leaf*
2 *tablespoons unsalted butter, cut*
into bits
Salt and freshly ground pepper

1. Place the steak in a large nonreactive dish or bowl. Add the tomatoes, broth, wine, onion, garlic, Worcestershire, thyme and bay leaf to the dish and turn the steak to coat evenly. Marinate for 4 hours at room temperature, turning several times, or cover and refrigerate overnight. Let the meat come to room temperature before cooking.

2. Preheat the broiler. Remove the meat from the marinade. Scrape all the marinade ingredients into a small nonreactive saucepan and cook over moderately high heat until the liquid has reduced to 1 cup, about 15 minutes. Strain the liquid into a small heavy saucepan, pressing the vegetables through the strainer. Discard the contents of the strainer.

3. Broil the steak 6 to 7 inches from the heat, turning once, for 10 minutes for rare, longer for medium. Transfer to a cutting board and cover lightly with foil.

4. Reheat the marinade over moderate heat, until hot but not boiling. Whisk in the butter and season with salt and pepper. Slice the meat against the grain and serve the sauce on the side.

—*Lee Bailey*

• • •

Fresh Ham with Rosemary-Pear
Marinade (p. 122) with side dishes of
Rutabaga and Potato Puree (p. 182) and
Marinated Cucumber Salad (p. 158).

Left, Mongolian Lamb Chops with Lemony Hummus
and Tortillas (p. 128). Above, Boiled Beef Stewed with
Potatoes (p. 108).

PEPPERED SIRLOIN SHELL STEAK WITH PAN-ROASTED POTATOES

🍷 A young Cabernet Sauvignon from California or the Médoc won't be overpowered by the pepper and spice of this dish, which echo the peppery bite and meatiness of the wine.

4 Servings

1 to 1½ teaspoons whole black peppercorns
1 teaspoon coriander seeds
1 teaspoon coarse (kosher) salt
3 pounds boneless whole sirloin shell steak cut from the top loin, trimmed of fat, but with a thin strip remaining
8 medium red potatoes, halved (1½ pounds)

1. Preheat the oven to 450°. In a mortar, pound the peppercorns to a coarse powder, working with a few at a time. Set aside in a small bowl. Add the coriander seeds to the mortar and pound to a fine powder; add to the peppercorns. Add the salt and mix well.

2. Place the shell steak in a roasting pan, fat-side up. Rub the pepper-coriander mixture into the fat and all over the top of the meat. Arrange the potatoes around the meat, cut-sides down. Roast in the oven for 20 minutes, then lower the temperature to 350°. Roast for about 25 minutes longer,

Sautéed Shrimp with Garlic and Herbs (p. 69) and a Pan-Broiled Pork Chop (p. 123).

or until a meat thermometer inserted in the center portion registers 125° for medium rare.

3. Transfer the potatoes to a large warmed platter. Place the roast in the center of the platter and let it sit for about 10 minutes before carving.

4. Meanwhile, set the roasting pan over high heat. When the juices sizzle, add ⅓ cup of water and scrape the browned bits from the bottom. Boil for 30 seconds to concentrate the flavor; pour into a sauceboat. Add accumulated meat juices from the platter. Carve the roast into ⅓-inch slices and serve with the potatoes. Pass the sauce separately.

—*Marcia Kiesel*

• • •

PEPPERED STEAK

The quantity of peppercorns listed below makes a pretty fiery steak, but you can decrease it to suit your taste.

2 Servings

¼ cup whole black peppercorns
Two 10-ounce trimmed boneless New York strip or shell steaks, 1 inch thick, at room temperature
½ teaspoon coarse (kosher) salt
1 tablespoon vegetable oil

1. Place the peppercorns on a work surface. Cover with a towel and, using a rolling pin or meat pounder, coarsely crush the peppercorns.

2. Lightly sprinkle both sides of the steaks with the salt. Lay the steaks on the pepper and press so that as much pepper adheres as possible. Turn the steaks and repeat on the other side.

3. In a large cast-iron skillet, heat the oil over high heat until hot, about 2 minutes. Add the steaks and cook for 3 minutes. Turn and cook for 2 minutes on the other side for rare, 3 minutes for medium. Transfer to large plates and let rest for 5 minutes before serving.

—*Mark Peel, Campanile, Los Angeles*

• • •

RIB STEAK WITH SALT AND PEPPER CRUST

Pan-broiling is a quick and delicious way to prepare thick cuts of meat, such as the popular *côte de boeuf*, or beef rib. This version, from Adrienne Biasin's homey Paris bistro Chez la Vieille (better known as Chez Adrienne), is coated with crushed black peppercorns and coarse sea salt and served with a marvelous shallot sauce. The beef is just as tasty the next day, cubed and tossed in a salad. Likewise, any leftover shallot sauce is great spread on toasted homemade bread.

🍷 This meaty dish, with its tangy sauce, needs a vigorous red with a firm, tannic bite of its own. A young California Cabernet Sauvignon, such as a 1986 Charles Krug or 1986 Chateau Montelena, would be an excellent choice.

2 to 3 Servings

2 teaspoons whole black peppercorns
One 2-pound beef rib steak with bone, 1½ inches thick, at room temperature
¼ cup coarse (kosher) or sea salt

117

6 tablespoons (3 ounces) unsalted
    butter
1 cup minced shallots (7 to 8
    medium)
¾ cup dry white wine
¾ cup beef or chicken stock or
    canned low-sodium broth
Salt and freshly ground white pepper
3 tablespoons peanut oil

1. On a work surface, crush the peppercorns with a heavy mallet or with the bottom of a heavy skillet. Alternatively, crush the peppercorns in a mortar with a pestle. Press onto both sides of the steak. Press the salt onto the meat, coating it well. Set aside for about 30 minutes at room temperature.

2. Meanwhile, make the shallot sauce. In a medium nonreactive saucepan, heat 3 tablespoons of the butter over moderately low heat until it begins to foam. Add the shallots and cook, stirring, until softened but not colored, about 5 minutes. Increase the heat to moderate, add the wine and the stock and simmer until the sauce is almost as thick as jam, 30 to 40 minutes. (*The sauce can be prepared up to 30 minutes ahead. Keep warm, covered, in the top of a double boiler over low heat. Just before serving, season with salt and pepper to taste.*)

3. Heat a very large cast-iron or heavy-bottomed skillet over high heat for 5 minutes. Add the remaining 3 tablespoons butter and the oil. When the butter has melted, add the steak and sear for 2 minutes on each side, turning with a two-pronged fork inserted into the side of the meat so that the coating is not disturbed. Reduce the heat to moderate and cook, without turning, about 8 minutes more for rare, 10 minutes for medium-rare, and 12 minutes

for medium. Transfer the steak to a cutting board, cover loosely with foil and let rest for 10 minutes.

4. To serve, carve the steak into ½-inch slices and arrange them on warmed serving plates. Spoon the shallot sauce alongside.

—Patricia Wells

• • •

PEPPERED RIB STEAK WITH PAN-FRIED WATERCRESS

4 Servings

Four 4- to 6-ounce rib-eye steaks,
    ¾ inch thick, trimmed of most fat
2 teaspoons coarsely ground pepper
¼ cup dry red wine
2 tablespoons unsalted butter
2 bunches of watercress, large stems
    removed
Salt

1. Coat each side of the steaks with ¼ teaspoon of the pepper, lightly pounding it in with your hands.

2. Heat a large cast-iron skillet over moderately high heat. When the pan is hot, add the steaks and cook for 4 minutes. Turn and cook until browned, about 2 minutes longer for medium-rare. Transfer the steaks to a large platter and cover with foil. Add the red wine to the skillet and boil until reduced by half, about 1 minute. Pour the sauce over the steaks.

3. Wipe out the skillet and add the butter. Increase the heat to high. Add the watercress and toss constantly until wilted, about 1 minute. Season with salt to taste. Serve alongside the steaks.

—Jim Fobel

• • •

GRILLED SHELL STEAK WITH LIME

❦ The shell steak demands a substantial red. A full-bodied California Merlot, such as 1987 Robert Keenan or 1987 Rutherford Hill, would fit the bill.

4 Servings

Four 12-ounce shell steaks, 1 inch
    thick, with bone
2 tablespoons fresh lime juice
Salt and freshly ground pepper
Lime wedges, for serving

1. Light the grill. Place the steaks on a large plate and drizzle the lime juice on top. Turn the steaks to coat. Set aside to marinate for 15 to 20 minutes.

GRILLED DINNER

Serves 4

Grilled Shell Steak with Lime (p. 118)

Grilled Red Potatoes (p. 177)

❦ *California Merlot*

*Red Cabbage Coleslaw with Jalapeño
    Vinaigrette (p. 156)*

Grilled Pineapple

—Stephanie Lyness

2. Preheat the broiler, if using. Season both sides of the steaks with salt and pepper and grill or broil, turning once, for about 8 minutes for medium-rare, 10 minutes for medium. Let rest for 10 minutes. Serve with lime wedges.

—*Stephanie Lyness*

• • •

HUNGARIAN-STYLE STUFFED CABBAGE

Stuffed cabbage is ubiquitous in central and eastern Europe. This recipe is from a friend's mother, Martha Singer. Non-kosher cooks can add two heaping tablespoons of sour cream to one cup of the reduced sauce and pass the resulting gravy at the table. This dish reheats beautifully and makes great leftovers.

🍷 The richness of the stuffed cabbage would harmonize with a full-flavored red, such as 1986 Château Greysac or 1986 Gundlach-Bundschu Merlot.

8 Servings

1 large head of green cabbage (about 3 pounds), cored
1½ pounds lean ground round
½ cup rice
2 eggs, lightly beaten
2 small onions, finely chopped
2 teaspoons salt
1 teaspoon freshly ground black pepper
2 teaspoons imported sweet Hungarian paprika
2 cans (8 ounces each) tomato sauce
1 pound sauerkraut

1. Bring a large pot of water to a boil over high heat. Add the cabbage, cored-end down. Reduce the heat to moderate, cover and simmer until the leaves are softened, about 12 minutes.

2. Transfer the cabbage to a bowl filled with cold water. Pour 1 quart of the cabbage cooking water into a large nonreactive saucepan; discard the rest. Separate 16 large leaves from the head of cabbage. Trim the tough ribs on the back of the leaves, if necessary, so that they will roll up easily. Finely chop enough of the remaining cabbage to measure 1 cup and set aside.

3. In a large bowl, combine the meat, rice, eggs, onions, salt, black pepper and paprika. Place a generous ¼ cup of the meat mixture at the bottom of a cabbage leaf and roll up like a cigar. Trim the ends of the leaves if they are very long. Tuck in the ends to form tight packages. Repeat with the remaining meat mixture and cabbage leaves.

4. Arrange enough rolls in the cabbage cooking water, seam-side down, to cover the pot in a single layer. Cover with half of the tomato sauce and half of the sauerkraut. Arrange the rest of the cabbage rolls on top. Cover with the remaining tomato sauce and sauerkraut. Scatter the reserved chopped cabbage over the top. The top layer of rolls should be at least half immersed in liquid; if necessary, add more water. Cover and cook over moderately low heat, simmering gently until a cabbage roll feels firm when pressed in the center, about 1½ hours.

5. Transfer the cabbage rolls to a large warmed platter and cover to keep warm. Boil the sauce over high heat until it has reduced to about 4 cups and is thick, about 10 minutes. Pour the sauce over the stuffed cabbage and serve 2

rolls per person. *(The recipe can be prepared up to 1 day ahead. Cover and refrigerate; reheat before serving.)*

—*Susan Shapiro Jaslove*

• • •

CORNED BEEF AND SHALLOT SMØRREBRØD WITH EGGS AND DILL

These open-faced sandwiches are a good bet for a Sunday brunch party. Corned beef varies in saltiness, so you may or may not need to season with additional salt.

Makes 16 Sandwiches

1½ cups mayonnaise
5 tablespoons plus 2 teaspoon Dijon mustard
1 large shallot, very thinly sliced
¼ cup finely chopped dill, plus about 48 small dill sprigs
1 pound cold thinly sliced corned beef, trimmed of all fat
Freshly ground pepper
Salt (optional)
16 slices of rye bread with caraway seeds
8 hard-cooked eggs, sliced or chopped

1. In a large bowl, combine the mayonnaise, 3 tablespoons of the mustard, the shallot and chopped dill. *(The dressing can be made up to 1 day ahead; cover and refrigerate.)*

2. Fold the corned beef into the dressing. Season well with pepper and, if desired, with salt. Stir gently, being careful not to break up the meat.

3. Trim the crusts from the bread to form 3-inch squares. Divide the corned beef evenly among the bread squares. Spread about ½ teaspoon of mustard on top of the corned beef on each sandwich. Cover the meat with dill sprigs. Top each sandwich with a few egg slices and another sprig of dill.

—*David Rosengarten*

• • •

GREEN PEPPERCORN PORK WITH CHINESE CABBAGE

❦ Alsace Gewürztraminer is the wine of choice for this dish. Try 1988 Hugel or 1987 Trimbach.

4 Servings

1 small garlic clove, minced
3 tablespoons plus 1 teaspoon coarse (kosher) salt
1½ teaspoons sugar
2 teaspoons brine-packed green peppercorns, rinsed
Three 8-ounce pork tenderloins
2 tablespoons olive oil
1 medium onion, halved and thinly sliced
½ large head of Chinese cabbage, thinly sliced crosswise (about 5 cups)
2 tablespoons unsalted butter
1 teaspoon yellow mustard seeds
¼ cup coarsely chopped flat-leaf parsley
⅓ cup chopped celery leaves
Salt and freshly ground pepper

1. In a small bowl, mix together the garlic, coarse salt, sugar and green peppercorns. Place the tenderloins in a shallow glass dish and rub them all over with the peppercorn marinade. Cover and refrigerate for 2 days, turning the meat once or twice to allow the peppercorn mixture to penetrate evenly.

2. Preheat the oven to 500°. Let the pork come to room temperature. In a large skillet, heat 1 tablespoon of the olive oil over high heat until it begins to smoke. Add the pork tenderloins and cook, turning, until well browned on all sides, about 8 minutes. Transfer the tenderloins to a heavy baking sheet and roast on the top shelf of the oven for about 8 minutes, until an instant-reading thermometer inserted in the thickest part reads 140°. Do not overcook. Transfer the meat to a platter and set aside.

3. Meanwhile, wipe out the skillet and add the remaining 1 tablespoon oil. Add the onion slices in an even layer and cook over high heat, without stirring, until they start to brown, about 1 minute. Add the cabbage, reduce the heat to moderate and add ¼ cup of water. Cover and cook until the cabbage is tender but still has a slight crunch, about 5 minutes.

4. In a small saucepan, cook the butter over moderately high heat until brown speckles begin to appear, about 3 minutes. Add the mustard seeds and cook, stirring, until they brown slightly and pop, about 30 seconds. Remove from the heat and set aside. When the cabbage is cooked, stir in the mustard seed butter, parsley and celery leaves. Season with salt and pepper to taste and set aside.

5. To serve, slice the pork into ⅓-inch slices, spoon the warm cabbage onto serving plates and top with the pork.

—*Marcia Kiesel*

• • •

PORK LOIN WITH WILD MUSHROOM-SAGE STUFFING

Since pork is much leaner these days, it requires shorter cooking times. For a succulent flavor, it is important to baste often while cooking. The internal temperature will rise 5 to 10 degrees as it sits after it is removed from the oven. Ask your butcher to cut a lengthwise pocket in the roasts for stuffing. When preparing the mushrooms for the stuffing, be sure to leave them fairly large and cook them quickly over brisk heat so that they will not release too much liquid. Prepare the mushrooms ahead of time so that they can cool completely before stuffing.

❦ This dish calls for a rather rich red, and the hint of sage points to one with herbaceous notes. Try a fine Bordeaux, such as 1982 Château Prieuré-Lichine, or a flavorsome California Cabernet Sauvignon, such as 1982 Simi Reserve.

12 Servings

Two 2½-pound boneless center-cut pork loins, about 10 inches long, with a lengthwise pocket for stuffing cut in each
1 garlic clove, halved
Wild Mushroom-Sage Stuffing (recipe follows)
1 tablespoon unsalted butter
2 tablespoons olive oil
½ cup Calvados or apple brandy
1½ cups chicken stock or canned low-sodium broth
1 teaspoon red currant jelly
2 tablespoons finely chopped fresh sage plus 1 fresh sage sprig, for garnish

¾ teaspoon thyme
½ teaspoon freshly ground pepper

1. Rub the surface of the pork loins with the garlic halves; reserve the garlic. Fill each pocket with half of the Wild Mushroom-Sage Stuffing, pushing the stuffing through with the handle of a wooden spoon if necessary. Tie each loin with 4 crosswise pieces of string. *(The recipe can be prepared to this point several hours ahead. Cover the pork loins and refrigerate.)*

2. Preheat the oven to 350°. In a large heavy skillet, melt the butter in the olive oil over moderately high heat. Add the reserved garlic and cook for 1 minute; discard the garlic. Add the stuffed pork loins to the skillet, one at a time, and cook, turning, until well browned all over, about 8 minutes per loin. Transfer to a large roasting pan.

3. Increase the heat to high and add the Calvados to the skillet. Boil until slightly thickened, about 3 minutes. Stir in the chicken stock, red currant jelly, chopped sage, thyme and pepper. Pour this liquid over the meat.

4. Insert a meat thermometer almost through one of the pork loins. Roast in the middle of the oven for about 50 minutes, until the temperature reaches 150°. Transfer the roasts to a large platter, cover loosely with foil; let rest for 15 minutes.

5. Degrease the pan juices and pour into a sauceboat. Carve the roasts into ½-inch slices and arrange on a warmed platter. Garnish with the sprig of sage and pass the sauceboat at the table.

—*Sheila Lukins*

• • •

A CHRISTMAS FEAST

Serves 12

Fennel Tart with Rosemary (p. 25)

🍷 *Champagne or Sparkling Wine*

Parsnip Vichyssoise (p. 34)

Pork Loin with Wild Mushroom-Sage Stuffing (p. 120)

Gingered Cranberry Relish (p. 260)

Pear and Apple Compote (p. 241)

Fragrant Barley (p. 145)

Spiced Butternut Squash (p. 184)

Glazed Roasted Shallots and Garlic (p. 182)

🍷 *Bordeaux or Cabernet Sauvignon*

Christmas Bread Pudding and Amaretto Sauce (p. 258)

Chocolate Raspberry Fudge Cake (p. 227)

🍷 *Muscat de Beaumes de Venise*

—*Sheila Lukins*

WILD MUSHROOM-SAGE STUFFING

Makes About 4 Cups

2 pounds fresh wild mushrooms, such as shiitakes and chanterelles, stems removed
2 tablespoons extra-virgin olive oil
4 large shallots, coarsely chopped
8 large garlic cloves, coarsely chopped
1¼ teaspoons thyme
½ cup coarsely chopped fresh sage
2 tablespoons unsalted butter
1½ teaspoons freshly ground pepper
1 to 1½ tablespoons finely grated lemon zest
Salt

1. Wipe the stemmed mushrooms with a damp cloth and cut into ½-inch pieces; set aside.

2. In a large nonstick skillet, heat the olive oil over moderately low heat. Add the shallots, garlic and thyme and cook, stirring, until the shallots soften slightly, about 3 minutes. Increase the heat to moderately high and stir in the mushrooms. Cover and cook until the mushrooms soften, 5 to 6 minutes.

3. Add the sage, butter, pepper and lemon zest. Cook, stirring, until the mushrooms give off some of their liquid, 4 to 5 minutes. Season with salt and additional pepper to taste. Transfer the stuffing to a large bowl and let cool to room temperature before using. *(The stuffing can be made up to 1 day ahead. Cover and refrigerate.)*

—*Sheila Lukins*

• • •

MEAT

ROAST PORK LOIN WITH FENNEL

This simple, satisfying main-course dish was inspired by the arrival of fresh fennel in the market. It has the added benefit of scenting the entire house with a lovely anise fragrance right before the meal. Leftovers make great sandwiches the next day.

6 Servings

3 pounds fennel bulbs (4 large)—quartered, cored and very thinly sliced crosswise
2 medium red onions, thinly sliced
2 tablespoons olive oil
2 pounds trimmed boneless pork loin
1½ tablespoons minced garlic
¾ teaspoon freshly ground pepper
3 tablespoons chopped parsley

1. Preheat the oven to 400°. In a medium roasting pan, toss the fennel, onions and olive oil. Rub the pork loin all over with the garlic and pepper. Place the loin fat-side up on top of the fennel and onions and roast in the middle of the oven for 30 minutes, until browned on top.

2. Remove the pan from the oven and reduce the temperature to 350°. Stir the fennel mixture and turn the pork over. Continue roasting for about 45 minutes longer, until an instant-read thermometer inserted in the center of the roast reads 140° and the fennel mixture is lightly browned. Turn the oven off.

3. Transfer the loin to a warm platter, cover loosely and let rest for 10 minutes. Return the fennel mixture to the oven to keep warm. Carve the pork into ¼-inch slices and arrange on the platter. Stir the parsley into the fennel mixture and spoon it around the pork. Serve hot.
—*Ann Chantal Altman*

• • •

FRESH HAM WITH ROSEMARY-PEAR MARINADE

Fresh ham—not really a ham but a hind-leg pork roast that has not been cured or smoked—is a delicious and generous cut of pork. Most butchers will sell a cut section of the whole ham. A ham with a short plump shape, with a stubby rather than elongated shank, is the most desirable. For this recipe, buy the butt portion—the upper thigh—rather than the shank end. Though sometimes more difficult to carve, the butt half is meatier than the shank. There should be plenty of leftovers if serving six.

❦ A light, fruity red would contrast nicely with the ham and accommodate the sweet, tart tastes of the chutney. Look for a Beaujolais, such as 1989 Château de la Chaize Brouilly from France, or a California Gamay Beaujolais, such as 1989 Monterey Vineyard.

6 to 8 Servings

1 ripe Anjou or Bosc pear—peeled, cored and cut into 1-inch chunks
1 tablespoon olive oil
2 teaspoons salt
2 teaspoons rosemary
1 teaspoon poultry seasoning
One 7½-pound bone-in butt-end fresh ham, rind removed
Grandma Jones's Pear Chutney (p. 260)

1. In a food processor, combine the pear chunks, oil, salt, rosemary and poultry seasoning. Process, scraping down the bowl as necessary, to form a paste.

2. Place the ham in a roasting pan. Slather the pear paste all over the ham, coating it well. Set aside for at least 1 hour. (*The ham can be prepared ahead to this point; cover with a damp towel and refrigerate overnight. Let sit at room temperature for 1 hour before roasting.*)

3. Preheat the oven to 400°. Insert a meat thermometer into the ham at its thickest point, making sure the thermometer does not touch the bone. Roast the ham for 15 minutes. Reduce the temperature to 325° and continue roasting for about 2 hours and 45 minutes (or 22 minutes per pound), until the internal temperature reads 165° to 170°. (If the ham begins to brown excessively before it is done, cover it loosely with aluminum foil.) Transfer the ham to a platter or carving board, cover loosely with aluminum foil and let rest for 10 to 15 minutes.

4. Using a thin sharp carving knife, slice the ham ¼ inch thick, cutting toward the bone against the grain. Pass the Pear Chutney separately.

—*Jessica B. Harris*

• • •

SAUTEED PORK MEDALLIONS WITH MUSTARD, SHALLOTS AND CAPERS

Baked apples and steamed broccoli would complement the tangy pork nicely.

4 to 6 Servings

2 pounds pork tenderloin, trimmed and sliced ½ inch thick
2 teaspoons coarsely ground pepper
¼ cup olive oil
½ pound shallots, thinly sliced
1½ cups dry white wine
1½ cups crème fraîche
2½ tablespoons drained capers
1½ tablespoons grainy mustard
1½ teaspoons anchovy paste
1 teaspoon fresh lemon juice
Salt

1. Preheat the oven to 200°. Place a heatproof platter in the oven to warm. Rub the pork medallions with the pepper and set aside at room temperature for at least 5 and up to 15 minutes.

2. In a large, high-sided nonreactive skillet, heat 1 tablespoon of the olive

oil over high heat until it just begins to smoke. Add half of the pork medallions and sauté for 1½ minutes on each side. Transfer the pork to the warmed platter and cover loosely with foil. Repeat with another tablespoon of oil and the remaining meat. Place the pork in the oven.

3. Add the remaining 2 tablespoons oil to the skillet, and when it begins to smoke, add the shallots. Sauté until browned, about 3 minutes. Add the wine and deglaze the pan, scraping up any browned bits from the bottom. Bring to a boil and cook until reduced by half, about 2½ minutes. Stir in the crème fraîche, capers, mustard, anchovy paste and lemon juice. Continue cooking until the sauce lightly coats the back of a spoon, 5 to 6 minutes.

4. Add the pork and any accumulated meat juices to the sauce and stir to coat. Season with salt and pepper to taste. Transfer the medallions and sauce to a platter or warmed plates and serve hot.

—*Bob Chambers*

• • •

PAN-BROILED PORK CHOPS

Pork chops have less fat in the muscle these days. It may be better for the heart, but it's drier on the palate, and with the fat, out went some of the flavor. This method of marinating the garlic- and thyme-rubbed meat in olive oil produces moist and tasty chops. Overcooking pork will make it dry, but cooking it quickly in a hot skillet insures that it will be crusty on the outside and juicy within. Make sure to choose a pan large enough to accommodate the chops comfortably. Center-cut chops fit easily and work

well but they are a little drier than loin chops. If you'll be using loin chops, ask the butcher to trim two inches from the bony ends. Don't turn the chops during the first six minutes or the crust will be spoiled. When it's time to turn them, use tongs to avoid piercing the meat and losing juices. These chops are good with unsweetened applesauce, peas, sautéed onions or cabbage, and mashed potatoes.

4 Servings

Four 8-ounce trimmed loin or center-cut pork chops, 1 inch thick
2 garlic cloves, smashed and peeled
1 tablespoon minced fresh thyme or 1 teaspoon dried
½ teaspoon freshly ground pepper
¼ cup fruity olive oil
½ teaspoon salt
Thyme sprigs, for garnish

1. Place the pork chops in a shallow dish just large enough to hold them. Deeply pierce the chops 10 times on each side with a fork. Rub the chops on both sides with the garlic, thyme and pepper. Pour the olive oil over the chops and turn to coat them well. Cover and set aside at room temperature for 1 hour. Turn the chops again, cover and refrigerate for at least 6 hours or overnight. Let the chops return to room temperature before cooking.

2. Heat a 10-inch cast-iron skillet over moderately high heat until very hot, about 4 minutes. Meanwhile, pat the chops dry with paper towels. Season them on both sides with the salt. Arrange the chops in the skillet and fry, without moving them, until browned and crusty on the bottom, about 6 minutes. Turn the chops over and fry until nicely browned, 5 to 6 minutes longer. The meat will be just slightly pink throughout. Serve the chops on warmed plates, garnished with thyme sprigs.

—*Diana Sturgis*

• • •

PORK CHOPS WITH RED ONIONS AND FENNEL SEEDS

4 Servings

1 tablespoon vegetable oil
Four 8-ounce boneless loin pork chops, ¾ to 1 inch thick, trimmed of excess fat
Salt and freshly ground pepper
2 tablespoons unsalted butter
2 large red onions, thinly sliced
1 teaspoon sugar
½ teaspoon fennel seeds
3 tablespoons red wine vinegar

1. Preheat the oven to 375°. In a large, nonreactive ovenproof skillet, heat the oil over moderately high heat. Season the chops on both sides with salt and pepper and cook until lightly browned, about 2 minutes a side. Transfer to a platter. Discard the fat and wipe out the skillet.

2. In the same skillet, melt the butter over moderate heat. Add the onions, sugar and fennel seeds. Cook, stirring frequently, until the onions are softened and browned, 7 to 10 minutes. Add the vinegar and cook for 1 minute more, stirring. Season with salt and pepper to taste and stir in 3 tablespoons of water.

3. Place the chops on top of the onion mixture along with any of their accumulated juices. Cover and bake for about 15 minutes, until the chops are cooked through. Season the onions with additional salt and pepper to taste and serve alongside the chops.

Stephanie Lyness

• • •

PORK CHOPS WITH SWEET AND SOUR RED CABBAGE

6 Servings

Six 8-ounce trimmed, center-cut pork chops, 1-inch thick
½ teaspoon thyme
1 teaspoon freshly ground pepper
½ cup olive oil
3 tablespoons cider or raspberry vinegar
1½ teaspoons salt
1 head of red cabbage (2 pounds), cored and finely shredded
1 medium onion, coarsely chopped
2 medium carrots, thinly sliced
1 medium Granny Smith apple— peeled, quartered, cored and sliced lengthwise ¼ inch thick
½ teaspoon marjoram

1. With a fork, deeply pierce each chop several times on both sides. Rub both sides with the thyme and ½ teaspoon of the pepper. Place the chops in a large, sturdy plastic bag with the olive oil and 1 tablespoon of the vinegar. Turn the chops in the bag to coat well. Set aside to marinate for 3 hours at room temperature or overnight in the refrigerator. (Return the chops to room temperature before proceeding.)

2. Remove the chops from the bag, reserving the marinade. Sprinkle the chops on both sides with 1 teaspoon of the salt. In a large nonreactive skillet, fry the chops over high heat, in batches if necessary, until browned, about 2 minutes per side. Transfer the chops to a plate, leaving the drippings in the pan.

3. In a large bowl, combine the cabbage, onion, carrots, apple and marjoram. Add the remaining 2 tablespoons vinegar and the remaining ½ teaspoon each of salt and pepper and toss well.

4. Add 1 tablespoon of the reserved marinade and half of the vegetables to the drippings in the skillet. Cook over moderately high heat, stirring frequently, until the cabbage is wilted and the carrots are tender, about 7 minutes. Transfer the vegetables to a nonreactive 9-by-13-inch baking dish. Arrange the chops and any accumulated meat juices on top of the vegetables.

5. Add 1 more tablespoon of the reserved marinade to the skillet (discard the remainder). Add the remaining vegetables and cook over moderately high heat, stirring, until softened, about 7 minutes. Spread the vegetables over the chops in the baking dish. (*The recipe can be prepared to this point up to 6 hours ahead. Cover loosely with foil and refrigerate. Let return to room temperature before proceeding.*)

6. Preheat the oven to 375°. Cover the baking dish tightly with aluminum foil. Bake in the lower third of the oven until the chops show no sign of red when pierced with a sharp knife at the bone, about 30 minutes. Remove from the oven and let stand for 5 minutes. Serve the pork and cabbage hot from the baking dish, spooning the juices over the chops.

—*Rick Rodgers*

• • •

SMOKY SPARERIBS

These ribs marinate overnight.

2 to 4 Servings

*3½ pounds pork spareribs in one
   piece
Seeds of 4 cardamom pods
4 garlic cloves, halved
2 tablespoons fresh lime juice
¼ teaspoon finely grated lime zest
2 tablespoons light brown sugar
2 tablespoons tomato paste
1 tablespoon finely grated
   fresh ginger
5 scallions, minced
2 chipotle chiles in adobo (see Note)*

1. Set the ribs on a work surface, underside facing up. Using a small sharp
knife, make a small cut at the top of the
bones and pull off the thick membrane
that covers the ribs. Next, trim off as
much excess fat on both sides as you
can, leaving some fat to keep the
ribs moist. Place the ribs in a large nonreactive dish.

2. In a mortar, crush the cardamom
seeds to a powder. Add the garlic and
pound to a coarse paste. Stir in the lime
juice and lime zest and scrape the mixture into a bowl. Stir in the brown sugar,
tomato paste, ginger and scallions.

3. Split the chipotles and remove
and discard the cores and seeds. Coarsely
chop the chipotles and add to the marinade. Spread the marinade over the ribs
to coat completely. Cover the meat and
refrigerate overnight. Let return to room
temperature before proceeding.

4. Preheat the oven to 300°. Transfer the spareribs to a broiling pan and
roast for 3½ to 4 hours, until the meat is

COMFORTING WINTER MENU

Serves 6

*Three-Mushroom Soup with Port and
Tarragon (p. 32)*

Coarse Peasant Bread

---

*Pork Chops with Sweet and Sour Red
Cabbage (p. 124)*

Crisp Potato-Scallion Roast (p. 178)

🍷 *Light, tart California Pinot Noir,
such as 1987 Iron Horse or 1987 Clos
du Bois*

Raspberry-Chocolate Tart (p. 217)

Coffee

Port

Hazelnut Biscotti

—Rick Rodgers

crusty on the surface and falling off the
bone. Cut in between the ribs and serve.

NOTE: *Available at Latin markets or
specialty food shops, chipotle chiles (red
jalapeños that have been smoked and dried)
are most often sold reconstituted in cans
in a sauce called adobo. If you find loose
chipotles, soften 2 of them in ½ cup hot
water for about 20 minutes; drain, reserving the soaking liquid. Split the chiles, discarding the cores and seeds, and coarsely
chop. Add them and their soaking liquid to
the marinade and proceed.*

—Marcia Kiesel

• • •

GRILLED SAUSAGE, APPLE AND ONION ON PUMPERNICKEL BREAD

These make-your-own sandwiches are
just the thing for alfresco eating.

Makes 12 Sandwiches

*3 Golden Delicious apples—peeled,
   quartered, and each quarter cut
   crosswise into 6 chunks
3 small red onions, cut into eighths
2 tablespoons olive oil
12 large sweet Italian sausages
   (about 1½ pounds)
24 slices of pumpernickel bread
Hot or sweet mustard*

1. Light a grill or preheat the broiler.
Thread 6 apple chunks and 2 onion
pieces onto each of twelve 8-inch bamboo or metal skewers. Place the skewers
on a large baking sheet. Drizzle with the
olive oil and turn to coat them well.

2. Using the tip of a knife, pierce
the sausages all over. Grill the sausages
on a moderately hot grill, turning occasionally, until browned and cooked
through, about 10 minutes. Alternatively, place the sausages on a broiling
pan and broil 9 inches from the heat,
turning once, until browned, about 10
minutes. Transfer to a plate and set
aside.

3. Grill the apple-onion skewers,
turning occasionally, until dark brown
and tender, about 12 minutes. Alternatively, broil them 9 inches from the
heat, turning occasionally, until dark
brown and tender, about 12 minutes.

4. Meanwhile, slice the sausages in
half lengthwise (or butterfly them) and
place 1 sausage on each of 12 slices of

125

MEAT

bread. Layer the apples and onions from 1 skewer on top of each sausage. Spread the remaining 12 slices of bread with mustard to taste and place on top of the sandwiches.

—David Rosengarten

• • •

ROASTED LEG OF LAMB WITH MUSTARD AND ROSEMARY

Some of my family want their lamb well done; others like it medium, and one likes it rare. This cooking method satisfies everyone. We all agree that we want a tasty outside crust and are willing to forgo the fat- and flour-thickened gravy of our slender youth.

Trim every last bit of fat from the surface of the meat. Tasty, greaseless pan juices will be your reward. The mustard, rosemary and garlic paste that's rubbed over the leg seals the meat and flavors it nicely. Let the roast relax for 15 minutes when finished to evenly redistribute the juices before carving. Serve the lamb with green beans, spinach or asparagus; buttered orzo or mashed potatoes; and broiled tomatoes.

▼ The somewhat nutty sweetness of lamb has a distinct affinity for lean, dry reds. Full-flavored Spanish reds, such as 1987 Torres Coronas or 1985 Marqués de Cáceres Rioja, have the requisite bite and balance for the lamb and its pungent seasonings.

6 to 8 Servings

⅓ cup Dijon mustard
1 tablespoon minced fresh rosemary, plus some sprigs for garnish
2 teaspoons minced garlic
½ teaspoon salt

½ teaspoon freshly ground pepper
One 6½-pound well-trimmed leg of lamb, at room temperature

1. Preheat the oven to 450°. In a small bowl, combine the mustard, rosemary garlic, salt and pepper. Spread the mixture all over the lamb and set the leg in a roasting pan. Insert a meat thermometer deep into the thickest part without touching the bone. Position the thermometer so that it can be easily read.

2. Roast the lamb in the middle of the oven for 35 minutes, then reduce the temperature to 325° and continue roasting for 45 minutes longer, or until the surface of the meat is browned and crusty and the thermometer reads 165°.

3. Remove the lamb from the oven. Tilt the pan and baste the meat with the small amount of pan juices. Cover the meat loosely with foil and set it aside for 15 minutes before carving.

4. Meanwhile, warm a large platter. Transfer the leg to a carving board and carve across the grain of each muscle. Arrange overlapping slices of meat on the warmed platter and cover loosely with foil.

5. Pour all the accumulated meat juices from the carving board and ¼ cup of water into the roasting pan and cook over moderately high heat stirring, until slightly reduced, about 1 minute. Spoon the juices over the meat and garnish with rosemary sprigs.

—Diana Sturgis

• • •

BUTTERFLIED LEG OF LAMB WITH PAPRIKA MARINADE

In this tannin-neutralizing recipe, a zesty paprika paste is rubbed on the lamb, which is then left to sit for several hours, even overnight. The result is succulent meat with a spicy crust that takes the sting out of tannic red wines. This lamb is delicious served with cooked white beans, drizzled with extra-virgin olive oil, and with a light green salad.

4 Servings

6 tablespoons tomato paste
2 tablespoons extra-virgin olive oil
1 large leek, white part only
1 tablespoon plus 1 teaspoon imported sweet paprika
1 tablespoon plus 1 teaspoon red wine vinegar
¼ teaspoon salt
½ teaspoon freshly ground pepper
One 4-pound shank-end leg of lamb, boned and butterflied

1. In a food processor, combine the tomato paste, olive oil, leek, paprika, vinegar, salt and pepper. Puree until a smooth paste forms, then thoroughly coat both sides of the meat with the paste. Place the lamb on a large platter. Cover tightly and refrigerate for several hours or overnight. Let the lamb return to room temperature before cooking.

2. Preheat the broiler. Transfer the lamb to a broiling pan and broil 7 inches from the heat for about 6 minutes per side, or until the lamb is brown on the outside and medium-rare on the inside (125° to 130°); rotate the pan once as each side cooks. Alternatively, grill the lamb over white coals 7 inches from the heat until medium-rare, about 6 minutes per side. Transfer to a large serving platter and cover loosely with foil; let rest for 10 minutes.

3. Slice the lamb ½ inch thick against the grain and serve immediately, drizzled with its juices.

—David Rosengarten

• • •

SKILLET-ROASTED LAMB WITH ROSEMARY BUTTER

6 Servings

4 tablespoons unsalted butter, at room temperature
2 teaspoons minced fresh rosemary plus some sprigs for garnish
1½ teaspoons plus a pinch of salt
¾ teaspoon freshly ground pepper
Three 10-ounce boned racks of lamb, trimmed of all fat
1 tablespoon olive oil

1. Preheat the oven to 450°. In a small bowl, mix the butter, minced rosemary and a pinch of salt until blended. Set aside at room temperature. *(The butter can be made up to 2 days ahead. Cover and refrigerate. Let return to room temperature before serving.)*

2. Rub ½ teaspoon of the salt and ¼ teaspoon of the pepper on each of the racks of lamb. In a large cast-iron skillet, heat the oil over high heat until almost smoking. Add the lamb and cook, turning, until well seared on all sides, about 6 minutes total.

3. Place the skillet with the lamb in the oven and roast the meat for 5 minutes. Turn the lamb over and roast for 5 minutes longer, or until its interior temperature reaches about 140°.

LAMB DINNER

Serves 6

Skillet-Roasted Lamb with Rosemary Butter (p. 127)

Cauliflower and Red Pepper Puree (p. 166)

Green Beans

🍷 *1986 Fetzer Barrel Select Cabernet Sauvignon*

Light Bread Pudding (p. 257)

—Lee Bailey

4. Transfer the lamb to a carving board and cover loosely with foil. Set aside for 15 minutes. Slice the lamb ¼ inch thick and arrange on a platter or on individual plates. Pour any meat juices on top

5. Spoon a small dollop of the rosemary butter on each piece of meat and garnish with the rosemary sprigs.

—Lee Bailey

• • •

STEWED LAMB SHANKS WITH FRESH DILL

🍷 Serving rich white wine with almost any kind of long-cooked meat stew is a great idea. And certain herbs—such as dill, tarragon and sage—complement white wine pairings. With this lamb shanks and dill stew, try a rich Sauvignon Blanc from California, such as 1988 Matanzas Creek from Sonoma or 1988 Ferrari-Carano Fumé Blanc, also from Sonoma.

2 Servings

1 tablespoon plus 2 teaspoons unsalted butter
1 tablespoon extra-virgin olive oil
Two 1-pound lamb shanks
Salt and freshly ground pepper
2 teaspoons all-purpose flour, plus more for dusting the meat
2 medium onions
2 medium carrots
1 garlic clove, smashed
2 cups beef stock or canned low-sodium broth
6 tablespoons finely chopped fresh dill

1. In a medium casserole, melt 1 tablespoon of the butter in the olive oil over moderate heat. Season the lamb shanks with salt and pepper and dust generously all over with flour. Add the lamb shanks to the casserole, and cook, turning once, until lightly browned, about 3 minutes per side. Meanwhile, finely chop 1 of the onions and add it to the casserole. Cut 1 of the carrots into ½-inch chunks and add to the casserole along with the garlic. Cook, stirring, until the vegetables are softened slightly, about 2 minutes. Increase the heat to high, add the stock and bring to a boil. Reduce the heat to low, cover partially and simmer until the meat is tender but not falling off the bone, about 2 hours.

2. Transfer the shanks to a platter. Strain the cooking liquid through a sieve set over a large glass measuring cup, pressing on the vegetables to extract all the juices. Skim all the fat from the surface of the liquid; reserve 1 tablespoon of the fat and 1¼ cups of the stock.

3. Quarter the remaining onion, then separate the quarters into single layers.

MEAT

Cut the remaining carrot on the bias into ¼-inch slices. In a large, heavy skillet, heat the reserved tablespoon of lamb fat over high heat. Add the onion and carrot and cook, stirring, until browned, about 3 minutes. Reduce the heat to low and add ½ cup of the reserved lamb stock. Cover and cook until the vegetables are just tender, 8 to 10 minutes. Meanwhile, cut the shank meat into 1½-inch pieces.

4. Wipe out the casserole. Add the remaining 2 teaspoons butter and melt over moderately high heat. Stir in the 2 teaspoons flour and cook, stirring, for 1 minute. Whisk in the remaining ¾ cup lamb stock and bring to a boil. Add 3 or 4 tablespoons of dill and boil for 1 minute. Add the lamb, onion and carrot and simmer for 2 minutes. Season with salt and pepper to taste and serve hot, sprinkled with the remaining dill.

—*David Rosengarten*

• • •

MONGOLIAN LAMB CHOPS WITH LEMONY HUMMUS AND TORTILLAS

"This is the most versatile marinade I know," says chef Roxsand Scocos of Roxsand's in Phoenix. "Use it on any meat or chicken, or brush it over vegetables, such as eggplant or peppers. If you want these lamb chops to remain pink inside, marinate them for no longer than 45 minutes."

♟ This dish needs an uncomplicated red, but one with equal bite and spice. A fruity red California Zinfandel, such as 1989 Kendall-Jackson "Dupratt Vineyard," 1989 Quivira or 1989 Ravenswood "Vintner's Blend" would be just the ticket.

---
4 Servings
---

2 cups Chinese mushroom soy sauce*
1 cup wine vinegar
¾ cup sugar
¾ cup Oriental sesame oil
2 medium heads of garlic, minced (about ¾ cup)
½ cup minced scallions
3 tablespoons plus 1 teaspoon crushed red pepper
1½ tablespoons Chinese hot bean paste*
1½ tablespoons Chinese sweet bean paste or sauce*
12 frenched rib lamb chops (about 3 pounds)
Lemony Hummus (p. 15)
Four 8-inch flour tortillas, warmed
***Available at Chinese markets**

1. In a 9-by-11-inch glass baking dish, combine the soy sauce, vinegar, sugar, sesame oil, garlic, scallions, red pepper and hot and sweet bean pastes. Stir well to dissolve the sugar and blend in the bean pastes. Add the chops to the marinade and turn to coat thoroughly. Let marinate at room temperature for about 45 minutes, turning once. Transfer the chops to a rack set over a platter to drain.

2. Light the grill. When the coals are hot, sear the chops for 1½ minutes on each side. Then grill for 3 to 5 minutes longer, turning the chops several times and basting with the marinade until the meat firms up slightly. Alternatively, preheat the broiler. Place the chops on a broiling pan and broil for 5 minutes. Turn and broil for about 3 minutes longer, until the meat feels slightly firm when pressed.

3. Arrange 3 chops on each plate and place some of the Lemony Hummus and a folded warm tortilla on the side.

—*Linda Burum*

• • •

LAMB MEDALLIONS IN AN HERBED POTATO CRUST

Don't be tempted to rinse the grated potatoes—the starch helps bind them together.

♟ Herbs, such as parsley, thyme and rosemary, and lamb are natural complements to spicy reds, like the 1986 Burgess Zinfandel, or herbaceous Cabernet Sauvignon blends, such as 1986 Dry Creek Heritage from California.

---
4 Servings
---

3 medium garlic cloves, finely chopped
1 tablespoon finely chopped parsley
1 tablespoon finely chopped fresh rosemary or 1 teaspoon dried
1 tablespoon finely chopped fresh thyme or 1 teaspoon dried
3 medium baking potatoes (1 pound)
½ teaspoon freshly ground pepper
Two 12-ounce boneless loins of lamb, cut crosswise into 1½-inch-thick medallions
Salt
2 eggs
½ cup all-purpose flour
About ½ cup olive oil, for frying

1. Mince together the garlic, parsley, rosemary and thyme. Peel the potatoes and grate on the large holes of a box grater into a bowl. Add the garlic and herb mixture and toss. Add the pepper and mix thoroughly.

2. Season the lamb medallions on both sides with salt and pepper. In a shallow bowl, beat the eggs with a fork. Place the flour in another shallow bowl. Working in small batches, coat the lamb medallions with the flour and shake off the excess. Then dip them in the beaten egg and again in the flour. The lamb should be thoroughly but lightly coated.

3. On a work surface, using a ¼-cup measure, scoop the potato mixture into 12 mounds. Place a medallion on each mound and use your palms to completely cover the meat with the mixture.

4. Preheat the oven to 250°. In a large heavy skillet, heat 2 tablespoons of the olive oil over moderately high heat. Lightly sprinkle the coated lamb medallions with salt and pepper. When the oil is hot but not smoking, add 4 of the medallions and fry until crusty and browned on the bottom, about 3 minutes. Turn with tongs and fry for 3 minutes on the other side, adjusting the heat as necessary so that the potatoes cook evenly but do not burn. Then turn the medallions on their sides and fry until well browned and crisp all over.

5. Transfer the medallions to a rack set over a baking sheet and keep warm in the oven while you fry the remaining 2 batches, adding more oil to the pan as necessary. Serve hot.

—*Andrea Hellrigl, Palio,*
New York City

• • •

EARLY AUTUMN CELEBRATION

Serves 4

Whiskey Sours

Spiced Peanuts

Field Salad with Goat Cheese

Lamb Sauté with Bell Peppers and Basil (p. 129)

Pressure-Cooker Butternut Squash and Parsnip Puree (p. 183)

Steamed Snow Peas

🍷 *Cabernet Sauvignon, such as 1986 Fetzer Barrel Select, or Bordeaux, such as 1985 Château Talbot*

Maple Sugar Crème Caramel

Espresso

Armagnac

LAMB SAUTE WITH BELL PEPPERS AND BASIL

Here, all that's needed in the way of accompaniment is a simple starch, such as orzo tossed with olive oil and fresh thyme.

---

4 Servings

---

3 tablespoons all-purpose flour
1½ teaspoons salt
1 teaspoon freshly ground black pepper
1½ pounds trimmed boneless leg of lamb, cut into ½-inch cubes
½ cup olive oil
1 red bell pepper, sliced into 1-by-⅛-inch strips
1 yellow bell pepper, sliced into 1-by-⅛-inch strips
4 scallions, thinly sliced
2 garlic cloves, crushed through a press
⅓ cup Madeira
2 teaspoons fresh lemon juice
1 pint cherry tomatoes, halved lengthwise
1 cup shredded basil leaves

1. In a medium bowl, toss the flour with the salt and black pepper. Add the lamb cubes and toss well to coat.

2. In a large, high-sided nonreactive skillet, heat 2 tablespoons of the olive oil over high heat until it just begins to smoke. Add one-third of the lamb cubes and sauté until lightly browned, about 1½ minutes. Transfer the meat to a bowl and cover loosely with foil. Repeat with the remaining 2 batches of meat, using 2 tablespoons of oil per batch.

3. Add the remaining 2 tablespoons olive oil to the skillet and heat until just beginning to smoke. Add the bell peppers and sauté until crisp-tender, about 1½ minutes. Add the scallions and garlic and sauté for 1 minute longer.

4. Deglaze the pan with the Madeira and lemon juice, scraping up any browned bits from the bottom. Add the lamb and any accumulated juices as well as the cherry tomatoes and basil. Bring to a simmer and cook until heated through. Serve hot.

—*Bob Chambers*

• • •

MEAT

LAMB MEATBALLS STUFFED WITH SUN-DRIED CHERRIES

These are the meatballs I grew up with. They are northern Indian, of aristocratic Persian lineage. These meatballs were stuffed with special sun-dried sour plums known as *aloo Bokhara* (the plums of Bokhara). The plums are hard to find today even in India, but sun-dried cherries, either sour or slightly sweet, are a fine substitute.

You can make this dish a day ahead and then reheat it; its flavor only improves. The cinnamon stick and cardamom pods are not meant to be eaten. The whole green chiles, on the other hand, can be eaten by those who like them. They are there primarily for the flavor of their skin.

6 Servings

Meatballs:
1¼ *pounds ground lamb*
2 *tablespoons plain yogurt*
2 *teaspoons ground cumin*
2 *teaspoons ground coriander*
¾ *teaspoon salt*
½ *teaspoon Garam Masala (p. 260)*
½ *teaspoon freshly ground black pepper*
⅛ *teaspoon cayenne pepper*

Stuffing:
⅓ *cup sun-dried cherries,* coarsely chopped (2 ounces)*
2 *tablespoons minced onion*
1 *to 2 fresh green chiles, finely chopped*
3 *tablespoons finely chopped fresh coriander (cilantro)*
Generous pinch of salt

Sauce:
2 *pieces (1 inch each) fresh ginger, peeled and coarsely chopped*
5 *large garlic cloves*
3 *medium onions—1 coarsely chopped, 2 minced*
¼ *cup plus 3 tablespoons vegetable oil*
1 *cinnamon stick*
7 *cardamom pods*
1 *tablespoon ground coriander*
2 *teaspoons ground cumin*
½ *teaspoon cayenne pepper*
2 *medium tomatoes (fresh or drained canned), peeled and chopped*
2 *tablespoons plain yogurt*
1 *teaspoon salt*
½ *teaspoon Garam Masala (p. 260)*
3 *whole fresh green chiles*
**Available at specialty food shops*

1. For the meatballs: Combine all the ingredients in a medium bowl. Mix well. Using wet hands, form the mixture into 25 balls.

2. For the stuffing: Mix all the ingredients in a small bowl.

3. Flatten each meatball slightly and spoon about ½ teaspoon of the stuffing in the center. Using wet hands, roll up the meatballs to enclose the stuffing.

4. For the sauce: In a blender, combine the ginger, garlic, coarsely chopped onion and 3 tablespoons of water. Blend until a paste forms.

5. In a large, wide, flameproof casserole, heat the oil over moderately high heat. When hot, add the cinnamon and cardamom, stir for a few seconds and then add the 2 minced onions. Stir-fry until the onions are a rich medium-brown, about 7 minutes.

6. Add the ginger-onion paste and stir-fry until droplets of oil begin to separate out, about 2 minutes. Stir in the

coriander, cumin and cayenne, then add the tomatoes and cook, stirring, for 2 minutes. Add the yogurt and stir until the oil begins to separate out again, about 2 minutes. Stir in 2 cups of water and the salt and bring to a simmer.

7. Add all the meatballs to the sauce in a single layer, cover and return to a simmer. Reduce the heat to low and cook for 40 minutes, shaking the pot gently now and then to distribute the sauce over the meatballs.

8. Uncover and cook for 15 minutes, shaking the pot or stirring gently from time to time. Stir in the Garam Masala and whole green chiles and cook for another 5 minutes. (*The recipe can be prepared to this point up to 1 day ahead. Let cool, then cover and refrigerate. Reheat before proceeding.*) Just before serving, transfer the meatballs to a bowl with a slotted spoon. Degrease the sauce and pour it over the meatballs. Serve hot.

—Madhur Jaffrey

• • •

PRESSURE-COOKER LAMB CHILI WITH BLACK BEANS

Serve this chili over plain boiled rice. ❦ This spicy, substantial dish needs a flavorsome, hearty red. A young California Zinfandel would be just right. Look for 1987 Beringer or 1988 Ravenswood Vintner's Blend.

6 to 8 Servings

1 *tablespoon olive oil*
2 *small garlic cloves, minced*
2 *medium onions, coarsely chopped*
1 *large red bell pepper, seeded and diced*

1 to 3 jalapeño peppers, seeded and chopped

2 pounds boneless lamb shoulder, trimmed of excess fat and cut into 1-inch cubes

1 can (28 ounces) Italian plum tomatoes, drained and coarsely chopped, juices reserved

1 teaspoon cumin seeds

1 teaspoon oregano

½ teaspoon cinnamon

2 bay leaves

1½ to 2 tablespoons chili powder

1 teaspoon salt

2 cups Pressure-Cooker Black Beans (p. 186)

1 cup (packed) minced fresh coriander (cilantro)

Freshly ground black pepper

1. In a 6-quart pressure cooker, heat the olive oil. Add the garlic and onions and cook over moderately high heat, stirring, until softened, about 3 minutes. Stir in the bell and jalapeño peppers. Add the lamb, tomatoes and their juices, cumin seeds, oregano, cinnamon, bay leaves, chili powder and salt.

2. Lock the lid in place and bring to high (15 pounds) pressure over high heat. Reduce the heat to maintain high pressure and cook for 12 minutes.

3. If time permits, let the pressure drop naturally. Alternatively, quick-release the pressure according to the manufacturer's instructions, or set the pot under cold running water until all the pressure is released. Remove the lid, tilting it away from you to allow any excess steam to escape. Test the meat for doneness; if it is not tender, lock the lid in place and return to high pressure for a few more minutes.

4. When the lamb is done, remove the bay leaves and stir in the black beans. Cook over moderate heat until the beans are warmed through. Stir in the coriander and season to taste with salt and black pepper before serving.

—Lorna Sass

• • •

RABBIT A L'ORANGE

Chicken can be substituted for the rabbit in this dish. Serve with rice to sop up all the sauce.

🍷 The hearty flavors in this dish, including the tartness of the sauce, would be nicely matched by a red. Try a modest Bordeaux, such as a 1988 Château Poujeaux, or a Washington State Merlot, such as a 1987 Arbor Crest Cameo Reserve or 1987 Chateau Ste. Michelle.

4 to 6 Servings

1 cup dry white wine

¼ cup plus 2 tablespoons olive oil

10 garlic cloves—7 sliced, 3 whole

2 tablespoons rosemary, crushed

2½ teaspoons salt

¾ teaspoon freshly ground pepper

4¼ pounds fresh or thawed frozen rabbit, cut into 7 or 8 pieces, liver reserved

One 3-inch strip of orange zest plus 2 teaspoons finely grated orange zest

2 tablespoons flour

3 slices of bacon, chopped

1 large onion, thinly sliced

1 tablespoon thyme

3 bay leaves

3 to 4 tablespoons fresh lemon juice

½ cup black Niçoise olives

1. In a large nonreactive bowl, combine the wine, 2 tablespoons of the olive oil, the sliced garlic, rosemary, 2 teaspoons of the salt and ½ teaspoon of the pepper. Add the rabbit, cover and refrigerate, turning twice, for 8 to 12 hours.

2. Preheat the oven to 300°. Place the strip of orange zest on a pan and bake for about 10 minutes.

3. Remove the rabbit from the marinade, pat dry with paper towels and season with the remaining ½ teaspoon salt and ¼ teaspoon pepper. Reserve the marinade.

4. In a large, heavy, nonreactive skillet, heat the remaining ¼ cup olive oil over moderately high heat. Working in 2 batches if necessary, cook the rabbit, turning, until lightly browned, 8 to 10 minutes.

5. Sprinkle the flour on top. Stir in the bacon, the remaining 3 whole garlic cloves, the onion and the thyme. Cook over moderately high heat, turning, until the garlic and onion are golden, about 3 minutes. Stir in the marinade and orange zest strip and the bay leaves.

6. Transfer the contents of the skillet to a heavy nonreactive casserole. Cover and cook over low heat until the rabbit is tender, 50 minutes to 1 hour.

7. Stir in the rabbit liver, grated orange zest, lemon juice and olives; cook for 2 minutes longer and serve.

—Mireille Johnston

• • •

SAUTEED CALF'S LIVER
WITH RED WINE
AND TOMATO SAUCE

Soaking the liver in milk for a few hours or overnight eliminates any possible bitterness. Creamy mashed potatoes and buttered green beans would be fine partners for this hearty dish.

6 Servings

2 cups milk
Six slices (⅜-inch-thick) trimmed
calf's liver (about 2 pounds)
½ cup olive oil
1 pound red onions, halved
lengthwise and thinly sliced
crosswise
2 garlic cloves, crushed through a
press
⅔ cup full-bodied red wine
1½ pounds fresh tomatoes—peeled,
seeded and chopped—or 2 cans
(14 ounces each) Italian plum
tomatoes with their juice, chopped
1½ cups chicken stock or canned
low-sodium broth
¼ cup tomato paste
1 teaspoon thyme
1 teaspoon fresh lemon juice
1 teaspoon sugar
¾ teaspoon salt
1½ teaspoons freshly ground pepper

1. In a large bowl or shallow glass dish, pour the milk over the calf's liver. Cover with plastic wrap and refrigerate for at least 4 hours or overnight.

2. In a large, high-sided nonreactive skillet, heat ¼ cup of the olive oil over high heat until it just begins to smoke. Add the onions and toss to coat with the hot oil. Cover, reduce the heat to moderately high and cook, stirring frequently, until beginning to brown, 5 to 7 minutes. Stir in the garlic and cook for 1 minute longer.

3. Increase the heat to high, add the wine and bring to a boil; boil until reduced by half, about 3 minutes. Stir in the tomatoes, chicken stock, tomato paste, thyme, lemon juice, sugar and ½ teaspoon each of the salt and pepper and return to a boil.

4. Reduce the heat to moderate. Cover the sauce and simmer, stirring occasionally, for 20 minutes. Uncover and simmer until thickened and all the watery liquid has evaporated, about 10 minutes longer. Transfer the sauce to a medium nonreactive saucepan and keep warm over low heat. Rinse and dry the skillet.

5. Drain the liver and pat dry with paper towels. Season with the remaining ¼ teaspoon salt and 1 teaspoon pepper.

6. Add 1½ tablespoons of the olive oil to the skillet and heat over high heat until it begins to smoke. Add 2 slices of liver and sauté for 1 minute on each side. Transfer to a warmed platter and cover with foil. Repeat twice, using 1½ tablespoons oil for the first batch of liver and the remaining 1 tablespoon for the second.

7. Add any accumulated juices from the liver to the tomato sauce and season with salt and pepper to taste. Spoon some of the sauce over the liver and pass the rest separately.

—*Bob Chambers*

• • •

PASTA, RICE & GRAINS

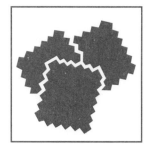

PASTA, RICE & GRAINS

SPAGHETTI MARINARA

There couldn't be a simpler, more fla-vorful sauce than marinara. It requires only ripe tomatoes, garlic and olive oil. Once the garlic has been simmered very slowly until golden in a generous amount of good olive oil, the tomatoes are added. The sauce is then cooked quickly to boil off the water and intensify the tomato flavor. The best time to make this sauce is when fresh plum tomatoes are in sea-son. Otherwise, canned Italian toma-toes, preferably from San Marzano (the can will say), work beautifully.

Ten cloves of garlic may sound ex-cessive, and if they were minced and cooked they would be too strong. But the garlic cloves are very thinly sliced with a sharp paring knife and cooked slowly to mellow them. The cooked gar-lic gives the sauce its irresistibly good flavor. One-quarter cup of olive oil may also sound like a lot, but as it boils, it eventually emulsifies this thick, rich sauce.

To embellish the basic sauce, you can cook thinly sliced mushrooms with the garlic until they are golden brown. Mushrooms add a great earthy flavor to the sauce without interfering with the tomato taste. If you like herbs, use only fresh mild ones and add them at the last moment to spark the sauce. Try chopped basil, parsley, marjoram or mint, which is especially compatible with the flavor of tomatoes.

---

4 to 5 Servings

---

1 can (35 ounces) Italian plum tomatoes or 3 pounds ripe plum tomatoes—peeled, seeded and chopped
¼ cup extra-virgin olive oil
10 medium garlic cloves, peeled and very thinly sliced
Salt and freshly ground pepper
1 pound spaghetti

1. Bring a large pot of salted water to a boil. If using canned tomatoes, empty the tomatoes with the juice into a large bowl. Remove and discard the stem end from the tomatoes. Squeeze the tomatoes with your hands to break them up.

2. In a large nonreactive skillet, com-bine the oil and garlic. Cook gently over low heat, stirring occasionally, until the garlic is deep golden but not brown, about 8 minutes. Increase the heat to high, wait for 30 seconds and then add the fresh or canned tomatoes with their liquid. Bring to a boil over high heat and cook, stirring occasionally, until most of the watery liquid has evaporated and the sauce is thick, about 12 min-utes. Remove from the heat and season with salt and pepper to taste.

3. Meanwhile, cook the spaghetti in the boiling water, stirring frequently with a fork, until al dente, about 8 min-utes. Drain well. In a large serving bowl, toss the spaghetti with the sauce. Serve immediately.

—*Marcia Kiesel*

• • •

RATATOUILLE WITH FRESH PASTA

The ratatouille is better made ahead of time and reheated. If thin-skinned Japanese eggplants are not available, substitute American eggplants and peel them.

---

8 Servings

---

1 pound Japanese eggplants, cut into ¼-inch dice
2 teaspoons coarse (kosher) salt
⅓ cup extra-virgin olive oil
5 ounces very lean bacon, cut into ¼-inch dice
3 medium red bell peppers, cut into ¼-inch dice
1 medium onion, coarsely chopped
1 tablespoon minced garlic
2 medium zucchini, cut into ¼-inch dice
3 large, juicy tomatoes, peeled and cut into ¼-inch dice, juices reserved
1 teaspoon table salt
½ teaspoon freshly ground black pepper
1½ pounds fresh fettuccine

1. Put the diced eggplant in a non-reactive colander and sprinkle with the coarse salt. Toss well and set aside. Meanwhile, in a large enameled dutch oven, heat 3 tablespoons of the olive oil over moderately low heat. Add the bacon and cook, stirring occasionally, until lightly browned, about 10 minutes. Mix in the red peppers, onion and garlic. Cover and cook over moderately low heat, stirring occasionally, until the veg-etables are soft, about 25 minutes.

2. Stir in the zucchini, cover and cook until just tender, about 10 minutes. Rinse off the eggplant, pat dry and add to the dutch oven, along with the tomatoes and their juices. Stir in the remaining 2 tablespoons plus 1 teaspoon oil and the table salt and black pepper. Cover and cook over moderately low heat until soft, about 20 minutes.

3. Drain the vegetables in a large strainer set over a bowl. Pour the juices into a medium nonreactive saucepan and boil over moderately high heat, adding any additional liquid that drains from the vegetables, until the sauce is slightly syrupy, about 10 minutes. Add the vegetables to the sauce and mix well. Season to taste with additional salt and pepper. (*The ratatouille can be made up to 5 days ahead and refrigerated, covered. Reheat before proceeding.*)

4. Bring a large saucepan of salted water to a boil over high heat. Add the fettuccine and cook until al dente, about 3 minutes after the water returns to a boil. Drain well. In a large bowl, toss the fettuccine with the ratatouille and serve immediately.

—*Lydie Marshall*

• • •

END-OF-SUMMER PASTA

The long, golden days of summer beckon even the most devoted cook away from the stove and into the glorious outdoors. When it comes time to cook for a crowd, this sunny pasta, depending as it does on seasonal vegetables, fresh herbs and minimal time in the kitchen, is a fitting way to cut down on the heat and still come up with something tasty and satisfying. This dish should be quite redolent of herbs; ½ cup of the basil

could be replaced with ¼ cup chopped fresh tarragon, 2 tablespoons chopped sage and 1 tablespoon chopped rosemary. Serve the pasta with a large green salad, a creamy goat cheese and a fresh loaf of crusty bread.

❦ A crisp, herbaceous white, such as California Sauvignon Blanc, would underscore the flavors of the scallions, bell peppers, basil and Parmesan. Look for 1988 Estancia or 1988 Parducci.

---

8 Servings

½ *cup olive oil*
8 *garlic cloves, peeled*
2 *pounds plum tomatoes, seeded and chopped*
2 *medium zucchini, cut into thin matchsticks*
2 *medium green bell peppers, cut into thin strips*
2 *medium red bell peppers, cut into thin strips*
1 *pound fusilli or rotelle*
8 *large scallions, white and 2 inches of green, thinly sliced*
1½ *cups coarsely chopped fresh basil*
1 *teaspoon salt*
1 *teaspoon freshly ground black pepper*
2 *cups freshly grated Parmesan cheese*

1. Preheat the oven to 375°. In a large casserole or baking dish, combine the olive oil and garlic cloves. Bake for 10 to 15 minutes, until the garlic is golden. Remove from the oven and, using a slotted spoon, discard the garlic.

2. Add the tomatoes, zucchini and red and green bell peppers to the casserole and toss well. Return to the oven and bake for 10 minutes, or until the vegetables are slightly softened.

3. Meanwhile, in a large pot of boiling salted water, cook the pasta until al dente, about 6 minutes. Drain the pasta and add it to the casserole.

4. Add the scallions, basil, salt, pepper and 1 cup of the Parmesan cheese and toss very well. Season with additional salt and pepper to taste. Serve warm or at room temperature and pass the remaining Parmesan cheese at the table.

—*W. Peter Prestcott*

• • •

PROVENÇAL MACARONI GRATIN

This is chef Philippe de Givenchy's recipe, which he serves with succulent braised veal at the small Parisian Left Bank restaurant La Timonerie. The gratin is also a fine accompaniment for roast chicken or baked fish.

---

4 to 6 Servings

---

10 *ounces short tubular pasta (3½ cups)*
1½ *cups brine-cured imported black olives, such as Niçoise, pitted and chopped*
5 *medium tomatoes—peeled, seeded and coarsely chopped*
2 *teaspoons chopped fresh thyme leaves or 1 teaspoon dried*
¼ *cup extra-virgin olive oil*
½ *teaspoon salt*
½ *teaspoon freshly ground pepper*
½ *cup freshly grated Parmesan cheese*

1. Preheat the oven to 400°. Cook the pasta in a large saucepan of boiling salted water just until al dente, about

10 minutes. Drain well and transfer to a large bowl. Add the olives, tomatoes, thyme and olive oil. Season with the salt and pepper.

2. Transfer the mixture to a 9-by-13-by-2-inch baking dish. Sprinkle the Parmesan cheese on top. Bake for about 10 minutes, until warmed through and brown on top. Serve hot.

—*Patricia Wells*

• • •

NAVY BEAN AND PASTA GRATIN

The pasta in this recipe lightens the beans, and the parsley and tomatoes add a bright, fresh taste. When basil is available, it can be substituted for the parsley.

4 to 6 Servings

1 cup dried navy beans or cannellini (7 ounces), picked over
1 tablespoon light olive oil
½ of a medium onion, finely chopped
1 small bay leaf
Pinch of thyme
1 cup boiling water
1¼ teaspoons salt
3 medium garlic cloves, coarsely chopped
2 cups (loosely packed) flat-leaf parsley leaves
⅓ cup plus 1 tablespoon extra-virgin olive oil
1¼ cups freshly grated Parmesan cheese
½ teaspoon freshly ground pepper
1½ cups small pasta shapes, such as shells or butterflies

2 medium tomatoes—peeled, seeded and chopped—or 1 cup drained canned Italian plum tomatoes, chopped, juice reserved
1 cup ricotta cheese
⅔ cup fine dry bread crumbs

1. In a large saucepan, soak the beans in plenty of cold water for at least 6 hours or overnight. Pour off the water, re-cover the beans with fresh water and bring to a boil. Boil the beans vigorously for 5 minutes. Drain the beans in a colander and rinse well to remove any scum.

2. In a medium saucepan, heat the light olive oil over moderate heat. Stir in the onion, bay leaf and thyme and cook until softened, about 4 minutes. Add the beans and 4 cups of cold water and bring to a boil over high heat. Reduce the heat to moderately low and simmer gently until the beans are nearly tender, about 1¼ hours. During cooking, gradually add the 1 cup boiling water as necessary to keep the beans submerged. Stir in 1 teaspoon of the salt and continue cooking until the beans are very tender, about 15 minutes longer. Drain the beans and reserve the broth. (*The recipe can be prepared to this point up to 2 days ahead. Cover and refrigerate the beans and broth.*)

3. In a food processor, pulse the garlic and parsley until coarsely chopped; scrape down the sides. With the machine on, gradually add ⅓ cup of the extra-virgin olive oil. Scrape down the sides again, add the Parmesan and process until you have a rough puree. Add the remaining ¼ teaspoon salt and the pepper and pulse briefly to mix.

4. Preheat the oven to 350°. Meanwhile, cook the pasta in a large pot of boiling salted water, just until al dente,

about 8 minutes. Drain and rinse under cool water to stop the cooking. Drain the pasta again and place in a medium bowl. Add the reserved beans and their broth, the parsley sauce and the tomatoes and their juice. Season the mixture to taste with salt and pepper and place in a 7-by-12-inch baking dish.

5. Drop tablespoons of the ricotta onto the beans, poking it beneath the surface. In a small bowl, combine the bread crumbs with the remaining 1 tablespoon extra-virgin olive oil. Crumble the crumbs evenly over the gratin. (*The gratin can be prepared to this point up to 1 day ahead and refrigerated, covered.*) Bake the gratin for about 35 minutes, until heated through, browned on top and bubbling around the edges. Let stand for a few minutes before serving.

—*Deborah Madison*

• • •

DOUBLE-CRISPED NOODLE PANCAKE

4 Servings

½ pound dried capellini (angel hair pasta)
3 tablespoons peanut oil
1 tablespoon soy sauce

1. In a large pot of boiling salted water, cook the pasta until al dente, about 3 minutes; drain thoroughly. Transfer the pasta to a bowl and toss with 1 tablespoon of the peanut oil and the soy sauce.

2. Place a large cast-iron skillet or wok over high heat. Add the remaining 2 tablespoons oil. Swirl in a handful of the pasta, then add the remainder, patting it down to make an even layer.

Poke a wooden spoon handle in 6 spots to make steam vents. Reduce the heat to moderately high and cook until the pancake is golden brown on the bottom, about 10 minutes. Loosen the edges and flip the pancake over with a spatula. Cook until golden brown on the second side, about 10 minutes longer. Slide the pancake onto a plate, cover it to keep warm and cut it into quarters before serving.

—Jim Fobel

• • •

MOM'S THREE-CHEESE MACARONI

The addition of Roquefort cheese to this dish puts a flavor spin on the traditional macaroni and cheese.

6 Servings

1½ cups medium elbow macaroni
2 tablespoons unsalted butter
2 tablespoons all-purpose flour
1 cup plus 2 tablespoons milk
2 ounces extra-sharp Cheddar cheese, shredded (½ cup)
2 ounces freshly grated Parmesan cheese (½ cup)
2 ounces Roquefort cheese, crumbled (½ cup)
⅛ teaspoon salt
½ teaspoon freshly ground pepper
¼ cup fine dry bread crumbs

1. Preheat the oven to 350°. Lightly grease a shallow 6-cup oval gratin dish and set aside. In a medium saucepan of boiling salted water, cook the macaroni, stirring occasionally, until al dente, 8 to 10 minutes. Drain well and transfer to the prepared dish.

2. In a small saucepan, melt the butter over moderate heat. Whisk in the flour and cook until thick and pasty, about 2 minutes. Gradually add the milk, whisking constantly, and cook until the sauce is thickened, 7 to 8 minutes. Remove from the heat and cover to keep warm.

3. In a small bowl, combine 1 tablespoon each of the Cheddar, Parmesan and Roquefort cheeses; set aside. Add the remaining Cheddar, Parmesan and Roquefort to the white sauce and stir until smooth. Return the pan to low heat, if necessary, to melt the cheese. Season with the salt and pepper.

4. Pour the sauce over the macaroni in the gratin dish and toss to coat thoroughly. Add the bread crumbs to the bowl of reserved cheese and stir to combine. Sprinkle the mixture over the top of the macaroni. Bake for 35 to 40 minutes until hot, bubbly and lightly browned. Let cool for about 10 minutes before serving.

—Jessica B. Harris

• • •

GREEN CHILE MACARONI AND CHEESE

4 Main-Course or 6 Side-Dish Servings

3 large pieces of dried New Mexican, or Sandia, chile—each about 3 to 4 inches long, halved (less than ½ ounce total)
½ cup boiling water
3 tablespoons unsalted butter plus 2 teaspoons, melted
1 medium onion, finely chopped
3½ tablespoons all-purpose flour
5 cups milk
1 bay leaf, broken in half

2½ cups grated extra-sharp white Cheddar cheese
1¼ teaspoons salt
½ teaspoon freshly ground black pepper
½ cup fresh bread crumbs
¾ pound medium pasta shells (5 cups)

1. In a medium bowl, cover the chiles with the boiling water and set aside to soften, about 10 minutes. Drain the chiles, stem and seed. Finely chop the chiles and set aside.

2. In a medium saucepan, melt the 3 tablespoons of butter over moderately high heat. Add the onion and cook, stirring until wilted, about 2 minutes. Whisk in the flour and cook until smooth, about 30 seconds. Increase the heat to high and add the milk 1 cup at a time, whisking constantly until smooth and bringing the mixture to a boil before adding the next cupful. Add the bay leaf. Reduce the heat to very low and simmer, whisking to prevent a skin from forming on top and to prevent the bottom from scorching, until the flour is cooked and the sauce is smooth and shiny, about 20 minutes.

3. Transfer the sauce to a coarse strainer and press it firmly through with a rubber spatula. Whisk in the reserved chiles and set aside for 5 minutes. Whisk in the cheese and season with the salt and black pepper.

4. Preheat the oven to 350°. Meanwhile, bring a large saucepan of salted water to a boil. In a small bowl, combine the melted butter with the bread crumbs. Set aside.

5. Add the pasta shells to the boiling water, stirring vigorously to separate them. Boil for exactly 7 minutes, stirring occasionally. Drain.

6. Butter a large shallow baking dish, about 13 by 10 inches. Add the shells and pour the chile-cheese sauce on top. Stir to coat the shells; smooth evenly. Sprinkle the buttered crumbs on top.

7. Bake on the top rack of the oven for 30 minutes, just until the sauce starts bubbling around the edges. Remove from the oven and preheat the broiler for 2 minutes. Broil, turning the dish a few times, for about 2 minutes, or until lightly browned and crisp on top. Let rest for 5 minutes before serving.

—*Marcia Kiesel*

• • •

ORANGE PISTACHIO COUSCOUS

Makes About 3½ Cups

2¼ cups chicken stock or canned
  low-sodium broth
Finely grated zest of 1 medium
  orange
2 tablespoons unsalted butter
¾ teaspoon salt
1½ cups instant couscous
2¼ teaspoons orange flower water*
½ cup shelled roasted pistachios,*
  coarsely chopped (about
  2½ ounces)
*Available at Middle Eastern
  markets

1. In a medium saucepan, combine the stock, orange zest, butter and salt. Bring to a boil over high heat. Add the couscous; stir well. Cover, remove from the heat and let stand for 5 minutes.

2. Sprinkle the orange flower water over the couscous and add the pistachios. Fluff lightly with a fork.

—*Linda Burum*

• • •

WHOLE WHEAT COUSCOUS

Whole wheat couscous, which is available in health food stores, has a wonderful nutty flavor, but feel free to use the more traditional refined product and follow the package directions.

4 Servings

2 tablespoons unsalted butter
½ teaspoon salt
1 cup whole wheat or other quick-
  cooking couscous

In a medium saucepan, combine 1½ cups of water with the butter and salt and bring to a boil over high heat. Stir in the couscous. Reduce the heat to low, cover and cook for 5 minutes. Fluff the couscous with a fork before serving.

—*Susan Shapiro Jaslove*

• • •

BASIC COOKED RICE

In this formula, washing and soaking the rice accounts for the small amount of water used in cooking it.

6 Servings

2 cups rice
1¾ cups plus 2 tablespoons cold
  water, chicken stock or canned
  broth

1. In a large saucepan, combine the rice and enough water to cover. Rub the rice between your hands a few times. Drain well in a colander. Repeat this procedure 2 more times. Return the rice to the pan and then add the 1¾ cups plus 2 tablespoons water (or chicken stock). Set aside to soak for 2 hours before cooking.

2. Place the saucepan over high heat and bring to a boil. Boil, stirring, until most of the water evaporates, about 4 minutes. The rice will still be quite hard. Reduce the heat to very low, cover and cook, stirring occasionally, until tender, about 8 minutes.

3. Fluff the rice with a fork. Serve at once or cover tightly until ready to use.

—*Eileen Yin-Fei Lo*

• • •

THAI JASMINE RICE

This is a fried-rice dish from Thailand. It is made with an extremely fragrant long-grain variety from Thailand called jasmine rice. If you cannot find jasmine rice, substitute another aromatic rice type, such as basmati, or one of the domestic aromatics.

6 Servings

2 tablespoons oyster sauce
1 teaspoon sugar
½ pound thick-sliced bacon
2½ tablespoons peanut oil
5 eggs, beaten
Pinch of freshly ground white pepper
3 medium shallots, minced
4 large broccoli stalks, peeled and
  cut into ¼-inch dice (about 1¼
  cups)

*Basic Cooked Rice (p. 138)—made
with jasmine rice* and chicken
stock or broth—cooled, uncovered*
6 medium scallions, thinly sliced
Salt
**Available at Asian markets and
specialty food shops*

1. In a bowl, combine the oyster sauce and sugar. Set aside.

2. Using a small sharp knife, cut the fat from the bacon. Cut the meat into ½-inch pieces and the fat into ¼-inch dice. Set aside separately.

3. Heat a wok over high heat for 40 seconds. Add the diced bacon fat and stir-fry until golden brown and crisp, about 2 minutes. Remove the wok from the heat. Using a slotted spoon, transfer the cracklings to paper towels to drain. Pour off the fat. Rinse and dry the wok and spatula.

4. Heat the wok over high heat for 40 seconds. Add 1½ tablespoons of the peanut oil and swirl the oil around the wok with the spatula until a wisp of white smoke appears, about 1 minute. Add the eggs and the pepper and scramble until firm, about 2 minutes. Remove the wok from the heat and, using the spatula, cut the eggs into ½-inch pieces. Transfer to a plate and set aside. Again, rinse and dry the wok and spatula.

5. Heat the wok over high heat for 40 seconds. Add the remaining 1 tablespoon peanut oil and swirl the oil around with the spatula until a wisp of white smoke appears, about 1 minute. Add the meaty bacon and spread in a single layer. Cook for 1 minute, flip over and cook until well browned, 1 to 1½ minutes. Stir in the shallots and cook until softened, about 2 minutes. Add the broccoli stalks, mix well and cook for 2 minutes more.

6. Stir in the rice and cook until heated through, about 2 minutes. Add the reserved oyster sauce mixture and stir until the rice is thoroughly coated. Stir in the reserved eggs. Add the scallions and mix well; season to taste with salt. Transfer the rice to a warm platter, sprinkle the reserved fat cracklings on top and serve.

—Eileen Yin-Fei Lo

• • •

CURRIED BASMATI RICE

In the Indian kitchen, rice is served mostly as an accompaniment and rarely as a main course.

6 Servings

2 cups basmati rice
*2¼ cups plus 3 tablespoons beef
    stock or canned broth*
*2½ tablespoons curry powder (see
    Note)*
¼ cup peanut or other vegetable oil
1 tablespoon minced fresh ginger
1 medium garlic clove, minced
2 large onions, finely chopped
¾ teaspoon salt
*½ of a medium green bell pepper, cut
    into ¼-inch dice*
*½ of a medium red bell pepper, cut
    into ¼-inch dice*
*¼ cup minced fresh coriander
    (cilantro)*

1. In a large saucepan, combine the rice and enough water to cover. Rub the rice between your hands a few times. Drain well in a colander. Repeat this procedure 2 more times. Return the rice to the saucepan, add 2 cups of the beef stock and set aside to soak for 1 hour.

2. In a small bowl, mix the curry powder with 2 tablespoons of the beef stock to form a thick paste. Set aside.

3. In a small saucepan, heat 1½ tablespoons of the peanut oil over high heat until a wisp of white smoke appears, about 1 minute. Add the ginger and garlic and cook, stirring constantly, until the garlic is golden, about 2 minutes. Stir in the reserved curry paste and the remaining 5 tablespoons beef stock. Reduce the heat to low, cover and simmer for 15 minutes, stirring occasionally. Remove from the heat and set aside, covered.

4. In a medium skillet, heat the remaining 2½ tablespoons peanut oil over moderate heat until a wisp of white smoke appears, about 1 minute. Add the onions and cook, stirring occasionally, until soft, about 7 minutes. Increase the heat to moderately high and stir-fry until lightly browned, about 8 minutes.

5. Add the onions, the reserved curry mixture and the salt to the rice and mix well. Bring to a boil over high heat and cook, stirring often to prevent sticking, for 3 minutes. Reduce the heat to moderately low, cover and cook until the rice is tender but firm, 8 to 10 minutes.

6. Stir in the diced green and red bell peppers and the coriander. Transfer to a bowl and serve hot.

NOTE: *Curry powder loses its potency quickly. If you have an old jar of it, purchase a new one from a good source.*

—Eileen Yin-Fei Lo

• • •

PASTA, RICE & GRAINS

INDONESIAN RICE WITH RAISINS

On the island of Sumatra, this savory, perfumed rice main dish is accompanied occasionally with pickled vegetables.

If made the day before, the stock will be easier to degrease.

6 to 8 Servings

3 pounds beef soup bones, rinsed
1 teaspoon whole cloves
1 teaspoon coriander seeds
1 teaspoon cumin seeds
1 whole nutmeg
2 cinnamon sticks
3 ounces fresh ginger (a 2-by-½-inch piece), peeled and coarsely chopped
1 stalk of lemon grass,* rinsed and cut into 1-inch pieces
1 tablespoon salt
1½ pounds London broil, rinsed
2½ cups extra-long-grain rice
2½ tablespoons peanut oil
5 large shallots, finely chopped
2 large garlic cloves, minced
⅔ cup raisins
*Available at Asian markets

1. In a large pot, place the beef bones and 10 cups of water. Add the cloves, coriander seeds, cumin seeds, nutmeg, cinnamon sticks, ginger, lemon grass and 2 teaspoons of the salt. Cover and bring to a boil over high heat. Reduce the heat to low and cover, leaving a slight opening. Simmer for 2¼ hours, skimming occasionally.

2. Add the London broil and bring to a boil over high heat. Reduce the heat to low and cover, leaving a slight opening. Simmer until the meat is tender, about 1 hour. Remove the meat and set aside on a platter to cool. Wrap the meat in plastic wrap and refrigerate overnight.

3. Strain the stock and discard the solids. Return the stock to the pot and bring to a boil over high heat; boil until reduced to 4 cups, about 20 minutes. Remove from the heat, let cool and refrigerate overnight.

4. Skim the fat from the stock and discard. Set aside at room temperature. Remove the London broil from the refrigerator and set aside at room temperature. In a medium bowl, combine the rice and enough water to cover. Rub the rice between your hands a few times. Drain well in a colander. Repeat this procedure 2 more times and set aside.

5. In a large saucepan, heat the peanut oil over high heat until hot, about 1 minute. Add the shallots and cook, stirring, until beginning to brown, about 2 minutes. Add the garlic and cook, stirring, until browned, 1 minute longer. Add the rice and stir until well coated.

6. Pour in the reserved stock and bring to a boil over moderately high heat; boil for 3 minutes. Stir, reduce the heat to very low, cover and cook until tender, about 15 minutes. Remove from the heat. Stir in the raisins and the remaining 1 teaspoon salt. Cover and let stand until the raisins are plump, about 5 minutes.

7. Meanwhile, slice the London broil against the grain ½ inch thick, then cut the slices into ½-inch dice. Lightly toss the meat with the rice and serve hot. (*The recipe can be prepared up to 2 days ahead; cover and refrigerate. Reheat in a wok over moderate heat, stirring.*)

—Eileen Yin-Fei Lo

• • •

TAIWANESE RICE WITH PINEAPPLE

If you wish to serve this in an authentic Taiwanese fashion, buy the largest pineapples you can find, lay each pineapple on its side and slice off one-quarter along the length. Scoop out the flesh and use the shell as the serving vessel.

6 to 8 Servings

2 tablespoons oyster sauce
3 teaspoons white wine
2 teaspoons Oriental sesame oil
1 teaspoon light (thin) soy sauce*
1½ teaspoons sugar
1 teaspoon cornstarch
1 teaspoon salt
Freshly ground white pepper
1 pound medium shrimp—shelled, deveined and cut crosswise into thirds
1 small ripe pineapple
3 tablespoons chicken stock or canned broth
2 teaspoons soy sauce
4 Chinese pork sausages*
About 2 tablespoons peanut oil
2 teaspoons minced fresh ginger
1½ teaspoons minced garlic
Basic Cooked Rice (p. 138), made with 2½ cups short-grain rice and 2¼ cups plus 1 tablespoon cold water
3 scallions, thinly sliced
*Available at Asian markets

1. In a medium bowl, combine 1 tablespoon of the oyster sauce, 2 teaspoons of the wine, 1 teaspoon of the sesame oil, the light soy sauce, 1 teaspoon of the sugar, the cornstarch, ½ teaspoon of the salt and a pinch of pepper. Add

the shrimp, toss to coat and set aside to marinate until ready to use.

2. Quarter and core the pineapple. Using a grapefruit knife, cut enough of the fruit into ⅓-inch pieces to make 1 cup, drained; set aside. Reserve the remainder for another use.

3. In a small bowl, combine the chicken stock, soy sauce and remaining 1 tablespoon oyster sauce, 1 teaspoon wine, 1 teaspoon sesame oil, ½ teaspoon salt, ½ teaspoon sugar and a pinch of pepper. Mix well and set the sauce aside.

4. Rinse the sausages and pat dry. Slice on the diagonal ¼ inch thick. Heat a wok over high heat for 30 seconds. Add 1 tablespoon of the peanut oil, swirl it around with a metal spatula and heat until a wisp of white smoke appears, about 1 minute. Add the sausages and stir-fry for 2 minutes. Using a slotted spoon, transfer the sausages to a plate and set aside.

5. Reheat the wok over high heat for 20 seconds. Stir in the ginger, then stir in the garlic and cook until golden brown, about 30 seconds. Add the shrimp and its marinade, spreading the shrimp in a single layer. Cook for 10 seconds, then flip the shrimp and cook until pink, another 10 seconds. Add the Basic Cooked Rice and mix well until very hot, about 2 minutes.

6. Stir in the reserved pineapple pieces; if the rice sticks to the wok, add the remaining 1 tablespoon peanut oil and mix well. Add the sausages and stir well. Stir the reserved sauce, then drizzle it over the rice, stirring with a wooden spoon. Toss thoroughly to coat all the rice. Add the scallions and mix well.

—*Eileen Yin-Fei Lo*

• • •

FLAGSTAFF GREEN RICE

Madeira gives this unusual version of green rice an extra dimension.

8 to 10 Servings

12 medium scallions
2 tablespoons olive oil
2 serrano chiles or small jalapeño peppers, seeded and finely chopped
2 tablespoons Madeira or sherry
2 cups rice
1 teaspoon salt
1 teaspoon freshly ground black pepper
2 cups canned chicken broth diluted with 1½ cups water
½ cup minced fresh coriander (cilantro)
½ cup minced parsley

1. Thinly slice the scallions; reserve the white and green parts separately. In a large saucepan, heat the olive oil over moderately high heat. Add the white portion of the scallions and the chiles and cook until softened but not browned, about 3 minutes.

2. Stir in the Madeira, rice, salt and black pepper. Add the diluted chicken broth and bring to a boil. Cover and reduce the heat to low and cook until the rice is tender and the liquid has been absorbed, about 20 minutes.

3. Fluff with a fork and stir in the coriander, parsley and reserved sliced scallion greens. Transfer to a serving dish and serve warm.

—*Susan Costner*

• • •

PRESSURE-COOKER RISOTTO WITH PORCINI AND PROSCIUTTO

The pressure cooker makes a splendid risotto with a delightfully chewy texture.

6 First-Course or
3 to 4 Main-Course Servings

¾ ounce dried porcini mushrooms (about ¾ cup)
1½ cups boiling water
2 to 2½ cups Pressure-Cooker Chicken Stock (p. 269) or canned low-sodium broth
2 tablespoons unsalted butter
1 tablespoon olive oil
2 medium leeks, white part only, finely chopped
1 small garlic clove, minced
½ teaspoon oregano
1½ cups arborio rice (10 ounces)
2½ ounces (about 6 paper-thin slices) prosciutto, coarsely chopped
2 tablespoons minced parsley
⅓ to ½ cup freshly grated Parmesan cheese
Salt and freshly ground pepper
Freshly grated nutmeg (optional)

1. Place the porcini in a food processor and pulse until coarsely chopped. Add the boiling water and set aside for 10 minutes. Drain the porcini and strain the liquid into a 1-quart measuring cup. Add enough of the Chicken Stock to reach the 3½-cup mark. Rinse the mushrooms to remove any grit. Cut off and discard any tough bits.

2. In a 6-quart pressure cooker, melt 1 tablespoon of the butter in the oil over moderate heat. Add the leeks and garlic and cook, stirring, until slightly softened, about 1 minute. Add the oregano and rice; stir to coat the rice thoroughly with the fat. Add the porcini and stir in the porcini-stock liquid.

3. Lock the lid in place and bring to high (15 pounds) pressure over high heat. Reduce the heat to maintain high pressure and cook for 6 minutes.

4. Set the pot under cold running water until all pressure is released. Remove the lid, tilting it away from you to allow any excess steam to escape. Taste the rice; if it requires more cooking, add a bit more stock and stir constantly over moderate heat for 1 to 2 minutes longer.

5. Stir in the prosciutto and parsley, then stir in all but 1 tablespoon of the Parmesan cheese. Stir in the remaining 1 tablespoon butter and season the risotto to taste with salt, pepper and nutmeg. Transfer the risotto to a serving dish and sprinkle the remaining 1 tablespoon Parmesan on top. Serve immediately.

—Lorna Sass

• • •

PRESSURE-COOKER SEAFOOD RISOTTO

6 Servings

1 pound mussels, scrubbed and debearded
1 cup dry white wine, preferably Italian
1 garlic clove, halved
½ pound small or medium shrimp, shelled and deveined

½ pound bay scallops or quartered sea scallops
1 bottle (8 ounces) clam juice
1 tablespoon olive oil
1 tablespoon unsalted butter
1 medium onion, minced
½ teaspoon thyme or oregano
1½ cups arborio rice (10 ounces)
2 tablespoons minced parsley
½ cup freshly grated Parmesan cheese
Salt and freshly ground pepper

1. In a 6-quart pressure cooker, combine the mussels, wine, garlic and ¾ cup water. Set the lid in place but do not lock it. Steam the mussels over high heat (but do not bring up to pressure) until they open, 3 to 4 minutes. Transfer the mussels to a large bowl with a slotted spoon.

2. If using medium shrimp, halve them lengthwise. Place the shrimp in the pressure cooker and cook over moderate heat, stirring, until opaque, about 30 seconds. Add the scallops and cook, stirring, for 30 seconds longer. With a slotted spoon, transfer the shrimp and scallops to another large bowl.

3. Remove the mussels from their shells; discard the shells and any unopened mussels. Add the mussels to the shrimp and scallops, cover loosely with plastic wrap and set aside.

4. Carefully pour the shellfish cooking liquid into a 1-quart measuring cup, leaving behind any sediment. Add the clam juice and enough water to reach the 3½-cup mark. Set aside.

5. Rinse and dry the pressure cooker. Add the oil and butter and heat over moderately high heat. Add the onion and cook, stirring, until soft but not brown, about 2 minutes. Add the thyme and rice; stir to coat the rice with fat.

6. Stir the reserved 3½ cups liquid into the rice. Lock the lid in place and bring to high (15 pounds) pressure over high heat. Reduce the heat to maintain high pressure and cook for 6 minutes.

7. Set the pot under cold running water until all pressure is released. Remove the lid, tilting it away from you to allow any excess steam to escape. Add the reserved shellfish and stir gently until warmed through. Stir in the parsley and Parmesan and season to taste with salt and pepper. Serve immediately.

—Lorna Sass

• • •

STEAMED BAMBOO LEAF RICE BUNDLES

Versions of this Cantonese dish exist throughout Asia. If you can't find bamboo leaves, you can substitute aluminum foil or cheesecloth, but the leaves lend a pleasant fragrance to the dish.

6 Servings

4 cups glutinous rice*
1½ pounds boneless pork loin in one piece, well trimmed
1 tablespoon cornstarch
2 teaspoons regular soy sauce
4 teaspoons Oriental sesame oil
2 teaspoons white wine
3½ tablespoons oyster sauce
1½ tablespoons sugar
1 teaspoon fresh ginger juice (see Note)
1¾ teaspoons salt
Freshly ground white pepper
¾ pound evenly sized shiitake mushrooms, stemmed and quartered, or 2 ounces dried Chinese mushrooms

2 tablespoons peanut oil
8 medium scallions, sliced on the
diagonal ½ inch long
6 peeled fresh water chestnuts or ⅓
cup canned (drained), finely diced
12 large dried bamboo or lotus
leaves* (see Note)
2 teaspoons light (thin) soy sauce*
2 teaspoons double black soy sauce*
*Available at Asian markets

1. In a medium bowl, combine the rice and enough water to cover. Rub the rice between your hands a few times. Drain well in a colander. Repeat this procedure 2 more times. Transfer the rice to a 9- or 10-inch round cake pan at least 2 inches high. Add 4 cups of water and set aside to soak for 1 hour.

2. Halve the pork loin lengthwise, then slice crosswise ¼ inch thick. Stack and quarter the slices.

3. In a bowl, whisk together the cornstarch, regular soy sauce, 2 teaspoons of the sesame oil, the wine, 1½ teaspoons of the oyster sauce, 1½ teaspoons of the sugar, the ginger juice, ¾ teaspoon of the salt and a pinch of pepper. Add the pork, toss well to coat and set aside to marinate for 30 minutes.

4. If using dried mushrooms, place in a small bowl and cover with 2 cups of boiling water. Set aside to soak for 30 minutes. Drain, squeeze out any excess water, stem and quarter.

5. Heat a wok over high heat for 45 seconds. Add the peanut oil, swirl it around the wok with a metal spatula and heat until a wisp of white smoke appears, about 1 minute. Add the pork

and its marinade, spreading the meat in a single layer. Cook for 1½ minutes. Flip over and cook, stirring, for 1 minute longer. Add the mushrooms and stir-fry until the meat has lost its pink color, about 2½ minutes. Add the scallions and water chestnuts and stir-fry for 1 minute. Transfer the pork and vegetables to a medium bowl and set aside. Rinse and dry the wok and spatula.

6. Place the wok over high heat. Add 6 cups of water and bring to a boil. Set a bamboo steamer or a large, round cake rack in the wok above the water. Set the cake pan of rice in the steamer or on the rack and cover tightly with aluminum foil or the wok lid or both. Steam the rice until soft and sticky, about 40 minutes. Remove the steamer from the wok, fluff the rice with a fork and set aside to cool for 5 minutes.

7. While the rice steams, place the bamboo leaves in a large bowl or in the sink and add hot water to cover. Let soak for at least 30 minutes or until ready to use.

8. In a large bowl, stir together the light and dark soy sauces, the remaining 3 tablespoons oyster sauce, 1 tablespoon sugar, 2 teaspoons sesame oil, 1 teaspoon salt and a pinch of pepper. Using a large spoon, blend in the rice. Divide the rice mixture into 6 equal portions and place on a baking sheet.

9. Divide the reserved pork and vegetable mixture into 6 equal portions and place on a separate baking sheet.

10. To assemble the bundles: Remove 2 bamboo leaves from the water and pat dry with paper towels. Lay the leaves lengthwise on a work surface, spine side down, with the long sides overlapping by a third of the width. Using your hands, form half a rice portion into a square or rectangular patty. Place

it in the center of the bamboo leaves and pat it down. Spread a portion of the pork evenly on top. Using scissors, trim off the pointed ends of the bamboo leaves. Take the remaining half of the rice portion, form it into another patty and place it on top of the pork filling. Fold the long sides of the bamboo leaves inward over the patty. Then fold the 2 short ends over the patty to form a bundle. Using kitchen string, tie each bundle as if you were wrapping a present. Repeat with the remaining bamboo leaves, rice and pork to make 6 bundles. *(The recipe can be prepared to this point up to 2 days ahead; cover and refrigerate. Let return to room temperature before steaming.)*

11. Place the wok over high heat, add 6 cups of water and bring to a boil. Reduce the heat to moderate. Arrange the bundles in a bamboo steamer or on a cake rack and set them in the wok. Cover tightly with aluminum foil or the wok lid, or both, and steam for 30 minutes. Remove the bundles from the wok and cut off the strings. Place a bundle on each of 6 plates and serve at once. Let everyone open his own.

NOTE: *Packages of dried bamboo leaves are available in Asian markets. Use the widest leaves possible. To make 1 teaspoon of ginger juice, grate a 1-by-1½-inch piece of ginger and squeeze in a garlic press.*
—Eileen Yin-Fei Lo

• • •

PASTA, RICE & GRAINS

BASIC AND BEAUTIFUL FRIED RICE

Just about the only requirement for good fried rice is that the rice be neither gummy nor dry. Rice that has been refrigerated overnight is ideal. It will break apart easily and will not stick to the pan. Overly dry rice requires a bit of stock or water, which can be added to the pan just after the rice is tossed in. Cover and steam over low heat until the liquid is absorbed.

4 Side-Dish Servings

2 to 6 tablespoons corn or peanut oil
1 small onion, cut into ¼-inch dice
1 small red bell pepper, cut into ¼-inch dice
1 small carrot, cut into ¼-inch dice
3½ cups cold cooked rice
½ pound cooked string beans or asparagus, cut into ½-inch pieces, or other cooked vegetable
¼ pound cooked chicken, beef, pork, fish or shellfish, slivered or cubed
1 teaspoon salt
3 medium scallions, thinly sliced on the diagonal

1. Heat a wok or large heavy skillet over high heat for 30 seconds. Add 1½ tablespoons of the oil and swirl to glaze the pan. Reduce the heat to moderately high, add the onion and stir-fry until partially softened, about 1 minute. Add the red pepper and carrot and stir-fry until crisp-tender, about 2 minutes. Drizzle a bit more oil down the side of the wok as needed to prevent sticking. Adjust the heat to maintain a sizzle without scorching the vegetables.

2. Add the rice, toss to blend and stir-fry until heated through, about 3 minutes. Add a bit more oil if needed to prevent sticking. Add the string beans and toss briskly for 30 seconds. Add the chicken and toss to combine and heat through, about 1 minute. Season with the salt and fold in the scallions.

—*Barbara Tropp, China Moon Cafe, San Francisco*

• • •

CAJUN RICE DRESSING WITH HAM AND SAUSAGE

This dressing resembles jambalaya; in fact, if you doubled the amount of ham and sausage, you'd *have* jambalaya. Like most good Cajun recipes, this one begins with a roux, which should be browned slowly so that it will develop the proper rich caramel flavor. Rushing the job is likely to produce a bitter taste. This dressing may seem like a lot of work, but it can all be done a day ahead. Begin the rice as the roux reduces so that both will be done at the same time.

10 to 12 Servings

Roux Mixture:
2 tablespoons vegetable oil, bacon drippings or lard
3 tablespoons all-purpose flour
1 medium onion, minced
1 medium green bell pepper, finely diced
1 celery rib, finely diced
¼ pound bulk sausage meat
¼ pound finely ground smoked ham

Rice Mixture:
2 tablespoons vegetable oil
1 garlic clove, minced
1 small onion, minced
1 large celery rib, diced
¼ to ½ teaspoon cayenne pepper
¼ teaspoon freshly ground black pepper
2½ cups converted rice (1 pound)
5 cups chicken stock or canned low-sodium broth
⅓ cup very thinly sliced scallion greens
3 tablespoons minced parsley
3 tablespoons unsalted butter

1. Make the roux mixture: In a large heavy saucepan, combine the vegetable oil and flour and cook over moderately low heat, stirring frequently to prevent sticking or scorching, until the roux is a rich rust brown, about 30 minutes. Mix in the onion, green pepper and celery and cook until they stop sizzling, about 5 minutes. Remove from the heat, cover and let stand for 15 minutes.

2. Add 2 cups of water to the roux and cook over moderate heat, stirring, until the mixture boils and thickens, about 3 minutes. Reduce the heat to moderately low so that the mixture bubbles gently; simmer, stirring frequently, until very thick and reduced by at least three-quarters with no more than one inch remaining in the pan, about 45 minutes.

3. Meanwhile, in a small heavy skillet, cook the sausage and ham over moderately high heat for 3 minutes, stirring to break up any clumps. Remove from the heat, cover and keep warm. When the roux has thickened properly, stir in the meats and set aside.

4. Make the rice mixture: While the roux is reducing, in a heavy medium casserole, heat the vegetable oil over moderate heat for 1 minute. Add the garlic, onion, celery, cayenne and black pepper and cook, stirring frequently, until the vegetables are slightly softened and fragrant, about 5 minutes. Add the rice and cook, stirring, until well coated and heated through, about 3 minutes. Add the stock and bring to a rolling boil over moderately high heat, stirring occasionally.

5. Reduce the heat to low so that the liquid bubbles gently; simmer for 15 minutes, stirring once. Stir well, cover and cook until all the liquid has evaporated and the rice is just tender, about 7 minutes longer. Stir in the scallion greens, parsley and butter. As soon as the butter melts, stir in the reserved roux mixture. Transfer the stuffing to a casserole or serving dish and serve immediately. *(The recipe can be prepared up to 1 day ahead. Let cool, then cover and refrigerate. Before serving, cover tightly with foil and bake at 375° for about 30 minutes, or until heated through.)*

—*Jean Anderson*

• • •

FRAGRANT BARLEY

Rarely would we think of putting a bowl of barley on a holiday table, but when decorated and enlivened with pasta bow ties, studded with toasted pine nuts and a confetti of carrots, these pearly grains belong on the most festive tables.

12 Servings

8 ounces bow-tie pasta
3 tablespoons extra-virgin olive oil
1 cup pine nuts (4½ ounces)
4 medium carrots, cut into ¼-inch dice
1 large onion, cut into ¼-inch dice
2 cups pearl barley (about 14 ounces)
4 cups beef stock or canned low-sodium broth
½ cup dried currants (optional)
1 cinnamon stick (optional)
1 teaspoon salt
½ teaspoon freshly ground pepper
2 tablespoons chopped fresh mint

1. In a large pot of boiling salted water, cook the pasta until al dente, about 11 minutes. Drain, rinse under cold running water and set aside. *(The pasta can be cooked up to 1 day ahead. Let cool, toss with a little olive oil to prevent sticking, cover and refrigerate overnight.)*

2. In a large heavy saucepan, heat the oil over moderately low heat. Add the pine nuts and cook, stirring, until just golden, about 5 minutes. Reduce the heat to low. Add the carrots and onion and cook, stirring occasionally, until the onion is translucent, about 5 minutes. Add the barley and stir until the barley is hot, about 2 minutes.

3. Add the stock, currants, cinnamon stick, salt, pepper and 2 cups of water. Increase the heat to high and bring to a boil. Reduce the heat to moderately low, cover and simmer until the liquid has been absorbed and the barley is tender but not mushy, about 55 minutes.

4. Stir in the cooked pasta and 1 tablespoon of the mint. Cover and simmer until the pasta is heated through, about 5 minutes. Spoon the barley into a serving bowl and garnish with the remaining 1 tablespoon mint.

—*Sheila Lukins*

• • •

BULGUR, TOASTED WALNUT AND DRIED FRUIT DRESSING

An acquaintance from California once served me a superb casserole of cracked wheat and dried fruits. It serves as the basis of this dressing, which also contains toasted walnuts, grated orange and lemon zests, fresh herbs and the woodsy-flavored dried Polish mushrooms that are available at many supermarkets in little plastic cups.

12 to 14 Servings

¼ cup olive oil, plus some for brushing
1½ cups walnuts (6 ounces)
1 ounce dried Polish mushrooms
3½ cups boiling water
2 cups bulgur (cracked wheat)
2 cups boiling chicken stock or canned low-sodium broth

PASTA, RICE & GRAINS

3 large garlic cloves, minced
1 large onion, coarsely chopped
4 large celery ribs, coarsely chopped
1 pound carrots, coarsely chopped
1 tablespoon minced fresh marjoram
    or 1 teaspoon dried leaf marjoram,
    crumbled
1 tablespoon minced fresh lemon
    thyme or ¾ teaspoon dried leaf
    thyme, crumbled
1 teaspoon minced fresh rosemary or
    ½ teaspoon dried rosemary,
    crumbled
1 teaspoon finely grated orange zest
1 teaspoon finely grated lemon zest
½ teaspoon freshly ground pepper
1 box (11 ounces) mixed dried fruits,
    coarsely chopped
1½ teaspoons salt

1. Preheat the oven to 350°. Brush a deep 3½-quart casserole with olive oil and set aside. Spread the walnuts in a pie tin and toast in the middle of the oven for about 12 minutes, until crisp and lightly browned. Coarsely chop and set aside. Increase the oven temperature to 375°.

2. Place the dried mushrooms in a small heatproof bowl, add 2 cups of the boiling water and let stand for 20 minutes. Place the bulgur in a large heatproof bowl, add the boiling chicken stock and the remaining 1½ cups boiling water and set aside until all the liquid has been absorbed, about 30 minutes.

3. Meanwhile, remove the mushrooms from the soaking liquid with a slotted spoon. Strain the liquid through a fine sieve lined with a moistened paper towel; set aside. Rinse the mushrooms and pat dry. Cut off any tough bits and discard; coarsely chop the mushrooms and set aside.

4. In a large heavy skillet, heat the ¼ cup olive oil over moderate heat for 1 minute. Add the garlic, onion and celery and cook, stirring frequently, until slightly softened, about 5 minutes. Add the carrots, marjoram, thyme, rosemary, orange and lemon zests, pepper and ½ cup of the reserved mushroom soaking liquid. Reduce the heat to low, cover and cook for 15 minutes.

5. When the bulgur is tender, add the dried fruits, chopped mushrooms, remaining mushroom soaking liquid and the salt; toss well to mix. Add the vegetable mixture and the reserved toasted walnuts and toss well again. Lightly spoon the dressing into the prepared casserole and cover tightly with foil. Bake in the middle of the oven for 40 minutes, until steaming hot. Fluff with a large fork and serve immediately.

—Jean Anderson

• • •

PRESSURE-COOKER WILD RICE WITH CHESTNUTS

Because the time and amount of water needed to prepare wild rice varies, the rice is pressure-cooked in ample liquid, then drained and returned to the pot to dry out for a minute or two.

5 to 6 Servings

3 tablespoons unsalted butter
5 medium shallots, minced
2 celery ribs, finely chopped
1 cup (about 6 ounces) wild rice,
    rinsed and drained
3 ounces dried chestnuts* (about 15)
¼ cup dried currants
2 teaspoons aniseed
¼ teaspoon salt

1 teaspoon grated orange zest
Freshly ground pepper
*Available at Italian groceries and
    specialty food stores

1. In a 6-quart pressure cooker, melt 2 tablespoons of the butter over moderate heat. Add the shallots and celery and cook, stirring, until softened slightly, about 1 minute. Stir in the rice, chestnuts, currants, aniseed, salt and 4 cups of water. Lock the lid in place and bring to high (15 pounds) pressure over high heat.

2. Reduce the heat to maintain high pressure and cook for 25 minutes. Set the pot under cold running water until all pressure is released. Remove the lid, tilting it away from you to allow any excess steam to escape. Taste the rice; if the grains are tough and have not burst open, lock the lid back into place and return to high pressure for another few minutes.

3. Drain the rice in a large strainer and return it to the pressure cooker. Add the orange zest and stir over moderately high heat with a wooden spoon until the rice is fairly dry. Stir in the remaining 1 tablespoon butter and season to taste with salt and pepper. Serve hot.

—Lorna Sass

• • •

SALADS

SALADS

FIELD SALAD WITH SHALLOTS AND CHIVES

This simple variation on a familiar theme comes from Marcel Baudis, chef at L'Oulette, the minuscule Parisian restaurant he runs with his wife, Marie-Noëlle. The combination of shallots and chives is often used in Baudis's native town of Montauban in the southwest of France. Marinating the shallots in oil softens their often harsh flavor.

4 to 6 Servings

¼ cup minced shallots
¼ cup extra-virgin olive oil
2 teaspoons red wine vinegar
2 teaspoons sherry wine vinegar
Salt and freshly ground pepper
6 cups bite-size pieces of mixed
    greens, such as curly endive,
    radicchio, watercress, mâche,
    dandelion greens and arugula
⅓ cup chopped fresh chives

1. In a small bowl, stir 2 tablespoons of the shallots into the oil. Set aside at room temperature for at least 1 hour and up to 24.

2. In another small bowl, combine the red wine and sherry wine vinegars. Add the shallot-oil mixture and stir to blend thoroughly. Season with salt and pepper to taste.

3. In a salad bowl, toss the salad greens with the remaining 2 tablespoons shallots and the chives. Pour the vinaigrette over the greens and gently toss until thoroughly and evenly coated. Adjust the seasonings, if necessary, and serve immediately.

—*Patricia Wells*

• • •

MIXED SALAD WITH CAPER VINAIGRETTE

This salad is a trio of assertive lettuces—arugula, watercress and radicchio—that stand up to the piquant vinaigrette with capers.

4 Servings

1 bunch of arugula, stems removed
½ bunch of watercress, large stems
    removed
1 very small head of radicchio, torn
    into bite-size pieces
½ of a small red onion, thinly sliced
2 tablespoons extra-virgin olive oil
2 tablespoons balsamic vinegar
1 tablespoon drained capers
Salt and freshly ground pepper

In a large salad bowl, combine the arugula, watercress and radicchio. Add the onion. Sprinkle the oil, vinegar and capers on top and toss. Season to taste with salt and pepper. (The capers will affect the amount of salt required.)

—*Stephanie Lyness*

• • •

ROMAINE AND AVOCADO SALAD

4 Servings

2 tablespoons fresh lemon juice
1 garlic clove, finely chopped
1 teaspoon grainy mustard
1 teaspoon honey
2 tablespoons safflower or other
    vegetable oil
1 large ripe avocado, preferably
    Hass, cut into ½-inch dice

Salt and freshly ground pepper
1 small head of romaine lettuce, torn
    into bite-size pieces

1. In a small bowl, whisk the lemon juice with the garlic, mustard and honey. Whisk in the oil and the diced avocado. Season with salt and pepper to taste.

2. Place the lettuce in a serving bowl, add the avocado dressing and toss.

—*Susan Shapiro Jaslove*

• • •

WARM ESCAROLE SALAD

This is not meant to be a wilted salad, so use sturdy greens like escarole or chicory that will not lose their crunchiness when mixed with the warm vinaigrette.

4 Servings

1 head of escarole or chicory (about
    1¼ pounds), torn into bite-size
    pieces
⅓ cup olive oil
2 tablespoons red wine vinegar
1 tablespoon fresh lemon juice
1 garlic clove, minced
Salt and freshly ground pepper

Place the escarole in a salad bowl. In a small nonreactive saucepan, combine the oil, vinegar, lemon juice and garlic. Cook over moderate heat until hot, 2 to 3 minutes. Pour the dressing over the escarole and toss. Season with salt and pepper and serve immediately.

—*Stephanie Lyness*

• • •

Salad of Winter Greens (p. 154).

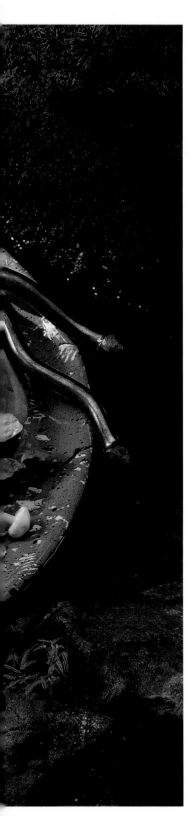

Left, Curried Salmon Salad with Lemon Grass Vinaigrette
(p. 162). Above, Taiwanese Rice with Pineapple (p. 140).

SALAD OF MIXED GREENS AND HERBS WITH ORANGES

8 Servings

2 navel oranges
1 tablespoon minced shallots
1 tablespoon honey mustard
2 teaspoons cider vinegar
1 teaspoon balsamic vinegar
¼ cup plus 1 tablespoon olive oil
Salt and freshly ground pepper
12 cups mixed baby lettuce leaves
1 cup (loosely packed) flat-leaf
    parsley leaves
1 cup (loosely packed) mint leaves
1 bunch of chives, cut into 2-inch
    lengths

1. Using a sharp knife, peel the oranges, making sure to remove all the bitter white pith. Working over a bowl, cut the oranges in between the membranes to release the sections.

2. In a small bowl, combine the shallots, mustard and vinegars. Gradually whisk in the olive oil. Season the dressing with salt and pepper to taste.

3. In a large salad bowl, combine the lettuce, parsley, mint and chives. Pour 3½ tablespoons of the dressing over the salad and toss well. Add the orange segments and toss lightly. Add more dressing if desired. Serve immediately.

—*Elizabeth Woodson*

• • •

Fresh Tuna Salade Niçoise (p. 162).

GRAPEFRUIT AND AVOCADO SALAD WITH TOMATO-CUMIN DRESSING

Bitter greens pair magically with avocado and grapefruit, creating a taste that is much more interesting than the sum of these simple ingredients.

8 to 10 Servings

5 large grapefruits
6 ripe avocados, preferably Hass
¼ cup fresh lemon juice
2 medium red onions, very thinly
    sliced
1 teaspoon coarse (kosher) salt
½ teaspoon freshly ground pepper
6 cups (loosely packed) stemmed
    arugula or watercress
24 Niçoise or other small black olives
Tomato-Cumin Dressing (p. 264)

1. Using a sharp knife, peel the grapefruits, making sure to remove all the bitter white pith. Working over a bowl, cut in between the membranes to release the sections.

2. Halve the avocados lengthwise and remove the pits. Using a large spoon, scoop out the flesh in one piece. Cut each half lengthwise into ¼-inch slices. Sprinkle with 2 tablespoons of the lemon juice and set aside until ready to use.

3. In a medium bowl, toss the onions with the remaining 2 tablespoons lemon juice and the salt and pepper.

4. Arrange the arugula around the rim of a large platter, then fill in to cover the surface. Fan the avocado slices around the outer edge of the platter, then arrange the grapefruit sections inside the ring of avocado and top with

the olives. Mound the onions in the center. Drizzle about ⅓ cup of the Tomato-Cumin Dressing over the grapefruit. Serve the remaining dressing alongside.

—*Susan Costner*

• • •

BOSTON LETTUCE WITH STUFFED ENDIVE SPEARS

6 Servings

2 tablespoons white wine vinegar
1 teaspoon grainy mustard
¼ cup plus 1 tablespoon olive oil
Pinch of salt
¼ teaspoon freshly ground pepper
1 large head of Boston lettuce, torn
    into bite-size pieces
4 ounces soft blue cheese, such as
    Saga, Gratte Paille or Pipo Crem'
24 endive spears

1. In a small bowl, whisk together the vinegar and mustard. Whisk in the oil in a fine stream until incorporated. Season with the salt and pepper.

2. In a large bowl, toss the lettuce with the dressing. Place the dressed lettuce on 6 salad plates.

3. Spoon about ½ teaspoon of the blue cheese on each of the endive spears. Place 4 spears on top of each salad.

—*Lee Bailey*

• • •

153

SALADS

TENDER GREENS WITH PROSCIUTTO, CROUTONS AND WALNUT OIL VINAIGRETTE

When making salads to be served with wine, avoid using bitter greens. Use a mild vinegar and dilute it with other liquids. Also, supply some textural bumps for the wine to grab on to, such as the croutons in the following recipe. Here's a perfect salad for wine.

2 Servings

½ *cup walnut oil*
3 *medium garlic cloves, smashed and peeled*
1 *cup bread cubes (½ inch)*
Salt and freshly ground pepper
1 *tablespoon red wine vinegar with 5 to 6 percent acidity*
1½ *teaspoons rich chicken stock or canned low-sodium broth*
1½ *teaspoons dry white wine*
4 *paper-thin slices of prosciutto di Parma (about 2 ounces)*
6 *loosely packed cups mild greens, such as Bibb, Boston or red-leaf lettuce*

1. In a heavy medium skillet, heat ¼ cup of the walnut oil over moderately low heat. Add the garlic and cook, stirring, until golden, about 10 minutes. Remove and discard the garlic. Increase the heat to moderately high. Add the bread cubes and sauté, turning, until golden brown and crisp on all sides, about 5 minutes. Season with a pinch each of salt and pepper and drain on paper towels; set aside.

2. In a small bowl, whisk the vinegar, chicken stock and wine. Add ⅛ teaspoon each of salt and pepper, then gradually whisk in the remaining ¼ cup walnut oil.

3. Cut each slice of prosciutto into 4 lengthwise strips. In a large bowl, lightly coat the greens with the dressing. Add the croutons and toss well. Place the salad on 2 large dinner plates and arrange the prosciutto strips decoratively on top. Serve immediately.

—*David Rosengarten*

• • •

SALAD OF WINTER GREENS

Based on a recipe from a farmer in California, this salad is made with lively winter greens, which have their own cheering and distinct character not present at any other time of year. They have a pleasant bitterness and meaty texture that are particularly satisfying when good, fresh vegetables are rare.

The keys to this salad are careful washing of the greens so absolutely no grit remains, drying them completely so the dressing will adhere, tearing them in bite-size pieces to get the most out of their flavor, and tossing them just before serving, so the dressing doesn't wilt and slightly "cook" the greens.

6 to 8 Serving;s

2 *tablespoons balsamic vinegar*
1 *garlic clove, minced*
½ *teaspoon salt*
¼ *teaspoon freshly ground pepper*
⅓ *cup extra-virgin olive oil*

1 *medium fennel bulb, cored and cut into ¼-inch dice (1 cup)*
7 *cups (loosely packed) mixed bitter greens—such as curly endive, escarole and broccoli raab (leaves and buds only), torn into bite-size pieces*
2 *cups radicchio leaves (from 1 medium head), torn into bite-size pieces*

1. In a large serving bowl, combine the vinegar, garlic, salt and pepper; whisk well. Whisk in the olive oil in a thin, steady stream so the dressing emulsifies. *(The dressing can be made up to 1 day ahead and refrigerated in a jar. Shake well before using.)* Add the fennel and toss to coat. Set aside to marinate for at least 15 minutes and up to 1 hour.

2. Add the greens and radicchio to the bowl and toss to coat thoroughly. Serve immediately.

—*Susan Hermann Loomis*

• • •

TOMATO-WATERCRESS SALAD

6 Servings

2 *tablespoons white wine vinegar*
1 *tablespoon grainy mustard*
½ *teaspoon anchovy paste*
¼ *cup plus 1 tablespoon olive oil*
Pinch of salt
½ *teaspoon freshly ground pepper*
2 *bunches of watercress, large stems removed*
1 *large tomato, cut into ½-inch dice*

In a small bowl, whisk the vinegar, mustard and anchovy paste. Whisk in the oil in a thin stream until incorporated.

Season with the salt and pepper. Place the watercress in a medium bowl and top with the tomato. Drizzle the dressing over the salad; toss and serve.

—Lee Bailey

• • •

FENNEL SALAD

6 Servings

6 medium fennel bulbs (about 5 pounds total), trimmed, feathery leaves reserved
2 navel oranges
2 small lemons
¼ cup plus 2 tablespoons extra-virgin olive oil
2 teaspoons salt
1 teaspoon coriander seeds
¼ teaspoon freshly ground pepper
1 tomato—peeled, seeded and diced
¼ cup black Niçoise olives in brine, pitted (and halved if large)

1. Halve the fennel bulbs lengthwise and remove the tough cores. In a food processor fitted with a slicing disk, thinly slice the fennel crosswise. Spread in a flat serving dish.

2. Using a small sharp knife, peel the oranges, removing all the bitter white pith. Working over the bowl of a food processor, cut between the membranes to release the sections. Discard the membranes. Repeat with the lemons. Add the olive oil, salt, coriander seeds and pepper to the citrus sections in the bowl and puree.

3. In a medium nonreactive saucepan, combine the citrus dressing with the tomato and cook over low heat until lukewarm, 2 to 3 minutes. Pour over the fennel and toss. Sprinkle the olives and the reserved feathery fennel leaves on top.

—Mireille Johnston

• • •

CHOPPED WINTER SALAD

6 Servings

4 cups shredded green cabbage (from a 1-pound head)
1 large red bell pepper, cut into ¼-inch dice
2 small carrots, shredded
½ cup mayonnaise
¼ cup plain yogurt
1 tablespoon white wine vinegar
½ teaspoon freshly ground black pepper
⅓ cup fresh coriander (cilantro) leaves, chopped
½ teaspoon salt

In a large salad bowl, toss the cabbage with the bell pepper and carrots. In a small nonreactive bowl, combine the mayonnaise, yogurt, vinegar, black pepper, coriander and salt until smooth. Pour the dressing over the vegetables and toss to coat.

—Lee Bailey

• • •

CARROT AND ORANGE SALAD WITH BLACK MUSTARD SEEDS

6 Servings

1 navel orange
1 pound carrots, coarsely grated
2 tablespoons fresh lemon juice
¼ teaspoon cayenne pepper
½ teaspoon sugar
1 teaspoon salt
2 tablespoons vegetable oil
1 teaspoon black mustard seeds

1. Using a sharp knife, peel the orange; make sure to remove all of the bitter white pith. Slice the orange crosswise ⅛ inch thick. Stack the slices and cut them into 6 wedges.

2. In a large serving bowl, combine the orange, carrots, lemon juice, cayenne, sugar and salt. Mix well.

3. In a small skillet, heat the oil over moderately high heat. When hot, add the mustard seeds. When the seeds begin to pop, scrape the oil and seeds over the salad. (*The recipe can be prepared to this point up to 4 hours ahead. Cover and refrigerate.*) Toss well before serving.

—Madhur Jaffrey

• • •

SALADS

CREAMY GARLIC COLESLAW

Makes About 2 Quarts

1½ pounds green cabbage, cored and shredded
1 tablespoon salt
¾ cup mayonnaise
½ teaspoon finely grated lemon zest
1 tablespoon plus 1 teaspoon fresh lemon juice
1 large garlic clove, minced
¾ teaspoon freshly ground pepper
2 medium carrots—shredded, rinsed and squeezed dry

1. In a large bowl, cover the shredded cabbage with cold water. Stir in the salt and let stand at room temperature for 1 hour. Drain well, cover and refrigerate until cold.

2. In a large bowl, combine the mayonnaise, lemon zest, lemon juice, garlic and pepper. Add the cabbage and carrots and toss well. Season with additional salt to taste. (*The slaw can be refrigerated, covered, for up to 1 day.*)
—Marcia Kiesel

• • •

RED CABBAGE COLESLAW WITH JALAPENO VINAIGRETTE

4 Servings

2 tablespoons red wine vinegar
2 teaspoons Dijon mustard
Salt
¼ cup plus 1 teaspoon vegetable oil
½ of a medium jalapeño pepper, seeded and finely chopped

1 small head of red cabbage (about 1 pound), cored and finely shredded
1 medium red bell pepper, sliced lengthwise into thin strips
1 medium green bell pepper, sliced lengthwise into thin strips
3 medium scallions, thinly sliced crosswise
¼ cup chopped fresh coriander (cilantro)
Freshly ground black pepper

1. In a large bowl, whisk together the vinegar, mustard and ⅛ teaspoon salt. Gradually whisk in the oil. Stir in the jalapeño.

2. Add the cabbage, red and green bell peppers, scallions and coriander. Toss with the vinaigrette. Season to taste with black pepper.
—Stephanie Lyness

• • •

GREEN MANGO SLAW

Makes About 6 Cups

3 green or semi-ripe mangoes or green papayas
½ of a red bell pepper, sliced lengthwise into ¼-inch strips
¼ cup mayonnaise
1 tablespoon sugar
¼ cup fresh lime juice
¼ teaspoon hot pepper sauce
½ teaspoon salt
¼ teaspoon freshly ground black pepper

1. Peel the mangoes and cut the flesh away from the large, flat inner seed in two portions. If the mango is very hard, shred it using a hand-held grater as you would shred cabbage for coleslaw. Al-

ternatively, place a pitted mango half, cut-side down, on a work surface. Slice lengthwise into ¼-inch strips. Stack the strips and slice again lengthwise to make thin matchstick strips about ¼ inch thick. Repeat with the remaining mango halves. (If using papaya, peel, halve and scrape out the seeds. Slice as for the mangoes.)

2. In a large bowl, combine the mangoes, bell pepper, mayonnaise, sugar, lime juice and hot pepper sauce. Stir to combine and season with the salt and black pepper. Cover and refrigerate for up to 2 hours before serving.
—Chris Schlesinger, *East Coast Grill, Cambridge, Massachusetts*

• • •

FENNEL AND BELL PEPPER SLAW

This slaw is designed to be served with Spiced Crabs with Fennel and Pepper Slaw (p. 80). The dressing for the slaw doubles as the sauce for the crabs, so serve any remainder alongside.

Makes About 8 Cups

1 cup apple cider vinegar
¼ cup sugar
½ teaspoon salt
1 large fennel bulb (1½ pounds)— trimmed, halved lengthwise, cored and very thinly sliced
1 yellow bell pepper, sliced lengthwise into very thin strips
1 red bell pepper, sliced lengthwise into very thin strips

1 green bell pepper, sliced lengthwise
into very thin strips
½ cup thinly sliced scallions
3 tablespoons mayonnaise
2 tablespoons Creole or other whole-
grain mustard
3 dashes of hot pepper sauce
¼ cup vegetable oil
2 tablespoons extra-virgin olive oil

1. In a small nonreactive saucepan, combine the vinegar, sugar and salt. Bring to a boil over high heat, stirring once or twice to dissolve the sugar. Place the fennel in a large bowl. Pour the hot vinegar over the fennel and toss well. Press the fennel down so the liquid almost covers it and set aside for 10 minutes, stirring occasionally.

2. Add the bell peppers and scallions to the fennel and toss well. Set aside for at least 10 minutes and up to 1 hour. Drain the vegetables well; cover and refrigerate. (The vegetables can be prepared to this point up to 1 day ahead. Drain them again before dressing them.)

3. In a small bowl, combine the mayonnaise with the Creole mustard, hot pepper sauce, vegetable oil and olive oil. Whisk well to blend. Stir 3 tablespoons of the dressing into the slaw. Reserve the remainder to serve alongside the crabs.

—Bob Chambers and Carl Parisi

• • •

GRILLED BREAD SALAD WITH TOMATOES, FENNEL AND GOAT CHEESE

4 Servings

3 large tomatoes, halved and sliced
¼ inch thick, juice and seeds
reserved
1 small fennel bulb—trimmed,
halved and thinly sliced crosswise
¼ cup thinly sliced red onion
¼ cup (loosely packed) basil leaves,
torn into bite-size pieces
⅓ cup crumbled goat cheese
¼ cup plus 1 tablespoon red wine
vinegar
½ cup extra-virgin olive oil
¼ teaspoon salt
¼ teaspoon freshly ground pepper
4 slices (½ inch to ¾ inch) white
country-style or sourdough bread,
crusts trimmed
1 garlic clove, halved

1. Light a grill or preheat the broiler.
2. In a wide, shallow salad bowl, combine the tomatoes, their juice and seeds with the fennel, onion, basil and goat cheese. Add the vinegar and ¼ cup plus 1 tablespoon of the olive oil. Season with the salt and pepper and toss well.

3. Brush both sides of the bread slices with the remaining 3 tablespoons olive oil. Grill or broil 4 inches from the heat for 4 minutes on each side, or until golden brown. Rub the cut garlic over both sides of the grilled bread. Let the bread cool, then cut it into 1-inch squares. Add the bread to the salad bowl and toss. Serve immediately.

—Stephanie Lyness

• • •

CITRUS SALAD WITH HONEY-LIME DRESSING

This refreshing fruit salad has the right balance of tartness and sweetness. The fruit here can be prepared a day ahead without damaging taste or texture.

8 Servings

4 large pink grapefruits
4 navel oranges
2 tablespoons honey
1 tablespoon fresh lime juice
½ teaspoon finely grated lime zest
Pinch of salt

1. Using a sharp knife, peel the grapefruits, removing all the bitter white pith. Working over a bowl, cut in between the membranes to release the sections. Discard the membranes.

2. Using a small sharp knife, peel the oranges, removing all the bitter white pith. Slice the oranges crosswise ¼ inch thick and add to the bowl of grapefruit sections. (The recipe can be prepared to this point up to 1 day ahead. Cover and refrigerate the fruit and its juice. Let return to room temperature for about 1 hour before proceeding.)

3. In a small bowl, whisk together the honey, lime juice, lime zest and salt until smoothly combined.

4. Arrange the fruit on a large platter: lay the orange slices in the center in an overlapping circle and surround with the grapefruit sections. Stir 2 tablespoons of the juice that has collected at the bottom of the fruit bowl into the honey-lime dressing and spoon it over the fruit just before serving.

—Tracey Seaman

• • •

157

SALADS

MARINATED CUCUMBER SALAD

6 Servings

2 medium cucumbers, very thinly
   sliced crosswise
2 small onions, halved and thinly
   sliced crosswise
½ cup distilled white vinegar
2 tablespoons (packed) dark brown
   sugar
Pinch of salt
6 coriander seeds
5 allspice berries, crushed
3 whole cloves
1 cinnamon stick

1. In a medium nonreactive bowl, layer the cucumbers and onions. Set aside.

2. In a small nonreactive saucepan, whisk the vinegar with the brown sugar and salt. Stir in the coriander seeds, allspice berries, cloves, cinnamon stick and ¼ cup of water. Bring to a boil over moderate heat. Reduce the heat to moderately low and simmer for 5 minutes.

3. Pour the liquid over the cucumbers and onions. Place a plate on top to weigh down the salad. Refrigerate for at least 6 hours or preferably overnight. Serve chilled or at room temperature.

—*Jessica B. Harris*

• • •

CUCUMBER RAITA

6 Servings

1 teaspoon cumin seeds
1½ teaspoons coriander seeds
1½ cups plain yogurt
Pinch of cayenne pepper
1 tablespoon finely chopped onion
½ teaspoon salt
½ teaspoon freshly ground black
   pepper
1 large European cucumber—peeled,
   halved lengthwise and thinly
   sliced

1. In a small dry skillet, toast the cumin and coriander seeds over high heat until fragrant, about 1 minute. Transfer the seeds to a mortar or a spice mill and grind to a powder.

2. In a medium bowl, combine the spice mixture with all the remaining ingredients and stir well. Refrigerate for 1 hour to blend the flavors.

—*Madhur Jaffrey*

• • •

SALAD OF FLAGEOLET BEANS WITH FENNEL AND WALNUTS

This salad is worth serving as a course by itself so that the flavors can be savored.

4 Servings

⅔ cup dried flageolet beans (4½
   ounces), picked over
1 large shallot, finely chopped
4 teaspoons Champagne vinegar or
   white wine vinegar, or more to
   taste
½ teaspoon salt

2 tablespoons walnut oil
1 tablespoon cream or crème fraîche
1 small fennel bulb (½ pound)—
   quartered, cored and thinly sliced
   crosswise
2 teaspoons finely chopped fennel
   fronds
2 teaspoons minced parsley
6 walnut halves, broken into small
   pieces
¼ teaspoon freshly ground white
   pepper
1 teaspoon snipped fresh chives

1. In a medium saucepan, soak the beans in plenty of cold water for at least 6 hours or overnight. Pour off the water, re-cover the beans with fresh water and bring to a boil. Boil the beans vigorously for 5 minutes. Drain the beans in a colander and rinse well to remove any scum.

2. Return the beans to the saucepan, cover with cold water and bring to a boil over high heat. Reduce the heat to moderately low and simmer until the beans are tender, about 1¼ hours. Drain the beans and place in a medium bowl. Let cool to tepid. Reserve the broth for another use.

3. In a small bowl, combine the shallot, vinegar and salt and let stand for a few minutes. Whisk in the walnut oil and cream. Taste and add more vinegar if necessary.

4. Add the dressing to the beans along with the fennel, fennel fronds, parsley and walnuts. Toss gently. Add the pepper and season to taste with salt. Arrange the salad on 4 plates and garnish with the chives.

—*Deborah Madison*

• • •

BLACK-EYED PEA AND MINT MARIGOLD SALAD

If you cannot find fresh or frozen black-eyed peas, use dried black-eyed peas, first cooking them until just tender.

6 Servings

*2 cups freshly shelled black-eyed
    peas or 1 package (10 ounces)
    frozen black-eyed peas, thawed*
3 ounces sliced smoked bacon
1 large garlic clove, minced
1 small onion, finely diced
*½ of a small red bell pepper, finely
    diced*
2 serrano chiles, seeded and minced
1 tablespoon balsamic vinegar
2 teaspoons finely chopped chives
*2 teaspoons finely chopped mint
    marigold or tarragon*
*1 tablespoon freshly ground black
    pepper*
Salt

1. In a medium saucepan, bring 4 cups of water to a boil over moderately high heat. Add the fresh or thawed peas and boil until tender, 15 to 20 minutes. Drain, refresh under cold running water and set aside.

2. In a medium nonreactive skillet, cook the bacon over moderate heat, turning once, until crisp, about 5 minutes. Using tongs, transfer the bacon to paper towels to drain. Coarsely chop and set aside.

3. Heat the bacon fat over low heat. Add the garlic, onion, red bell pepper and serrano chiles and cook, stirring, until softened, about 5 minutes. Add the reserved peas and bacon. (*The recipe can be prepared up to 1 day ahead. Cover and refrigerate. Rewarm over moderate heat before proceeding.*) Add the vinegar, chives, mint marigold and black pepper. Season to taste with salt. Serve hot.

—*Kevin Rathbun, Baby Routh, Dallas*

• • •

ASPARAGUS AND GOAT CHEESE SALAD

6 Servings

*1 pound pencil-thin asparagus,
    trimmed and cut into 1½-inch
    lengths*
2 tablespoons cider vinegar
½ teaspoon salt
¼ teaspoon freshly ground pepper
*¼ cup plus 2 tablespoons safflower or
    canola oil*
*1 large head of Boston or other mild
    lettuce, torn into large pieces*
2 ounces dry goat cheese, chilled

1. In a medium skillet, bring 1 inch of lightly salted water to a boil over high heat. Add the asparagus and cook briefly until bright green and crisp-tender, 30 seconds to 1 minute. Drain and let cool.

2. In a medium bowl, whisk the vinegar with the salt and pepper. Pour in the oil in a thin stream, whisking until incorporated. (*The recipe can be made up to 1 day ahead. Cover and refrigerate the asparagus and dressing separately. Bring to room temperature before proceeding.*) Add the asparagus and toss well to coat.

3. Mound the lettuce on 6 salad plates. Spoon the asparagus and dressing over the lettuce and crumble the goat cheese on top.

—*Lee Bailey*

• • •

SCALLOP, MUSSEL AND ASPARAGUS SALAD WITH ORANGE-SAFFRON DRESSING

🍷 Dry-style Rieslings are a fine foil for this dish. For ripe flavor and depth, try a top Californian, such as 1989 Trefethen White Riesling or 1989 Firestone "Dry."

4 First-Course Servings

*1 pound medium asparagus, tough
    ends snapped off, cut into 1-inch
    pieces*
*2 dozen small mussels, scrubbed and
    debearded*
1 pound small sea scallops
8 saffron threads
2 tablespoons minced shallots
2 tablespoons fresh orange juice
½ teaspoon finely grated orange zest
½ teaspoon salt
¼ teaspoon freshly ground pepper
*1 tablespoon rice vinegar or 2
    teaspoons white wine vinegar
    diluted with 1 teaspoon water*
2 tablespoons extra-virgin olive oil

1. Fill a medium saucepan with ½ inch of water and insert a steamer basket. Bring the water to a boil over high heat, add the asparagus pieces, cover and steam until bright green and just tender, about 4 minutes. Remove the basket and rinse the asparagus under cold running water until cool; set aside. Pour out the water.

2. Add another ½ inch of water to the saucepan and bring to a boil over high heat. Add the mussels, cover and steam until they open, about 2 minutes. Remove the mussels from the basket and set aside; discard any that have not opened. Add the scallops to the basket,

159

cover and steam until just opaque throughout, about 3 minutes. Remove the scallops and set aside. Measure 2 tablespoons of the steaming liquid into a small bowl. Crumble the saffron threads into the liquid and set aside to steep.

3. Remove the mussels from their shells and briefly rinse the mussels if they are sandy. Cut the scallops to the same size as the mussels, if necessary. In a large bowl, combine the mussels, scallops and asparagus and set aside.

4. In a medium bowl, whisk together the shallots, orange juice, orange zest, salt, pepper, vinegar and olive oil. Whisk in the reserved saffron liquid. Set aside to blend the flavors for about 20 minutes.

5. Up to 1 hour before serving, pour the dressing over the seafood and asparagus and mix well; stir occasionally until ready to serve. Serve at room temperature.

—*Marcia Kiesel*

• • •

SOFT-SHELL CRAB AND HAZELNUT SALAD

*8 First-Course or
4 Main-Course Servings*

1 cup hazelnuts (5 ounces)
¼ cup all-purpose flour
¾ teaspoon salt
½ teaspoon freshly ground pepper
8 cleaned soft-shell crabs
1 cup milk
3 tablespoons sherry wine vinegar
1 tablespoon Dijon mustard
2 tablespoons hazelnut oil
⅓ cup vegetable oil
½ cup olive oil
3 medium carrots, grated

*2 large bunches of arugula, large
    stems removed*
*3 medium Belgian endives, cored and
    sliced crosswise ¼ inch thick*
Lemon wedges, for serving

1. Preheat the oven to 350°. Spread the hazelnuts on a small baking sheet and roast in the middle of the oven for 10 to 12 minutes, until fragrant and the skins start to crack. Transfer the nuts to a kitchen towel and rub them against each other to remove the skins. Let the nuts cool completely. Reduce the oven temperature to 250°.

2. In a food processor, combine ½ cup of the cooled hazelnuts with the flour and ¼ teaspoon each of the salt and pepper. Pulse until the nuts are finely ground. Place on a plate. Coarsely chop the remaining ½ cup hazelnuts and set aside.

3. Place the crabs in a large shallow dish and pour the milk on top. Set aside to soak for 10 minutes. In a small bowl, combine the vinegar, mustard and the remaining ½ teaspoon salt and ¼ teaspoon pepper. Gradually whisk in the hazelnut oil, vegetable oil and ¼ cup of the olive oil. Set the dressing aside.

4. In a large skillet, preferably nonstick, heat 2 tablespoons of the olive oil over moderately high heat. Remove 4 crabs from the milk and shake gently. Dredge the crabs in the hazelnut flour, add to the skillet and fry, turning once, until browned and crisp, about 3 minutes per side. Transfer the crabs to a heatproof platter and place in the oven to keep warm. Repeat with the remaining 2 tablespoons olive oil and 4 crabs.

5. In a large bowl, combine the carrots, arugula and endives. Add all but ¼ cup of the dressing and toss well. Arrange the salad on plates and sprinkle the reserved chopped hazelnuts on top. Set the crabs on the salads and spoon some of the reserved dressing over each crab. Serve immediately, with lemon wedges on the side.

—*Bob Chambers and Carl Parisi*

• • •

WARM SHRIMP SALAD WITH TARRAGON DRESSING

8 Servings

¼ cup pure olive oil
*3 pounds large shrimp, shelled and
    deveined, shells reserved*
1 medium tomato, chopped
*⅔ cup dry white wine, preferably
    Chardonnay*
Salt
½ cup heavy cream
3 tablespoons minced fresh tarragon
Freshly ground pepper
*1 large bunch of watercress, large
    stems removed*
*1 large bunch of arugula, large stems
    removed, large leaves torn*
*1 small head of red leaf lettuce, torn
    into bite-size pieces*
*2 tablespoons plus 2 teaspoons red
    wine vinegar*
½ cup fruity extra-virgin olive oil
2 tablespoons plain yogurt

1. In a large nonreactive skillet, heat 2 tablespoons of the pure olive oil over high heat. Add the shrimp shells and cook, stirring, until they turn pink, about 1 minute. Add the tomato, wine, ¼ teaspoon salt and ½ cup water and bring to a boil. Reduce the heat to moderate and simmer for 10 minutes. Add the cream and 2 tablespoons of the tarragon and simmer for 10 minutes longer.

2. Strain the sauce into a small saucepan, pressing hard on the shells; discard the shells. Bring the sauce to a boil over high heat. Reduce the heat to moderate and simmer until it is reduced to about ⅓ cup and slightly syrupy, about 10 minutes.

3. In a large skillet, heat the remaining 2 tablespoons pure olive oil over high heat. Add the shrimp in 3 batches and cook each batch, turning once, until opaque throughout, about 5 minutes. In a large bowl, toss the shrimp with the tarragon sauce and season with salt and pepper to taste. Set aside in a warm place.

4. In a large bowl, toss the watercress with the arugula and red leaf lettuce. In a small bowl, combine 1 teaspoon salt with ¼ teaspoon pepper. Whisk in the vinegar; then whisk in the extra-virgin olive oil. Whisk in the yogurt and a pinch of the remaining minced tarragon. Add the dressing to the greens and toss.

5. Arrange the mixed greens around the rim of a large serving platter and mound the shrimp in the center. Sprinkle the remaining minced tarragon on top.

—Lydie Marshall

• • •

LOBSTER SALAD WITH TARRAGON AND SWEET PEPPERS

This recipe was inspired by a delicious molded lobster salad at Park Bistro in New York City. For lunch or a light dinner, serve a generous mound atop tender lettuce with a side of blanched green beans and sliced steamed artichoke bottoms, or sandwich the salad between thick slices of brioche. For a first course, spoon a half cup into an avocado half.

4 Main-Course or
8 First-Course Servings

Four 1¼- to 1½-pound cooked
 lobsters
¼ cup mayonnaise
1 tablespoon sour cream or crème
 fraîche
1 tablespoon fresh lime juice
2 teaspoons minced fresh tarragon
¼ teaspoon freshly ground white
 pepper
1 small red bell pepper
1 small yellow bell pepper
2 tablespoons minced fresh chives
Freshly ground black pepper
Lime wedges, for serving

1. Giving a twist and a pull, break off the tails from the lobsters. Then break off the knuckles and claws in 1 piece. Place 1 of the tails belly-up on a work surface and use sharp kitchen shears to cut through the thin underside shell. Remove the tail meat and set aside. Repeat with the remaining tails.

2. Using a lobster cracker or a nutcracker, crack the claws and knuckles, extract the meat and add it to the tail meat. Extract any other meat and discard all the shells. Cut all the meat into ½-inch pieces and transfer to a large bowl.

3. In a small bowl, whisk the mayonnaise with the sour cream, lime juice, tarragon and white pepper. Fold the mixture into the lobster.

4. Roast the red and yellow bell peppers directly over a gas flame or under the broiler as close to the heat as possible, turning frequently, until charred all over. Transfer the peppers to a paper bag and set aside to steam for 10 minutes. Using a small sharp knife, scrape off the blackened skins and remove the cores, seeds and ribs. Rinse the peppers and pat dry. Cut the peppers into ¼-inch dice. (*The recipe can be prepared to this point up to 1 day ahead. Cover the lobster salad and peppers separately and refrigerate overnight. Let return to room temperature before proceeding.*)

5. Stir the chives and 2 tablespoons each of the diced red and yellow bell peppers into the lobster salad. Season with black pepper to taste. Garnish with the remaining diced peppers and lime wedges. (If you are making sandwiches, reserve the remaining bell peppers for another use.)

—Tracey Seaman

• • •

SALADS

FRESH TUNA SALADE NICOISE

The availability of high-quality fresh tuna inspired Joseph Manzare to try this sparkling new twist on a classic salade niçoise, more often made with canned tuna. Use fine sashimi-quality tuna and cook it rare.

6 Servings

2 large garlic cloves, unpeeled
1½ tablespoons drained capers
3 anchovy fillets, drained
2 tablespoons chopped flat-leaf parsley, plus more for garnish
1 cup Niçoise olives (4 ounces), pitted
1 cup olive oil
2 tablespoons fresh lemon juice
2 tablespoons white wine vinegar
8 small shallots, minced
¾ teaspoon salt
½ teaspoon freshly ground pepper
1 pound green beans
12 small new potatoes (about 1 pound)
6 hard-cooked eggs
1¼-pound tuna steak, 1 inch thick, cut into 3 equal chunks
8 cups bite-size pieces of mixed greens, such as Bibb or frisée
2 tomatoes, sliced ¼ inch thick

1. Preheat the oven to 350°. Wrap the garlic cloves loosely in foil and roast on a baking sheet until very soft, about 35 minutes. Let cool slightly, then remove the foil and squeeze the garlic from the skins. In a blender or food processor, combine the garlic, capers, anchovies, parsley and olives; puree until smooth. With the machine on, gradually add ¼

cup of the olive oil until incorporated, scraping down the sides of the bowl as necessary. Transfer to a small bowl.

2. In a medium bowl, whisk together the lemon juice, vinegar, shallots, salt, pepper and ⅔ cup of the olive oil. *(The recipe can be prepared to this point 1 day ahead. Cover and refrigerate the olive paste and vinaigrette separately.)*

3. Bring a medium saucepan of water to a rolling boil over high heat. Add the green beans and cook until bright green and crisp-tender, about 5 minutes. With a slotted spoon, transfer the beans to a colander and refresh under cold running water. Drain thoroughly and add to the bowl with the vinaigrette. Toss well and set aside to marinate for at least 1 hour and up to 2 hours.

4. Add the potatoes to the boiling water and reduce the heat to moderate. Cook the potatoes until tender when pierced, about 15 minutes. Drain the potatoes and let cool slightly. Slice ¼ inch thick and set aside, covered. Using an egg slicer, slice the eggs and set aside, covered.

5. Preheat the broiler. Place the tuna chunks on a baking sheet or broiling pan and rub with the remaining 1 tablespoon plus 1 teaspoon olive oil. Season lightly with salt and pepper. Broil the tuna 6 inches from the heat for about 3 minutes, until medium-rare. Remove from the oven and let cool slightly on the baking sheet, then slice the tuna across the grain ⅓ inch thick. Set aside.

6. With a slotted spoon, remove the green beans from the vinaigrette and set aside. Add the mixed greens to the vinaigrette and toss well to coat.

7. To serve, arrange the tuna slices, tomato slices, potato and egg slices around the rims of 6 serving plates. Mound the tossed greens in the center

and top with the marinated beans. Top each slice of tuna with ½ teaspoon of the reserved olive paste. Garnish with chopped parsley and serve immediately.
—*Joseph Manzare, 44 restaurant, New York City*

• • •

CURRIED SALMON SALAD WITH LEMON GRASS VINAIGRETTE

This Thai-inspired salad is from Roy Yamaguchi of Roy's in Honolulu.

4 Servings

2 tablespoons Thai Mussaman curry paste*
1 tablespoon canned unsweetened coconut milk*
1 teaspoon finely grated fresh ginger
1 teaspoon minced garlic
1 teaspoon Oriental sesame oil
7 tablespoons vegetable oil
3½ teaspoons soy sauce
Four 5-ounce center-cut salmon fillets
2 stalks of fresh lemon grass,* white part only, minced
2 tablespoons strained fresh lemon juice
¼ cup light olive oil
Salt
½ head of romaine lettuce, torn into bite-size pieces
½ head of bronze-leaf lettuce, torn into bite-size pieces
2 medium Belgian endives, cored and sliced crosswise ½ inch thick
1 package enoki mushrooms or radish sprouts†
½ ripe medium papaya—peeled, seeded and cut into ½-inch dice

⅓ cup macadamia nuts, coarsely
   chopped (1½ ounces)
2 ounces pickled red ginger,† cut
   into matchsticks (See Note)
*Available at Thai markets
†Available at Asian markets

1. In a medium bowl, combine the curry paste, coconut milk, grated fresh ginger, garlic, sesame oil, vegetable oil and 2 teaspoons of the soy sauce. Whisk well. Pour half of the marinade into a 9-by-11-inch glass dish. Add the salmon and spoon the remaining marinade over the fish. Let marinate at room temperature for 1 hour, turning occasionally.

2. Meanwhile, in a small saucepan, combine the lemon grass with 1 cup of water and bring to a simmer over moderate heat. Simmer until only 1 teaspoon of liquid remains, about 30 minutes. In a small nonreactive bowl, whisk the lemon grass and its liquid with the lemon juice, olive oil, ½ teaspoon salt and the remaining 1½ teaspoons soy sauce. Set the dressing aside.

3. Keeping as much of the marinade solids clinging to the fish as possible, transfer the salmon to a rack set over a platter and let drain for 20 minutes, turning once.

4. Light a grill. When the fire is medium-hot, grill the salmon for 3 minutes, then turn and grill for 2 to 3 minutes longer, until the flesh, ½ inch from the center of a fillet, flakes with a fork. Lightly salt the salmon. Alternatively, preheat the broiler. Broil the fish for about 5 minutes, until the surface is firm and begins to sizzle. Turn and broil for 2½ to 3½ minutes longer.

5. While the salmon cooks, assemble the salad: In a large bowl, toss the romaine and bronze-leaf lettuces with the endives and three-quarters of the enoki mushrooms. Whisk the reserved dressing to blend. Toss the salad with the dressing and arrange on 4 plates.

6. Scatter the diced papaya over the salads and set a salmon fillet in the center of each one. Sprinkle with the macadamia nuts. Garnish the salads with the remaining enoki mushrooms and the pickled ginger. Serve immediately.

NOTE: *As a substitute, cut ½ of a medium red bell pepper into thin matchsticks and marinate overnight in 6 tablespoons unseasoned rice vinegar mixed with 2 tablespoons sugar. Drain well before using.*

—*Linda Burum*

• • •

BAKED GOAT CHEESE SALAD WITH GARLIC CROUTONS

Alice Waters has said that she would rather make salads than almost anything else. In the *Chez Panisse Menu Cookbook*, the San Francisco advocate of the freshest high-quality ingredients says that a salad's success depends in part on a harmonious blend of lettuces.

4 Servings

Four 2½-inch rounds of goat cheese,
   each about ½ inch thick
¾ cup extra-virgin olive oil
3 fresh thyme sprigs plus 1 teaspoon
   dried thyme
24 slices (¼ inch thick) of day-old
   baguette
4 tablespoons unsalted butter,
   melted
2 medium garlic cloves, peeled and
   halved
1 cup fine dry bread crumbs
2 to 3 tablespoons red wine vinegar
Salt and freshly ground pepper, to
   taste
8 cups (about 4 ounces) lightly
   packed lettuce leaves, such as
   small oak leaf, arugula and mâche

1. Place the goat cheese in a shallow glass dish and drizzle with ¼ cup of the olive oil; turn to coat completely. Sprinkle the fresh thyme on top. Cover and refrigerate overnight.

2. Preheat the oven to 350°. Brush both sides of the bread with the melted butter and place in a single layer on a baking sheet. Bake for 15 minutes, until golden. Rub the croutons with the cut garlic cloves while they are still slightly warm. Turn the oven up to 400°.

3. In a small bowl, combine the bread crumbs with the dried thyme. Remove the cheese from the oil and coat thoroughly with the bread crumb mixture. Transfer to a lightly greased baking sheet. Bake without turning until golden brown and bubbly, 10 to 12 minutes.

4. Meanwhile, place 2 tablespoons of the vinegar in a bowl and slowly whisk in the remaining ½ cup oil. Season with the salt and pepper.

5. Toss the lettuce leaves with enough of the vinaigrette to coat lightly and mound the greens on individual plates. Invert a round of warm goat cheese into the center and place the garlic croutons around the cheese. Serve immediately.

—*Alice Waters, Chez Panisse,
   Berkeley, California*

• • •

163

SALADS

CHINESE CHICKEN WITH CARROTS AND STAR ANISE

Use only the sweetest carrots for this light, room-temperature salad.

2 First-Course Servings

3 tablespoons light (thin) soy sauce
2 teaspoons sugar
⅜ teaspoon Oriental sesame oil
2 star anise pods, crumbled
1½-inch piece of fresh ginger, peeled and thinly sliced lengthwise
½ pound skinless boneless chicken breast halves, well trimmed
2 small carrots, thinly sliced on the diagonal
1 tablespoon rice vinegar
1½ tablespoons peanut oil
1 scallion, green part only, thinly sliced

1. In a bowl, combine the soy sauce, sugar and ⅛ teaspoon of the sesame oil. Stir in the star anise and the ginger. Add the chicken breasts, turning to coat with the marinade. Cover and refrigerate for at least 2 hours or overnight.

2. Transfer the chicken and marinade to a medium saucepan. Add 1 cup of water and bring to a boil over high heat. Reduce the heat to low, turn the chicken over and simmer for 3 minutes. Remove from the heat and set aside to cool.

3. Transfer the chicken to a work surface and thinly slice crosswise; set aside. Return the poaching liquid to a boil over high heat and cook until reduced to ¼ cup, about 3 minutes. Strain the liquid into a small bowl and let cool to room temperature.

4. Meanwhile, in a small saucepan of boiling salted water, cook the carrots until barely tender, about 2 minutes. Drain and set aside to cool.

5. Whisk the wine vinegar into the reduced poaching liquid, then gradually whisk in the remaining ¼ teaspoon sesame oil and the peanut oil.

6. To serve, decoratively arrange the chicken and carrots on 2 small plates. Spoon the dressing over the salads and let stand for about 5 minutes to let it soak in. Sprinkle the scallion on top.

—David Rosengarten

• • •

CRUNCHY CHICKEN SALAD

Be sure the noodles and sesame seeds are not added until the last minute; otherwise they will get soggy.

10 Servings

2½ tablespoons olive oil
1½ pounds skinless boneless chicken breasts
1 teaspoon salt
¾ teaspoon freshly ground pepper
1 cup fresh bean sprouts (about 3 ounces)
1 large celery rib, cut into ½-inch dice
¾ cup mayonnaise

2 tablespoons fresh lemon juice
1½ tablespoons soy sauce
1 head of romaine lettuce, torn into bite-size pieces
1½ cups Chinese fried noodles
2 tablespoons sesame seeds (optional)

1. Preheat the oven to 350°. Coat the bottom of a large shallow casserole or baking sheet with ½ tablespoon of the oil. Sprinkle the chicken breasts with ¾ teaspoon of the salt and the pepper. Place the chicken in a single layer in the casserole, turn to coat in the oil and bake for about 20 minutes, just until opaque throughout. Set aside until cool to the touch. Using your fingers, shred the meat into bite-size pieces.

2. In a large bowl, toss the chicken with the bean sprouts, celery and the remaining ¼ teaspoon salt. In a small bowl, mix the mayonnaise with the lemon juice, soy sauce and the remaining 2 tablespoons olive oil. Spoon on top of the chicken and toss to combine. Refrigerate for 15 minutes.

3. In a large salad bowl, combine the lettuce, chicken salad, Chinese noodles and sesame seeds. Toss and serve.

—Annie Gilbar

• • •

VEGETABLES

VEGETABLES

BRAISED ARTICHOKES WITH SPINACH

6 Servings

6 large artichokes (1 pound each)
¼ cup fresh lemon juice
4 pounds fresh spinach, large stems removed
2 tablespoons unsalted butter
6 medium garlic cloves, minced
¼ cup virgin olive oil
¼ teaspoon freshly ground pepper
½ cup plus 2 tablespoons freshly grated Parmesan cheese (about 2 ounces)
1¾ cups chicken stock or canned low-sodium broth

1. Place the artichokes and lemon juice in a large bowl and add water to cover. Let soak for 30 minutes. With a small sharp knife, trim the artichokes: Cut off the stems and then peel off all the dark outer leaves. Cut off the leaves about 2 inches from the base (you should be able to see the rose-colored centers). Trim off the remaining leaves and any dark outer skin from the artichoke bottoms. Using a teaspoon, scrape out the hairy chokes. As each artichoke is trimmed, drop it back into the bowl of water and lemon juice.

2. Fill a large nonreactive flameproof casserole with water and bring to a boil over high heat. Reduce the heat to moderate, add the artichoke bottoms and simmer until fork-tender but still slightly firm, about 10 minutes. Drain and pat dry. Pour the water out of the casserole.

3. Rinse the spinach very well in several changes of water. Place the spinach (with some of the water still clinging to the leaves) in the casserole. Cover and steam over high heat, turning occasionally, until wilted, about 8 minutes. Drain the spinach and rinse with cold water to cool it down. Squeeze as much water as possible from the spinach, then coarsely chop.

4. Wipe the casserole dry, then add the butter and melt over moderate heat. Add the spinach, garlic and 2 tablespoons of the olive oil. Cook, stirring, until the garlic is fragrant, about 5 minutes. Remove from the heat. Stir in the pepper and ½ cup of the Parmesan cheese. Let cool.

5. Mound the spinach mixture in the artichoke bottoms. Set the casserole over moderately low heat. Add the remaining 2 tablespoons olive oil, the stuffed artichoke bottoms and the chicken stock. Cover and braise gently over low heat until the artichokes are just tender, about 30 minutes. Sprinkle the remaining 2 tablespoons Parmesan on top of the artichokes and serve warm, with some of the broth spooned on top.

—*Ann Chantal Altman*

• • •

SPICY BRUSSELS SPROUTS

This recipe was created using leftover brussels sprouts to challenge anyone who wouldn't eat them in the first place. Expand this into a pilaf by folding in two cups of cooked rice.

6 Servings

1 tablespoon vegetable oil
3 tablespoons slivered almonds (1 ounce)
½ teaspoon yellow mustard seeds, crushed
¼ teaspoon cumin seeds
¼ teaspoon fennel seeds
3 cups cooked brussels sprouts, halved
⅛ teaspoon cayenne pepper
1 tablespoon finely chopped fresh ginger or Japanese pickled ginger
About 1 tablespoon fresh lime juice
½ teaspoon salt

1. In a large, heavy, nonreactive skillet, heat the oil over moderately high heat for about 30 seconds. Add the almonds and the mustard, cumin and fennel seeds. Cook, stirring, until the nuts and spices are fragrant and dark, about 15 seconds.

2. Reduce the heat to moderate and add the brussels sprouts, cayenne and ginger. Cook and stir until the vegetables are heated through and the spices are well distributed, about 4 minutes. Add a few tablespoons of water if the vegetables look dry. Season to taste with up to 1 tablespoon of lime juice and the salt and serve hot. (*The sprouts can be covered tightly and refrigerated for up to 1 day; reheat before serving.*)

—*Julie Sahni*

• • •

CAULIFLOWER AND RED PEPPER PUREE

6 Servings

4 large shallots, unpeeled
1 tablespoon olive oil
1 medium red bell pepper
5 cups cauliflower florets (from a 1½-pound cauliflower)
1½ tablespoons unsalted butter

¾ *teaspoon salt*
½ *teaspoon freshly ground black*
  pepper

1. Preheat the oven to 400°. Cut the top ¼ inch off the shallots and place them in the center of a 10-inch square of aluminum foil. Drizzle the oil over the shallots and wrap the foil tightly to enclose them. Roast the shallots for 45 minutes, or until the flesh is soft.

2. Meanwhile, roast the red pepper directly over a gas flame, turning frequently, until blackened all over. Place the pepper in a small paper bag and let steam for 10 minutes. Under gently running water, peel off the blackened skin. Halve the pepper and remove the core, seeds and membranes. Cut the pepper into 1-inch pieces.

3. Fill a large saucepan with 1 inch of water. Add the cauliflower florets and bring to a boil over moderately high heat. Cover, reduce the heat to low and simmer until tender, about 12 minutes. Drain well and cover to keep warm.

4. In a food processor, combine the red pepper, butter, salt, black pepper and drained cauliflower. Squeeze in the flesh from the shallots and process to a fine puree. Transfer to a warm serving dish and serve immediately.

—*Lee Bailey*

• • •

ELLA'S DRIED CORN

This recipe, a family Thanksgiving tradition when I was growing up, comes from my maternal grandmother, Ella Ferris. Her original recipe called for shucking and cleaning a bushel and a half of sweet corn. Once cut from the cob, the fresh kernels were seasoned with salt and pepper, spread out on screens, covered with cheesecloth and left to dry in the rafters of the barn. The dried kernels were stored until winter in cheesecloth bags that Ella had sewn.

When my grandmother moved from the farm, she resorted to drying her corn in an oven warmed by a pilot light. Somewhere along the way, a little sugar and some heavy cream were added to the corn before it was dried.

To simplify my grandmother's recipe, I use frozen corn. After boiling the corn with cream and seasonings, I gradually dry it in an oven set at successively lower temperatures. As the corn dries, the cream and sugar caramelize to give it its nutty flavor. One cup of dried corn will make six half-cup servings when reconstituted with water.

Makes About 6 Cups

12 *packages (10 ounces each) frozen*
   corn kernels
1 *tablespoon salt*
1 *tablespoon freshly ground pepper*
1 *tablespoon sugar*
1 *cup heavy cream*

1. Preheat the oven to 400°. Combine all the ingredients in a large saucepan and bring to a rolling boil over high heat, stirring occasionally with a large wooden spoon. Boil, stirring frequently, until the liquid has evaporated and the corn begins to adhere to the pan, about 20 minutes.

2. Transfer the corn to 2 jelly-roll pans and spread out in an even layer. Set the pans in the oven on the top and middle shelves and bake for 20 minutes. Stir the corn well, switch the pans and bake for 20 minutes longer. Stir again.

3. Reduce the oven temperature to 350° and bake the corn for 40 minutes, stirring and switching the pans at halftime, after 20 minutes.

4. Reduce the oven temperature to 300°. Stir the corn and bake for another 40 minutes, stirring and switching the pans at halftime. The corn should be golden with some browned kernels and should have a nutty aroma. Turn off the oven and leave the corn to dry out overnight.

5. The next day, transfer the corn to an airtight container. (The dried corn can be refrigerated for up to 2 months or frozen for up to 6 months.)

6. To reconstitute: Use 2 cups of water for each cup of corn. In a saucepan, bring the water and corn to a boil over high heat. Reduce the heat to moderate and simmer, partially covered, until most of the liquid has evaporated and the corn is tender, 20 to 25 minutes.

—*Bob Chambers*

• • •

VEGETABLES

CORN CHILI

Fresh jalapeño, chili powder and hot sauce give this warm, buttery side dish just the right kick.

6 Servings

4 cups fresh corn kernels (cut from 6 ears) or 2 packages (10 ounces each) frozen corn, thawed
4 tablespoons unsalted butter
1 medium red bell pepper, cut into ¼-inch dice
2 scallions, white and green portions thinly sliced separately
½ teaspoon pure mild chili powder
½ teaspoon salt
½ teaspoon freshly ground black pepper
1 small jalapeño pepper—seeded, deribbed and minced (about 1 tablespoon)
½ cup (loosely packed) fresh coriander (cilantro) leaves, finely chopped
Hot pepper sauce, to taste

1. In a medium saucepan, combine the corn with ½ cup of water. Cover and bring to a boil over moderately high heat. Cook the corn for 3 minutes, then drain in a colander and set aside.

2. Add the butter to the saucepan and melt over moderately low heat. Add the red bell pepper and the scallion whites and cook, stirring occasionally, until softened, about 3 minutes. Stir in the corn, chili powder, salt and black pepper and cook, stirring occasionally, until heated through, about 3 minutes.

3. Stir in the jalapeño and the scallion greens. Remove from the heat and stir in the coriander. Season to taste with salt and hot sauce and serve warm.

—*Tracey Seaman*

• • •

TOASTED CASCABEL CHILE BUTTER ON FRESH CORN

You can also use the chile butter on grilled chicken or steak, on pasta with fresh tomatoes, or on rice with Spanish olives.

4 Servings

3 dried Mexican cascabel chiles
5 tablespoons unsalted butter, softened
1 garlic clove, minced
⅛ teaspoon salt
6 medium ears of corn (about 3½ cups kernels)
2 large plum tomatoes—peeled, seeded and chopped

1. Break open the chiles with your hands, discard the stems and all but ½ teaspoon of the seeds. Tear the chile into large, flat pieces.

2. In a small skillet, toast the chile pieces and seeds over high heat until fragrant and the chile pieces are blistered but not too dark, about 1 minute. Transfer to a mortar and set aside until cool and brittle, about 5 minutes. Using a pestle, pound the chiles into a coarse powder (a few larger bits may remain). Alternatively, using a large knife, finely chop the chiles to a coarse powder. Transfer the powder to a coarse strainer set over a small bowl and push the powder through with a small spoon. Add the butter, garlic and salt and blend thoroughly; set aside.

3. Slice the corn kernels from each cob. Transfer to a steamer over high heat, cover and steam over boiling water until tender, about 4 minutes.

4. Transfer the corn to a serving bowl, add the tomatoes and toss. Add the chile butter by the tablespoonful until the dish is creamy and tastes spicy. (Reserve the remainder for another use.) Season with salt and serve at once.

—*Marcia Kiesel*

• • •

ROASTED CORN ON THE COB WITH BASIL

For a decorative touch, drape a cooked basil leaf or two over the corn when serving.

4 Servings

4 medium ears of corn, husked
24 fresh basil leaves
4 tablespoons unsalted butter, cut into bits

Preheat the oven to 475°. Place each ear of corn on a large square of aluminum foil. Tuck 3 basil leaves under each ear and arrange 3 on top. Scatter the butter over the corn and wrap tightly in the foil, twisting the ends to seal. Place on a baking sheet and roast for 25 minutes. Leave the ears wrapped in the foil until ready to serve.

—*Jim Fobel*

• • •

Carrot and Orange Salad with Black Mustard Seeds (p. 155).

CALIFORNIA RANCHO-STYLE HOMINY

Hominy is puffed kernels of corn that have been soaked in a lye solution and washed to remove the hulls. For this recipe buy cooked hominy, which is sold canned in most grocery stores.

8 to 10 Servings

⅓ cup olive oil
2 large onions, coarsely chopped
4 garlic cloves, minced
1 tablespoon chili powder
1 tablespoon cumin
3 cans (16 ounces each) hominy, preferably yellow, drained and rinsed
½ teaspoon salt
1 teaspoon freshly ground pepper
½ pound Monterey Jack cheese, freshly grated (about 2 cups)
Fresh coriander (cilantro) leaves, for garnish

1. In a large skillet, heat the olive oil over moderately high heat. Add the onions and cook, stirring, until slightly softened, about 5 minutes. Add the garlic, chili powder and cumin; cook, stirring frequently, until the onions are soft and beginning to brown, about 10 minutes longer. Add the hominy and cook, stirring, until heated through, about 5 minutes. Season with the salt and pepper. *(The recipe can be prepared to this point up to 1 day ahead. Cool, then cover and refrigerate. Reheat before proceeding.)*

Salad of Flageolet Beans with Fennel and Walnuts (p. 158).

2. To serve, fold the cheese into the warm hominy. Transfer to a serving dish, garnish with the coriander and serve warm.

—*Susan Costner*

• • •

MEXICAN POLENTA PIE

Cooked, shredded chicken or leftover beans are good alternatives to black beans in this recipe.

4 Servings

2 tablespoons safflower oil
1 small onion, coarsely chopped
8 ounces mushrooms, thinly sliced
1 teaspoon cumin seeds
1 teaspoon chili powder
¼ teaspoon crushed red pepper
1 can (28 ounces) Italian plum tomatoes, drained
1 can (4 ounces) chopped mild green chiles, drained
1 can (16 ounces) black beans, rinsed and drained
¾ teaspoon salt
⅔ cup instant polenta*
½ cup (packed) grated sharp Cheddar cheese (about 2½ ounces)
*Available at specialty food stores

1. Preheat the oven to 400°. In a large nonreactive skillet, heat the oil over moderately high heat. Add the onion and cook, stirring occasionally, until slightly softened, about 3 minutes. Add the mushrooms, cumin seeds, chili powder and crushed red pepper. Cook, stirring occasionally, until the mushrooms soften and release their juices, about 3 minutes.

2. Add the tomatoes to the skillet and crush them. Stir in the green chiles and black beans. Reduce the heat to moderate and simmer for at least 10 minutes. Stir in ¼ teaspoon of the salt.

3. Meanwhile, in a 10-inch cast-iron skillet, combine 2 cups of water and the remaining ½ teaspoon salt. Bring to a boil over high heat and stir in the polenta. Reduce the heat to moderately high and cook, stirring, until the polenta holds its shape, about 5 minutes. Remove from the heat and spread the polenta evenly in the skillet. Set aside for 5 minutes.

4. Spread the black-bean chili evenly over the polenta. Sprinkle the cheese on top. Bake for 12 to 15 minutes, until the chili is bubbling and the cheese is melted. Let stand for 15 minutes before serving.

—*Susan Shapiro Jaslove*

• • •

MELTED CUCUMBERS WITH CREAM

The cucumbers for this side dish are briefly cooked to intensify their mild flavor, with just a bit of heavy cream and butter added to offset their slight bitterness.

4 Servings

2 European cucumbers (about 1¾ pounds total), unpeeled
3 tablespoons unsalted butter
½ teaspoon salt
¼ teaspoon freshly ground pepper
⅓ cup heavy cream

1. Using a large knife, halve the unpeeled cucumbers lengthwise. Cut each

VEGETABLES

half crosswise into ¼-inch-thick slices and set aside.

2. In a large skillet, melt the butter over moderate heat. Add the cucumbers, salt and pepper, cover and cook, stirring occasionally, until the cucumbers are tender, about 10 minutes. Stir in the cream and cook until slightly reduced and thickened, about 2 minutes.

—*Stephanie Lyness*

• • •

EGGPLANT AND MUSHROOMS WITH BALSAMIC GLAZE

❦ The sweet and sour elements in this dish would be united by a young Cabernet Sauvignon, such as 1986 Beringer Knights Valley, 1987 Silverado Vineyards or a vigorous one from the Médoc, like 1985 Château Léoville Barton.

---

4 First-Course Servings

2½ tablespoons extra-virgin olive oil
4 small Japanese eggplants (about
  1½ pounds total), halved
  lengthwise
3½ tablespoons balsamic vinegar
Salt and freshly ground pepper
½ pound fresh shiitake mushrooms,
  stems discarded, caps quartered
1 tablespoon coarsely chopped flat-
  leaf parsley

1. In a large nonreactive skillet, heat 1 tablespoon of the oil over moderate heat until almost smoking. Reduce the heat to low. Add half of the eggplants, cut-sides down, cover and cook until browned and soft, about 4 minutes. Sprinkle in 1 tablespoon of the balsamic vinegar and boil to glaze the eggplants and evaporate the vinegar, about 10 sec-

onds. Using a spatula, transfer the eggplant halves to a large serving platter, cut-sides up, and set aside. Repeat with another tablespoon of oil, the remaining eggplants and another tablespoon of vinegar. Season the eggplants with salt and pepper to taste.

2. Add the remaining ½ tablespoon olive oil to the skillet and when hot, add the mushrooms in an even layer. Cover and cook until wilted and browned, about 3 minutes. Uncover, sprinkle in the remaining 1½ tablespoons balsamic vinegar and cook to reduce slightly, about 10 seconds. There should be some liquid remaining. Season the mushrooms with salt and pepper to taste and pour the mushrooms over the eggplants, sprinkle the parsley on top and serve.

—*Marcia Kiesel*

• • •

GREEN BEANS WITH COCONUT AND POPPED RICE

Browned, semi-popped rice is used here as a seasoning for the beans. As the rice cooks, it becomes an exotic spice with a deep-roasted taste. The other main flavoring here is coconut. This dish comes from South India, where vegetables are frequently parboiled before being stir-fried with seasonings.

---

6 Servings

¼ cup dried unsweetened shredded
  coconut or 6 tablespoons freshly
  grated
⅓ cup boiling water
2 tablespoons coarse (kosher) salt
1½ pounds green beans, trimmed
  and cut into 1-inch lengths

¼ cup vegetable oil
½ teaspoon cumin seeds
1 teaspoon black mustard seeds
1 tablespoon long-grain rice,
  preferably basmati
3 dried red chiles
¼ teaspoon cayenne pepper
1 teaspoon sugar
1 teaspoon table salt
2 tablespoons chopped fresh
  coriander (cilantro)

1. If using dried coconut, place it in a small bowl, cover with the ⅓ cup boiling water and set aside for at least 15 minutes. Drain well.

2. In a large pot, bring 5 quarts of water to a rolling boil. Add the coarse salt and the beans and boil rapidly until the beans are just cooked slightly but still crisp, 2 to 3 minutes. Drain the beans and rinse under cold water; drain again.

3. In a large skillet, heat the oil over moderately high heat. Add the cumin and mustard seeds. When the mustard seeds start to pop, stir in the rice. When the rice browns (some grains might pop), after about 1 minute, stir in the dried chiles. Add the green beans, cayenne, sugar and table salt; reduce the heat to moderate and stir-fry for 3 minutes. Stir in the fresh or drained coconut and fresh coriander, cover and reduce the heat to low. Cook for 1 minute. Transfer the beans to a bowl and serve hot.

—*Madhur Jaffrey*

• • •

GREEN BEANS WITH WALNUTS AND LEMON

This simple recipe makes green beans, such as Kentucky Wonders or Blue Lakes, come alive. Though they remain a lovely bright green, the beans are cooked enough to remove the raw, grassy taste they sometimes have, leaving them tender and full of flavor. Use the same dressing with other green vegetables, such as broccoli or small leeks.

Serve the beans immediately after they're dressed so that the acid of the lemon juice won't make their bright green color fade.

4 Servings

⅓ *cup walnut halves (⅔ ounce)*
1 pound green beans, cut on the
    diagonal into 2-inch pieces
3 tablespoons unsalted butter
1 tablespoon fresh lemon juice
1 teaspoon finely grated lemon zest
Salt and freshly ground pepper

1. Preheat the oven to 450°. Toast the walnuts on a baking sheet until golden, about 3 minutes. Chop coarsely.

2. In a steamer, bring 2 inches of water to a boil. Steam the beans until tender but still bright green, about 8 minutes. Drain well. Transfer the beans to a medium bowl and add the butter, lemon juice and lemon zest. Toss until the butter melts. Season to taste with salt and generous amounts of pepper and toss again.

3. Transfer the beans to a serving dish, sprinkle the walnuts on top and serve.

—*Susan Hermann Loomis*

• • •

HARICOTS VERTS WITH PERSILLADE

For hearty appetites, consider increasing the amount of beans.

8 Servings

1 pound haricots verts
Salt
1 teaspoon minced garlic
1 tablespoon minced parsley
1 tablespoon olive oil
Freshly ground pepper

1. Bring a large saucepan of water to a boil over high heat. Add the beans and when the water returns to a boil, add 1 teaspoon salt. Boil the beans for 1 minute and taste. If they are too crunchy, boil for 1 to 2 minutes longer. Drain the beans quickly and rinse under cold running water to stop the cooking. Drain well. (*The beans can be prepared to this point up to 1 day ahead.*)

2. In a small bowl, toss the garlic with the parsley. In a large nonstick skillet, heat the olive oil over moderately high heat. Add the beans and ¼ teaspoon salt and cook for 1 minute. Add the garlic and parsley and cook, tossing until heated through, about 1 minute longer. Season with salt and pepper to taste.

—*Lydie Marshall*

• • •

RICHLY GLAZED PEARL ONIONS

6 Servings

⅔ *cup boiling water*
⅓ *cup dried porcini (or cèpes)*
    mushrooms (about 1 ounce)
3 tablespoons unsalted butter
2 pints pearl onions, peeled
1 cinnamon stick, broken
1 cup dry red wine
1 cup chicken or beef stock or
    canned broth
½ *cup chopped canned Italian plum*
    tomatoes with some of their liquid
Salt and freshly ground pepper
Pinch of sugar (optional)

1. In a heatproof bowl, combine the boiling water and mushrooms. Set aside to soak until softened, about 20 minutes. Rinse the mushrooms in the soaking liquid and squeeze dry. Cut off any tough bits of stem. Coarsely chop the mushrooms and set aside. Set the soaking liquid aside to allow the grit to settle.

2. In a large nonreactive skillet, melt the butter over moderate heat until hot, about 2 minutes. Add the onions in an even layer. Add the cinnamon stick and cook, without stirring, until the onions are browned on one side.

3. Using tongs, turn each onion over and cook until dark brown on the other side, another 4 minutes. Pour in the red wine and boil for 2 minutes, then pour in the stock. Bring to a boil, cover and cook until the onions are tender and the liquid has reduced and thickened, about 20 minutes.

4. Uncover and stir in the reserved mushrooms and the tomatoes with their liquid. Pour in the porcini soaking liquid, stopping when you reach the grit on the bottom. Return to a boil, cover and simmer until the sauce is dark and syrupy, about 4 minutes. Season with the salt, pepper and sugar if desired. (*The onions can be prepared up to 2 days ahead; cover and refrigerate. Reheat in a saucepan over moderately low heat, adding a little water if the sauce is too thick.*)

—*Marcia Kiesel*

• • •

TEMPURA ONION RINGS

4 to 6 Servings

4 cups vegetable oil, for frying
1½ cups cornstarch
3 large red onions (about 1¼
    pounds), peeled and sliced
    crosswise ⅓ inch thick
1½ cups all-purpose flour
1 teaspoon salt, plus more for
    sprinkling
1½ cups coarsely crushed ice
Lemon wedges, ketchup or soy sauce,
    for serving

1. In a deep fryer or large saucepan, heat the oil to 350°. Meanwhile, put 1 cup of the cornstarch in a brown paper bag. Add the onion slices and shake well to coat. Transfer the coated onion rings to a large baking sheet.

2. In a large bowl, mix the remaining ½ cup cornstarch with the flour and 1 teaspoon salt. Add 1½ cups of cold water to the ice and dump the ice water all at once into the flour mixture. Stir vigorously with chopsticks or a fork to make a slightly thick but lumpy batter. Do not overmix. There will be pieces of ice and lumps the size of a nickel in the batter.

3. When the oil is hot, add as many coated onion rings to the batter as will fit comfortably in the fryer. (You will have to do this in about 5 batches.) Using chopsticks or a large fork, lift the rings out of the batter; make sure that there aren't any pieces of ice clinging to the onions. Add the rings to the hot oil and separate any that cling together. Fry the onion rings until golden brown all over, about 3 minutes. Transfer to paper towels or a paper bag to drain well. Repeat with the remaining onion rings and batter. Sprinkle the onion rings with salt if desired. Serve hot, warm or at room temperature with lemon, ketchup or soy sauce on the side.

—*Marcia Kiesel*

• • •

BUTTERED OKRA

In this simple preparation, suggested by Anne Friar Thomas, from Cuero, Texas, the gentle cooking brings out the flavor and incomparable texture of the okra. When buying okra, look for small—three- to four-inch-long—buds that are evenly green. Trim the stem ends, but don't cut into the body of the okra bud itself. The tiny amount of vinegar in this recipe was suggested to keep the okra from developing its characteristic slippery texture, but there's little likelihood of slipperiness as long as you don't cut into the bud. Regardless, use the vinegar because it adds a subtle tang. Serve this with just about any roast meat or fish.

4 to 6 Servings

1 pound okra
½ teaspoon apple cider vinegar

2 tablespoons unsalted butter
½ teaspoon salt
½ teaspoon freshly ground pepper

1. In a medium nonreactive saucepan, combine the okra, vinegar and ½ cup of water. Cover and bring to a boil over moderately high heat. Reduce the heat to moderate. Add the butter, salt and pepper, cover partially and cook, stirring occasionally, until the okra changes from bright to olive green and is tender, about 8 minutes.

2. Season with salt and pepper to taste. Transfer to a platter, and pour any cooking juices on top. Serve hot.

MICROWAVE OVEN VARIATION: Place the okra, water and cider vinegar in a microwave-proof bowl. Cover tightly, and cook on High, or full, power for 6 minutes, until the okra has softened. Remove from the oven and let stand, covered, until the okra is crisp-tender, about 3 minutes. Season with the butter, salt and pepper and serve immediately.

—*Susan Hermann Loomis*

• • •

ROASTED RED POTATOES

Some people like these potatoes cooked longer—until the skins are crisper and the pulp is drier. It is best to serve these as soon as they come out of the oven.

6 Servings

2 pounds small red potatoes, halved
3 tablespoons olive oil
½ teaspoon salt
½ teaspoon freshly ground pepper
½ teaspoon sweet paprika

Preheat the oven to 425°. In a small roasting pan, toss the potatoes with the oil and arrange them in the pan, cut-sides down. Sprinkle the salt, pepper and paprika on top and bake for 25 minutes, until the potatoes are tender inside and the undersides are crusty brown. Serve immediately.

—Lee Bailey

• • •

GRILLED RED POTATOES

4 Servings

**6 medium red potatoes (about 1½
  pounds), halved lengthwise
1 to 2 tablespoons olive oil
Salt and freshly ground pepper**

1. In a saucepan, combine the potatoes and enough cold salted water to cover. Bring to a boil over high heat. Reduce the heat to moderate and simmer until tender, 20 to 25 minutes. Drain; do not rinse.

2. Prepare the grill or preheat the broiler. Drizzle the potatoes with the oil and season with salt and pepper to taste. Place cut-sides down on the grill or cut sides up on a broiler pan, if using. Cook undisturbed for about 5 minutes, until crusty and browned.

—Stephanie Lyness

• • •

POTATO AND WILD MUSHROOM GRATIN

6 Servings

**¼ pound pancetta or lean bacon,
  sliced ⅛ inch thick and cut into
  matchsticks
1 pound fresh wild mushrooms, such
  as chanterelles, morels and
  shiitakes
4 tablespoons unsalted butter
2 medium leeks, white and tender
  green, finely chopped
¾ teaspoon salt
¾ teaspoon freshly ground pepper
2 pounds red bliss or other waxy
  potatoes
1 cup heavy cream
1 cup milk
¼ teaspoon thyme
2 tablespoons freshly grated
  Parmesan cheese**

1. In a large heavy skillet, cook the pancetta over moderate heat, stirring occasionally, until browned, about 10 minutes. Using a slotted spoon, transfer to paper towels to drain. Wipe out the pan.

2. Clean the mushrooms. Remove and discard any tough stems. Slice the mushrooms ¼ inch thick. Melt 2 tablespoons of the butter in the skillet and add the mushrooms. Cook over moderate heat, stirring, until softened and beginning to brown, about 15 minutes. Scrape the mushrooms into a medium bowl and add the pancetta.

3. Add the remaining 2 tablespoons butter to the skillet and melt over moderately low heat. Add the leeks and cook, stirring frequently, until thoroughly softened, about 10 minutes. Add the leeks to the mushrooms and pancetta. Stir in ¼ teaspoon each of the salt and pepper.

4. Preheat the oven to 350°. Peel the potatoes and slice them as thin as possible. Lightly butter a 2½- to 3-quart shallow gratin dish and evenly layer half of the potatoes in the bottom. Sprinkle with ¼ teaspoon each of the salt and pepper and spread the mushroom mixture on top. Cover with the remaining potatoes.

5. In a bowl, combine the cream and milk and pour over the potatoes. Sprinkle with the thyme, the remaining ¼ teaspoon each of salt and pepper and the Parmesan cheese. Cover loosely with foil and bake on the upper rack of the oven for 45 minutes. Uncover and bake for about 15 minutes longer, until the gratin is bubbling, the potatoes are very tender and the top is brown. Serve hot.

—Nancy Harmon Jenkins

• • •

POTATO AND JERUSALEM ARTICHOKE GRATIN

Rich with the nutty flavor of Jerusalem artichokes, this is no ordinary potato gratin. The French tired of Jerusalem artichokes during World War II, but they are now back in fashion. This recipe is from Claude Udron (chef at Pile ou Face in Paris), who makes it with Jerusalem artichokes from his garden in Normandy.

6 to 8 Servings

**2 medium baking potatoes, peeled
  and sliced ⅛ inch thick
6 medium Jerusalem artichokes
1 tablespoon fresh lemon juice**

177

VEGETABLES

2¼ cups heavy cream
1¼ teaspoons salt
½ teaspoon freshly ground white
   pepper
⅛ teaspoon freshly grated nutmeg

1. Preheat the oven to 375°. Rinse the potato slices in a colander to rid them of starch. Pat thoroughly dry, cover and set aside.

2. Peel the Jerusalem artichokes and drop them into a medium bowl of cold water mixed with the lemon juice. Slice them ⅛ inch thick and rinse in a colander under cold running water. Pat thoroughly dry.

3. Place a layer of the potatoes in a 9-by-13-by-2-inch baking dish and cover with a layer of Jerusalem artichokes; repeat with the remaining potatoes and Jerusalem artichokes. In a small bowl, combine the cream, salt, pepper and nutmeg; pour over the vegetables. Bake the gratin in the middle of the oven for about 1 hour, until the potatoes and Jerusalem artichokes are tender and the top is golden brown. Serve hot.

—Patricia Wells

• • •

SCALLOPED POTATOES WITH BACON AND CHEESE

On a farm in Pennsylvania, Barbara Fischer cooks three meals a day for her family of nine. She serves this variation of scalloped potatoes in winter, and sometimes she makes it into a main course, adding beef, ham, corn or peas. In this version, the flavor of the potatoes is heightened by bacon and celery seed.

Get top-quality potatoes. Baking potatoes give a fluffy result, but try Urgenta or Maine potatoes, which fall somewhere between a fluffy and waxy potato. Depending on their age and quality, the potatoes may not always absorb all the milk and cream. You may want to add only the milk at first. Check the potatoes halfway through cooking. If they have absorbed all the milk, then add the cream and continue baking.

---

6 to 8 Servings

---

1 garlic clove, halved lengthwise
8 large baking potatoes (about 4
   pounds total), peeled and halved
   crosswise
6 ounces thick-sliced bacon, cut
   crosswise into ¼-inch strips
¾ teaspoon salt
¾ teaspoon freshly ground pepper
2 cups milk
½ cup heavy cream
Heaping ¼ teaspoon celery seeds
2 ounces Gruyère cheese, shredded
   (about ½ cup, packed)
2 ounces sharp Cheddar cheese,
   shredded (about ½ cup, packed)

1. Preheat the oven to 350°. Rub the garlic clove over the inside of a 12-by-8-inch or 13-by-9-inch nonreactive baking dish.

2. In a large steamer, steam the potatoes over high heat until nearly cooked through but still slightly firm in the center, about 15 minutes. Remove from the heat and set aside to cool.

3. In a heavy medium skillet, fry the bacon over moderately high heat until lightly golden but not crisp, about 5 minutes. Using a slotted spoon, transfer the bacon to paper towels; reserve the bacon fat.

4. Grate half the potatoes into the prepared baking dish using the large holes of a box grater. Season with half of the salt and pepper and sprinkle half of the bacon and 2 teaspoons of the bacon fat on top. Repeat with the remaining potatoes, salt, pepper, bacon and 2 more teaspoons of the bacon fat.

5. Combine the milk and cream and pour evenly over the potatoes. Sprinkle the celery seeds and then the cheeses on top. Cover with aluminum foil and bake in the middle of the oven for 25 minutes. Remove the foil and bake for 20 minutes longer, until the cheese has melted and the potatoes are golden at the edges. Set aside to cool for 5 minutes before serving.

—Susan Hermann Loomis

• • •

CRISP POTATO-SCALLION ROAST

---

6 Servings

---

6 large baking potatoes (about 3
   pounds), peeled and cut into
   1-inch cubes
3 tablespoons unsalted butter
3 tablespoons vegetable oil
3 medium scallions, white and green
   parts coarsely chopped separately
¾ teaspoon salt
½ teaspoon freshly ground pepper

1. Bring a large saucepan of lightly salted water to a boil over high heat. Add the potatoes, return to a boil and boil for 5 minutes. Drain the potatoes in a colander and rinse under cold running water; drain well. (*The potatoes can be parboiled up to 4 hours ahead and refrigerated, covered.*) Pat the potatoes as dry as possible with paper towels.

2. Preheat the oven to 375°. In a 10-by-15-inch jelly-roll pan, combine the butter and the oil and place in the upper third of the oven until just melted, about 3 minutes. Add the potatoes, white part of the scallion, salt and pepper and toss to coat.

3. Bake the potatoes on a rack in the top third of the oven for 1 hour. Stir the potatoes well and bake them for 40 minutes longer, or until golden brown and crisp. Transfer to a bowl, sprinkle with the chopped scallion greens and serve hot.

—*Rick Rodgers*

• • •

SAUTEED POTATOES WITH THYME

4 Servings

4 medium boiling potatoes (1 to 1¼ pounds)
1 tablespoon unsalted butter
1 tablespoon olive oil
1 teaspoon chopped fresh thyme, plus some sprigs for garnish
Salt and freshly ground pepper

1. In a large pot of boiling salted water, cook the potatoes until just tender, about 20 minutes. Drain well and cut into ½-inch chunks.

2. In a medium skillet, melt the butter in the oil over moderately high heat. Add the potatoes and sauté, shaking the pan occasionally, for 4 minutes. Add the chopped thyme and season with salt and pepper to taste. Sauté until the potatoes are lightly browned, about 3 minutes. Garnish with thyme sprigs and serve.

—*Stephanie Lyness*

• • •

POTATO-TURNIP CAKE

For crisp vegetable cakes, the food writer Paula Wolfert suggests that you occasionally wipe dry the underside of the pan lid during cooking.

4 Servings

2 medium white turnips, peeled
2 large baking potatoes, peeled
1 teaspoon salt
¼ teaspoon freshly ground pepper
3 tablespoons vegetable oil

1. In a food processor, coarsely grate the turnips; transfer to a bowl. Then coarsely grate the potatoes and transfer them to a bowl of cold water. Let soak for about 1 minute.

2. Drain the potatoes and dry thoroughly with paper towels. Add the potatoes to the turnips. Season with the salt and pepper and toss well to combine.

3. In a medium nonstick skillet or cast-iron pan, heat 2 tablespoons of the oil over moderately high heat. Add the potato-turnip mixture to the pan and press to pack evenly. Cover and cook, occasionally shaking the pan so that the cake doesn't stick, until the bottom is golden brown, about 20 minutes.

4. Invert a plate on top of the cake and flip the pan over to turn the cake out. Add the remaining tablespoon of oil to the skillet and slide the cake back in, browned-side up. Continue to cook, uncovered, until the bottom is golden, about 20 minutes. Invert a serving plate over the pan, then flip the pan over to release the cake. Cut into quarters and serve immediately.

—*Stephanie Lyness*

• • •

POTATO LATKES

Serve the *latkes* hot from the pan or, if serving them all at once, keep warm in a 200° oven on a rack set over a baking sheet.

Makes About 45 Latkes

6 large baking potatoes (3½ pounds), peeled and cut into small chunks
2 medium onions, cut into small chunks
5 eggs
2 teaspoons fresh lemon juice
About ¾ cup all-purpose flour
1 tablespoon salt
½ teaspoon freshly ground pepper
About 1 cup vegetable oil, for frying
Cinnamon Applesauce (p. 241)
Sour cream, for serving

1. In a food processor fitted with a shredding disk, shred the potatoes and onions. Transfer to a large strainer and squeeze out the excess moisture.

2. In a large bowl, beat the eggs. Stir in the lemon juice and the squeezed onions and potatoes. Gradually stir in enough of the flour to make a thin batter. Season with the salt and pepper. (*The recipe can be prepared to this point up to 30 minutes ahead. Refrigerate the batter with a piece of plastic wrap pressed directly on top.*)

3. Pour enough vegetable oil into a large heavy skillet to reach ¼ inch up the sides of the pan. Heat over moderately high heat until the oil begins to shimmer and a small spoonful of batter sizzles when added, about 5 minutes.

4. Stir the batter. To form each *latke,* drop a heaping tablespoon of the batter into the hot oil and flatten it slightly with the back of a spoon. Form several more *latkes* in the pan without overcrowding. Fry until golden brown on one side, about 3 minutes. Flip the *latkes* and fry on the other side until golden brown, about 2 minutes longer. Transfer to paper towels to drain. Stir the remaining batter well before making the next batch of *latkes*. Serve them hot or warm with Cinnamon Applesauce and sour cream on the side.

—*Susan Shapiro Jaslove*

• • •

FRENCH FRIES

2 Servings

4 cups vegetable oil, for frying
2 large Idaho potatoes (4 to 5 inches long), unpeeled
Coarse (kosher) salt

1. In a deep fryer or a large heavy saucepan, heat the oil over moderately high heat to 350°, about 15 minutes.

2. Meanwhile, slice the potatoes lengthwise ½ inch thick. Cut the slices into ½-inch sticks. Place the potatoes in a bowl and cover with cold water.

3. When the oil is hot, spread half of the potatoes out on a kitchen towel. Pat dry. Fry the potatoes in a fryer basket until slightly golden, about 8 minutes. Remove and drain on paper towels. Repeat with the remaining potatoes. (*The recipe can be prepared to this point up to 6 hours ahead.*)

4. Heat the oil to 385°. Add half of the potatoes to the hot oil and fry until crisp and well browned, 11 to 13 minutes. Drain on paper towels. Repeat with the remaining potatoes. Sprinkle with coarse salt and serve immediately.

—*Mark Peel, Campanile, Los Angeles*

• • •

POTATO CRISPS

When we made these fried potatoes, some preferred the crisp, thick-chip version, while others liked the chewy ones better. If you like yours chewy too, see the adjustments at the end of the recipe. The method for both types of crisps is the same; only the temperature of the oil and the cooking times vary.

4 to 6 Servings

1½ pounds Idaho potatoes, unpeeled
4 cups corn oil, for frying
Salt and freshly ground pepper
Malt vinegar, for serving

1. Using a sharp knife or a mandoline, slice the potatoes into ⅛-inch-thick rounds. Place in a large bowl of ice water and let soak for at least 45 minutes, adding more ice as necessary.

2. In a large skillet, heat the oil to 375° over high heat. Meanwhile, lay a clean kitchen towel on a work surface. Remove half of the potatoes from the ice bath and spread them out on a kitchen towel in a single layer. Cover with a second towel and pat thoroughly dry.

3. When the oil is hot, carefully add the drained potatoes and spread them out with tongs. Fry, turning occasionally, until well browned and crisp, about

10 minutes. As the potatoes are done, transfer them to paper towels to drain. Blot well. Repeat with the remaining potatoes. (*The potatoes can be fried up to 2 days ahead and stored in an airtight container.*) Serve the crisps warm or at room temperature, sprinkled with salt, pepper and malt vinegar.

CHEWY POTATO CRISPS:
Heat the oil to 350°. Fry each batch of potatoes, turning, until evenly browned, 12 to 15 minutes. Drain well, sprinkle with salt and pepper and serve hot.

—*Tracey Seaman*

• • •

GARLIC MASHED POTATOES

6 Servings

1 large head of garlic
1 teaspoon olive oil
2 pounds baking potatoes, peeled and cut into 1-inch chunks
1½ teaspoons salt
3 tablespoons unsalted butter
¼ cup low-fat (2%) milk
1 cup low-fat cottage cheese, at room temperature
Pinch of freshly grated nutmeg
¼ to ½ teaspoon freshly ground pepper, to taste

1. Preheat the oven to 350°. With a sharp knife, cut off the top third of the head of garlic. Place the garlic, cut-side up, on a 6-inch square of aluminum foil. Drizzle the olive oil over the top and wrap snugly in the foil. Bake for 1 hour. Remove and set aside to cool slightly.

2. In a large saucepan, combine the potatoes with 1 teaspoon of the salt. Add water to cover and bring to a boil over high heat. Reduce the heat to moderately high and boil until fork-tender, 12 to 15 minutes. Drain and return to the pan. Place the pan over high heat for about 30 seconds, shaking it once or twice to dry out the potatoes. Transfer the potatoes to a large bowl and add the butter.

3. In a medium saucepan, warm the milk over moderate heat, 1 to 2 minutes. Squeeze the soft garlic pulp into the milk and add the remaining ½ teaspoon salt. Pour this mixture over the potatoes and mash with a hand-held masher.

4. Add the cottage cheese, nutmeg and pepper and continue mashing until well blended and smooth. Serve hot. *(The potatoes can be kept warm in a 300° oven for up to 1 hour.)*

—Lee Bailey

• • •

FOIE GRAS WHIPPED POTATOES

Executive Chef Brian Whitmer offers this incredibly simple but ethereal first course as a special.

4 Servings

3 large baking potatoes (1½ pounds), peeled and cut into 1-inch chunks
2 teaspoons salt
1 stick (4 ounces) plus 1 tablespoon unsalted butter, softened
¼ cup warm milk
1 teaspoon freshly ground pepper
5 nappa cabbage leaves, finely chopped
2 medium scallions, thinly sliced
4 ounces chilled fresh foie gras, cut into ½-inch dice (see Note, p. 103)

1. Place the potatoes in a medium saucepan with water to cover and 1 teaspoon of the salt. Bring to a boil over moderately high heat and cook until the potatoes are tender, about 15 minutes; drain well. Puree the potatoes in a food mill set over a medium bowl or mash until very smooth with a potato masher.

2. Using a wooden spoon, beat the stick of butter, warm milk, pepper and the remaining 1 teaspoon salt into the potatoes until thoroughly incorporated.

3. In a medium skillet, melt the remaining 1 tablespoon butter over moderately high heat. Add the cabbage and cook, stirring, until slightly softened but still green, about 1 minute. Stir the cabbage and the scallions into the potatoes and set aside in a warm place.

4. Place a large cast-iron skillet over high heat until hot, about 5 minutes. Add the diced foie gras and cook, turning once or twice, until well browned, 1 to 1½ minutes. Using a slotted spoon, transfer the foie gras to paper towels to drain. Gently fold into the potatoes and serve.

—Brian Whitmer, Highlands Inn, Carmel, California

• • •

BASIL MASHED POTATOES

6 Servings

8 medium baking potatoes, unpeeled
2 teaspoons salt
2 cups (packed) basil leaves
½ cup freshly grated hard sheep's milk cheese, Parmesan or aged Gouda cheese (about 2 ounces)
3 tablespoons extra-virgin olive oil
¼ teaspoon freshly ground pepper
1½ to 2 cups milk, heated

1. Place the potatoes in a large heavy saucepan. Add 1 teaspoon of the salt and enough cold water to cover and bring to a boil over moderately high heat. Reduce the heat to moderate and simmer until tender, 35 to 40 minutes.

2. Meanwhile, in a food processor or blender, combine the basil, cheese, 2 tablespoons of the olive oil and ⅛ teaspoon of the pepper and puree, scraping as necessary.

3. Drain the potatoes and peel them while they are still warm. Pass them through a ricer or a food mill. Return the potatoes to the saucepan and add the remaining ⅛ teaspoon pepper. Using a wooden spoon, stir in 1½ cups milk, then add up to ½ cup more milk until the potatoes are as soft as you like them. Season with the remaining 1 teaspoon salt and stir over low heat until hot, about 5 minutes. Stir in the reserved basil puree. Transfer the potatoes to a dish and drizzle the remaining 1 tablespoon oil on top.

—Mireille Johnston

• • •

181

VEGETABLES

MASHED POTATOES WITH ROMANO CHEESE

4 Servings

3 large baking potatoes (1½ pounds), peeled and cut into ¾-inch chunks
¾ cup milk
2 tablespoons unsalted butter
1 teaspoon salt
¼ teaspoon freshly ground black pepper
⅛ teaspoon cayenne pepper
¼ cup freshly grated Romano cheese
Pinch of paprika (optional)

1. In a large pot of boiling salted water, cook the potatoes, partially covered, until tender, 15 to 18 minutes. Drain the potatoes and return them to the pot.

2. Reduce the heat to moderate and cook for a few seconds to dry out the potatoes. Add the milk and butter and bring to a boil. Remove from the heat and add the salt, black pepper and cayenne.

3. Mash with a potato masher. Stir in the cheese until just incorporated. Mound the potatoes in a large serving bowl and dust with a pinch of paprika if desired. Serve hot.

—*Jim Fobel*

• • •

RUTABAGA AND POTATO PUREE

6 Servings

6 slices of bacon
1 large rutabaga (2 pounds), peeled and cut into ½-inch chunks
2 large baking potatoes (1 pound), peeled and cut into 1-inch chunks
1 teaspoon salt
1 tablespoon unsalted butter
1 teaspoon sugar
½ teaspoon freshly ground pepper

1. In a heavy medium saucepan, fry the bacon over moderately high heat until it begins to brown and the fat is rendered, about 6 minutes. Add the rutabaga and 4 cups of water and bring to a boil over moderately high heat. Cook until very tender, about 40 minutes. Drain the rutabaga and discard the bacon.

2. Twenty minutes before the rutabaga is done, in a medium saucepan, combine the potato chunks, ½ teaspoon of the salt and enough water to cover. Bring to a boil over high heat. Reduce the heat to moderately high and cook until tender, about 15 minutes. Drain well.

3. Place the rutabaga in a food mill fitted with a medium disk and puree into a medium bowl. Puree the potatoes through the food mill into the same bowl. Stir to combine. Alternatively, use a potato masher to thoroughly mash the rutabaga and potatoes.

4. Beat in the butter, sugar, pepper and the remaining ½ teaspoon salt. Serve warm. (*The puree can be transferred to a heatproof serving dish and kept in a low oven for up to 30 minutes.*)

—*Jessica B. Harris*

• • •

GLAZED ROASTED SHALLOTS AND GARLIC

Be sure to buy large firm shallots and heads of garlic; avoid any that are sprouting. Roast the shallots and garlic with a sprinkling of sugar to release their nutty sweetness. When tender and caramelized, quickly sauté with butter to add the final glaze.

10 to 12 Servings

3¾ pounds large shallots, peeled
2 large heads of garlic (about 32 cloves), separated into cloves and peeled
¾ cup chicken stock or canned low-sodium broth
2 tablespoons fresh lemon juice
2 tablespoons sugar
1 teaspoon salt
½ teaspoon freshly ground pepper
3 tablespoons unsalted butter

1. Preheat the oven to 375°. Place the shallots and garlic in a single layer in a shallow baking pan. In a small non-reactive saucepan, combine the chicken stock and lemon juice and bring to a boil over high heat. Pour the hot stock over the shallots and garlic and sprinkle with the sugar, salt and pepper. Cover with aluminum foil and bake for 45 minutes.

2. Remove the foil, stir gently and bake uncovered for 20 to 30 minutes, until the shallots are very tender.

3. In a large nonstick skillet, melt 1½ tablespoons of the butter over moderate heat. Add half of the shallots and garlic and some of their cooking liquid. Increase the heat to moderately high and cook, shaking the pan frequently until the shallots and garlic are golden brown and caramelized all over, 5 to 7 minutes. Transfer to an ovenproof serving dish. Rinse out the skillet and repeat with the remaining butter, shallots, garlic and cooking liquid. Serve hot. *(The recipe can be prepared up to 1 day ahead. Let cool, cover and refrigerate. Let return to room temperature before baking in a 375° oven for about 10 minutes, until heated through. Serve warm.)*

—*Sheila Lukins*

• • •

SPINACH AND CHEESE CASSEROLE

This recipe has been handed down in my cousin Karen Shabetai's family for generations. It is a simple vegetarian preparation that resembles a Middle Eastern crustless spinach pie. Many Sephardic Jews from Spain and Portugal migrated to the Middle East during the Inquisition and adopted the local style of cooking.

8 to 10 Servings

2 tablespoons olive oil
2 medium onions (about 1 pound), coarsely chopped
3 pounds fresh spinach—washed, stemmed and coarsely chopped
6 eggs
1 teaspoon salt
½ teaspoon freshly ground black pepper
¼ teaspoon freshly grated nutmeg
1¾ cups grated sharp Cheddar cheese (½ pound)
¼ teaspoon cayenne pepper

1. Preheat the oven to 400°. Lightly grease a large shallow casserole. In a large nonreactive saucepan, heat the oil over moderate heat. Add the onions and cook, stirring occasionally, until softened but not browned, about 5 minutes. Transfer to a large bowl. Add one-third of the spinach to the saucepan, cover and cook in its own steam over moderate heat until just wilted, about 1 minute. Transfer the spinach to the bowl with the onions and mix well. Repeat with the remaining two batches of spinach.

2. In a medium bowl, beat the eggs with the salt, black pepper and nutmeg. Add the egg mixture to the spinach and stir until thoroughly mixed. Transfer to the prepared casserole.

3. In a small bowl, toss the cheese with the cayenne and sprinkle evenly over the spinach. Bake the casserole for about 35 minutes, until the spinach has puffed and the cheese is very brown and crusty. Let sit for about 10 minutes before serving.

—*Susan Shapiro Jaslove*

• • •

PRESSURE-COOKER BUTTERNUT SQUASH AND PARSNIP PUREE

4 Servings

1 butternut squash (1½ pounds)
1 pound medium parsnips, peeled and sliced ½ inch thick
2 tablespoons unsalted butter, at room temperature
Salt
Freshly grated nutmeg

1. Halve the squash lengthwise and scoop out the seeds. Cut each half into quarters and peel the pieces. Slice the squash ½ inch thick.

2. Set a rack or a steamer basket in a 6-quart pressure cooker. Add 1 cup of water (or 2 cups if that is the minimum liquid required by the manufacturer) and bring to a boil over high heat. Place the squash and parsnips on the rack. Lock the lid in place and bring to high (15 pounds) pressure. Reduce the heat to maintain high pressure and cook for 4 minutes.

3. Quick-release the pressure according to the manufacturer's instructions, or set the pot under cold running water until all pressure is released. Remove the lid, tilting it away from you to allow any excess steam to escape.

4. Transfer the vegetables to a food processor. Add the butter and puree until just smooth. (Don't overprocess or the puree will become gummy.) Season with salt and nutmeg to taste and serve hot.

—*Lorna Sass*

• • •

VEGETABLES

SPICED BUTTERNUT SQUASH

Butternut squash is a winter vegetable that lends itself to a wide range of flavors and preparations while still retaining its integrity. This spices in this warming puree are reminiscent of the winter holiday season.

12 Servings

4 pounds butternut squash (4 medium)—halved, peeled, seeded and cut into 2-inch chunks
1 cup chicken stock or canned low-sodium broth
6 tablespoons unsalted butter, cut into small pieces
½ teaspoon ground ginger
¼ teaspoon mace
¼ teaspoon ground coriander
Pinch of cayenne pepper
½ teaspoon salt
¼ teaspoon freshly ground black pepper
1 to 2 tablespoons fresh lemon juice
3 tablespoons crème fraîche or sour cream

1. In a large heavy saucepan, combine the squash, chicken stock and 3 cups of water. Bring to a boil over high heat. Reduce the heat to moderately low, cover partially and simmer until the squash is tender, about 20 minutes. Drain, reserving ¼ cup of the cooking liquid.

2. In a large bowl, combine the squash, butter, ginger, mace, coriander, cayenne, salt, black pepper, 1 tablespoon of the lemon juice and the reserved squash cooking liquid.

3. Preheat the oven to 350°. In a food processor, puree the squash mix-

ture in 2 batches just until smooth; do not overprocess. Transfer the puree to an ovenproof 3-quart serving dish and fold in the crème fraîche. Season with additional lemon juice, and salt and pepper to taste. *(The recipe can be prepared to this point up to 2 days ahead. Let cool, then cover and refrigerate. Let return to room temperature before baking.)*

4. Cover the dish with foil and bake until heated through, about 25 minutes. If desired, uncover and broil about 5 inches from the heat for 1 minute, or until lightly browned. Serve hot.

—*Sheila Lukins*

• • •

SWEET POTATO SHAM

The recipe for this sweet side dish hails from Don Patterson in Texas. The cooking time for the potatoes depends on their age. At the beginning of the season—early fall—they will cook more quickly because they are still quite full of moisture. As the year progresses they lose moisture and take longer to cook.

If you have a source for good sweet potatoes, buy and store them in a cool place to have the year through.

8 to 10 Servings

6 sweet potatoes (about 12 ounces each)
1 tablespoon plus ¾ teaspoon salt
4 tablespoons unsalted butter, softened
½ cup granulated sugar
½ cup (packed) brown sugar
1 egg
½ cup milk
½ teaspoon freshly grated nutmeg
½ teaspoon cinnamon

1. Preheat the oven to 350°. Place the sweet potatoes in a large saucepan and add enough water to cover. Add 1 tablespoon of the salt. Bring to a boil over high heat and cook until the potatoes are soft, 30 to 50 minutes. Drain well.

2. When the potatoes are cool enough to handle, peel them and place in a large bowl. Using a potato masher or a fork, mash the potatoes until smooth.

3. In a medium bowl, mix the butter and the granulated and brown sugar. Whisk in the egg until blended, then add the milk and mix well. Add to the potatoes and mix thoroughly. Season with the nutmeg, cinnamon and the remaining ¾ teaspoon salt.

4. Transfer the mixture to a large baking dish and smooth the top. Bake for about 1 hour, or until lightly golden. *(The sham can be made up to 1 day ahead and refrigerated covered. Return to room temperature and reheat in a 350° oven.)*

—*Susan Hermann Loomis*

• • •

SLOW-BAKED TOMATOES

This long method of cooking improves the flavor of out-of-season tomatoes.

6 Servings

¼ cup plus 1 tablespoon olive oil
6 large tomatoes
1½ teaspoons sugar
¼ teaspoon salt
Freshly ground pepper
3 medium garlic cloves, minced
½ cup finely chopped parsley

1. Preheat the oven to 300°. Pour ¼ cup of the oil into a 9-by-13-inch nonreactive baking dish. Slice off the top quarter (stem end) of each tomato and discard. Arrange the tomatoes, cut-side down, in the pan and bake for 30 minutes. Turn with a spatula and cook, basting occasionally with the pan juices, for another 30 minutes.

2. Sprinkle the sugar, salt and plenty of pepper on top and bake until the tomatoes are soft and flattened, about 1½ hours longer.

3. Meanwhile, in a small skillet, cook the garlic in the remaining 1 tablespoon oil over moderately low heat until softened, about 4 minutes. Remove from the heat and stir in the parsley.

4. When the tomatoes are ready, spoon about 1 teaspoon of the garlic-parsley mixture over each one. Serve warm or at room temperature.

—Lee Bailey

• • •

WHITE LIMA BEANS WITH SORREL AND PARSLEY

This recipe is for a delicious side dish. The sorrel provides a tart bite that is just right with the creaminess of the beans. Big white limas, Great Northern and cannellini beans are all wonderful here, but the limas are especially good because they're so plump and moist and have a strong shape. Large limas require some special care in cooking because they can easily be overcooked. Before draining the soaked beans, run your hands through them and remove any skins that have loosened.

This side dish can be turned into a soup by simply adding two more cups of the reserved bean broth along with the beans in Step 4. Often there's a starchy residue at the bottom of the broth; if you're making soup, be sure to include it for body.

4 Side-Dish Servings

2 cups dried white lima beans (14 ounces), picked over
1½ teaspoons salt
1 tablespoon unsalted butter
½ medium red or yellow onion, finely chopped
1 cup chopped parsley
6 ounces fresh sorrel leaves, large stems removed, leaves finely chopped
¼ cup heavy cream, or more to taste
1 teaspoon freshly ground pepper

1. In a large saucepan, soak the beans in plenty of cold water for at least 6 hours or overnight. Pour off the water, re-cover the beans with fresh water and bring to a boil. Boil the beans vigorously for 5 minutes. Drain the beans in a colander and rinse well to remove any scum.

2. Return the beans to the saucepan. Add 4 cups of water and bring to a boil over high heat. Reduce the heat to moderately low and simmer the beans very gently until tender, about 1 hour. Keep an eye on them to make sure they don't overcook. Toward the end of the cooking time, add 1 teaspoon of the salt. Drain the beans in a colander set over a bowl. Reserve the broth.

3. In a large skillet, melt the butter over moderate heat. Add the onion and ¾ cup of the parsley and cook, stirring occasionally, until the onion is softened, about 3 minutes. Add the sorrel and cook, stirring, until wilted, about 2 minutes. Stir in 1 cup of the reserved bean broth. Bring to a simmer and cook until the onion is soft and most of the broth has evaporated, about 12 minutes.

4. Stir in the cream, pepper, the remaining ½ teaspoon salt and the beans. Cook gently, stirring, until the beans are heated through, about 2 minutes. Stir in the remaining ¼ cup parsley and season with salt to taste. Serve hot.

—Deborah Madison

• • •

SPICY BLACK-EYED PEAS

These black-eyed peas are seasoned three times, producing three quite different effects. First, cumin seeds are sautéed in oil with onion and garlic and left in the sauce to stew. Then cumin and mustard seeds are popped in hot oil and stirred into the peas. At the very end, a kind of salsa of raw seasonings is added. If you make this dish a day ahead, prepare the raw seasonings shortly before serving.

6 Servings

Peas:
¼ cup vegetable oil
1 teaspoon cumin seeds
1 medium onion, finely chopped
4 garlic cloves, finely chopped
5 plum tomatoes (fresh or drained canned), peeled and chopped
2 packages (10 ounces each) frozen black-eyed peas, partially thawed
1½ teaspoons salt
¼ teaspoon cayenne pepper
1 teaspoon ground coriander

Raw seasonings:
1 tablespoon fresh lemon juice
1 fresh green chile, finely chopped
1 tablespoon finely chopped onion
2 tablespoons finely chopped fresh coriander (cilantro)

VEGETABLES

⅛ teaspoon salt

Cooked seasonings:
3 tablespoons vegetable oil
½ teaspoon cumin seeds
½ teaspoon black mustard seeds
3 dried red chiles
1 garlic clove, finely chopped

1. To cook the peas: In a medium saucepan, heat the oil over moderately high heat. When hot, put in the cumin seeds. Ten seconds later, add the chopped onion and garlic and fry, stirring frequently, until the onion turns brown at the edges, about 3 minutes. Stir in the tomatoes and cook for 1 minute.

2. Add the black-eyed peas, salt, cayenne, ground coriander and 2 cups of water. Stir well and bring to a boil. Cover partially, reduce the heat to low and cook until the peas are tender, about 40 minutes.

3. For the raw seasonings: Combine all the ingredients in a small bowl; set aside.

4. For the cooked seasonings: When the peas are tender, in a small skillet, heat the oil over moderately high heat. Add the cumin and mustard seeds. As soon as the mustard seeds begin to pop, after a few seconds, stir in the dried chiles. Add the garlic and when it begins to brown, scrape the oil and seasonings into the black-eyed peas and stir to blend. (The recipe can be prepared to this point up to 1 day ahead. Let cool, then cover and refrigerate. Reheat before proceeding.) Mix in the raw seasonings just before serving.

—Madhur Jaffrey

• • •

SAUTEED WATERCRESS WITH WALNUTS

4 Servings

1 tablespoon olive oil
2 large bunches of watercress (about ¾ pound), large stems removed
Salt and freshly ground pepper
2 tablespoons chopped walnuts

In a large skillet, heat the oil over moderately high heat. Add the watercress and sauté until wilted, 1 to 2 minutes. Season with salt and pepper to taste. Sprinkle with the walnuts and serve hot.

—Stephanie Lyness

• • •

SHREDDED ZUCCHINI

The technique used here brings out the sweetness of the vegetable.

6 Servings

6 medium zucchini
1 teaspoon salt
3 tablespoons unsalted butter
1 small onion, chopped

1. In a food processor fitted with a shredding disk, shred the zucchini. Alternatively, grate the zucchini on the large holes of a box grater. Place the zucchini in a colander and toss with the salt. Place the colander in the sink or over a bowl and let the zucchini drain for 1 hour. Using your hands, squeeze as much liquid as possible from the zucchini. Set the zucchini aside.

2. In a large skillet, melt the butter over moderately high heat. Add the onion and cook, stirring, until wilted and browned, about 5 minutes. Stir in the zucchini and cook, stirring frequently, until tender, about 5 minutes longer. Serve warm.

—Lee Bailey

• • •

PRESSURE-COOKER BLACK BEANS

Makes About 2 Cups

1 cup dried black (turtle) beans, rinsed and picked over
1 tablespoon oil

1. In a 6-quart pressure cooker, combine the beans with the oil and 4 cups of water. Lock the lid in place and bring to high (15 pounds) pressure over high heat. Reduce the heat to maintain the high pressure and cook for 20 minutes.

2. Set the pot under cold running water until all pressure is released. Remove the lid, tilting it away from you to allow any excess steam to escape. Test the beans for doneness; if they are not tender, lock the lid in place and return to high pressure for a few more minutes. Drain the beans and set aside until needed.

—Lorna Sass

• • •

BREAD & BREADSTUFFS

BREAD & BREADSTUFFS

KAISER ROLLS

What's in a name? Known as bulkies in Boston and kaisers in Philly, these seeded rolls with crunchy crusts are marvelous for deli sandwiches or burgers.

Makes 6 Rolls

1 envelope active dry yeast
1 teaspoon sugar
1½ cups lukewarm water (105° to 115°)
3½ cups bread flour
1½ teaspoons salt
Oil and cornmeal, for baking sheet
1 to 2 tablespoons poppy seeds

1. In a small bowl, sprinkle the yeast and sugar over the warm water. Stir to mix, then let stand until foamy, 5 to 10 minutes.

2. In a food processor, combine the flour and salt. With the machine on, add the yeast mixture. When the dough forms a ball, let the machine run for 30 seconds to knead the dough; it should be sticky.

3. With floured hands, shape the dough into a ball and transfer it to a large, oiled, nonmetallic bowl. Turn to coat. Cover with plastic wrap and let rise in a warm, draft-free place until almost doubled in bulk, about 1 hour.

4. Punch down the dough and then turn out onto a lightly floured surface and cut the dough into 6 equal pieces. Shape each piece into a smooth ball; then flatten each one slightly.

5. Lightly oil a large baking sheet and sprinkle with cornmeal. Set the rolls on the baking sheet, cover with a towel and let rise in a warm place until almost doubled in bulk, 30 to 45 minutes.

6. Meanwhile, preheat the oven to 425°. Using a sharp knife or razor blade, deeply score the top of each roll 5 times from the center to the edge in a pin-wheel pattern. Spray or lightly brush the rolls with water and sprinkle the poppy seeds on top. Place the rolls in the oven and mist once. Two minutes later, mist again and bake for 20 minutes, or until the rolls are lightly browned and sound hollow when tapped. Transfer to a rack and let cool completely.

—Linda Drachman and
Debra Rosman

• • •

BUTTER-BOTTOM YEAST ROLLS

Makes 32 Rolls

2 cups buttermilk
1 stick (4 ounces) plus 1 tablespoon unsalted butter
2 tablespoons sugar
2 teaspoons salt
¼ cup lukewarm water (105° to 115°)
1 envelope active dry yeast
6 to 7 cups unbleached all-purpose flour
½ teaspoon baking soda

1. In a small nonreactive saucepan, combine the buttermilk, 3 tablespoons of the butter, 1 tablespoon of the sugar and the salt. Cook over moderate heat, stirring occasionally, until the mixture is warmed through and the butter has melted. Set aside to cool slightly.

2. In a small bowl, combine the lukewarm water with the remaining 1 tablespoon sugar. Sprinkle the yeast on top and set aside until foamy. Mean-

while, in a large bowl, toss 5½ cups of the flour with the baking soda.

3. Whisk the dissolved yeast mixture into the buttermilk mixture and pour over the flour. Stir with a wooden spoon until the dough loosely masses together.

4. On a floured surface, knead the dough, adding the remaining flour as necessary, until smooth and slightly sticky, about 10 minutes. Cover with a towel and set aside for 3 minutes.

5. In a small saucepan, melt the remaining 6 tablespoons butter over moderate heat. Pour the butter into two 8-inch square metal baking pans, dividing it evenly. Tilt the pans to coat the bottoms and sides with butter.

6. Using a large sharp knife, cut the dough in half. Working with one half while the other remains covered, cut the dough into 16 even pieces. Roll each piece into a ball, using the heel of your hand and rolling loosely in a clockwise motion. (The dough will stick slightly as it forms into a ball.) Add the balls to one of the prepared pans and turn to coat each one with the butter. Arrange the balls in 4 rows of 4, leaving equal space between them. Repeat with the remaining dough and pan. Cover with kitchen towels and let rise in a warm place for 1 hour.

7. Preheat the oven to 375°. Bake the rolls for 25 to 30 minutes, or until golden brown. Serve warm. (*The rolls can be made up to 2 weeks ahead and frozen, well wrapped. Reheat in a warm oven before serving.*)

—Lee Bailey

• • •

Spaghetti Marinara (p. 134).

At left (clockwise from center): Green Beans
with Coconut and Popped Rice (p. 174), Fresh
Coriander Chutney (p. 260) with assorted
breads, Lamb Meatballs Stuffed with Sun-Dried
Cherries (p. 130). Above, Simple Stew of
Lima Beans, Corn and Tomatoes (p. 30).

CRESCENT ROLLS

There is a secret to the tenderness of my grandmother's rolls. Because the dough is very soft, you will want to add more flour than the recipe calls for, but resist the temptation, or they will toughen. Also, avoid working the dough too much. Just mix it enough so that the flour is thoroughly incorporated; then knead the dough a few times. Let it rise slowly. The final rising of four hours, once the rolls are shaped, is important. Don't stint on it.

Makes 32 Rolls

1 cup milk, scalded
1 stick (4 ounces) unsalted butter, softened
1 envelope active dry yeast
½ cup sugar
4½ cups all-purpose flour
2 eggs
1 teaspoon salt

1. In a large bowl, combine the scalded milk and the butter. Stir until the butter melts and let stand until lukewarm. Stir in the yeast and sugar. Whisk in 1 cup of the flour. Add the eggs, 1 at a time, whisking well after each addition. Add the salt and 1 more cup of flour. Mix vigorously with a wooden spoon until the dough is elastic and smooth, about 6 minutes. Alternatively, mix the dough at medium-high speed for 3 minutes.

Basic and Beautiful Fried Rice (p. 144).

2. Work in the remaining 2½ cups flour until the dough is a little firmer; it will still be very soft. Turn the dough out onto a lightly floured work surface and knead just until smooth, about 2 minutes. Place the dough in a bowl, cover and let rise in a warm place until doubled in bulk, about 2 hours.

3. Punch down the dough and turn out onto a well-floured work surface and divide it in half. Roll each half into a disk about 16 inches in diameter. Cut each disk into quarters, then cut each quarter into 4 equal wedges. Beginning at the wide ends, roll up the wedges. Seal the pointed end of each wedge underneath so it won't pop up during rising and baking.

4. Arrange the rolls 2 inches apart on 3 lightly floured baking sheets. Cover with a dry kitchen towel and set aside to rise in a warm place until nearly doubled in size, about 4 hours.

5. Preheat the oven to 350°. Bake the rolls in 2 batches in the middle of the oven for 10 to 12 minutes, until golden. Serve immediately.

—*Susan Hermann Loomis*

• • •

ONION BOARDS

These flat breads are soft and chewy when warm. As they cool, they become slightly crisp. Either way, they are best slathered with sweet butter. They can also be topped with cream cheese and smoked salmon, cut into small wedges and served as hors d'oeuvres.

Makes 4 Boards

1 envelope active dry yeast
1 tablespoon sugar

¾ cup lukewarm water (105° to 115°)
3 to 3¼ cups bread flour
2 teaspoons salt
¼ teaspoon freshly ground pepper
3 tablespoons vegetable oil
5 tablespoons unsalted butter, melted
¼ cup dried minced onion flakes
¼ cup poppy seeds
1 egg
Oil and cornmeal, for baking sheets

1. In a small bowl, sprinkle the yeast and sugar over the warm water. Stir to mix, then let stand until foamy, 5 to 10 minutes.

2. In a food processor, combine 3 cups of the flour with the salt and pepper. With the machine on, add the yeast mixture and the oil. When the dough forms a ball, process for an additional 30 seconds to knead the dough. (If the dough seems wet, add the remaining flour, 1 tablespoon at a time and process after each addition, until the dough pulls away from the sides of the bowl.)

3. Turn the dough out onto a lightly floured surface and knead until smooth and shiny, about 1 minute. Transfer the dough to a large, oiled, nonmetallic bowl and turn to coat. Cover with plastic wrap and let rise in a warm, draft-free place until almost doubled in bulk, about 1 hour.

4. In a medium bowl, combine the butter, onion flakes and poppy seeds. In a small bowl, beat the egg with 1 tablespoon of water.

5. Punch down the dough and divide it into 4 equal pieces; cover all but 1 of the pieces with a towel. Gently stretch the uncovered dough to form a thin disk. Brush with the egg wash and sprinkle one-quarter of the onion mixture on top; press it into the dough to help it adhere. Repeat with the remaining dough, egg wash and onion mixture.

6. Preheat the oven to 375°. Lightly oil 2 large baking sheets and sprinkle with cornmeal. Place 2 onion boards on each sheet. Cover with a towel and let rise in a warm place until almost doubled in bulk, about 30 minutes.

7. Place the onion boards in the oven and mist once. Two minutes later, mist again and bake for 20 minutes, or until the onion boards are puffed and golden. Transfer to racks and let cool completely.

—Linda Drachman and
Debra Rosman

• • •

SOURDOUGH RYE BREAD

This is the ultimate sandwich bread; its firm texture and slightly sour tang will stand up to any filling. The bread takes time to make because the starter requires two days to develop, but it is certainly worth the wait.

Makes 2 Loaves

1 envelope active dry yeast
1 tablespoon sugar
1⅓ cups lukewarm water (105° to 115°)
1 tablespoon salt
Sourdough Starter (recipe follows)
3 tablespoons caraway seeds

2 tablespoons dark molasses
2 cups medium rye flour
3 to 3½ cups bread flour
Oil and cornmeal, for baking sheet

1. In a small bowl, sprinkle the yeast and sugar over ⅓ cup of the warm water. Stir to mix, then let stand until foamy, 5 to 10 minutes.

2. In a large mixing bowl, combine the salt with the remaining 1 cup warm water. Stir the Sourdough Starter and add it to the bowl. Using an electric mixer at medium speed, beat in the yeast mixture, caraway seeds, molasses and ½ cup of the rye flour.

3. On a work surface, toss the remaining 1½ cups rye flour with 2 cups of the bread flour. Form the flours into a mound and make a wide well in the center. Pour in the sourdough mixture. Using your fingertips, gradually work in the flours, beginning with the inside of the well. The dough will be very moist and sticky. Work in enough of the remaining bread flour, ¼ cup at a time, until the dough is no longer tacky. Flour the work surface as necessary. Knead the dough until smooth and shiny, 8 to 10 minutes; it will still be slightly sticky.

4. Transfer the dough to a large, oiled, nonmetallic bowl and turn to coat. Cover with plastic wrap and let rise in a warm, draft-free place until almost doubled in bulk, about 1½ hours.

5. Punch down the dough in the bowl. Cover and let sit for 20 minutes. Meanwhile, oil a large baking sheet and sprinkle with cornmeal.

6. Divide the dough in half and shape into oval loaves that are tapered at the ends. Place the loaves on the prepared baking sheet. Cover with a towel and let rise in a warm place until almost doubled in bulk, about 45 minutes.

7. Meanwhile, preheat the oven to 400°. Place the loaves in the oven and mist once. Two minutes later, mist again and bake for 55 minutes, or until the loaves are dark brown and the bottoms sound hollow when tapped. Transfer to a rack and let cool completely.

—Linda Drachman and
Debra Rosman

• • •

SOURDOUGH STARTER

The starter will keep for weeks in the refrigerator.

Makes About 2 Cups

3 cups bread flour
1 tablespoon sugar
1 envelope active dry yeast
2 cups lukewarm water (105° to 115°)

In a large nonmetallic bowl, combine the bread flour, sugar and yeast. Gradually stir in the warm water. Using a whisk or an electric mixer, beat until smooth. Cover the bowl loosely with plastic wrap and let stand at room temperature for 2 days.

—Linda Drachman and
Debra Rosman

• • •

RAISIN PUMPERNICKEL BREAD

Dense, dark and delicious, this hearty bread is terrific plain, toasted for sandwiches or spread with sweet butter or cream cheese.

Makes 1 Loaf

¼ cup dark molasses
2 tablespoons cider vinegar
2 tablespoons unsalted butter
1 tablespoon unsweetened cocoa
   powder
1 envelope active dry yeast
1 tablespoon sugar
½ cup lukewarm water (105° to
   115°)
1½ cups bread flour
1½ cups medium rye flour
½ cup whole wheat flour
¼ cup bran flakes
2 teaspoons salt
2 teaspoons powdered instant coffee
Oil and cornmeal, for baking sheet
1 cup raisins

1. In a small nonreactive saucepan, combine the molasses, vinegar, butter, cocoa powder and 1 cup of cool water. Cook over low heat, stirring frequently, until the butter is completely melted, about 4 minutes. Remove from the heat, stir again and let cool to lukewarm (105° to 115°), about 10 minutes.

2. Meanwhile, in a small bowl, sprinkle the yeast and sugar over the warm water. Stir to mix, then let stand until foamy, about 5 minutes.

3. In a medium bowl, combine the bread, rye and whole wheat flours with the bran flakes, salt and instant coffee. Mix well. Measure out 2 cups of this flour mixture into a large bowl. Add the molasses mixture and the yeast. Using an electric mixer at low speed, beat until smooth. Increase the speed to medium and mix for 5 minutes longer. On low speed, stir in the remaining flour mixture, ½ cup at a time, until the dough pulls away from the sides of the bowl. (If the dough is too heavy for your mixer, beat in the flour with a wooden spoon.)

4. Turn the dough out onto a lightly floured surface and knead until smooth and shiny, 8 to 10 minutes. Transfer the dough to a large, oiled, nonmetallic bowl and turn to coat. Cover with plastic wrap and let rise in a warm, draft-free place until almost doubled in bulk, about 1 hour.

5. Preheat the oven to 375°. Oil a baking sheet and sprinkle it lightly with cornmeal. Punch down the dough and knead in the raisins. Shape the dough into a round loaf and place on the prepared baking sheet. Cover with a towel and let rise in a warm, draft-free place until almost doubled in bulk, about 45 minutes.

6. Slash the top of the loaf a few times with a sharp knife. Place the loaf in the oven and mist once. Two minutes later, mist again and bake for 45 minutes, or until the bottom of the loaf sounds hollow when tapped. Transfer to a rack and let cool completely.

*—Linda Drachman and
Debra Rosman*

• • •

CHALLAH

Challah, a braided egg bread, is always on hand at Jewish holidays and celebrations. The sesame seeds sprinkled on top recall the manna that fell from heaven to nourish the Israelites as they wandered through the Sinai desert searching for the Promised Land. This version is simpler and lower in cholesterol than traditional loaves, which are packed with egg yolks. Although best when fresh, challah makes wonderful french toast the next day.

Makes 1 Large Loaf

1 envelope active dry yeast
1 cup lukewarm water (105° to
   115°)
⅛ teaspoon sugar
2 tablespoons honey
1 teaspoon salt
¼ cup plus 1 teaspoon vegetable oil
2 eggs
About 4 cups unbleached all-purpose
   flour
1 tablespoon cornmeal
1 egg yolk
1 tablespoon sesame seeds

1. In a large bowl, combine the yeast and lukewarm water. Sprinkle the sugar on top and set aside until the yeast begins to bubble, 5 to 10 minutes. Add the honey, salt and ¼ cup of the oil and beat with an electric mixer on medium speed until blended, about 30 seconds. Add the eggs, 1 at a time, beating well after each addition. Gradually beat in 2 cups of the flour at moderately high speed for 3 minutes. Mix in 1 cup of the flour by hand.

2. Turn the dough onto a floured work surface and knead, using the remaining 1 cup flour as necessary, until the dough is very smooth and soft and has lost most of its stickiness, about 15 minutes.

3. Coat a large bowl with the remaining 1 teaspoon oil. Form the dough into a ball and place it in the bowl. Cover with plastic wrap and let rise in a warm place until doubled in bulk, about 1½ hours.

4. Dust a large baking sheet with the cornmeal and set aside. Punch the dough down. Cut off one-third of the dough, cover it with plastic wrap and set aside. Divide the remaining dough into three pieces. Using your hands, roll each piece into a 14-inch rope. Pinch the ends together and braid the ropes. Pinch the end of the braid to seal it closed. Transfer the braid to the prepared baking sheet.

5. Divide the reserved third of the dough into 3 even pieces. Roll each piece into a 10-inch rope and form a second braid. Center this braid on top of the larger braid. Let rise, uncovered, at room temperature in a draft-free place until doubled in bulk, about 1 hour.

6. Preheat the oven to 350°. In a small bowl, beat the egg yolk with 1 teaspoon of water. Brush the egg wash over the bread and sprinkle the sesame seeds on top. Bake for about 30 minutes, or until golden brown and the bread sounds hollow when tapped on the bottom. Transfer to a rack to cool completely.

—*Susan Shapiro Jaslove*

• • •

FOCACCIA

Julia Boorstin, who is 12, has been making focaccia since she was eight, so by now she's an expert on both technique and tips for toppings. Says Julia, "Don't get into a rut. Choose different toppings, and you'll feel like it's different every time." Nevertheless, thyme and rosemary are her favorites. For a totally different taste, use poppy or sesame seeds.

As the bakers of Genoa, Italy, do, dimple the dough with your fingertips to leave indentations for trapping little pools of oil and salt to flavor the surface of the bread. Focaccia is best eaten when it's warm on the same day it's baked. Never refrigerate focaccia; it simply will not taste right.

*Makes 3 Round or
2 Rectangular Focaccias*

2 envelopes active dry yeast
**2¼ cups lukewarm water (105° to
    115°)**
5 to 6 tablespoons olive oil
1 teaspoon table salt
**About 7½ cups unbleached all-
    purpose flour or 3¾ cups each all-
    purpose flour and bread flour**
1 tablespoon chopped fresh rosemary
**1½ to 2 teaspoons coarse (kosher)
    salt**

1. In a large bowl, combine the yeast and the warm water. Set aside until dissolved, 5 to 10 minutes. Stir in 3 tablespoons of the olive oil and the table salt. Gradually add the flour, stirring with a wooden spoon until it becomes hard to mix (you may not need all the flour). Turn the dough out onto a lightly floured surface and knead until smooth and elastic, 5 to 7 minutes. The dough should be soft but not sticky.

2. Place the dough in a lightly oiled bowl and cover tightly with plastic wrap. Set aside to rise in a warm draft-free place until doubled in bulk, about 1½ hours.

3. To make round focaccias, turn the dough out onto a lightly floured surface and cut into 3 equal pieces. Roll 1 piece into a ball, pat into a thick disk and then gently pull and stretch with your fingers to form a 9- or 10-inch round. Place in an oiled 9- or 10-inch pie plate. Repeat with the remaining dough. Alternatively, to make rectangular focaccias, cut the dough in half and pat and stretch out each piece to fit 2 oiled 10½-by-15½-inch jelly-roll pans.

4. Cover the dough with damp towels and set aside to rise in a warm draft-free place until almost doubled in bulk, about 1 hour.

5. Preheat the oven to 400°. Dimple the dough with your fingertips, leaving deep indentations. Brush the focaccias with the remaining 2 to 3 tablespoons olive oil, as desired. Sprinkle a little water on the surface, then sprinkle the rosemary and coarse salt on top.

6. Bake the focaccias in the middle of the oven for 20 to 25 minutes, until golden brown, spraying or sprinkling with water 3 times during the first 10 minutes. Immediately transfer the focaccias to racks to cool slightly so that the bottom crusts won't get soggy.

—*Annie Gilbar*

• • •

196

PERFECT PIZZA

Jean Brady has been running her own cooking school in Los Angeles for many years. At her cooking classes for children, this delicious, easy-to-make pizza is a favorite recipe. Let the children pick the topping for the pizzas. Kids particularly love the kneading part and can do it all by themselves, but you may need to supervise them at the end to be sure the texture of the dough is just right.

Jean uses a pizza stone, available in most cookware stores, to cook the pizza evenly. But if you don't have one, a baking sheet will do.

Makes 6 Individual Pizzas

1 envelope active dry yeast
¼ cup lukewarm water (105° to 115°)
1 tablespoon honey
3 tablespoons extra-virgin olive oil
¾ teaspoon salt
About 3½ cups all-purpose flour
1 pound mozzarella cheese, shredded
3 ounces thinly sliced cooked ham
3 ounces thinly sliced pepperoni
¼ cup chopped pitted olives (about 1½ ounces)

1. Preheat the oven to 500°. If using a pizza stone, place it in the oven to preheat for at least 45 minutes.

2. In a large bowl, combine the yeast, lukewarm water and ¼ teaspoon of the honey and stir well. Set aside until foamy, about 10 minutes.

3. Using a wooden spoon, stir in the olive oil, salt, the remaining 2¾ teaspoons honey and 1 cup of warm water. Gradually stir in about 3 cups of the flour until incorporated. Transfer the dough to a floured surface. Knead the dough, adding just enough of the remaining ½ cup flour to prevent sticking, until it is smooth and elastic, about 7 minutes.

4. Cover the dough with plastic wrap and let rest for 10 minutes. Divide it into 6 even pieces. Roll each piece into a ball and place several inches apart on a lightly oiled large baking sheet. Cover and set aside to rise in a warm, draft-free place until doubled in bulk, about 1 hour.

5. Using your hands, flatten and stretch 1 of the balls of dough on a lightly floured surface into a disk about 6 inches in diameter and ¼ inch thick. Form a little rim around the edge. Transfer to a pizza paddle—or a baking sheet turned bottom-side up—lightly dusted with cornmeal. Repeat with another ball of dough.

6. Top the 2 disks of dough with one-sixth each of the mozzarella, ham, pepperoni and olives. Slide the pizzas onto the pizza stone in the oven and bake for 8 to 12 minutes, until the cheese is bubbly. Repeat with the remaining dough and toppings. If you don't have a pizza stone, assemble 2 pizzas at a time on a baking sheet sprinkled lightly with cornmeal and bake in the middle of the oven.

—Annie Gilbar

• • •

CHEESE SCONES

Flavored with both Cheddar and Gruyère, these cheesy scones also have a light peppery bite, a crunchy, flaky crust and, because of the addition of some chopped onion, a slightly moist interior.

Makes 8 Scones

6 tablespoons cold unsalted butter
1 medium onion, finely chopped
2 cups all-purpose flour
1 tablespoon baking powder
½ teaspoon salt
4 ounces Gruyère cheese, shredded (1 cup)
2 ounces extra-sharp Cheddar cheese cut into ¼-inch dice (½ cup)
¼ teaspoon freshly ground white pepper
¼ teaspoon cayenne pepper
¾ cup milk

1. Preheat the oven to 425°. Lightly grease a large baking sheet. In a medium skillet, melt 2 tablespoons of the butter over moderate heat. Add the onion and cook, stirring occasionally, until softened, about 5 minutes. Transfer the onion to paper towels to drain and cool.

2. In a medium bowl, mix the flour, baking powder and salt together thoroughly. Using 2 knives or a pastry blender, cut in the remaining 4 tablespoons butter until the mixture is mealy. Stir in the Gruyère, Cheddar, white pepper, cayenne and the reserved onion. Using a fork, stir in ½ cup plus 2 tablespoons of the milk to form a shaggy

BREAD & BREADSTUFFS

dough. Knead briefly on a work surface just until the cheese is evenly incorporated. Do not overwork.

3. On a lightly floured surface, form the dough into a disk and roll it out into an 11-inch circle, about ¾ inch thick. Using a 3-inch round or fluted biscuit cutter, cut the dough into 8 scones. Transfer to the prepared baking sheet. Brush with the remaining 2 tablespoons milk. Bake for 15 to 17 minutes, until the scones are golden brown.

4. Let cool on a rack for at least 15 minutes before serving. Serve warm or at room temperature.

—*Tracey Seaman*

• • •

HOT PEPPER SKILLET CORN BREAD

6 Servings

4 tablespoons unsalted butter
1 cup yellow cornmeal
1 cup all-purpose flour
2 tablespoons sugar
½ teaspoon salt
2 teaspoons baking powder
1 teaspoon crushed red pepper
1 cup milk
2 eggs

1. Preheat the oven to 425°. Place the butter in a 9- or 10-inch ovenproof skillet, preferably cast iron, and heat in the oven until the butter has completely melted, about 2 minutes.

2. Meanwhile, in a medium bowl, combine the cornmeal, flour, sugar, salt, baking powder and crushed red pepper and toss to mix.

3. In a medium bowl, lightly whisk the milk with the eggs. Pour most of the melted butter into the egg mixture—leaving enough behind to generously coat the skillet—and stir to combine.

4. Add the egg mixture to the dry ingredients and stir until just blended. Scrape the batter into the skillet and smooth the surface with a spoon. Bake for 15 minutes, or until lightly golden. Let cool for a few minutes before serving directly from the pan.

—*Stephanie Lyness*

• • •

GREEN CHILE SPOON BREAD

This spoon bread is especially delicious served with the sauce or any gravy.

6 Servings

2 cups milk
3 eggs
2 tablespoons unsalted butter
⅔ cup yellow or white cornmeal
¼ teaspoon salt
1 can (4 ounces) chopped mild green chiles
1½ teaspoons baking powder

1. Preheat the oven to 400°. Lightly grease a 6-cup soufflé dish and set aside. In a medium bowl, whisk ⅔ cup of the milk with the eggs.

2. In a medium saucepan, warm the remaining 1⅓ cups milk over moderate heat. Add the butter and simmer for 3 minutes. Gradually sprinkle in the cornmeal, whisking constantly until incorporated. Season with the salt and remove from the heat.

3. Gradually add the egg mixture to the cornmeal, stirring until combined. Stir in the chopped green chiles and the baking powder. Scrape the batter into the prepared soufflé dish and bake for 40 minutes, or until golden and puffed. Serve immediately.

—*Lee Bailey*

• • •

GRANDMA HARRIS'S HOECAKES

Grandma Harris used to make one skillet-size cake that she deftly turned out of the pan. Unfortunately, that technique never got passed down, so I make individual cakes.

Makes 12 Hoecakes

1 cup white or yellow cornmeal
¼ teaspoon salt
6 tablespoons corn oil or rendered bacon fat
Unsalted butter, for serving

1. In a medium bowl, combine the cornmeal and salt. Whisk in 1 cup of cold water to make a thick batter.

2. In a large cast-iron skillet, heat 2 tablespoons of the oil over high heat until ripples appear on the surface, 1 to 2 minutes. Working in batches, for each cake, drop about 1 tablespoon of the batter into the skillet and flatten slightly with a spatula, allowing room for each cake to spread to 2 inches. Fry, turning once, until browned, about 1½ minutes per side. Transfer to a plate lined with paper towels and keep warm. Repeat with the remaining oil and batter.

3. Blot the tops of the corn cakes with paper towels, dot with butter and serve.

—*Jessica B. Harris*

• • •

CORN-KERNEL PANCAKES

Makes 14 Pancakes

1¼ *cups cornmeal*
¼ *cup all-purpose flour*
½ *teaspoon salt*
½ *teaspoon freshly ground pepper*
½ *teaspoon baking soda*
2 *cups buttermilk*
2 *eggs, lightly beaten*
3 *tablespoons vegetable oil*
1½ *cups frozen corn kernels, thawed*

1. In a large bowl, sift together the cornmeal, flour, salt, pepper and baking soda. In another bowl, whisk the buttermilk with the eggs and oil until blended. Stir the buttermilk mixture into the dry ingredients. Stir in the corn just until incorporated; be careful not to overmix.

2. Heat a large, greased, nonstick skillet over moderately high heat. Add 2 tablespoons of the batter to form each pancake. Fry the pancakes in batches until golden, about 2 minutes on each side.

—*Lee Bailey*

• • •

MOM'S FRIED DRESSING

The corn bread recipe (Steps 1 through 4) for these pan-fried patties can be made ahead of time. Or use store-bought corn bread and dry it in the oven, as instructed in Step 4.

Makes 16 Patties

1 *cup yellow cornmeal*
½ *cup all-purpose flour*
1½ *teaspoons salt*
¾ *teaspoon baking soda*
1½ *cups buttermilk*
1 *egg*
¼ *cup vegetable oil*
2 *tablespoons unsalted butter*
3 *small leeks, white part with 2 inches of green, finely chopped*
1½ *cups chicken stock or canned low-sodium broth*
2 *teaspoons finely grated lemon zest*
2 *teaspoons chopped fresh tarragon*
1 *teaspoon chopped fresh marjoram*
1 *teaspoon chopped fresh thyme*
¼ *teaspoon freshly ground pepper*
1½ *cups stale white bread crumbs*
2 *eggs, lightly beaten*
Oil, for frying

1. Preheat the oven to 400°. Grease an 8-inch square baking pan and set aside.

2. In a large mixing bowl, combine the cornmeal, flour, 1 teaspoon of the salt and the baking soda. In a large measuring cup, combine the buttermilk, egg and oil and whisk until blended. Pour all at once over the dry ingredients and stir briskly until just combined.

3. Scrape the batter into the prepared pan and bake in the middle of the oven for 20 to 25 minutes, until firm and lightly browned. Let cool in the pan for 2 to 3 minutes, then turn out onto a wire rack to cool completely. Turn the oven down to 325°.

4. Coarsely crumble the corn bread and spread the crumbs out in a pan. Bake for about 20 minutes, stirring frequently, until the crumbs are dry and crisp. Let cool completely before using.

5. Meanwhile, in a large nonstick skillet, melt the butter over moderate heat. Add the leeks and cook, stirring, until tender, 8 to 10 minutes. Add ½ cup of the stock and simmer until the pan is almost dry, about 4 minutes. Remove from the heat and add the lemon zest, tarragon, marjoram, thyme, remaining ½ teaspoon salt, the pepper and the remaining 1 cup stock.

6. In a large bowl, toss the corn bread crumbs with the white bread crumbs. Pour the leek and herb mixture over the crumbs, add the eggs and stir until the crumbs are evenly moistened. Using a scant ¼ cup for each, shape the mixture into patties ½ inch thick.

7. Pour ¼ inch of oil into a large nonstick skillet and heat over moderate heat until hot. Add as many of the patties as fit comfortably and cook, turning once, until crisp and golden brown, about 3 minutes per side. Drain on paper towels. Repeat with the remaining patties. Serve hot. (*The patties can be fried up to 1 day ahead. Cover and refrigerate when cool. Reheat in a 350° oven for about 10 minutes.*)

—*Elizabeth Woodson*

• • •

BREAD & BREADSTUFFS

SOUTHWEST CORN AND PEPPER STUFFING

This stuffing makes a fine accompaniment to barbecue.

12 to 14 Servings

6 slices of bacon (6 ounces), very
    thinly sliced crosswise
1 large onion, coarsely chopped
1 large red bell pepper, finely diced
4 tablespoons unsalted butter, melted
1 package (16 ounces) frozen corn
    kernels or 4 cups fresh kernels
½ cup pine nuts (3 ounces)
Old-Fashioned Corn Bread for
    Stuffing (recipe follows), dried and
    crumbled
2 cups coarsely shredded longhorn or
    sharp white Cheddar cheese (6
    ounces)
⅓ cup chopped fresh coriander
    (cilantro)
1½ tablespoons poultry seasoning
1½ teaspoons rubbed sage
1½ teaspoons chili powder
1 teaspoon leaf oregano, crumbled
¾ teaspoon ground cumin
¾ teaspoon salt
¼ teaspoon freshly ground black
    pepper
1 can (4 ounces) chopped mild green
    chiles, drained
1½ cups chicken stock or canned
    low-sodium broth

1. In a heavy medium skillet, fry the bacon over moderately high heat, separating the pieces, until crisp and browned, about 7 minutes. Using a slotted spoon, transfer the bacon to paper towels to drain.

2. Add the onion and red bell pepper to the bacon drippings and cook, stirring frequently, until the onion is limp and golden, about 10 minutes. Using a slotted spoon, transfer the onion-and-pepper mixture to a small bowl and set aside.

3. Preheat the oven to 350°. Butter a deep 4-quart casserole and a large square of heavy-duty aluminum foil; set aside.

4. Add 2 tablespoons of the melted butter to the skillet and reduce the heat to low. Add the corn and cook, stirring often, until tender, about 15 minutes.

5. Meanwhile, spread the pine nuts in a pie pan and toast them in the middle of the oven until pale tan, about 7 minutes. Let the pine nuts cool slightly, then coarsely chop them.

6. In a very large mixing bowl, combine the crumbled corn bread, bacon, pine nuts, cheese, coriander, poultry seasoning, sage, chili powder, oregano, cumin, salt and black pepper. Toss well to mix. Add the chiles, reserved onion-and-pepper mixture and corn, the remaining 2 tablespoons melted butter and 1 cup of the stock; toss again.

7. Lightly spoon the mixture into the prepared casserole and drizzle the remaining ½ cup stock evenly over all. Cover with the foil, buttered-side down, and crumple around the casserole to seal snugly. Bake in the middle of the oven for 40 to 45 minutes, until steaming hot. Serve at once.

—*Jean Anderson*

• • •

OLD-FASHIONED CORN BREAD FOR STUFFING

This basic corn bread is firm enough to use for all kinds of stuffings. It's good to eat out of hand too. For best results when making stuffing, turn the slightly cooled corn bread out onto a rack and let air dry uncovered for two days at room temperature or for three in the refrigerator before crumbling and using. Better still, make it up to one month ahead and freeze, covered with a double layer of freezer wrap.

*Makes About 10 Cups Coarsely
Crumbled Corn Bread*

2 cups sifted all-purpose flour
2 cups cornmeal
2 tablespoons baking powder
1 tablespoon sugar
1½ teaspoons salt
2 eggs, lightly beaten
2 cups milk
½ cup vegetable oil, bacon drippings
    or melted lard

1. Preheat the oven to 400°. Spray a 13-by-9-by-2-inch baking pan with non-stick vegetable cooking spray and set aside.

2. In a large mixing bowl, combine the flour, cornmeal, baking powder, sugar and salt. Make a well in the center. In a large measuring cup, whisk the eggs, milk and oil until blended. Pour all at once into the well of the dry ingredients and stir briskly until just combined; the batter will be slightly lumpy.

3. Scrape the batter into the prepared pan and bake in the middle of the oven for 30 minutes, or until firm and lightly browned. Cut the corn bread into large squares if serving right away. Or, let cool on a rack for 10 minutes, then turn it out of the pan and air dry thoroughly before crumbling.

—*Jean Anderson*

• • •

CHESAPEAKE OYSTER STUFFING

This recipe was double-starred in Mother's recipe file. It came from an old farm woman who lived near our summer cottage on Chesapeake Bay.

10 to 12 Servings

1½ *pints shucked oysters with their liquor (3 dozen)*
5 *cups dry, coarsely crumbled Old-Fashioned Corn Bread for Stuffing (p. 200)*
4 *cups coarsely crumbled saltines (about 6 ounces)*
4 *medium celery ribs, coarsely chopped*
1 *medium onion, coarsely chopped*
¼ *cup minced parsley*
1 *tablespoon snipped fresh dill*
2 *teaspoons poultry seasoning*
1 *teaspoon freshly ground pepper*
½ *teaspoon finely grated lemon zest*
½ *teaspoon salt*

1½ *sticks (6 ounces) unsalted butter, melted*
1 *tablespoon fresh lemon juice*

1. Preheat the oven to 350°. Butter a deep 3-quart casserole and a large square of heavy-duty aluminum foil and set aside.

2. Pour the oysters into a strainer set over a bowl. Measure out 1 cup of oyster liquor and set aside; if there isn't enough liquor, add enough water to equal 1 cup. Coarsely chop the oysters.

3. In a large bowl, combine the oysters with the corn bread, saltines, celery, onion, parsley, dill, poultry seasoning, pepper, lemon zest and salt; toss to mix. Add the melted butter, lemon juice and ½ cup of the reserved oyster liquor and toss again. Season with additional salt and pepper if necessary.

4. Spoon the stuffing lightly into the prepared casserole and drizzle the remaining ½ cup oyster liquor evenly on top. Lay the foil on top of the stuffing, buttered-side down, and crumple around the casserole dish to seal. Bake in the middle of the oven for 40 minutes, until steaming hot.

—*Jean Anderson*

• • •

TEN THOUSAND LAKES WILD RICE, MUSHROOM AND CARROT DRESSING

More than 25 years ago when I was researching my first cookbook, *The Art of American Indian Cooking*, a Chippewa from Minnesota gave a wild rice casserole recipe to my Indian co-author, the late Yeffe Kimball. We featured it in the book, and it's still a favorite of mine. I then got to thinking that with an addition here and a subtraction there, it could be turned into a casserole dressing. Quite so. This version is better if made a day ahead and then reheated at 350° for 35 to 40 minutes.

10 to 12 Servings

2 *cups wild rice (12 ounces), rinsed and drained*
1½ *teaspoons salt*
¼ *cup corn oil*
1 *large onion, coarsely chopped*
6 *medium scallions, thinly sliced*
3 *large celery ribs, coarsely diced*
2 *medium carrots, coarsely chopped*
1 *teaspoon leaf marjoram, crumbled*
½ *teaspoon rosemary, very finely crumbled*
½ *teaspoon leaf thyme, crumbled*
½ *teaspoon freshly ground pepper*
1 *pound small mushrooms, thinly sliced*
2 *tablespoons unsalted butter*
3 *tablespoons all-purpose flour*
1⅔ *cups chicken or beef stock or canned low-sodium broth*
2 *cups Melba Toast Cubes (p. 204)*

201

1. In a large heavy saucepan, combine the wild rice, salt and 7 cups of water and bring to a rolling boil over moderately high heat. Reduce the heat to moderately low and simmer, partially covered, until the rice has popped and the grains are tender but slightly chewy, about 55 minutes. Drain well and set aside.

2. Meanwhile, in a large heavy skillet, heat the oil over moderately high heat for 1 minute. Add the onion, scallions and celery and cook, stirring frequently, until limp and golden, about 10 minutes. Add the carrots, marjoram, rosemary, thyme and pepper and reduce the heat to low. Cover and cook for 10 minutes. Using a slotted spoon, transfer the vegetables to a large bowl and set aside.

3. Add the mushrooms to the skillet and increase the heat to moderately high. Cook, stirring occasionally, until the mushrooms have released their juices and the juices have evaporated, about 7 minutes. Add the mushrooms to the bowl of vegetables.

4. Preheat the oven to 350°. Butter a large oval casserole and a large square of heavy-duty aluminum foil.

5. In a small heavy saucepan, melt the butter over moderate heat. Whisk in the flour until the mixture is smooth and hot. Whisk in the stock and cook, stirring frequently, until the sauce boils and thickens, about 3 minutes. Reduce the heat so that the sauce bubbles gently; simmer, stirring, until the sauce is as thick as gravy, about 5 minutes longer.

6. Add the sauce to the large bowl along with the Melba Toast Cubes and the reserved wild rice; toss very well.

Lightly spoon the dressing into the prepared casserole and cover with the foil; crumple around the casserole to seal tightly. Bake in the middle of the oven for 1 hour and serve at once.

—Jean Anderson

• • •

POTATO, CELERY AND MELBA TOAST STUFFING

In the old days on the Eastern Shore of Maryland, a simple bread-and-potato mixture was used to stuff fowl, especially game birds. This version is a bit fancier but still is easy to make. If the flavor is to be right, however, you must make the melba toast yourself. Also, use fresh herbs if they're available; they give the stuffing a bouquet no dried herbs can.

10 to 12 Servings

8 ounces stale, sliced firm-textured
  white bread (about 7 slices)
6 tablespoons unsalted butter, melted
3 large bay leaves, preferably fresh
2½ teaspoons fresh lemon thyme or
  ½ teaspoon dried leaf thyme,
  crumbled
2 teaspoons minced fresh rosemary or
  ½ teaspoon dried rosemary,
  crumbled
4 large baking potatoes (2½ pounds),
  peeled and cut into ½-inch cubes
¼ teaspoon freshly grated nutmeg
¼ teaspoon freshly ground pepper
2 medium onions, minced
3 large celery ribs, finely diced
⅓ cup minced parsley
2½ cups hot milk
1¾ teaspoons salt

1. Make the melba toast crumbs: Preheat the oven to 300°. Spread the bread out on a large baking sheet and bake in the middle of the oven for 30 minutes, or until crisp and golden brown. Let cool to room temperature, then break the toast into chunks and place in a food processor. Pulse until the mixture is the texture of coarse crumbs with some large pieces remaining. Set aside.

2. Increase the oven temperature to 425°. Butter a high-sided 3-quart flameproof casserole. Place 2 tablespoons of the melted butter and the bay leaves in the bottom. If using fresh herbs, add the thyme and rosemary (if using dried herbs, wait and then sprinkle them over the potatoes). Add the potatoes and sprinkle with the nutmeg, pepper (and dried herbs, if using). Scatter the onion and celery evenly on top. Cover and bake in the middle of the oven for 20 minutes.

3. Stir the potatoes up from the bottom, cover and bake for 20 minutes longer, or until the potatoes are just tender. Remove the casserole from the oven and preheat the broiler. Remove the bay leaves and discard. Add the parsley and 2 more tablespoons of the butter and toss lightly but thoroughly. Combine the hot milk and salt and gently fold into the potatoes alternately with 2 cups of the melba toast crumbs; the mixture will be very moist. Transfer the stuffing to a 14-inch oval gratin dish.

4. In a small bowl, using a fork, toss the remaining melba toast crumbs with the remaining 2 tablespoons melted butter. Scatter the crumbs evenly over the stuffing and broil 7 inches from the heat for about 30 seconds, or until tipped with brown. Serve at once.

—Jean Anderson

• • •

PLANTATION-STUFFING PATTIES WITH PECANS

The idea for this recipe comes from a South Carolina friend who shapes a moist dressing (as stuffing is known down South) into burgers and bakes them. She uses a half-and-half mix of bread stuffing mix and crumbled home-made corn bread plus "gobs of chopped onion, celery and giblet stock." Here melba cubes are substituted for the stuffing mix and chicken stock for the giblet stock (but by all means use giblet stock if you have it on hand). I also added pecans, which, my friend admits, are a nifty addition.

Makes 18 to 20 Patties

Melba Toast Cubes (p.204)
6 cups dry, coarsely crumbled Old-Fashioned Corn Bread for Stuffing (p. 200)
1½ cups finely chopped pecans (6 ounces)
2 tablespoons poultry seasoning
1 teaspoon salt
¼ teaspoon freshly ground pepper
¼ cup corn oil
1½ large onions, finely chopped
6 large celery ribs, finely chopped
1 stick (4 ounces) unsalted butter, melted
3¾ to 4 cups chicken stock or canned low-sodium broth

1. Lightly spray two baking sheets with nonstick vegetable cooking spray and set aside.

2. In a very large bowl, combine the Melba Toast Cubes, Corn Bread, pecans, poultry seasoning, salt and pepper; toss well and set aside.

3. In a large heavy skillet, heat the corn oil over high heat for 1 minute. Add the onion and celery and cook, stirring occasionally, until golden but still a bit crisp, about 5 minutes. Add to the bowl along with the melted butter; toss well.

4. Stir in 3¾ cups of the chicken stock; the stuffing should be very moist, about like porridge, but should hold together nicely when you squeeze a bit of it in your hand. Season with additional salt and pepper to taste and let stand for 10 minutes. If the mixture seems dry at this point, add a bit more chicken stock.

5. Preheat the oven to 400°. Using a ½-cup measure, lightly scoop up the stuffing mixture and shape it into patties about 3 inches across and ½ inch thick. Arrange the stuffing patties on the prepared baking sheets, spacing them evenly. *(The patties can be prepared to this point up to 1 day ahead. Cover and refrigerate.)*

6. Bake the stuffing patties on the middle and lower racks of the oven for 15 minutes. Turn the patties over, switch the baking sheets and bake for about 15 minutes longer, until the patties are lightly browned. Serve hot.

—Jean Anderson

• • •

YANKEE HAM AND LEMON STUFFING BALLS

Once when researching early New England recipes, I came across stuffing balls that were served at Old Sturbridge Village in Massachusetts. They contained nearly a pound of ground suet—in addition to half a pound of ham and two egg yolks. What follows is a lower-cholesterol version that's every bit as good as the original. These are traditionally cooked covered; if you prefer a very crusty exterior, however, cook them uncovered.

Makes 16 Stuffing Balls

¼ pound thick-sliced bacon, cut into ¼-inch dice
4½ cups soft, fresh white bread crumbs (from a 14-ounce loaf)
½ pound ground smoked ham
2 tablespoons unsalted butter, melted
2 tablespoons fresh lemon juice
1 teaspoon leaf marjoram, crumbled
½ teaspoon leaf thyme, crumbled
½ teaspoon finely grated lemon zest
¼ teaspoon freshly ground pepper
¼ teaspoon freshly grated nutmeg
1 egg
3 tablespoons vegetable oil

1. Preheat the oven to 325°. Heat a large heavy skillet over moderately high heat. Add the bacon and fry, stirring frequently, until crisp, about 5 minutes. Drain well on paper towels. Pour off the bacon fat from the skillet and wipe clean.

2. In a medium bowl, combine the bacon with the bread crumbs, ground ham, melted butter, lemon juice, mar-

203

joram, thyme, lemon zest, pepper, nutmeg, egg and 2 tablespoons of water. Mix lightly with your hands until well blended. Shape the stuffing into 16 balls about the size of golf balls.

3. In the skillet, heat the oil over moderate heat until bubbly, about 1 minute. Add half of the stuffing balls and fry, turning frequently, until evenly browned and crisp, about 7 minutes. As the stuffing balls are done, transfer them to an ungreased 9-by-13-inch baking pan. Make sure that they do not touch each other or the sides of the pan. Repeat with the remaining stuffing balls.

4. Cover the pan snugly with aluminum foil and bake in the middle of the oven for 35 minutes, until piping hot. Transfer the stuffing balls to a platter and serve at once.

—*Jean Anderson*

• • •

GREAT PLAINS SAGE AND SAUSAGE STUFFING

Many of the settlers of America's breadbasket were Germans who doted on the sausages of their homeland. Not surprisingly, the Thanksgiving stuffings they developed were rich ones filled with sausage. It's important that you use a firm-textured bread for this particular stuffing and that the bread be good and dry; otherwise it will turn to mush when you mix everything together.

10 to 12 Servings

1 pound bulk sausage
1 stick (4 ounces) unsalted butter, melted
1 large onion, coarsely chopped

3 large celery ribs, finely diced
10 cups stale ½-inch cubes from a ¾-pound loaf of firm-textured white bread
½ cup minced parsley
2 teaspoons rubbed sage
2 teaspoons poultry seasoning
½ teaspoon leaf thyme, crumbled
½ teaspoon salt
½ teaspoon freshly ground pepper
¾ cup chicken stock or canned low-sodium broth

1. Preheat the oven to 375°. Butter a deep 3-quart casserole and a large square of heavy-duty aluminum foil; set aside.

2. In a large heavy skillet, fry the sausage meat over moderately high heat, breaking up the clumps, until lightly browned and no trace of pink remains, about 5 minutes. Using a slotted spoon, transfer the sausage to paper towels to drain.

3. Add 2 tablespoons of the butter to the skillet along with the onion and celery. Cook over moderate heat, stirring frequently, until the onion is soft and golden, about 15 minutes.

4. Scrape the vegetable mixture into a large bowl and add the bread cubes, parsley, sage, poultry seasoning, thyme, salt and pepper and toss well. Add the reserved sausage meat and the remaining 6 tablespoons butter and toss again. Drizzle ½ cup of the chicken stock over the stuffing and toss.

5. Lightly spoon the stuffing into the prepared casserole and drizzle the remaining ¼ cup stock evenly on top. Lay the foil on top of the stuffing, buttered-side down, and crumple around the casserole to seal tightly. (*The recipe can be prepared to this point up to 1 day ahead and refrigerated.*) Bake the stuffing in the middle of the oven for 40 to 45 minutes, until steaming hot. Serve at once.

—*Jean Anderson*

• • •

MELBA TOAST CUBES

Small cubes of melba toast impart a nutty flavor and welcome crunch to stuffings. The cubes couldn't be easier to make, and they can be double-bagged in plastic and stored in a 0° freezer for up to three months. These little croutons can also be tossed into green salads or scattered on top of soups.

Makes 6 Cups

1 loaf (1 pound) firm-textured white bread

1. Preheat the oven to 250°. Stack 3 slices of bread and cut into ¼-inch strips with a large serrated knife; then cut the strips crosswise at ¼-inch intervals to form ¼-inch cubes. Repeat with the remaining bread.

2. Spread the cubes out in a roasting pan or jelly-roll pan and bake in the middle of the oven, stirring occasionally, for 1 hour or until uniformly crisp and golden. Let cool to room temperature; then store in an airtight container.

—*Jean Anderson*

• • •

PIES, CAKES & COOKIES

PIES, CAKES & COOKIES

PUMPKIN CUSTARD PIE

This recipe comes from Linda Stoltzfus, a young Amish woman from northern Pennsylvania. It produces a pie that is light and airy, with a subtle pumpkin taste and delicate edge of cinnamon. The pie is best made with freshly cooked pumpkin, but pumpkin from a can works well too. You might want to double the recipe and make two pies, thereby using a full recipe of the pastry dough and—if using canned pumpkin—a whole can of pumpkin puree.

Makes One 9-Inch Pie

½ recipe *Farmhouse Pie Pastry
  (recipe follows)*
1 cup fresh or unsweetened canned
  pumpkin puree (see Note)
2 eggs, separated
1⅓ cups milk
¼ cup plus 2 tablespoons granulated
  sugar
¼ cup plus 2 tablespoons (loosely
  packed) light brown sugar
1 tablespoon unsalted butter, melted
¾ teaspoon vanilla extract
Pinch of salt
3 tablespoons all-purpose flour
¼ teaspoon cinnamon

1. Preheat the oven to 425°. On a lightly floured surface, roll out the pie pastry into a 12-inch circle. Place the dough in a 9-inch pie plate, fitting it evenly into the plate without stretching; crimp the edge. Line the pastry with aluminum foil or parchment paper and fill with pie weights, dried beans or rice.

2. Bake the pastry for 15 to 20 minutes, until the edge begins to turn golden. Remove the foil and weights and bake for about 10 minutes longer, until lightly browned all over. Transfer to a rack to cool. (*The pie shell can be prebaked up to 1 day ahead; store at room temperature.*)

3. In a medium bowl, combine the pumpkin puree and egg yolks and whisk until blended. Whisk in the milk, granulated and light brown sugars, butter, vanilla and salt. Sift the flour over the mixture and whisk in until smooth.

4. In another medium bowl, whisk the egg whites just until they are bright white and form very soft peaks. Lightly whisk them into the pumpkin mixture, then pour the filling into the prebaked pie shell. Sprinkle the cinnamon on top.

5. Bake the pie in the middle of the oven for 10 minutes, then reduce the heat to 350° and bake for 25 to 30 minutes longer, until the filling is nearly set but still moves slightly in the center. Transfer to a rack to cool to room temperature before serving.

NOTE: *To make 1 cup of fresh pumpkin puree, steam 7 ounces of peeled fresh pumpkin chunks over 2 cups boiling water until very soft throughout, about 15 minutes. Puree in a food processor until smooth. Transfer the puree to a medium saucepan and cook over moderately high heat until thick enough to hold its shape up on a spoon, 8 to 10 minutes.*

—Susan Hermann Loomis

• • •

FARMHOUSE PIE PASTRY

This light, buttery and flaky pastry will make any pie a spectacular success. The most important rules to follow when making it are: do not overmix it once the water is added, and be sure to chill it for at least an hour before rolling. It is quite delicate and can be difficult to work with if the dough is the least bit warm.

Makes One 9-Inch Double-Crust

1¾ cups unbleached all-purpose
  flour
1 tablespoon sugar
1 teaspoon salt
1 stick (4 ounces) plus 3 tablespoons
  cold unsalted butter, cut into bits
2 tablespoons cold lard, cut into bits
About 3 tablespoons ice water

1. In a food processor fitted with a plastic dough blade, combine the flour, sugar and salt. Pulse just to mix. Add the butter and lard and pulse on and off about 10 times, until the mixture is the texture of coarse meal with a few pea-size pieces of fat remaining.

2. Pour in some of the ice water, 1 tablespoon at a time, and pulse to incorporate it into the flour mixture. Add just enough water for the pastry to hold together in a very loose ball.

3. Turn the dough out onto a large sheet of wax paper and press it into a 5-inch disk. Wrap tightly and refrigerate for at least 1 hour. (*The pastry dough can be made up to 1 week ahead and frozen. Wrap first in wax paper and then in aluminum foil so it doesn't dry out.*)

—Susan Hermann Loomis

• • •

WARM LEMON SOUFFLE PIE

This recipe is from Sue Crouse, who says that it was handed down from her great-grandmother. "My ancient recipe card calls for the whites to be made into meringue to top the cake," she writes, "but truthfully, I am not too crazy about meringue and think the pie is excellent without it." (She's right.) We both think this recipe beats the cornstarch-thickened version all to pieces. Serve it warm or at room temperature on the same day it is baked.

8 Servings

Basic Pie Pastry (p. 208)
3 whole eggs, separated
3 egg yolks
¾ cup sugar
2 teaspoons finely grated lemon zest
3 tablespoons fresh lemon juice

1. Preheat the oven to 350°. On a lightly floured work surface, roll the pastry into an 11-inch circle about ⅛ inch thick. Line a 9-inch pie pan with the pastry and fit it against the bottom and the sides without stretching. Trim the overhang to ½ inch, then fold the extra dough under and crimp decoratively. Bake for 25 minutes until golden brown, pricking any air bubbles in the pastry with a fork after 10 minutes. Transfer to a wire rack and let cool completely in the pan.

2. Meanwhile, in a medium stainless steel bowl set over simmering water, whisk all 6 egg yolks until foamy, about 20 seconds. Gradually whisk in the sugar, lemon zest and lemon juice. Cook, whisking constantly, until the mixture thickens, about 8 minutes. Remove from the heat and continue whisking for 1 minute. Set aside.

3. Using an electric mixer, beat the egg whites on medium speed until glossy and firm. Fold the whites into the yolk mixture until just blended. Gently pour the filling into the cooled crust and bake for 20 minutes, or until puffed and golden. Let cool slightly on a wire rack and serve warm.

—*Richard Sax*

• • •

CRANBERRY PIE

This marvelous recipe is from Elizabeth Ryan, a farmer and baker in New York's Hudson Valley. It's one of her most popular Thanksgiving pies, vying with apple and pumpkin. "It's my version of mince pie," she says, "And I like it a lot better."

Makes One 9-Inch Double-Crust Pie

Farmhouse Pie Pastry (p. 206)
1 cup sugar
¼ cup all-purpose flour
1 bag (12 ounces) fresh or frozen cranberries
½ cup golden raisins
⅓ cup coarsely chopped walnuts
¼ cup fresh orange juice
3 tablespoons unsalted butter, melted
½ teaspoon finely grated orange zest
1 egg mixed with 2 teaspoons water, for brushing

1. Preheat the oven to 400°. On a lightly floured surface, roll out half of the pie pastry into a 12-inch circle. Place the dough in a 9-inch pie plate, fitting it evenly into the plate without stretching; leave the edge overhanging and refrigerate. On a sheet of wax paper, roll out the remaining pie pastry into another 12-inch circle; transfer the pastry on the wax paper to a baking sheet and refrigerate.

2. In a small bowl, mix the sugar with the flour and set aside.

3. In a food processor, chop the cranberries until some are finely ground and the largest pieces are the size of peas, about 2 minutes for frozen and several pulses for fresh.

4. Transfer the cranberries to a medium bowl and add the raisins, walnuts, orange juice, melted butter and orange zest. Thoroughly combine.

5. Sprinkle ¼ cup of the reserved sugar and flour mixture on the bottom of the pastry-lined pie plate. Pile in the cranberry filling and sprinkle the remaining sugar and flour mixture on top. Cover with the rolled out pie pastry and crimp the edges together to seal. Brush the top of the pie with the egg wash and cut several slits for steam to escape.

6. Place the pie plate on a baking sheet and bake in the middle of the oven for about 50 minutes, until the pastry is golden and the filling bubbles up through the steam vents. Transfer to a rack and let cool to room temperature before serving.

—*Susan Hermann Loomis*

• • •

PIES, CAKES & COOKIES

BASIC PIE PASTRY

Makes One 9- or 10-Inch Pie Shell

1½ cups all-purpose flour, preferably
    unbleached
1 teaspoon sugar
½ teaspoon salt
6 tablespoons cold unsalted butter,
    cut into small pieces
1 tablespoon cold vegetable
    shortening
2 to 3 tablespoons ice water

1. In a food processor, combine the flour, sugar, salt, butter and shortening. Pulse until the mixture resembles coarse meal.

2. Add 2 tablespoons of the ice water, 1 tablespoon at a time, pulsing briefly after each addition. Pulse just until the dough barely comes together. Add the remaining 1 tablespoon cold water if the dough is too dry. Transfer the dough to a lightly floured work surface and gather it into a ball, handling it as little as possible. Flatten it slightly, wrap tightly and refrigerate until chilled, at least 30 minutes, before rolling out. (*The dough can be refrigerated for up to 1 day.*)

—*Richard Sax*

• • •

ALSATIAN APPLE TART

6 to 8 Servings

Flaky Pie Pastry (recipe follows)
2 eggs
1 cup Crème Fraîche (p. 267)
½ cup vanilla sugar (see Note)
2 medium cooking apples, such as
    Golden Delicious or Cortland
¼ teaspoon cinnamon
⅓ cup finely chopped walnuts

1. On a lightly floured work surface, roll the pastry into a 12-inch round about ⅛ inch thick. Transfer the dough to an 11-inch tart pan with a removable bottom, fitting it evenly without stretching. Fold the overhang in to reinforce the sides, pressing the pastry against the rim. Trim off excess dough. Cover with plastic wrap and refrigerate until well chilled, at least 1 hour.

2. Preheat the oven to 400°. Prick the bottom of the pastry all over with a fork. Bake the tart shell for about 30 minutes, until well browned. Transfer to a rack and let cool completely before filling.

3. In a medium bowl, combine the eggs, crème fraîche and vanilla sugar and whisk until frothy.

4. Peel, quarter and core the apples and cut lengthwise into ¼-inch slices. Fill the tart shell with the apple slices in an even layer. Pour the crème fraîche mixture over the apples and sprinkle the cinnamon and walnuts on top.

5. Bake the tart in the middle of the oven for 25 minutes, until the filling is set, the apples are tender and the nuts are golden. Let cool; serve warm or at room temperature.

NOTE: *To make vanilla sugar, place 4 cups granulated sugar in a clean 1-quart glass jar. Push a whole vanilla bean down into the sugar, cover the jar tightly and set aside for at least 1 week.*

—*Susan Herrmann Loomis*

• • •

FLAKY PIE PASTRY

Makes One 11-Inch Tart Shell

1¼ cups plus 2 tablespoons
    unbleached all-purpose flour
¼ teaspoon salt
1 tablespoon sugar
1 stick (4 ounces) cold unsalted
    butter, cut into ½-inch pieces
3 to 4 tablespoons ice water

In a food processor, combine the flour, salt and sugar and pulse once or twice. Add the butter and pulse until the mixture resembles coarse meal. Add 3 tablespoons of the ice water and pulse until the dough just begins to hold together but does not form a ball. If necessary, add the remaining 1 tablespoon of water, 1 teaspoon at a time. Transfer the dough to a lightly floured surface and gather it into a ball, handling it as little as possible. Pat into a flat 6-inch disk; wrap tightly. Refrigerate until chilled, at least several hours and preferably overnight, before rolling out.

—*Susan Herrmann Loomis*

• • •

Heavenly Puff Angels (p. 233).

Above, Fall Linzer Tart (p. 216).
Right, Mom's Citrus Meringue Pie (p. 213).

MOM'S CITRUS MERINGUE PIE

Makes One 8-Inch Pie

¼ cup cornstarch
3 tablespoons fresh lemon juice
2 tablespoons fresh lime juice
1⅓ cups sugar
Finely grated zest of 1 large lemon
1 tablespoon unsalted butter
Salt
2 eggs, separated
Prebaked Orange Pastry Shell
  (recipe follows)
Pinch of cream of tartar

1. Preheat the oven to 350°. In a medium nonreactive saucepan, combine the cornstarch, lemon juice and lime juice, and stir until the cornstarch dissolves. Stir in 1½ cups of water, 1 cup of the sugar, the lemon zest, butter and a pinch of salt. Bring to a boil over moderately low heat, stirring constantly with a wooden spoon. Remove from the heat.

2. Place the egg yolks in a medium bowl. Gradually whisk in the hot lemon-lime mixture. Set aside to cool slightly, then pour into the pastry shell. Set aside.

3. In a medium bowl, using an electric mixer, beat the egg whites with a pinch of salt at medium speed until frothy, about 1 minute. Continue to beat, gradually sprinkling in the cream of tartar and the remaining ⅓ cup sugar, until stiff, glossy peaks form, about 2 minutes longer.

Pear and Red Wine Custard Tart in a Hazelnut Crust (p. 215).

4. Gently dollop the meringue over the lemon-lime filling. Using the back of a spoon, completely cover the pie with the meringue, sealing the edge all around and swirling decoratively with the spoon. Bake for 25 minutes, until the meringue is golden brown. Let cool to room temperature on a rack, then refrigerate until well chilled, about 3 hours.

—*Jessica B. Harris*

• • •

PREBAKED ORANGE PASTRY SHELL

Because lard is used in the dough, this pastry gets very soft as it comes to room temperature, so roll it out as quickly as possible.

Makes Enough for One 8- or 9-Inch Single-Crust Pie

1 cup all-purpose flour
½ teaspoon salt
⅓ cup chilled lard or 7 tablespoons
  vegetable shortening
2 to 3 tablespoons chilled fresh
  orange juice

1. In a medium bowl, toss the flour and salt together. Using a pastry blender or 2 knives, cut in the lard until the mixture is mealy. Using a fork, gradually stir in 2 tablespoons of the orange juice; continue to stir until the dough comes together. (If the dough seems too dry and crumbly, add some of the remaining orange juice, 1 teaspoon at a time, as necessary.)

2. Flatten the dough into a disk, wrap in wax paper and refrigerate until chilled, about 30 minutes.

3. Preheat the oven to 350°. On a lightly floured surface, roll out the dough, rotating and flouring it as necessary, into a 10-inch round about ⅛ inch thick. Place the dough in an 8- or 9-inch pie plate, fitting it evenly without stretching. Roll up the overhang and crimp the edges. Prick all over the bottom of the pastry with a fork. Bake the shell for about 30 minutes, until golden brown. Transfer to a rack and let cool completely before filling.

—*Jessica B. Harris*

• • •

FRESH RHUBARB TART

Rhubarb is readily available throughout the year in the Paris markets. In the early spring months it comes from hothouses in Holland and is generally more tender and sweeter than the field-grown kind, which appears by late spring. When buying rhubarb, look for young stalks. Always discard the leaves (they are full of poisonous oxalic acid) and, if necessary, peel the stalks to remove the coarse strings before cooking. Although rhubarb is naturally tart, I like to add lemon zest and candied ginger to emphasize its unusual acidic flavor.

8 Servings

1½ cups unbleached all-purpose
  flour
Pinch of salt
1 cup plus 2 tablespoons sugar
1 stick (4 ounces) plus 2 tablespoons
  cold unsalted butter, cut into
  small dice
1 teaspoon almond extract

213

2 pounds fresh rhubarb stalks,
    trimmed and cut into ½-inch dice
2 tablespoons finely chopped candied
    ginger, plus fine slivers of candied
    ginger for garnish
1 teaspoon finely grated lemon zest
1 cup crème fraîche, for serving
Fresh mint sprigs, for garnish

1. In a food processor, combine the flour, salt and 2 tablespoons of the sugar. Pulse briefly to combine. Add the butter and process until crumbly, about 15 seconds. With the machine on, pour in the almond extract and 1 tablespoon of cold water and process until the dough just barely forms a ball.

2. Press and pat the dough evenly into 9½-inch tart pan with a removable bottom; make sure to press the dough into the grooved sides of the pan. With a fork, prick the bottom of the tart shell at 1-inch intervals. Wrap well and freeze for at least 30 minutes or overnight.

3. Preheat the oven to 400°. Remove the tart shell from the freezer and bake in the middle of the oven for 15 minutes. Reduce the temperature to 375° and bake for about 15 minutes longer, until light golden brown all over. Remove the tart shell from the oven and reduce the temperature to 325°.

4. Meanwhile, in a heavy medium nonreactive saucepan, combine the rhubarb, chopped candied ginger and the remaining 1 cup sugar. Cover tightly and cook over moderate heat until the rhubarb is very soft, about 15 minutes. Uncover, increase the heat to high and cook, stirring constantly, until a thick puree forms, about 5 minutes longer. Let the puree cool for 10 minutes, then stir in the lemon zest.

5. Spread the rhubarb puree in the tart shell and bake for 20 minutes. Let

cool to room temperature on a rack. Garnish the tart with the slivered candied ginger.

6. Remove the sides of the pan and serve the tart in wedges, garnished with a large dollop of crème fraîche and fresh mint sprigs.

—Ann Chantal Altman

• • •

BLUEBERRY TART

8 Servings

¼ cup whole almonds (1½ ounces)
⅓ cup granulated sugar
2 tablespoons all-purpose flour
Unbaked Tart Shell (recipe follows)
1½ pints blueberries (4 cups)
1 tablespoon confectioners' sugar
Sweetened sour cream or vanilla ice
    cream, for serving

1. Preheat the oven to 425°. In a food processor, combine the almonds, 2 tablespoons of the granulated sugar and the flour. Process until the almonds are finely ground. Sprinkle the mixture evenly into the tart shell. Spread the blueberries over the almond mixture. Sprinkle the berries with the remaining 1 tablespoon plus 1 teaspoon granulated sugar.

2. Place the tart on the bottom rack of the oven and reduce the temperature to 400°. Bake for about 45 minutes, until the crust is golden brown. Transfer to a rack to cool completely.

3. Before serving, lightly sift the confectioners' sugar over the tart. Serve in wedges, accompanied with sweetened sour cream or vanilla ice cream.

—Lydie Marshall

• • •

UNBAKED TART SHELL

It is difficult to make a butter pastry crust in the summer because the butter softens so quickly. To remedy this problem, keep a bag of flour in the freezer during hot weather. Cut the butter into small pieces and freeze it for at least 15 minutes before making pastry.

Makes One 11½-Inch Tart Shell

1½ cups very cold all-purpose flour
1 stick (4 ounces) plus 4 tablespoons
    cold unsalted butter, cut into
    small pieces and frozen
1 tablespoon sugar
Pinch of salt
3 to 4 tablespoons ice water

1. In a food processor, combine the flour, butter, sugar and salt. Process just until coarse crumbs form. Sprinkle 3 tablespoons of the ice water over the crumbs and process for 5 seconds.

2. Transfer the crumbs to a work surface. Working with about 3 tablespoons at a time, use the heel of your hand to quickly knead the crumbs into a cohesive dough. Sprinkle up to 1 tablespoon more water on the dough if necessary. Shape the dough into a 5-inch disk, wrap in wax paper and refrigerate for 15 minutes.

3. Generously flour a work surface. Using a floured rolling pin, roll out the dough into a 13-inch circle about ⅛ inch thick. Brush off all excess flour and fold the dough in quarters. Place the dough in an 11½-by-1-inch tart pan with a removable bottom and unfold. Press lightly on the dough to evenly line the pan. Trim the dough flush with the rim. Prick the bottom of the shell all over with a fork. Wrap the shell well and freeze for at least 1 hour and up to 2 days.

—Lydie Marshall

• • •

PEAR AND RED WINE CUSTARD TART IN A HAZELNUT CRUST

This tart should be served the day it is made. Once baked, it can be set under the broiler for a few seconds to lightly brown the custard.

❦ There's an acidic zip to this tart that comes from the orange and lemon juice; it calls for a dessert wine with acid. The rich flavor of the crust, and of the pears, further requires a richly flavored wine. A fine solution is a 1981 Tokay Aszú from Hungary (a sweet one, with 5 *puttonyos* on the label); it tastes something like a cross between Sauternes and cream sherry, but with more acidity than either one. —David Rosengarten

8 Servings

1 cup granulated sugar
1 bottle (750 ml) dry red wine
1 cup fresh orange juice
⅓ cup fresh lemon juice
2 cinnamon sticks
8 Bartlett pears
1 cup hazelnuts (5 ounces)
1 cup flour
½ cup confectioners' sugar
Pinch of salt

6 tablespoons cold unsalted butter, cut into tablespoons
1 egg yolk
3 whole eggs, lightly beaten

1. Preheat the oven to 350°. In a large nonreactive saucepan, combine ⅔ cup of the granulated sugar with the wine, orange juice, lemon juice and cinnamon sticks and bring to a boil over high heat. Boil until the liquid reduces to 3½ cups, about 12 minutes.

2. Meanwhile, cut a circle of parchment paper to fit just inside the saucepan. Peel, quarter and core the pears. Add them to the pan and lightly press the parchment paper on top. Bring to a boil over moderately high heat. Reduce the heat to low and simmer for 10 minutes. Remove from the heat and let the pears cool in the poaching liquid.

3. Preheat the oven to 350°. Place the hazelnuts in a pie pan and bake for about 15 minutes, until their skins crack. Transfer the hot nuts to a kitchen towel and rub them together to loosen their skins. Let cool completely.

4. In a food processor, combine the cooled hazelnuts with the remaining ⅓ cup granulated sugar and process to a fine powder. Add the flour, confectioners' sugar and salt and pulse to blend. Add the butter and pulse until only a few large pieces remain. Add the egg yolk and process just until a dough forms. Gather the dough into a ball.

5. Press the dough into an even ¼-inch layer over the bottom and up the side of a 9-by-1-inch fluted tart pan with a removable bottom. Trim off any excess dough. Pierce the bottom all over with a fork. Cover the tart shell and freeze for 1 hour. (*The recipe can be prepared to this point up to 2 days ahead. Cover and refrigerate the pears.*)

6. Preheat the oven to 350°. Line the frozen tart shell with parchment paper and fill with pie weights or dried beans. Bake for 30 minutes, or until the crust is set and golden. Remove from the oven and let cool, then carefully remove the paper and weights.

7. Using a slotted spoon, transfer the pears to a plate lined with paper towels. Strain the wine syrup through a fine sieve and return it to the saucepan. Bring to a boil over high heat. Reduce the heat to moderately low and simmer until the syrup has reduced to ¾ cup, about 15 minutes. Pour the syrup into a bowl and let cool until just warm.

8. Arrange the pear quarters in the baked tart shell on their sides in 2 concentric circles, overlapping them slightly if necessary. Beat the whole eggs into the warm wine syrup until blended. Pour the mixture evenly over the pears and bake for 40 to 50 minutes, until the custard is just set. Transfer to a rack to cool. Serve at room temperature.

—Bob Chambers

• • •

CREAMY LEMON CHEESE TART

6 to 8 Servings

Flaky Pie Pastry (p. 208)
3¼ cups cottage cheese
½ cup sour cream
6 tablespoons vanilla sugar (see Note, p. 208)
1 teaspoon vanilla extract
1 teaspoon finely grated lemon zest
2 eggs, lightly beaten
1 tablespoon all-purpose flour

1. On a lightly floured work surface, roll the pastry into a 12-inch round about ⅛ inch thick. Transfer the dough to an 11-inch tart pan with a removable bottom, fitting it evenly without stretching. Fold the overhang in to reinforce the sides, pressing the pastry against the rim of the pan. Trim off any excess dough. Cover and refrigerate until well chilled, at least 1 hour.

2. Preheat the oven to 400°. Prick the bottom of the pastry all over with a fork. Bake the tart shell for about 30 minutes, until well browned all over. Transfer to a rack and let cool completely before filling.

3. Reduce the oven temperature to 325°. Put the cottage cheese in a food processor and process until smooth. Add the sour cream, vanilla sugar, vanilla extract and lemon zest and process to mix. Add the eggs and process until blended. Add the flour and process until the mixture is very smooth, 2 to 3 minutes.

4. Place the tart shell on a baking sheet and pour in the cheese filling. Bake in the middle of the oven for about 35 minutes, until the filling is set and a cake tester inserted in the center comes out clean. Transfer to a wire rack and let cool to room temperature. Refrigerate until well chilled, at least 1 hour. Serve chilled.

—*Susan Herrmann Loomis*

• • •

FALL LINZER TART

Nancy Silverton admits that "it may sound trite, but simplicity is the key to desserts." She believes that a restaurant dessert menu should make diners think "This sounds great" not "What is this?" Her luscious Fall Linzer Tart fits the bill.

12 Servings

3 hard-cooked egg yolks
½ cup whole blanched almonds (3 ounces)
1½ cups sugar
2½ cups all-purpose flour
1 tablespoon cinnamon
1½ teaspoons freshly grated nutmeg
½ teaspoon plus a pinch of ground cloves
3 sticks (12 ounces) plus 1 teaspoon cold unsalted butter
3 tablespoons finely grated lemon zest (from 4 large lemons)
2 teaspoons almond extract
1 teaspoon finely grated orange zest
2 cinnamon sticks
Pinch of fresh, coarsely ground black pepper
1 bag (12 ounces) fresh cranberries
¾ cup fresh orange juice
½ cup blackberry or boysenberry preserves

1. Press the egg yolks through a strainer set over a small bowl and set aside. In a food processor, grind the almonds with 1 tablespoon of the sugar until fine. Transfer to a medium bowl and mix in the flour, cinnamon, 1 teaspoon of the nutmeg and ½ teaspoon of the cloves; set aside.

2. Cut the 3 sticks of cold butter into tablespoons. In a large bowl, beat the butter with the lemon zest at high speed until light in color, fluffy and soft peaks form, about 10 minutes. Beat in the sieved egg yolks and 1 cup of the sugar until well blended. Beat in the almond extract. Mix in the flour mixture by hand until a dough forms. Divide the dough in half and shape into two 6-inch disks. Wrap tightly and refrigerate until well chilled, at least 2 hours or overnight.

3. In a heavy, medium, nonreactive saucepan, combine ¼ cup of the sugar with ⅓ cup of water and bring to a boil over moderately high heat. Boil just until the sugar dissolves, about 30 seconds. Stir in the orange zest, cinnamon sticks, pepper and the remaining ½ teaspoon nutmeg and pinch of ground cloves. Increase the heat to high and boil until the mixture is thick and syrupy and turns a light caramel color, about 3 minutes.

4. Add the cranberries and stir to coat with the syrup. Cook until some of the berries begin to pop, about 2 minutes. Stir in the orange juice and 2 tablespoons of the sugar. Reduce the heat to moderate and cook, stirring occasionally, until most of the cranberries have popped and the mixture is thick, about 10 minutes. Remove from the heat and set aside to cool.

5. Grease an 11-by-1-inch fluted tart pan with a removable bottom with the remaining 1 teaspoon butter. Between 2 sheets of wax paper, roll one disk of the chilled dough into a 13-inch circle, about ⅛ inch thick. Transfer to a cookie sheet and refrigerate until firm enough to handle, about 10 minutes. Peel off the top layer of wax paper and invert the dough into the prepared tart pan. Peel off the other layer of wax paper and carefully pat the dough into the pan. Trim the excess dough from the rim. Refrigerate until chilled, at least 30 minutes.

6. Meanwhile, preheat the oven to 350°. Between 2 sheets of wax paper, roll the remaining dough into a 13-inch circle, about ⅛ inch thick. Transfer to a cookie sheet and refrigerate until firm enough to handle, about 10 minutes.

7. Remove the cinnamon sticks from the cranberry mixture and stir in the preserves. Spoon the filling into the tart pan and spread evenly over the bottom.

8. Peel off the top layer of wax paper from the chilled dough; invert the dough over the filling. Peel off the other layer of wax paper and crimp to seal the edges. Trim off any excess dough even with the rim. With a small sharp knife, cut out about eight 1½-inch diamonds from the top crust. Mist or brush the top crust lightly with water and sprinkle the remaining 1 tablespoon sugar on top. Bake for about 55 minutes, until well browned. Transfer to a rack to cool slightly before unmolding and serving.

—Nancy Silverton, Campanile
Los Angeles

• • •

RASPBERRY-CHOCOLATE TART

6 to 8 Servings

⅓ *cup sliced blanched almonds (1 ounce)*
¼ *cup sugar*
1¼ *cups all-purpose flour*
⅛ *teaspoon salt*
6 *tablespoons unsalted butter, at room temperature*
¼ *teaspoon almond extract*
2½ *ounces bittersweet or semisweet chocolate, finely chopped*
1 *pint fresh raspberries*
⅓ *cup red currant jelly*

1. Preheat the oven to 400°. In a food processor, combine the almonds and sugar and process until the nuts are very finely ground. Add the flour and salt and pulse just to blend. Add the butter and almond extract. With the machine running, add 2 to 3 teaspoons of water through the feed tube and process until the dough just begins to form a mass.

2. Gather the dough into a ball and, with your fingers, press it evenly into an ungreased 9-by-1-inch fluted tart pan with a removable bottom. Prick the dough well with a fork. Bake the crust for 20 to 25 minutes, or until golden brown.

3. While the crust is hot, sprinkle the chopped chocolate evenly over the bottom. Let stand until the chocolate melts, about 5 minutes. With the back of a spoon, spread the melted chocolate evenly over the bottom of the crust. Let cool completely on a wire rack.

4. Remove the side of the pan and transfer the tart shell to a serving plate. Arrange the raspberries in the shell. In a small saucepan, melt the red currant jelly over moderate heat, stirring constantly, for about 1 minute. Using a small pastry brush, brush the melted jelly on the raspberries. Serve at room temperature. *(The tart can be assembled up to 1 day ahead. Cover tightly and refrigerate. Let return to room temperature for 1 hour before serving.)*

—Rick Rodgers

• • •

BITTERSWEET CHOCOLATE TART

This is an exquisitely elegant tart that has a satiny dark sheen and a wonderful play of chocolate against the delicate sweet pastry. It's also a cinch to make. At Joël Robuchon's Paris restaurant, Jamin, this tart is prepared at the very last minute and served warm, dusted with cocoa powder or accompanied with a scoop of vanilla ice cream. The tart may, however, be prepared several hours in advance. Offer slender slices, for it's very rich.

Makes One 9-Inch Tart

¾ *cup heavy cream*
⅓ *cup milk*
7 *ounces imported bittersweet chocolate, grated or finely chopped*
1 *egg, lightly beaten*
Shortbread Pastry Shell (recipe follows)
½ *teaspoon unsweetened cocoa powder, preferably Dutch process, for garnish*

1. Preheat the oven to 375°. In a medium saucepan, combine the cream and milk and bring to a simmer over moderate heat. Remove from the heat, add the chocolate and stir until thoroughly melted, about 1 minute. Set aside and let cool to lukewarm. When cooled, whisk in the egg until thoroughly blended.

2. Pour the mixture into the baked pastry shell. Bake in the middle of the oven until the filling is almost firm but

217

still trembling in the center, 12 to 15 minutes. Transfer to a wire rack to cool. Dust with unsweetened cocoa powder. Serve warm or at room temperature.

—*Patricia Wells*

• • •

SHORTBREAD PASTRY SHELL

Shortbread pastry is one of my favorites, and this version, flecked with vanilla seeds and enriched with egg and almonds, is particularly delicious. The same dough can be used to prepare shortbread cookies. This is exceptional as a base for Joël Robuchon's extraordinary chocolate tart, making a marvelous alliance of "bread and chocolate."

Makes One 9-Inch Tart Shell

1 *plump vanilla bean*
1 *egg yolk, at room temperature*
2 *tablespoons whole blanched
    almonds*
½ *cup confectioners' sugar, sifted*
¾ *cup all-purpose flour, sifted*
Pinch of salt
5 *tablespoons unsalted butter, at
    room temperature*

1. Flatten the vanilla bean and cut it in half lengthwise. With a small spoon, scrape the seeds into a small bowl. Add the egg yolk and stir to blend. Set aside.

2. In a food processor, combine the almonds and sugar and process until finely ground. Add the flour and salt and process to blend. Add the butter and process just until the mixture resembles coarse crumbs. Add the egg yolk and vanilla seeds and pulse until the dough just begins to hold together, about 10 times. Do not overprocess; the dough

should not form a ball.

3. Transfer the dough to a sheet of wax paper. With your hands, gently form the dough into a ball, handling it as little as possible, and flatten it into a disk. Wrap and refrigerate until well chilled, at least 1 hour or overnight.

4. Butter the bottom and sides of a 9-inch fluted tart pan with a removable bottom. On a lightly floured surface, roll out the dough into an 11-inch circle. Transfer the dough to the prepared tart pan. Using your fingertips, gently press the dough against the fluted sides of the pan. Allow about ½-inch overhang to drape naturally over the rim of the pan. Generously prick the bottom of the dough all over with a fork. Refrigerate until well chilled, at least 1 hour, or wrap loosely in foil and refrigerate for up to 24 hours.

5. Preheat the oven to 375°. Place the tart pan on a baking sheet and bake in the middle of the oven for about 5 minutes, until the pastry just begins to firm up. Remove from the oven and with a sharp knife, carefully cut off and discard the overhanging pastry to make a smooth, even rim. Return the shell to the oven and bake for about 15 minutes longer until the pastry is well browned all over. Transfer to a wire rack and let cool before filling.

—*Patricia Wells*

• • •

CHOCOLATE-CINNAMON TARTLETS WITH RICOTTA AND HONEY

Makes 24 Tartlets

4½ *tablespoons unsalted butter,
    softened*
3½ *tablespoons sugar*
3 *tablespoons unsweetened cocoa
    powder, plus more for dusting*
1 *teaspoon cinnamon, plus more for
    dusting*
⅔ *cup all-purpose flour*
Pinch of salt
⅔ *cup ricotta cheese (see Note)*
2 *tablespoons mild honey*

1. In a large bowl, cream the butter with the sugar. Stir in the 3 tablespoons cocoa and 1 teaspoon cinnamon. Add the flour and salt and stir until completely blended. Pat the dough into a disk and refrigerate until firm, about 30 minutes.

2. Preheat the oven to 350°. On a lightly floured surface, roll out the dough about ¼ inch thick. Using a 2-inch round biscuit cutter or glass, cut out 24 disks. Press the disks into 24 mini-muffin molds. Bake for about 10 minutes, until firm but not too dark. Set aside to cool for a few minutes before turning out onto a rack to cool completely.

3. Fill each tartlet shell with a heaping teaspoon of the ricotta cheese and drizzle each generously with some of the honey. Put a small amount of cinnamon and cocoa in a fine strainer and dust the tops of the tartlets.

NOTE: *If possible, use freshly made ricotta available at Italian markets, cheese stores and specialty food stores.*

—Marcia Kiesel

• • •

CRUSTLESS PEAR AND ALMOND TART

This dessert has the look of a tart from a fancy French bakery, but it doesn't require pastry-making skills. In place of a crust, a ground almond-based batter is spread in a tart pan, then sliced pears are fanned out on top. As the tart bakes, the almond mixture rises up around the pears. If you want the tart to glisten, glaze the top after baking with melted and strained apricot preserves. This tart is best served the day it is made, either warm or at room temperature.

8 Servings

1¼ cups whole blanched almonds (6 ounces)
½ cup plus 1½ tablespoons sugar
⅓ cup all-purpose flour
⅛ teaspoon salt
2 eggs, at room temperature
¼ cup milk
4 tablespoons unsalted butter, melted, plus 1 tablespoon, cut into small bits
2 large evenly sized ripe Bartlett or Bosc pears (about ½ pound each)

1. Preheat the oven to 350°. Butter a fluted 9½-by-1-inch ceramic baking dish or tart pan.

2. In a food processor, combine the almonds and ½ cup of the sugar and process until finely ground. Do not overprocess to a paste. Transfer the mixture to a medium bowl and stir in the flour and salt until blended.

3. In another medium bowl, whisk the eggs until frothy. Whisk in the milk and melted butter until well blended.

4. Add the egg mixture to the almonds and stir to blend well. Pour the batter into the prepared dish and spread to form an even layer.

5. Peel, quarter and core the pears. Cut each pear quarter crosswise into thin slices, keeping the slices assembled as you go. Slide one of the sliced pear quarters onto a metal palette knife and set it on top of the batter like the spoke of a wheel. Repeat with the remaining sliced pear quarters.

6. Press the fanned pears down into the batter so that only the surface of the pears is showing. Sprinkle the remaining 1½ tablespoons sugar evenly over the pears and batter. Scatter the cut-up pieces of butter over the top.

7. Bake the tart in the upper third of the oven until the batter is puffed and golden brown, 40 to 45 minutes. Let the tart cool on a rack and serve it directly from the baking dish.

—Diana Sturgis

• • •

HONEY-ROASTED PECAN NAPOLEONS

Dazzling desserts are a big attraction at Aureole in New York City and for good reason. Pastry chef Richard Leach says that he amuses himself by coming up with sophisticated combinations of textures and tastes.

6 Servings

1½ sticks (6 ounces) butter
2 cups (10 ounces) pecan halves
8 sheets of phyllo dough
2 tablespoons confectioners' sugar
Pecan Pastry Cream (recipe follows)
Vanilla Custard Sauce (p. 268)
Candied Pecans (p. 258)

1. In a small saucepan, melt the butter over low heat. Pour the clear melted butter into a small bowl, discarding the milky solids; keep warm.

2. Preheat the oven to 350°. Finely chop the pecans and set aside. Line a baking sheet with parchment paper.

3. Place one sheet of the phyllo dough on a work surface; keep the rest covered with a damp towel as you work. Brush the sheet lightly with some of the clarified butter. Sprinkle ¼ cup of the finely chopped pecans over the phyllo. Place another sheet of phyllo on top and repeat the process until there are 4 stacked layers of buttered pastry, topped with nuts. Press down lightly on the layers so that they stick together. Using a 4-inch round cookie cutter, cut out 12 rounds and transfer to the prepared baking sheet. Repeat with the remaining 4 sheets of phyllo dough, melted butter and chopped pecans.

4. Sprinkle the top of each phyllo round lightly with the confectioners' sugar. Cover with another sheet of parchment paper and bake for about 8 minutes, or until golden brown. Let cool thoroughly on the baking sheet.

5. To assemble the napoleons, place a scant teaspoon of the Pecan Pastry Cream in the center of 6 large plates and top with 1 pastry round. Spread 2 tablespoons of the pastry cream on top. Cover with another pastry round and spread with 2 more tablespoons of pastry cream. Continue layering until there are 4 layers of pastry and 3 layers of pastry cream. Drizzle about ¼ cup of the Vanilla Custard Sauce around each of the napoleons and scatter the Candied Pecans around the plates.

—*Richard Leach, Aureole,*
New York City

• • •

PECAN PASTRY CREAM

This custard mixture is infused with pecans and thickened with cornstarch so that it will hold its shape without making the crisp phyllo layers soggy. The custard should be well chilled before using, so it is best to make it a day ahead.

Makes About 2½ Cups

½ cup pecan halves
2 cups milk
½ cup plus 2 tablespoons granulated sugar
3 tablespoons mild honey
2 tablespoons unsalted butter
8 egg yolks
3 tablespoons cornstarch

1. Preheat the oven to 350°. Spread the pecans on a baking sheet and bake until well toasted, about 10 minutes. Let cool to room temperature and then chop coarsely.

2. In a medium saucepan, combine the toasted chopped pecans with the milk, ¼ cup of the granulated sugar, honey and butter. Bring to a boil over moderate heat. Remove from the heat and set aside to cool for 20 minutes. Strain the milk mixture into a medium bowl and discard the nuts.

3. In a medium bowl, whisk the egg yolks with the cornstarch and the remaining 6 tablespoons granulated sugar. Gradually whisk in the warm milk until blended. Strain the mixture into a large stainless steel bowl.

4. Bring a large saucepan of water to a boil over moderately high heat; reduce the heat to moderate. Place the bowl with the milk-yolk mixture over the simmering water and cook, whisking constantly and turning the bowl frequently to insure even cooking, until the mixture thickens and no cornstarch taste remains, about 8 minutes. Remove the bowl from the heat and let the pastry cream cool to room temperature. Cover tightly to prevent a skin from forming and refrigerate until well chilled or overnight.

—*Richard Leach, Aureole,*
New York City

• • •

FOUR-LAYER STRAWBERRY TORTE

6 to 8 Servings

1½ cups cake flour
¼ cup plus 2 tablespoons sugar
¼ teaspoon salt
6 tablespoons cold unsalted butter, cut into bits
1 egg yolk
1 tablespoon ice water
1 pint strawberries
1½ cups heavy cream
1 tablespoon bourbon
½ cup toasted chopped walnuts or pecans

1. In a food processor, combine the flour, 3 tablespoons of the sugar and the salt. Pulse briefly to sift. Add the butter and process until mealy crumbs form.

2. In a small bowl, lightly beat the egg yolk with the ice water. With the machine running, add the yolk and process until the dough just begins to form a ball. (Do not overprocess, or the dough will be tough.) Divide the dough into 4 sections; form each into a disk. Wrap the disks separately in wax paper and refrigerate for 15 minutes.

3. Preheat the oven to 350°. Place each disk between 2 sheets of wax paper and roll out into an 8-inch circle. Refrigerate for 15 minutes.

4. Working with 1 disk at a time, peel off the top sheet of wax paper and invert the dough onto a very large baking sheet or jelly-roll pan. Peel off the other sheet of wax paper. Repeat with a second disk and place on the baking sheet. Bake for 16 minutes, or until the edges are golden. Let cool for 5 minutes on the sheet, then carefully transfer the rounds to racks to cool completely. Repeat with the remaining 2 disks. (*The recipe can be prepared to this point up to 1 day ahead. Wrap well and store at room temperature.*)

5. Reserve 4 of the largest strawberries and halve the rest. In a small bowl, combine them with 1½ tablespoons of the sugar and mash with a fork. In a medium bowl, combine the heavy cream, bourbon and the remaining 1½ tablespoons sugar and beat until stiff.

6. To assemble, place 1 round on a cake platter and cover with about ¾ cup of the bourbon cream. Top with one-third of the strawberries. Sprinkle with 2 tablespoons of the nuts. Repeat with the second and third layers. (You will have used up all the strawberries, but there will still be cream and nuts remaining.) Place the fourth layer on top and cover with the remaining cream. Arrange the 4 reserved strawberries on top and sprinkle with the remaining nuts. Refrigerate, uncovered, for at least 3 hours or for up to 6 hours.

—Lee Bailey

• • •

MERINGUE CAKE WITH CHOCOLATE BOURBON SAUCE

For those who are not chocolate lovers, this versatile, easy-to-make cake can also be served with vanilla ice cream, white chocolate sauce or a berry puree.

8 Servings

3 egg whites
¼ teaspoon cream of tartar
¾ cup plus 1 tablespoon superfine sugar

¼ cup sliced almonds
3 ounces semisweet chocolate, coarsely chopped
¼ cup heavy cream
1 tablespoon unsalted butter
1 tablespoon bourbon
2 tablespoons strongly brewed coffee

1. Preheat the oven to 300°. Line a round 8-inch cake pan with a large sheet of aluminum foil. Fold the excess foil over the sides of the cake pan and spray the inside with vegetable cooking spray.

2. In a medium bowl, using a hand-held electric mixer, beat the egg whites at high speed until frothy, about 30 seconds. Add the cream of tartar and beat until soft peaks form. Gradually beat in the sugar. Continue beating at high speed until firm, glossy peaks form.

3. Scrape the egg whites into the prepared pan and smooth the surface with a rubber spatula. Sprinkle the almonds evenly on top and bake for 1 hour and 15 minutes, or until puffy and golden. Carefully remove the meringue from the pan by lifting it out with the foil. Set aside to cool on a rack.

4. In a small saucepan, combine the chocolate and cream and cook over moderate heat, stirring constantly, until the chocolate has melted, 3 to 4 minutes. Remove from the heat and beat in the butter until incorporated. Stir in the bourbon and coffee.

5. With a serrated knife, cut the meringue cake into wedges and place on dessert plates. Drizzle some of the chocolate sauce on top and pass the remaining sauce at the table.

—Lee Bailey

• • •

HAZELNUT JAM CAKE

This cake is very sweet, so I like to glaze it with a tart jelly. Every fall my aunt sends me mayhaw jelly, which tastes like quince. Seedless boysenberry or raspberry jam are also good choices.

12 Servings

1 cup chopped skinned hazelnuts
1¾ cups sifted all-purpose flour
¼ teaspoon baking soda
1 stick (4 ounces) unsalted butter, softened
1½ cups sugar
3 eggs, separated
⅔ cup sour cream
1 teaspoon vanilla extract
8 to 12 ounces seedless mayhaw, boysenberry or raspberry jam
Lightly whipped cream, for serving

1. Preheat the oven to 325°. Grease and flour two 8-inch round cake pans.

2. In a small dry skillet, toast the hazelnuts over moderate heat until fragrant, about 3 minutes. In a large bowl, sift the flour with the baking soda. Set aside a few tablespoons of the flour mixture. In a medium bowl, cream the butter with the sugar until light and fluffy, about 3 minutes. Add the egg yolks, 1 at a time, beating well after each addition.

3. Add the dry ingredients to the egg and butter mixture, alternating with the sour cream, and beginning and ending with the flour. Stir in the vanilla and mix well.

4. Lightly dredge the hazelnuts in the reserved flour. Fold the hazelnuts and any excess flour into the batter.

5. In a medium nonreactive bowl, beat the egg whites until stiff peaks form.

Fold one-third of the egg whites into the batter. Gently fold in the remainder. Pour the batter into the prepared pans and bake for 40 to 50 minutes, or until a cake tester inserted in the center comes out clean. Let the layers cool for a few minutes, then turn them out of the pans.

6. Meanwhile, in a small saucepan, melt the jelly over moderate heat, about 2 minutes. Place 1 cake layer upside down on a plate. Spread half of the jelly on the top. Place the second layer, upside down, on the first layer. Hold the layers together with toothpicks, if necessary, and coat the top with the remaining jelly, letting it run down the side. Serve warm or at room temperature with the whipped cream.

—*Lee Bailey*

• • •

SPONGECAKE WITH LEMON CURD AND TOASTED COCONUT

This is a big, showy cake with simple, homey flavors.

8 to 10 Servings

Spongecake:
1¾ cups sifted all-purpose flour
8 eggs, at room temperature
1¼ cups sugar
1 teaspoon finely grated lemon zest
¼ cup melted butter, at room temperature
¾ cup sweetened shredded coconut

Lemon Curd:
2 teaspoons minced lemon zest
1¾ cups plus 2 tablespoons fresh lemon juice (5 to 6 lemons)
2 cups sugar
2 whole eggs
6 egg yolks
1 stick (4 ounces) unsalted butter, cut into 12 pieces

1. Lightly butter a 10-by-3-inch springform pan. Line the bottom of the pan with parchment or wax paper. Lightly butter the paper. Flour the pan; tap out any excess.

2. Make the cake: Sift the flour twice onto a sheet of wax paper; set aside.

3. Preheat the oven to 350°. In a large bowl, combine the eggs, sugar and lemon zest. Set the bowl over—not in—a large saucepan one-quarter filled with hot water. Warm the mixture over low heat, whisking occasionally, until smooth and syrupy, deep yellow and warm to the touch, 5 to 8 minutes. Remove from the heat.

4. Using an electric mixer, beat the egg and sugar mixture at high speed until it is pale yellow, has tripled in volume and holds a ribbon on the surface for a full 10 seconds when the beaters are lifted. (This will take 10 to 15 minutes using a stationary mixer and 15 to 20 minutes with a hand-held beater.)

5. Working quickly, scoop about 1½ cups of the beaten egg mixture into a medium bowl. Fold in the melted butter with a rubber spatula until no visible streaks of butter remain; set aside.

6. Sift the flour over the remaining beaten egg mixture and, using a balloon whisk, fold quickly until incorporated. Add the reserved egg mixture to the batter and quickly fold it in. Pour the batter into the prepared pan.

7. Bake the cake in the middle of the oven for 40 to 45 minutes, until golden brown on top and a cake tester inserted in the center comes out clean. Transfer the cake to a wire rack to cool for 5 minutes.

8. Increase the oven temperature to 400°. Spread the coconut in a small pan and toast for about 4 minutes, stirring twice, until golden. Remove from the oven and let cool.

9. Remove the sides of the pan and invert the cake on the rack. Remove the pan bottom and peel off the parchment. Turn the cake right side up and let cool on the rack for 2 to 3 hours. (*Once thoroughly cooled, the cake can be tightly wrapped in plastic and stored in a cool, dry place for up to 3 days or frozen for up to 1 month.*)

10. Make the lemon curd: In a medium nonreactive saucepan, combine the lemon zest, lemon juice and sugar. Let stand until the sugar is partially dissolved, about 10 minutes.

11. Beat in the whole eggs and egg yolks. Add the butter pieces. Cook over low heat, stirring occasionally, until the butter is melted and the mixture is warm, about 10 minutes. Continue to cook, stirring constantly and scraping the bottom of the pan frequently, until the curd is thick enough to coat the back of a spoon, about 10 minutes longer. Do not let the curd boil. Scrape the curd into a bowl and let cool. Cover and refrigerate until chilled. (*The lemon curd can be prepared up to 3 days ahead.*)

12. Using a long serrated knife, cut the cake horizontally in thirds. Place the bottom layer on a large serving plate, cut-side up, and spread a generous layer of lemon curd on top. Cover with the middle cake layer and spread again with curd. Place the last layer on top and spread an even layer of curd over the top. Sprinkle the toasted coconut in a ring around the edges of the cake.

—*Marcia Kiesel*

• • •

BOBBIE'S FAMOUS LEMON POUND CAKE

Like all true southern belles, my sister, Bobbie Parham, knows how to make a perfect pound cake. She says that the lemon glaze helps keep the cake moist, especially when it is baked a few days ahead.

10 to 12 Servings

3 sticks (12 ounces) unsalted butter, softened
3⅓ cups sugar
5 eggs
2 teaspoons vanilla extract
3⅓ cups sifted cake flour
½ teaspoon baking powder
1 tablespoon finely grated lemon zest
1 cup buttermilk
¼ cup fresh lemon juice (2 lemons)

1. Preheat the oven to 300°. Butter and lightly flour a 10-inch tube pan. In a large mixing bowl, using an electric mixer, combine the butter with 3 cups of the sugar and beat at high speed until light and fluffy, about 3 minutes. Add the eggs, 1 at a time, beating well after each addition. Beat in the vanilla.

2. In a medium bowl, combine the flour, baking powder and lemon zest. Beat the flour mixture into the butter in 3 batches, alternating with the buttermilk. Scrape down the sides of the bowl and beat for 20 seconds after each addition. Continue to beat for 1 minute longer after all the buttermilk and flour have been added.

3. Pour the batter into the prepared pan and smooth the surface with a spatula. Bake for 2 hours, or until the top is golden brown and a metal cake tester or a wooden skewer inserted in the center of the cake comes out clean.

4. Meanwhile, make the lemon glaze: In a small nonreactive saucepan, combine the lemon juice with the remaining ⅓ cup sugar. Cook over moderate heat, stirring with a wooden spoon until the sugar dissolves, about 2 minutes.

5. As soon as the cake is done, transfer the pan to a wire cake rack set over a baking sheet. With a cake tester or skewer, pierce through the cake in several places. Brush with half of the warm lemon glaze. Let the cake cool in the pan for about 10 minutes, then free the sides of the cake from the pan with a thin, sharp knife. Invert the cake onto a large plate or platter, then brush the top and sides with the remaining glaze. Cool to room temperature. Wrap the glazed cake tightly in plastic wrap and set aside at room temperature for at least 1 day and up to 3 days.

—*Susan Costner*

• • •

ST. LOUIS ORANGE RING CAKE

When Sue Crouse sent me this cake recipe from Warren, Ohio, she wrote, "My grandmother would never give this recipe to anyone—she always said that it came from St. Louis. Then, in the middle 1950s, Clementine Paddleford published it. She wrote that it originally came from The Shaw House Cookbook, a book inspired by the Henry Shaw Mansion, which is in the garden Mr. Shaw presented to St. Louis in 1859. No matter, its past lives, it's a very old recipe indeed—and wonderful."

10 to 12 Servings

1¾ cups sifted all-purpose flour, preferably unbleached
1 teaspoon baking powder
1 teaspoon baking soda
2 sticks (8 ounces) unsalted butter, softened
1½ cups sugar
2½ teaspoons finely grated orange zest
3 eggs, separated, at room temperature
1 cup plain yogurt
1½ teaspoons vanilla extract
Pinch of salt
½ cup fresh orange juice
3 tablespoons fresh lemon juice

1. Preheat the oven to 325°. Lightly butter and flour a 12-cup bundt, kugelhopf or tube pan; tap out any excess flour and set aside.

2. In a medium bowl, sift the flour with the baking powder and baking soda three times; set aside.

3. In a large bowl, using an electric mixer, beat the butter on medium-high speed until it is very light and fluffy. Gradually add 1 cup of the sugar and the orange zest and continue beating until the sugar is thoroughly dissolved and the mixture is very light, about 8 minutes. Add the egg yolks, beating until fully incorporated, then add the yogurt and vanilla; continue beating until very light and fluffy, about 2 minutes. Using a wooden spoon, gently stir in the sifted dry ingredients until just blended.

4. In a large bowl, using an electric mixer on medium speed, beat the egg whites with the salt until firm. Using a large spatula, fold the whites into the batter just until blended. Transfer the batter to the prepared pan and smooth the surface.

5. Bake the cake for 1 hour, until golden brown and a wooden skewer or cake tester inserted in the center comes out clean. Let the cake cool on a wire rack for about 10 minutes.

6. Meanwhile, in a small nonreactive saucepan, combine the orange juice, lemon juice and the remaining ½ cup sugar. Bring to a boil over moderate heat, stirring. Reduce the heat to moderately low and simmer gently until the syrup has reduced to about ½ cup, 8 to 10 minutes.

7. Run a thin sharp knife around the inside rim of the pan to loosen the cake; invert the cake onto a serving plate. Brush the hot syrup over the entire cake. Serve the cake warm or at room temperature. *(The cake can be prepared up to 2 days ahead and kept tightly covered at room temperature.)*

—*Richard Sax*

• • •

BROWN SUGAR BUTTER CAKE WITH VANILLA-HONEY GLAZE AND PISTACHIOS

This delicate pound cake is best served the day it is made.

Makes One 9-Inch Loaf Cake

1 vanilla bean, at least 6 inches long
2 teaspoons vanilla extract, preferably Tahitian
2 sticks (8 ounces) unsalted butter, softened
1 cup (firmly packed) light brown sugar, sifted
4 eggs, at room temperature
2 cups cake flour
½ teaspoon baking powder
½ teaspoon salt
½ cup mild creamed honey (see Note)
⅓ cup finely chopped unsalted pistachios

1. Preheat the oven to 325°. Butter and flour a 9-by-5-inch loaf pan. Halve the vanilla bean crosswise and reserve 1 half. Using a small sharp knife, split open the remaining vanilla bean. With the tip of the knife, scrape the seeds from the bean into a small bowl (reserve the bean itself for another use). Pour the vanilla extract over the seeds, stir well and set aside.

2. In a medium bowl, using an electric mixer, beat the butter at medium speed until fluffy. Add the brown sugar and beat on high speed until very light and fluffy, about 4 minutes. Add the reserved vanilla mixture. Then beat in the eggs, 1 at a time, beating well after each addition to fully incorporate.

3. Sift together the flour, baking powder and salt, then add in 3 batches to the butter and sugar mixture, folding in each addition with a rubber spatula until just incorporated. Do not overmix.

4. Scrape the batter into the prepared pan and smooth the surface lightly. Bake in the middle of the oven for about 1 hour, or until risen and a cake tester inserted in the center comes out clean (the cake will have a large crack running down the center). Let the cake cool for about 5 minutes in the pan before turning it out onto a rack. Turn the cake right-side up to cool slightly before glazing.

5. Meanwhile, make the glaze: Spoon the honey into a small bowl. Cut a 3-inch length from the reserved vanilla bean half; save any remainder for another use. Split the bean lengthwise and scrape the seeds into the honey (add the bean itself to the scraps you are saving to reuse).

6. When the cake is still slightly warm, gently spread 2 tablespoons of the glaze on top of the cake, allowing some to drizzle down the sides. Reserve the remaining honey glaze, or pass separately along with the cake. Sprinkle the top of the cake with the pistachios.

NOTE: *You can buy good-quality creamed honey in specialty food shops. An excellent variety to look for is Rare Hawaiian White Honey from Volcano Island Honey Company.*

—Marcia Kiesel

• • •

MORAVIAN SUGAR CAKE

Moravians settled in Pennsylvania and North Carolina in the 18th century. This cake is based on an old recipe pointed out to me by Karyl Bannister, who writes "Cook & Tell," an engaging monthly food newsletter. It is a deliciously moist yeast cake, baked in a sheet pan. (The potato in the dough is the secret to its moistness.) The top of the dough is dimpled with shallow holes, then topped with a generous blanket of spiced brown sugar and melted butter. It is best eaten warm from the oven.

12 Servings

1 medium baking or all-purpose
  potato, peeled and cut into ½-inch
  chunks
¼ cup milk
2 envelopes active dry yeast
⅓ cup granulated sugar
3 cups all-purpose flour, preferably
  unbleached
10 tablespoons (5 ounces) plus 1
  teaspoon unsalted butter
2 eggs
½ teaspoon salt
½ cup (packed) light brown sugar
1½ teaspoons cinnamon

1. In a small saucepan, cover the potato chunks with cold water and bring to a boil over moderately high heat. Cook until tender when pierced with a knife, about 10 minutes. Drain, reserving ¼ cup of the cooking liquid. In a small bowl, mash the potato chunks until smooth and set aside to cool.

2. In a small saucepan, warm the milk over low heat to 105° to 115°, about 1 minute. In a large bowl, combine the yeast with 1 tablespoon of the sugar and the warm milk. Set aside until foamy, about 5 minutes.

3. Add 1½ cups of the flour, ½ cup of the mashed potato, the reserved potato cooking liquid, 6 tablespoons of the butter, the eggs, salt and the remaining sugar to the yeast mixture. Using an electric mixer, beat on medium speed until well blended, about 3 minutes. Stir in 1 cup of the flour with a wooden spoon. Transfer the dough to a work surface sprinkled with the remaining ½ cup flour. Knead the dough until smooth, about 10 minutes. The dough will remain sticky; use a metal scraper to release the dough from the work surface as you knead.

4. Lightly grease a large bowl. Place the dough in the bowl and cover loosely with plastic wrap. Let the dough rise in a warm place until it has doubled in bulk, about 1 hour.

5. Butter a 9-by-13-by-2-inch baking pan with 1 teaspoon of the butter. Punch the dough down and place it in the center of the prepared pan. Cover loosely with plastic wrap and set aside in a warm place until partially risen (but not doubled in bulk), about 30 minutes.

6. Meanwhile, in a small saucepan, melt the remaining 4 tablespoons butter and let cool slightly.

7. Using your fingertips, gently spread the dough so that it covers the bottom of the pan evenly. In a small bowl, combine the brown sugar and cinnamon; sprinkle the mixture evenly over the dough. With your fingers, carefully poke shallow dents all over the surface of the dough and drizzle the melted butter over the top. Let the dough rise, uncovered, in a warm place until doubled in bulk, about 30 minutes.

8. Meanwhile, preheat the oven to 375°. Bake the cake for 20 to 25 minutes, until deep golden brown. Let cool slightly; then cut into rectangles and serve warm.

—Richard Sax

• • •

MARSALA APPLE CAKE

❢ Since there's a brownness to this dessert, owing to the caramelized apples and the cooked Marsala, a brown wine with the flavors of treacle and nuts would be an ideal match. You could serve Marsala, but there's another much more complex and interesting southern Italian wine called Moscato Passito di Pantelleria. The 1986 Bukkuram is a delicious choice with this light cake.
—David Rosengarten

10 to 12 Servings

4 tablespoons unsalted butter
6 medium Golden Delicious apples—
  peeled, cored and cut into ½-inch
  chunks
2 tablespoons granulated sugar
¼ cup Marsala
2 tablespoons grated lemon zest
1 teaspoon cinnamon
6 eggs, at room temperature,
  separated
1 cup superfine sugar
2 teaspoons vanilla extract
¼ teaspoon salt

½ cup unbleached all-purpose flour
¼ cup cornstarch
Whipped cream or vanilla ice cream,
   for serving

1. Preheat the oven to 350°. Butter a 10-by-2-inch springform pan. Line the bottom with a circle of parchment paper and butter the paper. Flour the pan, tapping out the excess.

2. In a large nonreactive skillet, melt the butter over moderately high heat. Add the apples and sauté, stirring frequently, until golden and slightly tender, about 8 minutes. Increase the heat to high. Add 1 tablespoon of the granulated sugar and cook, tossing, to caramelize the fruit, about 1 minute longer. Add the Marsala and stir until it evaporates, about 2 minutes. Remove from the heat and stir in the lemon zest. Let the apples cool to room temperature.

3. In a small bowl, combine the remaining 1 tablespoon granulated sugar with the cinnamon and set aside. In a large bowl, beat the egg yolks with ⅔ cup of the superfine sugar at high speed until the mixture is lemon-colored and thick enough to hold a ribbon on the surface when the beaters are lifted, 3 to 4 minutes. Stir in the vanilla.

4. In another large bowl, using clean beaters, beat the egg whites with the salt until doubled in volume. Beat in the remaining ⅓ cup superfine sugar and continue beating until stiff and glossy, about 1½ minutes. Using a large spatula, fold one-fourth of the beaten whites into the yolks until blended, then fold in the remaining whites. Sift the flour and cornstarch over the egg mixture and continue folding until just combined. Fold in the cooled apples until evenly distributed.

5. Scrape the batter into the prepared pan and sprinkle the cinnamon sugar on top. Bake in the middle of the oven for 20 to 25 minutes, or until a cake tester inserted in the center comes out clean. Transfer to a rack and let cool for 30 minutes.

6. Run a knife around the edge of the cake and remove the sides of the pan. Let the cake cool completely. Invert the cake on the rack; remove the pan bottom and the paper. Invert the cake on a platter and serve warm or at room temperature, with whipped cream or vanilla ice cream.

—*Bob Chambers*

• • •

DRIED CHERRY AND CURRANT DUNDEE CAKE WITH PORT

This recipe was inspired by the Scottish celebration cake called Dundee, made with dried and candied fruit and brandy. ❦ When dried fruits team up with brown sugar in a dense, dark cake, port is the perfect partner. The flavor of a magnificent, subtle, aged port would be compromised by the strong-flavored cake. But a vigorous young port, like Sandeman Founders Reserve, has enough straightforward flavor to stand up to the cake. —*David Rosengarten*

Makes One 10-Inch Cake

6 medium Bosc pears—peeled, cored
   and cut into ½-inch chunks
⅔ cup sugar
Juice of 1 lemon
4 tablespoons unsalted butter, plus 1
   stick (4 ounces), melted

1 box (10 ounces) dried currants
1 pound dried cherries, coarsely
   chopped
3 cups boiling water
1½ cups ruby port
⅓ cup plus 1 teaspoon blackstrap or
   other dark molasses
⅔ cup (packed) dark brown sugar
3 eggs, beaten
1 tablespoon plus 1½ teaspoons
   finely grated orange zest
1 tablespoon plus 1½ teaspoons
   finely grated lemon zest
3½ cups unbleached all-purpose
   flour
1 tablespoon baking soda
1 tablespoon cinnamon
½ teaspoon salt
3 cups walnuts, coarsely chopped

1. In a large nonreactive saucepan, combine the pears with the sugar, lemon juice and 4 tablespoons of the butter. Cook over moderate heat, stirring frequently, until the pears soften completely and become a thick sauce, 20 to 25 minutes. Increase the heat to high and cook, stirring constantly, until the mixture caramelizes slightly, about 4 minutes longer. Scrape the pear sauce into a large bowl and let cool to room temperature.

2. Meanwhile, in a heatproof bowl, combine the currants, dried cherries and boiling water. Set aside to plump for 10 minutes. Drain well and return the fruit to the bowl. Pour ½ cup of the port over the fruit and set aside.

3. Preheat the oven to 300°. Butter a 10-by-2-inch springform pan. Line the bottom with a circle of parchment paper and butter the paper. Flour the pan, tapping out the excess.

4. When the pear sauce has cooled, stir in the melted butter, molasses, brown sugar, eggs, orange zest and lemon zest. Mix well. Stir in the plumped dried fruits and their liquid.

5. In a medium bowl, sift together the flour, baking soda, cinnamon and salt. Stir in the walnuts. Add the dry ingredients to the fruit mixture and stir just until incorporated. Scrape the batter into the prepared pan and smooth the surface with a rubber spatula dipped in water.

6. Bake the cake in the middle of the oven for 2 hours, or until a cake tester inserted in the center comes out clean. Transfer the cake to a rack and let cool for 30 minutes. Remove the sides of the pan and let cool for 1 hour longer. Remove the pan bottom and peel off the paper.

7. Brush 2 tablespoons of the remaining port over the bottom of the cake. Return the cake to the rack, rightside up; brush the top and sides with ½ cup of the port. Set aside at room temperature until the port has been absorbed, about 1 hour. Tightly wrap the cake and set aside. The next day, brush the remaining 6 tablespoons port over the cake and let sit for 1 hour. Wrap tightly and refrigerate for at least 5 days. *(The cake will keep for up to 2 months in the refrigerator.)* Serve at room temperature.

—*Bob Chambers*

• • •

CHOCOLATE RASPBERRY FUDGE CAKE

Everyone should be treated to a bit of chocolate during the holidays. After the cake is glazed, let it sit at room temperature for at least two hours so that it retains its shine. Then refrigerate the cake overnight, loosely covered, so that the texture becomes fudgy and the flavors mellow.

10 Servings

4 ounces hazelnuts
1 stick (4 ounces) plus 1 tablespoon
*   unsalted butter, at room*
*   temperature*
½ cup plus 2 tablespoons sugar
5 eggs, separated
6 ounces imported semisweet
*   chocolate, finely chopped*
2 tablespoons unbleached all-purpose
*   flour*
1 tablespoon sirop de framboise or
*   cassis (optional)*
Pinch of salt
¼ teaspoon cream of tartar
Chocolate Glaze (recipe follows)
1 cup fresh raspberries
Crème fraîche, for serving

1. Preheat the oven to 350°. Place the hazelnuts on a small baking sheet and bake until the skins crack, about 10 minutes. Transfer the hot nuts to a kitchen towel and rub them together to remove the skins. Finely chop enough nuts to yield 3 tablespoons; set aside in a small bowl. Coarsely chop the remaining nuts, place in another small bowl and set aside.

2. Lightly butter the bottom of a 9½-by-3-inch springform pan and line the bottom with wax paper. Butter the paper and dust lightly with flour, tapping out any excess.

3. In a large bowl, using an electric mixer, cream the stick of butter with ½ cup plus 1 tablespoon of the sugar until pale and light, about 2 minutes. Add the egg yolks, 1 at a time, beating well after each addition; set aside. Rinse and dry the beaters.

4. In a small metal bowl set over simmering water or in a double boiler, melt the chocolate. Remove from the heat and let cool for 3 minutes. Stir the chocolate into the butter and egg mixture until blended.

5. Mix the flour into the finely chopped hazelnuts and fold into the batter. Fold in the framboise.

6. In a large bowl, using an electric mixer, beat the egg whites with a pinch of salt just until soft peaks form, about 1 minute. Add the cream of tartar and the remaining 1 tablespoon sugar and continue beating until stiff, glossy peaks form, about 1½ minutes. Gently fold the egg whites into the batter until thoroughly incorporated .

7. Pour the batter into the prepared pan and smooth the surface. Bake in the middle of the oven for 30 minutes, or until the cake puffs up and cracks appear on the surface. Transfer to a rack and let cool for 30 minutes.

227

8. Remove the sides of the springform pan and invert the cooled cake on a wire rack. Carefully remove the bottom of the pan and peel off the wax paper. Invert the cake on another rack and let cool completely before glazing. The cake will fall to about 1 inch as it cools.

9. Carefully transfer the cake to a large serving plate. Pour the warm glaze on the center of the cake and, using a long narrow spatula, spread it evenly over the top and sides of the cake. (*The cake can be prepared to this point up to 1 day ahead. Once the glaze sets, loosely cover the cake and refrigerate.*)

10. Before serving, sprinkle the reserved coarsely chopped hazelnuts over the cake. Decoratively arrange the raspberries on top. Serve in wedges and pass the crème fraîche separately.

—*Sheila Lukins*

• • •

CHOCOLATE GLAZE

Makes About 1⅓ Cups

¾ *cup heavy cream*
7 *ounces imported semisweet*
    chocolate
2 *teaspoons sirop de framboise or*
    cassis (optional)

In a medium saucepan, warm the cream over low heat, about 2 minutes. Add the chocolate and cook, stirring constantly, until smooth and creamy, about 2 minutes longer. Remove from the heat and stir in the framboise. Set aside covered at room temperature for up to 1 day. Warm before using.

—*Sheila Lukins*

• • •

COCONUT BROWNIES

These dense brownies chock-full of coconut are a snap because the recipe uses only one pot.

Makes 16 Brownies

6 *tablespoons unsalted butter*
2 *ounces unsweetened chocolate*
1 *cup sugar*
2 *eggs*
1 *teaspoon vanilla extract*
1 *cup all-purpose flour*
1 *teaspoon baking powder*
¼ *teaspoon salt*
¾ *cup sweetened shredded coconut*

1. Preheat the oven to 375°. Butter an 8-by-11½-inch baking pan.

2. In a double boiler, melt the butter and chocolate over warm water. Remove from the heat and stir in the sugar. Beat in the eggs 1 at a time. Stir in the vanilla.

3. In a small bowl, combine the flour, baking powder and salt. Add to the chocolate mixture all at once and mix until incorporated. Stir in the coconut.

4. Scrape the batter into the prepared pan and smooth the surface. Bake for about 17 minutes, or until a knife inserted in the middle comes out clean. Do not overbake. Transfer the pan to a rack to cool; then cut the brownies into bars.

—*Stephanie Lyness*

• • •

FRUITCAKE COOKIES

As with any good fruitcake, there is only enough batter in this recipe to hold the fruit together. Sticky Medjool dates and moist, plump figs are first choices, but you can substitute other dried fruits. The cookie supporting the fruit remains soft and cakey. These cookies are best eaten a couple of days after they are baked, when the flavors have had a chance to develop. They travel well and will keep for up to two weeks airtight.

Makes About 2 Dozen

1 *stick (4 ounces) plus 2 tablespoons*
    unsalted butter, softened
⅓ *cup (packed) dark brown sugar*
½ *teaspoon cinnamon*
½ *teaspoon ground ginger*
¼ *teaspoon freshly grated nutmeg*
Pinch of salt
1 *cup plus 2 tablespoons all-purpose*
    flour
½ *cup whole unblanched almonds*
3 *moist dried figs, cut into ½-inch*
    pieces (½ cup)
4 *large dates, preferably Medjool, cut*
    into ½-inch pieces (½ cup)
½ *cup pecans, coarsely chopped*
2 *tablespoons honey*
1 *teaspoon plus 1½ tablespoons dark*
    rum
1 *egg, at room temperature, lightly*
    beaten
½ *cup confectioners' sugar*

1. In a medium bowl, using an electric mixer on high speed, cream 6 tablespoons of the butter with the brown sugar, cinnamon, ginger, nutmeg and the salt until light and fluffy. Beat in ¾ cup of the flour on low speed just until incorporated. Wrap the dough tightly and refrigerate until chilled, about 15 minutes.

2. Preheat the oven to 400°. Place the almonds on a heavy baking sheet and toast for about 5 minutes, until golden brown. Let cool, then coarsely chop. In a bowl, combine the almonds with the figs, dates and pecans; set aside.

3. In a medium bowl, using an electric mixer on high speed, cream the remaining 4 tablespoons butter with the honey and 1 teaspoon of the rum until light and fluffy. Gradually beat in the egg, scraping down the bowl as necessary. Beat in the remaining 6 tablespoons flour on low speed until just combined. Fold the batter into the dried fruit and nuts until completely coated. Set aside.

4. Lightly butter a heavy baking sheet. On a lightly floured surface, roll out the chilled dough ¼ inch thick. Using a 2-inch fluted cookie cutter, stamp out rounds as close together as possible. Reroll the scraps and repeat.

5. Place the cookies on the prepared baking sheet about 1 inch apart. Using your fingers, mound 1 tablespoon of the fruitcake batter on each cookie. Bake the cookies for 10 minutes, until they begin to brown on top.

6. Sift the confectioners' sugar into a bowl and add the remaining 1½ tablespoons rum; stir until smooth.

7. When the cookies are baked, immediately drizzle about ½ teaspoon of the rum glaze over each one. Return to the oven and bake for about 1 minute, or until the glaze bubbles and cracks. Let the cookies cool on the baking sheet for about 5 minutes. Using a spatula, transfer to a rack to cool completely.

—*Peggy Cullen*

• • •

PISTACHIO MADELEINES

These little cakes were inspired by the miniature almond cakes called *financiers*, which are sold at every Parisian *pâtisserie* worth its salt. The madeleines are crisp and golden brown on the outside and rich, dense and nutty inside.

Makes 2 Dozen

1¼ cups unsalted pistachios (6 ounces)*
1 stick (4 ounces) plus 6 tablespoons unsalted butter, melted
1⅓ cups confectioners' sugar, plus more for dusting
½ cup unbleached all-purpose flour
2 tablespoons apricot jam
½ teaspoon vanilla extract
5 egg whites
***Available at specialty food shops**

1. Preheat the oven to 450°. Place the pistachios on a small baking sheet and bake for 2 minutes. Set aside to cool completely. Butter a 12-madeleine pan with 1 tablespoon of the melted butter.

2. In a food processor, combine the cooled pistachios and confectioners' sugar and pulse until the nuts are fairly finely ground, about 1½ minutes. Add the flour and pulse to combine. Add the apricot jam, vanilla and egg whites and process just until blended, scraping down the sides of the bowl with a rubber spatula. Add all but 1 tablespoon of the remaining melted butter to the bowl and process until thoroughly blended.

3. Spoon heaping tablespoons of the batter into the prepared molds to fill them. Set the pan on a heavy baking sheet and bake for 7 minutes. Reduce the temperature to 400° and bake for 9

minutes longer, until the madeleines are brown and firm to the touch. Turn them out onto a rack to cool completely.

4. Return the oven temperature to 450°. Brush the madeleine pan with the remaining 1 tablespoon melted butter and repeat with the remaining batter. Just before serving, dust the madeleines with confectioners' sugar.

—*Ann Chantal Altman*

• • •

CHOCOLATE-FILLED RUGELACH

This version of rugelach was inspired by Bea, an old family friend, who instructed me to add "a little of this" and "a little of that." I decided on a lot of chocolate.

Makes 48 Rugelach

2 sticks (8 ounces) unsalted butter, at room temperature
4 ounces cream cheese, at room temperature
½ cup sour cream
5 tablespoons sugar
1¾ cups unbleached all-purpose flour
8 ounces semisweet chocolate, coarsely chopped
1 cup walnuts (about 3 ounces), coarsely chopped
⅓ cup dried currants (about 1½ ounces)
1½ teaspoons cinnamon
½ cup plus 2 tablespoons apricot preserves, strained

1. In a large bowl, beat the butter and cream cheese with an electric mixer on high speed until soft and creamy,

229

PIES, CAKES & COOKIES

about 1 minute. Mix in the sour cream and 2 tablespoons of the sugar until well combined, about 1 minute. Stir in the flour by hand until well blended. Wrap the dough in plastic wrap and refrigerate for at least 2 hours or overnight.

2. In a medium bowl, combine the chocolate, walnuts, currants, cinnamon and the remaining 3 tablespoons sugar. Set aside at room temperature.

3. Preheat the oven to 350°. Divide the dough into 4 equal portions; refrigerate all but one. On a lightly floured surface, form the dough into a ball and flatten it out. Roll the dough into a circle about 10 inches in diameter and ⅛ inch thick.

4. Brush 2 tablespoons of the apricot preserves over the dough. Sprinkle ⅔ cup of the chocolate mixture evenly over the dough and press down gently. Cut the dough into 12 wedges. Starting at the wide end, roll a wedge of dough tightly, but carefully, toward the point. Place the rugelach, with the point underneath, on a large ungreased cookie sheet. Roll up the remaining wedges in the same manner and arrange them on the sheet, about ½ inch apart. Repeat with the remaining dough, preserves and chocolate mixture; the rugelach will fit on 2 large cookie sheets.

5. Lightly brush the tops of the rugelach with the remaining 2 tablespoons of apricot preserves. Bake, switching the sheets after 20 minutes, for 35 to 40 minutes, or until well browned. Immediately transfer the rugelach to a rack to cool. (*The rugelach can be frozen, well wrapped, for up to 2 weeks; let return to room temperature before serving.*)

—*Susan Shapiro Jaslove*

• • •

COCONUT MACAROONS

Do not attempt to double this recipe; the batter will be too loose.

Makes 16 Cookies

1⅔ cups moist unsweetened grated coconut* (about 5½ ounces)
⅓ cup sugar
2 eggs
1 tablespoon unsalted butter, melted and cooled
*Available at health food stores

1. Preheat the oven to 350°. Grease 2 cookie sheets. In a medium bowl, combine the coconut and sugar and toss well with a fork. In another bowl, whisk the eggs until very frothy, about 1 minute. Stir the eggs and the melted butter into the coconut mixture until blended.

2. Using a tablespoon, make 8 well-spaced mounds of the coconut mixture on each cookie sheet. Bake for about 18 minutes, until the cookies are set and golden, switching the sheets halfway through the baking time. Gently pry the cookies loose and set aside on a rack to cool completely. Store in an airtight container for up to 3 days.

—*Lydie Marshall*

• • •

CHOCOLATE-DIPPED SNOWBALLS

These flourless macaroons are somewhere between a cookie and a confection. They are crunchy on the outside, moist and chewy on the inside. The slight bitterness of semisweet chocolate is the perfect foil for the sweet toasted coconut. These cookies can be stored in an airtight container for about a week and are wonderful for mailing to cool climates.

Makes About 2 Dozen

2½ cups unsweetened medium shredded coconut*
1 tablespoon plus 2 teaspoons cornstarch
¾ cup sugar
2 tablespoons unsalted butter, cut into pieces
¼ cup light corn syrup
1 teaspoon vanilla extract
¼ teaspoon salt
2 egg whites, lightly beaten
5 ounces imported semisweet chocolate, chopped into ½-inch pieces (about 1 cup)
*Available at health food stores

1. Preheat the oven to 375°. Butter and flour a heavy baking sheet. In a medium bowl, combine the coconut and cornstarch; set aside.

2. In a medium nonreactive saucepan, combine the sugar, butter, corn syrup, vanilla and salt. Bring to a boil over high heat, stirring constantly. Boil for 10 seconds, then remove from the heat and stir in the coconut mixture. Add half of the beaten egg whites, stirring until thoroughly incorporated. Stir in the remaining whites. The mixture will form a ball. Return to high heat and cook, stirring, for 30 seconds. Let cool slightly.

3. With moistened hands, break off tablespoon-size pieces of the mixture and roll into 1-inch balls. Place on the prepared baking sheet about 1 inch apart.

4. Bake for 10 minutes, or until the tops just begin to turn golden brown. Turn the tray halfway through baking to insure even cooking. Let the cookies cool completely on the sheet.

5. Place the chocolate in a small bowl set over a small saucepan filled with ¾ inch of simmering water or in a double boiler. When the chocolate is nearly melted, remove from the heat and, using a rubber spatula, stir until the mixture is completely smooth. Set aside to cool, stirring occasionally. The chocolate is ready for dipping when a small drop placed just below your lower lip feels cool on the skin.

6. Line a baking sheet with parchment paper. Using your fingers, hold a snowball near the top and dip the bottom half into the cooled chocolate. Gently shake off the excess and lightly scrape the bottom over the rim of the bowl. Set the dipped snowball, chocolate-side up, on the parchment paper. By the time you are dipping the 10th one, the first one should have hardened. If not, the chocolate was not quite cool enough. Refrigerate the cookies for just 5 minutes to set the chocolate; store at room temperature.

—Peggy Cullen

• • •

ALMOND-OAT COOKIES

Makes 12

½ *cup raw or roasted whole*
  almonds, plus 12 for garnish
  (about 4 ounces)
½ *cup old-fashioned rolled oats*
⅛ *teaspoon salt*
¼ *cup (packed) dark brown sugar*
2 *tablespoons cold butter, cut into*
  bits
¼ *teaspoon almond extract*

1. Preheat the oven to 350°. Lightly grease a large cookie sheet. In a food processor, combine the ½ cup almonds with the oats, salt and brown sugar; process until finely ground and mealy. Add the butter, almond extract and 1 tablespoon water. Process until the dough just forms a ball.

2. Divide the dough into 12 equal portions. Form each into a ball and place on the cookie sheet. Flatten the balls into circles about ¼ inch thick. Press a whole almond into the top of each cookie. Bake for 13 minutes, or until the cookies are set and barely browned around the edges. Do not overbake. Let cool on the cookie sheet before serving.

—Susan Shapiro Jaslove

• • •

LINZER WREATHS

This all-hazelnut version of linzer dough is formed into miniature tartlets. Once baked, these little gems can be stored in an airtight container for a week to 10 days. They also stand up well for shipping.

Makes 2 Dozen

1 *cup hazelnuts (4½ ounces)*
1½ *cups plus 2 tablespoons all-*
  purpose flour
¾ *teaspoon baking powder*
¼ *teaspoon salt*
¾ *teaspoon cinnamon*
1 *stick (4 ounces) plus 4 tablespoons*
  unsalted butter, softened
¾ *cup sugar*
½ *teaspoon vanilla extract*
1 *egg, lightly beaten*
⅓ *cup good-quality raspberry jam*

1. Preheat the oven to 350°. Place the hazelnuts in a large baking pan. Bake, stirring occasionally, until the skins crack and the centers begin to turn golden brown, about 15 minutes. Then transfer the hot nuts to a terry cloth towel and rub vigorously to remove most of the skins. Let cool completely.

2. In a food processor, combine the toasted hazelnuts with 2 tablespoons of the flour. Pulse until the nuts are finely ground but not oily and pasty.

3. In a small bowl, sift the remaining 1½ cups flour with the baking powder, salt and cinnamon. Set aside.

4. In a medium bowl, using an electric mixer, combine the butter with the sugar and vanilla and beat on high speed until light and fluffy, about 2 minutes. Beat in the ground nuts. Add the egg and continue beating until incorporated, scraping the bowl occasionally. Add the flour mixture to the butter mixture in two batches, beating on low speed just to incorporate. Refrigerate the dough, tightly wrapped, until cold, at least 2 hours or overnight.

5. Divide the dough in half. On a lightly floured work surface, roll out half of the dough about ¼ inch thick. Using a 2-inch round cookie cutter, stamp out circles. Center each circle inside ungreased ½-cup muffin tins. Repeat with the remaining dough scraps to fill all the muffin cups.

6. Divide the reserved dough into 24 equal pieces; roll each piece into a 6-inch log about ½ inch thick. Using a small knife, cut each log into 12 slices, each about ½-inch thick. Roll the slices between your palms to make small balls. Press 12 balls around the perimeter of each dough circle. The fit should not be too tight. Alternatively, roll the reserved dough into 24 logs about 5 inches long and place each log around the perimeter of each circle. Or let the dough soften and pipe it around the perimeter of each cookie using a pastry bag fitted with a ¼-inch round tip.

7. Bake the tartlets until lightly browned and firm, about 17 minutes. Unmold immediately onto a cooling rack. While still very hot, drop about ½ teaspoon of raspberry jam into the center of each wreath. Let cool completely before serving.

—*Peggy Cullen*

• • •

GRASMERE GINGERBREAD SHORTBREAD

This is an excellent shortbread-type cookie—fragrant with ginger and gritty with oatmeal.

Laura Barton, of the Oregon Department of Agriculture, tells me that on walking trips in Britain with the Sierra Club, her father visited the town of Grasmere in the Lake District, where they make gingerbread that is hard and crisp, unlike American gingerbread.

Makes 16 Cookies

1 cup plus 2 tablespoons whole wheat flour
½ cup plus 1 tablespoon (firmly packed) light brown sugar
½ cup old-fashioned rolled oats
1¾ teaspoons ground ginger
½ teaspoon cream of tartar
¼ teaspoon baking soda
1 stick (4 ounces) plus 1 tablespoon cold unsalted butter, cut into teaspoons

1. Preheat the oven to 325°. Lightly butter an 8-inch square baking pan and set aside.

2. In a food processor, combine the flour, sugar, oats, ginger, cream of tartar and baking soda. Pulse to combine. Add the butter and pulse until the mixture is crumbly, about 10 times. Transfer the crumbly mixture to the prepared pan and, using your fingertips, pat to form a flat, even layer.

3. Bake the gingerbread for 35 minutes, or until the center is set and the top is just golden. Let cool on a wire rack for 20 minutes. While still warm, carefully cut into 2-inch squares and let cool completely before removing from the pan. (*The cookies can be kept in an airtight container for up to 3 days.*)

—*Richard Sax*

• • •

GILDED CHOCOLATE SHORTBREAD

The trick to baking a good shortbread with a tender, buttery bite is to use a minimal amount of flour—just enough to prevent the cookies from spreading while in the oven. Confectioners' sugar, rather than granulated, also helps them hold their shape. These shortbread cookies are shaped with crescent moon and star cutters. To really gild the lily, brush on powdered 24-karat gold dust before the cookies are baked. These cookies can be stored in an airtight container for up to one week.

Makes About 3 Dozen

2 sticks (8 ounces) unsalted butter, softened
¾ cup plus 2 tablespoons confectioners' sugar
½ cup unsweetened Dutch-process cocoa powder
1 teaspoon vanilla extract
¼ teaspoon salt
2 cups all-purpose flour
24-karat gold dust (see Note)

1. In a large bowl using an electric mixer, beat the butter with ¾ cup of the confectioners' sugar and the cocoa, vanilla and salt on medium speed until just blended, about 30 seconds.

2. On low speed, mix in the flour in three parts until just incorporated, scraping the bowl after each addition. Refrigerate the dough, tightly wrapped, until well chilled, about 1 hour.

3. Preheat the oven to 325°. Sprinkle a work surface with the remaining 2 tablespoons confectioners' sugar. Divide the dough in half; cover and refrigerate one piece. Roll the other piece into a 9½-inch square just under ½ inch thick. Using crescent moon and star cutters, stamp out cookies as close together as possible. Transfer to an unbuttered baking sheet. Combine the scraps and set aside. Repeat with the remaining piece of dough, using the remaining confectioners' sugar, if necessary, to prevent the dough from sticking. Combine the scraps, roll out and cut until all the dough has been used.

4. Using a small, stiff paintbrush or a flat pastry brush, lightly paint the surface of each cookie with the gold dust. Bake the cookies for 15 minutes, or until firm and beginning to crisp on the bottom; do not overbake. Let the cookies cool on the baking sheet for 5 minutes, then transfer to a rack to cool completely.

NOTE: *Gold dust, which is nontoxic, can be found at art-supply stores or at stores specializing in cake-decorating equipment.*
—*Peggy Cullen*

• • •

HEAVENLY PUFF ANGELS

Palmiers, known to some as elephant ears, are familiar French cookies made from puff pastry. Using good-quality, ready-made puff pastry dough, cut out these Christmas angels with a gingerbread-girl cookie cutter, then attach miniature *palmiers* to form the wings.

Since puff pastry is best when just baked, you can assemble the angels up to a week ahead and freeze them unbaked.

Makes 9 Angels

**1 package (1 pound) frozen,
    all-butter puff pastry, thawed
About 1 cup sugar**

1. On a lightly sugared work surface, unfold the puff pastry and sprinkle ¼ cup of the sugar on each side. With a sharp knife, cut out a rectangle that is one-fourth of the total sheet of puff pastry (about 8 by 6 inches). This piece is for the angel's wings.

2. Sprinkle each side of the wing piece with 1 to 1½ tablespoons of sugar. Fold in the top and bottom edges about ½ inch toward the center. Gently pat the folds flat, keeping the sides and the corners square and sprinkle with 1 tablespoon sugar. Fold in the top and the bottom edges again so that they meet in the center. Gently flatten and sprinkle with another tablespoon of sugar. Fold the bottom over the top and gently press the layers to adhere. Wrap tightly and refrigerate the wing piece until well chilled, about 20 minutes.

3. Line 2 heavy baking sheets with parchment paper and set aside. Using a 5-inch gingerbread-girl cutter, stamp 9 cookies out of the remaining puff pastry, pressing the cutter down firmly and evenly, cutting as close together as possible, reversing the cookie cutter each time. Sprinkle generously with more sugar to prevent sticking. Arrange the cookies on the prepared baking sheets, leaving as much space as possible between them. Using a fork, prick each cookie in 6 places.

4. Preheat the oven to 425°. Remove the wing piece from the refrigerator and cut crosswise into eighteen ¼-inch slices (reserve any leftover dough and bake separately if desired). To form the wings, pinch the non-seam side of a slice flat, and tuck the flattened end of the slice under the angel's shoulder. Press firmly to adhere. For guidance, see the photograph on page 209. *(The recipe can be prepared to this point and frozen, tightly wrapped, for up to 1 week. These go directly from the freezer to the oven.)*

5. Bake one sheet of cookies at a time in the middle of the oven until deep brown, puffed and crisp, about 15 minutes. Let the angels cool completely on the baking sheet, then gently peel off the paper; be careful to keep the wings intact.
—*Peggy Cullen*

• • •

LACY GINGER SNOWFLAKES

These lacy cookies have a caramel crunch that is offset by the chewy bite of candied ginger and pineapple. The ginger should be soft enough to tear, and the candied pineapple should be moist and pliable. These elegant but fragile wafers will keep for two to three days, stored in an airtight container.

Makes About 2 Dozen

½ *cup instant rolled oats*
½ *cup all-purpose flour*
2 *ounces candied ginger, cut into* ⅓-
  *inch dice (*⅓ *cup, packed)*
2 *ounces candied pineapple, cut into*
  ⅓-*inch dice (*⅓ *cup, packed)*
4 *tablespoons unsalted butter, cut*
  into ½-*inch pieces*
¼ *cup (lightly packed) light brown*
  sugar
¼ *cup light corn syrup*
1 *teaspoon ground ginger*
1 *teaspoon dark rum*

1. Preheat the oven to 350°. In a medium bowl, combine the oats and flour. Add the candied ginger and pineapple and toss to coat thoroughly with the flour.

2. In a medium saucepan, combine the butter, brown sugar, corn syrup, ground ginger and rum. Bring to a boil over high heat, stirring, until the butter is completely melted, about 2 minutes. Stir the hot syrup into the dry ingredients and let cool, stirring occasionally, until the batter is somewhat stiff, about 5 minutes.

3. Meanwhile, lightly butter a heavy baking sheet. Scoop out scant tablespoons of the dough and, with moistened hands, roll into 1-inch balls. Place the balls on the baking sheet about 3 inches apart. Bake for 8 minutes, or until the edges are golden. The centers will appear somewhat white and underbaked, but they will continue to cook on the hot baking sheet.

4. Let the cookies cool slightly until they begin to harden, about 3 minutes. Using a metal spatula, transfer the cookies to a rack and let cool completely.

—*Peggy Cullen*

• • •

MEXICAN ANISE AND ORANGE COOKIES

Crushed aniseed and fresh orange zest give these butter cookies a pleasing, south-of-the-border flavor.

Makes About 4 Dozen

2 *tablespoons brandy or water*
1 *tablespoon aniseed, crushed*
2 *teaspoons finely grated orange zest*
1 *stick (4 ounces) unsalted butter,*
  softened
½ *cup solid vegetable shortening*
¾ *cup sugar*
1 *egg, lightly beaten*
1 *teaspoon baking powder*
3 *cups all-purpose flour*

1. In a small bowl, combine the brandy, aniseed and orange zest. Set aside to infuse for 20 minutes.

2. In a large mixing bowl, using an electric mixer, beat together the butter, vegetable shortening and sugar until fluffy, 5 minutes. Beat in the egg and

the brandy mixture. Add the baking powder and flour and continue beating until a smooth dough forms. Wrap tightly and refrigerate until firm, at least 2 hours and up to 2 days.

3. Preheat the oven to 350°. Lightly grease a large baking sheet. Cut the dough into quarters; reserve one portion and refrigerate the remaining dough, tightly wrapped, until ready to use.

4. On a lightly floured surface, roll the dough into a 12-inch circle about ⅛ inch thick. Using a 2½-inch round or fluted cookie cutter, cut out the cookies as close together as possible. Place on the prepared baking sheet about 1 inch apart. Combine the scraps and refrigerate.

5. Bake the cookies in the middle of the oven for 16 minutes, or until lightly browned. Transfer the cookies to a rack to cool. Repeat with the remaining portions of dough, working with one at a time. Combine all the scraps, roll out and cut until all the dough has been used. (*The cookies can be stored in an airtight container for 2 days or frozen, tightly wrapped, for up to 2 weeks.*)

—*Susan Costner*

• • •

DESSERTS

DESSERTS

FRESH RASPBERRIES WITH CREAM AND CHOCOLATE

4 Servings

1 ounce semisweet chocolate, chopped into small pieces
1 cup heavy cream
1 tablespoon confectioners' sugar
2 half-pints of raspberries (about 2 cups)

1. Line a baking sheet with wax paper. In a small double boiler set over simmering water, melt the chocolate until smooth. (Alternatively, place the chocolate in a small microwaveable bowl. Melt in the microwave oven at medium power for 30 seconds. Stir and microwave for another 30 seconds, or until melted.)

2. Spread the chocolate on the prepared baking sheet as thin as possible. Place in the freezer until hard, about 10 minutes.

3. Meanwhile, in a medium bowl, whip the cream with the confectioners' sugar until just thickened.

4. Peel the chocolate off the wax paper; crumble or sliver the chocolate with a knife.

5. Spoon the berries into 4 dessert dishes or wineglasses. Top with the thickened cream and garnish with the chocolate. Serve immediately or refrigerate for up to 30 minutes.

—*Stephanie Lyness*

• • •

STRAWBERRIES WITH CHOCOLATE CREAM

You can gild the lily by sprinkling toasted slivered almonds over the chocolate cream.

6 Servings

2 pints strawberries, halved lengthwise
1 tablespoon sugar
3 ounces semisweet chocolate, chopped
1½ cups heavy cream

1. In a medium bowl, toss the berries with the sugar. Refrigerate for at least 1 or up to 3 hours.

2. In a double boiler over simmering water, melt the chocolate in ¼ cup of the cream, stirring occasionally until smooth. Set aside to cool to room temperature. (*The chocolate can be melted a few hours ahead. Keep in a warm spot; if it hardens, re-melt over low heat.*)

3. In a medium bowl, using an electric mixer, beat the remaining 1¼ cups cream at medium speed until soft peaks form, 1 to 2 minutes. Gently fold in the cooled chocolate.

4. Spoon the berries into individual dessert dishes and top with the chocolate cream.

—*Lee Bailey*

• • •

POACHED PLUMS AND CHERRIES

The basic poaching liquid here can be used for any combination of fruit.

These fruits look very striking left whole, so just let your guests know that the plums and cherries still have their pits. Serve cookies on the side.

6 Servings

1½ cups sugar
2 cups dry white wine
2 cinnamon sticks
12 whole black peppercorns
8 whole cloves
12 assorted medium plums (1½ to 2 pounds total)
1 cup fresh cherries with stems

1. In a large nonreactive saucepan, combine the sugar with 2 cups of water. Bring to a simmer over moderate heat and cook until the sugar is dissolved, about 4 minutes.

2. Add the wine, cinnamon sticks, peppercorns and cloves; increase the heat to moderately high and bring to a boil. Reduce the heat to moderate, add the plums and simmer for 5 minutes. Add the cherries and simmer until tender, about 5 minutes longer. Using a slotted spoon, transfer the fruit to a serving bowl and set aside to cool, about 20 minutes.

3. Meanwhile, boil the poaching liquid over high heat until syrupy, about 15 minutes. Let cool.

4. When the plums are cool enough to handle, peel them. Pour the cooled poaching liquid over the fruit. (*The recipe can be prepared up to 1 day ahead and refrigerated, covered. Let return to room temperature for at least 1 hour before serving.*)

—Lee Bailey

• • •

DRIED SOUR CHERRIES AND PINEAPPLE IN PORT

For a textural contrast, you can serve this with a hard cookie like biscotti. The dessert must marinate for at least 12 hours, so plan accordingly.

6 Servings

2 cups tawny port
¼ cup sugar
¼ teaspoon whole black peppercorns
6 whole cloves
2 strips of lemon zest
½ cup dried sour cherries*
    (3 ounces)
1 whole small pineapple, about
    1½ pounds, peeled and cut into
    1-inch chunks
*Available at specialty food shops

1. In a small nonreactive saucepan, combine the port, sugar, peppercorns, cloves and lemon zest and bring to a simmer over moderate heat. Simmer for 5 minutes, stirring occasionally. Remove from the heat, stir in the dried cherries and let cool.

2. Place the pineapple chunks in a medium bowl. Pour the port mixture over the pineapple and refrigerate for at least 12 hours. Let come to room temperature; then spoon the fruit into 6 bowls and serve.

—Lee Bailey

• • •

POACHED PEARS WITH CARAMEL ICE CREAM

Jacques Torres of Le Cirque in Manhattan was awarded the coveted title of Meilleur Ouvrier de France. He feels that it's much more difficult to please the clientele in New York than in Nice or Paris because New Yorkers have traveled and eaten all over the world and know what they want. His Poached Pears with Caramel Ice Cream are sure to please even the most demanding.

6 Servings

2¼ cups sugar
2 cups milk
7 egg yolks
1 vanilla bean, split lengthwise
2 teaspoons finely grated lemon zest
¼ cup fresh lemon juice
6 ripe, medium Anjou or Bosc pears
    (about 6 ounces each)
4 ounces semisweet chocolate,
    chopped
1 package (10 ounces) frozen
    unsweetened raspberries, thawed
Fresh mint sprigs, for garnish

1. In a heavy medium saucepan, combine ½ cup of the sugar with ½ cup of water and bring to a boil over moderately high heat without stirring. Continue to boil until the syrup turns a golden caramel color, about 8 minutes. (If necessary, brush down the sides of the pot with a pastry brush dipped in cool water to prevent sugar crystals from forming.)

2. Remove from the heat and gradually whisk in the milk, standing back as you stir because the mixture may sputter. Return to the heat and bring to a boil, stirring constantly, until any lumps of caramel have dissolved. Reduce the heat to low and keep warm.

3. In a large bowl, beat the egg yolks with ¼ cup of the sugar at high speed until thick and light, about 3 minutes. Whisk half of the warm caramel milk into the beaten yolks, then stir the mixture into the remaining caramel milk in the saucepan.

4. Increase the heat to moderate and cook, stirring constantly with a wooden spoon, until the custard reaches 165°, is slightly thickened and coats the back of the spoon, 8 to 10 minutes. (Do not boil or the custard will curdle.) Strain the caramel custard into a large bowl and let cool to room temperature. Freeze in an ice cream maker according to the manufacturer's instructions. (*The ice cream can be made up to 3 days ahead and kept covered in the freezer.*)

5. In a large, deep, nonreactive saucepan, combine the remaining 1½ cups sugar with the vanilla bean, lemon zest, lemon juice and 6 cups of water. Cook over moderately high heat until the sugar has dissolved, about 2 minutes.

6. Meanwhile, peel the pears and immerse them in the warm sugar syrup as soon as they are peeled. There should be enough syrup to cover the pears; add more water if necessary. Bring to a slow simmer over moderate heat and poach gently until the pears are tender when pierced with a sharp knife, 20 to 25 minutes. Remove from the heat and let the pears cool to tepid in the poaching syrup, about 1 hour. Stand the pears upright on a rack to drain and cool completely. Discard the poaching liquid.

7. In a small double boiler over simmering water, partially melt the chocolate. Remove from the heat and stir until completely melted and smooth. Spoon half of the melted chocolate into a small, sturdy, plastic bag; reserve the remaining chocolate. Squeeze the chocolate into the corner of the bag and secure with a twist tie. With sharp scissors, snip the very tip off the corner of the bag to make a small hole.

8. Gently squeeze the chocolate through the hole in the bag into 6 goblets or balloon wineglasses with a wide rim. Beginning at the bottom, make zigzag chocolate lines in each glass. Tilt the glass as you work, keeping the point close to the inside surface. Repeat 3 or 4 times and set aside in a cool place for at least 30 minutes to set the chocolate. (*The glasses can be decorated up to 4 hours ahead and kept in a cool place.*)

9. To serve, cut the top half off each pear and set aside. Using a small sharp knife and a teaspoon, cut out the core and hollow out the pear to make a cup, leaving a ½-inch rim of fruit. Place a pear cup in each of the prepared goblets. Reheat the reserved chocolate, if necessary, and spoon it into the plastic bag.

10. In a food processor, puree the raspberries. Press the puree through a nonreactive strainer set over a medium bowl; set aside.

11. Fill each pear with caramel ice cream. Reserve any remaining ice cream in the freezer for another use. Spoon 2 to 3 tablespoons of the raspberry puree around the pears. Squeeze the remaining chocolate in a zigzag pattern over the ice cream. Set a pear top against each of the pears. Garnish with mint sprigs and serve immediately.

—*Jacques Torres, Le Cirque,*
New York City

• • •

BLACKBERRY ALMOND-CREAM FOOL

4 Servings

½ *cup heavy cream*
½ *cup sour cream*
2 *tablespoons sugar*
3 *to 4 drops of almond extract*
1 *pint fresh blackberries*
4 *amaretti cookies*

1. In a medium bowl, beat the heavy cream until stiff. Fold in the sour cream, sugar and almond extract.

2. Reserve some of the berries for garnish. Place the rest of the berries in 4 dessert bowls or wineglasses and top with the almond cream. Crumble 1 cookie over each serving and garnish with the reserved berries. Serve immediately.

—*Jim Fobel*

• • •

SAUTERNES SABAYON AND TROPICAL FRUIT PARFAITS

These parfaits can be assembled in any wide glass or stemmed cup. If you can't find fresh raspberries, halved seedless red grapes would be just as nice.

❡ Sauternes, the late-harvest wine from Bordeaux, is often described as having a tropical fruit character. Perfect. In this match, the honey-melon-pineapple flavors in the dessert, and the quickly cooked Sauternes in the sabayon don't hurt the harmony. —*David Rosengarten*

8 Servings

½ *cup pecans (2 ounces)*
1 *tablespoon unsalted butter*
2 *small firm, ripe bananas, halved*
  lengthwise
⅔ *cup plus 2 teaspoons sugar*
½ *small pineapple—peeled, cored*
  and cut into ½-inch cubes
12 *egg yolks*
1¼ *cups Sauternes*
2 *tablespoons fresh lemon juice*
1 *tablespoon finely grated lemon zest*
2 *kiwi fruit, peeled and sliced*
  crosswise
½ *pint raspberries*

1. Preheat the oven to 350°. Spread the pecans on a baking sheet and bake in the middle of the oven for 10 minutes, until fragrant. Set aside to cool.

2. In a medium nonstick skillet, melt 2 teaspoons of the butter over moderately high heat. Sprinkle the bananas with 2 teaspoons of the sugar and place in the pan, cut-sides down. Cook, turning once, until browned, about 1 minute per side. Remove to a plate and keep warm.

3. Add the remaining 1 teaspoon butter to the skillet. Add the pineapple and cook, stirring, until the juices have evaporated and the fruit is beginning to brown, 4 to 5 minutes. Add the pineapple to the bananas and keep warm.

4. In a medium stainless-steel bowl, combine the egg yolks, Sauternes, lemon juice and the remaining ⅔ cup sugar. Set the bowl over a saucepan of gently simmering water and whisk until the mixture is thick and frothy and has doubled in volume, about 5 minutes. Stir in the lemon zest. Remove the bowl of sabayon from the water and set aside.

5. Cut the bananas into 1-inch chunks. Set aside ½ cup of the sabayon. Spoon half of the remaining sabayon into 8 parfait glasses. Scatter the pineapple and banana chunks on top and cover with the other half of the sabayon. Garnish the parfaits with the kiwis and raspberries. Place a dollop of the reserved sabayon on each parfait and sprinkle the toasted pecans on top.

—*Bob Chambers*

• • •

BANANA LUMPIA WITH LILIKOI SAUCE

Peter Deehan incorporates Hawaii's multiethnic heritage into a contemporary style with an exotic twist. Preparations are light, and Pacific ingredients are the focus. The *lilikoi*, or passion fruit sauce, for this dessert is a shining example.

6 Servings

6 heavy, ripe passion fruit
¼ cup plus 2 tablespoons sugar
¼ teaspoon cornstarch
½ teaspoon cinnamon
1½ ounces semisweet chocolate
6 small firm-ripe bananas (about 5 inches long), halved lengthwise
2 tablespoons coarsely chopped cashews (about 1 ounce)
Six 8- to 9-inch spring roll wrappers*
1 egg white, lightly beaten
4 cups vegetable oil, for frying
*Available at Asian markets

1. Cut the passion fruit in half and, using a teaspoon, scrape the seeds and pulp into a strainer set over a medium bowl. Using a wooden spoon, press the pulp and seeds against the strainer to extract all the juice.

2. In a small, heavy, nonreactive saucepan, combine the passion fruit juice with ¼ cup of the sugar and bring to a boil over moderate heat, stirring con-

stantly. Meanwhile, dissolve the cornstarch in ¼ teaspoon of water. Stir the cornstarch into the juice and bring back to a boil. Remove from the heat and set aside to cool to room temperature. (*The passion fruit sauce can be made up to 2 days ahead; cover and refrigerate. Bring to room temperature before using.*)

3. In a small bowl, mix the remaining 2 tablespoons sugar with the cinnamon and set aside. In a small double boiler over simmering water, partially melt the chocolate. Remove from the heat and stir until all the chocolate is melted and smooth.

4. Spread about 1 teaspoon of the melted chocolate on the cut-sides of 6 banana halves. Sprinkle 1 teaspoon of the chopped cashews over the chocolate and cover with the remaining 6 banana halves.

5. On a work surface, place a filled banana diagonally on a spring roll wrapper about 1 inch from a corner of the wrapper. Sprinkle about 1 teaspoon of the reserved cinnamon sugar over the banana. Bring the closest point of the wrapper up over the banana and roll it one or two turns. Fold in the sides of the wrapper over the ends of the banana and continue rolling. At the last fold, brush the point of the wrapper with some of the beaten egg white, then roll up and press to seal. Place the wrapped banana on a large plate, seam-side down. Repeat with the remaining bananas, cinnamon sugar and wrappers.

6. In a medium saucepan, heat the oil to 385° over moderately high heat. Deep-fry 3 *lumpia* at a time, turning once, until crisp and golden brown, about 4 minutes. Remove and drain on paper towels.

7. Using a serrated knife, cut each *lumpia* in half on an angle. Arrange one

half on a dessert plate with the other half leaning against it. Spoon about 1 tablespoon of the reserved passion fruit sauce in a pool on one side and serve immediately.

—*Peter Deehan,*
Mauna Lani Hotel, Hawaii

• • •

SAUTEED BEIGNETS WITH SUGARED PLUMS

In Alsace they use the abundant *quetsche*, but here I have used Italian prune plums, which have a similar sweet-tart flavor.

8 Servings

½ cup lukewarm milk (105° to 115°)
¼ cup granulated sugar
1½ teaspoons active dry yeast
2 cups unbleached all-purpose flour
2 eggs
½ teaspoon salt
6 tablespoons unsalted butter, cut into ½-inch pieces, at room temperature
2 pounds plums, preferably Italian prune plums, halved lengthwise and pitted
½ cup vanilla sugar (see Note, p. 208)
6 cups vegetable oil, for frying

1. In a large bowl, combine the milk, sugar and yeast. Using an electric mixer, beat at medium speed to combine. Beat in 1 cup of the flour. Add the eggs, 1 at a time, beating well after each addition. Gradually beat in the remaining 1 cup flour and the salt until thoroughly combined. The dough will be quite sticky. Continue beating at medium-high speed until the dough becomes slightly elastic, about 5 minutes. Add the butter, a few pieces at a time, beating until the dough is smooth and pulls away from the sides of the bowl, about 5 minutes longer. Cover the bowl loosely; set aside in a warm place until the dough has doubled in bulk, about 2 hours. Punch the dough down, cover and set aside until it begins to rise again, about 15 minutes.

2. Meanwhile, in a very large, heavy, nonreactive skillet, toss the plums with ¼ cup of the vanilla sugar. Cook over moderate heat, stirring occasionally, until the plums soften and exude their juices, about 8 to 10 minutes. Continue cooking until the juices thicken slightly, 4 to 5 minutes longer. Set aside.

3. In a dutch oven or deep fryer, heat the oil over moderately high heat until it reaches 350°, about 15 minutes. Line 2 wire cooling racks with a double layer of paper towels.

4. Meanwhile, pinch off teaspoons of dough and roll into small balls on a lightly floured work surface. Shake off any excess flour and drop the balls of dough into the hot fat, a few at a time, making sure not to crowd the pan. Fry, turning frequently, until golden brown and cooked through, about 2 to 3 minutes. Using a wire skimmer, transfer the beignets to the racks to drain thoroughly. Repeat with the remaining balls of dough.

5. Reheat the plums over moderately high heat until warm, about 1 minute. Add the beignets. Stir to coat with plum juices and sprinkle with the remaining ¼ cup vanilla sugar. Continue stirring occasionally until the beignets have absorbed some of the juices and are heated through, 4 to 5 minutes. Transfer the beignets to a warmed platter and serve immediately.

—Susan Herrmann Loomis

• • •

SAUTEED APPLES WITH CREAM AND CARDAMOM

Although this dessert is delicious on its own, it can also be served with gingersnaps, vanilla wafers or ice cream.

4 Servings

2 tablespoons unsalted butter
4 large Golden Delicious apples—
  peeled, cored and thinly sliced
3 tablespoons sugar
½ cup heavy cream
¼ teaspoon ground cardamom
2 tablespoons chopped walnuts

1. In a large skillet, melt the butter over high heat. Add the apples, sprinkle with the sugar and cook, stirring frequently, until the apples have caramelized, 10 to 12 minutes. If the apples begin to burn, reduce the heat slightly. (*The recipe can be made to this point up to 30 minutes ahead.*)

2. Reduce the heat to moderate. Add the cream and cardamom and bring to a boil. Reduce the heat slightly and simmer for 1 minute. Sprinkle with the walnuts and serve immediately.

—*Stephanie Lyness*

• • •

PEAR AND APPLE CLAFOUTI

Clafouti is a traditional peasant dessert from the Limousin region of France, where it is made with cherries. It is a cross between a popover and a bread pudding made with fruit. The riper the fruit you use, the better. It is lovely on its own, but for a sweeter accent, serve with a drizzle of maple syrup.

8 Servings

½ cup plus 2 tablespoons sugar
2 tablespoons unsalted butter
2 medium Anjou pears (about 1 pound)—peeled, quartered and cut crosswise ¼ inch thick
1 large Granny Smith apple (about 8 ounces)—peeled, quartered and cut crosswise ¼ inch thick
⅛ teaspoon allspice
6 eggs
½ cup heavy cream
⅔ cup all-purpose flour
Pinch of salt
1 tablespoon Poire Williams
1 tablespoon Calvados
1 teaspoon vanilla extract

1. Preheat the oven to 400°. Lightly butter a 10½-inch fluted ceramic or glass tart pan. Dust the inside well with 1 tablespoon of the sugar and set aside.

2. In a large skillet, melt the butter over moderately high heat. Add the pears and apple and cook, stirring occasionally, until crisp-tender and lightly browned, about 8 minutes. Remove from the heat.

3. In a small bowl, stir the allspice with 1 tablespoon of the sugar. Sprinkle over the fruit and toss to coat. Spoon the fruit into the tart pan and set aside.

4. In a medium bowl, whisk the eggs with the remaining ½ cup sugar until frothy. Stir in the cream. Sprinkle the flour and salt on top and stir to incorporate; do not overmix. Stir in the Poire Williams, Calvados and vanilla.

5. Pour the batter over the fruit in the dish and bake for 30 to 35 minutes, until puffy and golden and a cake tester inserted in the middle comes out clean. Let cool for about 20 minutes. Serve warm or at room temperature.

—*Tracey Seaman*

• • •

CINNAMON APPLESAUCE

This applesauce is simplicity itself—the apples aren't even peeled or cored.

Makes About 4½ Cups

10 large McIntosh or Empire apples (about 3½ pounds), quartered
1 cinnamon stick
2 teaspoons fresh lemon juice (optional)
2 tablespoons maple syrup (optional)

1. In a large nonreactive saucepan, bring ½ cup of water to a boil over high heat. Add the apples and cinnamon. Reduce the heat to moderately low, cover and cook, stirring occasionally, until the apples are tender, about 25 minutes.

2. Pass the apples through a food mill set over a large bowl. Refrigerate the applesauce until chilled. Stir in the lemon juice and maple syrup just before serving.

—*Susan Shapiro Jaslove*

• • •

PEAR AND APPLE COMPOTE

Comforting, familiar flavors and a chunky texture make this winter compote a favorite with younger as well as older members of the family. Gently fold the ingredients together so that the fruit will retain some of its texture. It is best served at room temperature.

Makes About 10 Cups

¼ cup fresh lemon juice (2 lemons)
6 large firm-ripe Anjou or Bartlett pears (about 3 pounds)
4 Granny Smith or other tart cooking apples (about 2 pounds)
⅔ cup sugar
1 cup Riesling or other semi-dry white wine
1 cinnamon stick
1 small vanilla bean, split lengthwise
1 tablespoon red currant jelly
2 teaspoons finely grated lemon zest

1. In a large bowl, combine 2 cups of water with the lemon juice. Peel, halve and core the pears and apples. Cut the fruit into ½-inch chunks, dropping them into the lemon water as they are cut.

2. In a large, heavy, nonreactive saucepan, combine the sugar and wine and bring to a boil over high heat. Stir in the fruit and lemon water and bring to a boil. Reduce the heat to moderate, cover partially and simmer, stirring occasionally, until the fruit is just tender but still in chunks, 10 to 15 minutes. With a large slotted spoon, transfer the fruit to a large bowl; set aside.

3. Add the cinnamon stick, vanilla bean and currant jelly to the liquid in the saucepan. Increase the heat to high and bring to a boil; boil until the liq-

uid reduces to 1½ cups, about 10 minutes. Strain the reduced liquid over the fruit. Stir in the lemon zest. Transfer the compote to a serving bowl and let cool. Cover and refrigerate for up to 3 days. Bring to room temperature before serving.

—*Sheila Lukins*

• • •

DRIED FRUIT COMPOTE IN CRISP MERINGUE SHELLS

The plain whipped cream garnish in this elegant dessert can be simply spooned on top or piped out using a pastry bag fitted with a star tip.

🍷 Dried fruits can go with many wines, but in this case the light meringue and whipped cream present a pairing challenge (many dessert wines would be too heavy). A good solution is a wine that is light and frothy, such as a sweet sparkling wine. One of the best for this dessert is Moscato d'Asti, a minty-peach delight made in Italy's Piedmont. Try the 1989 Cascinetta by Vietti. —*David Rosengarten*

8 Servings

2 cups dry white wine
½ cup sugar
2 tablespoons minced crystallized ginger
Zest strips from 1 lemon
⅓ cup fresh lemon juice
¼ cup dark raisins
¼ cup golden raisins
8 pitted prunes, quartered
12 dried Black Mission figs, stemmed and quartered (4 ounces)

DESSERTS

3 ounces dried apricots, thinly sliced
   (½ cup)
2 ounces dried pears, cut into ½-inch
   cubes (⅓ cup)
1½ ounces dried apples, cut into
   ½-inch cubes (½ cup)
¼ cup slivered blanched almonds
   (1 ounce)
2 cups heavy cream, chilled
Crisp Meringue Shells (recipe
   follows)
1 ounce semisweet chocolate, grated

1. In a medium nonreactive sauce-pan, combine the wine, sugar, ginger, lemon zest, lemon juice and 1 cup of water. Bring to a boil over high heat. Reduce the heat to low, cover and sim-mer for 10 minutes.

2. Add the raisins, prunes, figs, apri-cots, pears and apples and bring to a boil. Cover, reduce the heat to low and simmer for 15 minutes, stirring occa-sionally. Remove the saucepan from the heat and set aside to cool. (*The compote can be prepared up to 4 days ahead. Cover and refrigerate. Let return to room tem-perature and remove the lemon zest before serving.*)

3. Preheat the oven to 350°. Place the almonds in a pie pan and bake in the middle of the oven for 10 to 12 min-utes, until lightly browned. Set aside to cool completely.

4. In a medium bowl, beat the cream until stiff. Place a Crisp Meringue Shell on each plate and spoon the dried fruit compote and some of its liquid into the center. Garnish with the whipped cream, grated chocolate and toasted almonds and serve immediately.

—*Bob Chambers*

• • •

CRISP MERINGUE SHELLS

This stiff, glossy meringue can be shaped with a spoon or piped through a pastry bag fitted with a star tip. The shells can also be filled with fresh fruit or ice cream. It is best to choose a dry day for mak-ing meringue because humidity can pre-vent it from drying out as it should.

Makes 8 Shells

6 egg whites, at room temperature
½ teaspoon cream of tartar
1¼ cups superfine sugar

1. Preheat the oven to 250°. Line a large cookie sheet with parchment paper. Using a template as a guide, draw eight 3-inch circles on the paper, ½ inch apart.

2. In a large bowl, beat the egg whites with the cream of tartar on low speed until foamy. Increase the speed to high and continue beating until soft peaks form. Gradually beat in the sugar, ¼ cup at a time; beat well after each addition to dissolve the sugar. By the time all the sugar has been added, the whites will be firm and glossy.

3. Scoop the meringue into the cir-cles and spread to form a 1½-inch layer. Using the back of a small spoon, hol-low out the centers to make slight in-dentations to hold the compote. Alternatively, scoop the meringue into a pastry bag fitted with a medium star tip. Beginning with the outer rims, pipe spirals of meringue to completely fill in the circles on the parchment paper. Then pipe meringue around the rims 2 more times to form the sides.

4. Bake the meringue shells in the middle of the oven for 1 hour. Reduce the heat to 200° and bake for 1 hour

longer. Turn off the heat and leave the shells in the oven for 1 hour, or overnight. When the shells are com-pletely cool, peel off the paper. (*The shells can be stored in an airtight container for up to 1 week.*)

—*Bob Chambers*

• • •

CRANBERRY-APRICOT CHARLOTTES WITH ORANGE MUSCAT CREME ANGLAISE

The filling for these charlottes is per-fumed with Essencia—a fragrant dessert wine from California made from the Or-ange Muscat grape. The whole wheat bread that forms the crust works very nicely with the tart fruit filling, but feel free to use white bread if you prefer. The charlottes are served warm to contrast with the chilled sauce.

❡ When an uncooked wine is featured prominently in a dish, very often the same wine will be the right choice to serve with it (this is not necessarily the case if the wine is cooked). Quady's Essencia is very good with the orange flavors in this dessert, and it especially reaches out to the uncooked Essencia that flavors the crème anglaise.

8 Servings

4 navel oranges
1 cup Essencia
1 cup fresh orange juice
1 cup sugar
⅔ cup thinly sliced dried apricots (4
   ounces)
⅓ cup dried currants
5 cups fresh cranberries (1¼
   pounds)

24 thin slices of packaged whole
    wheat bread
1 stick (4 ounces) unsalted butter,
    melted
Orange Muscat Crème Anglaise
    (p. 268)

1. Finely grate the zest of 2 of the oranges and set aside. Using a sharp paring knife, peel all 4 oranges, making sure to remove all the bitter white pith. Working over a bowl, cut in between the membranes to release the sections. Cover the sections and refrigerate.

2. In a large nonreactive saucepan, combine ⅔ cup of the Essencia with the orange juice, grated orange zest and ⅔ cup of the sugar. Bring to a boil over high heat and boil for 30 seconds. Add the apricots, currants and 4 cups of the cranberries and bring to a boil. Reduce the heat to moderate and cook, stirring frequently, until very thick, about 5 minutes. Remove from the heat and add the remaining ⅓ cup Essencia. Let the cranberry-apricot filling cool to room temperature, stirring occasionally.

3. In a small nonreactive saucepan, combine the remaining ⅓ cup sugar with ⅓ cup water and bring to a boil over high heat, stirring until the sugar dissolves. Add the remaining 1 cup cranberries, bring to a boil and remove from the heat. Set aside to cool. (The recipe can be prepared to this point up to 1 day ahead. Cover and refrigerate the elements separately. Let return to room temperature before proceeding.)

4. Preheat the oven to 450°. Using the rim of a ½-cup ramekin as a guide, cut out 1 circle from 16 of the bread slices. Trim the crusts from the remaining 8 slices of bread. Cut these slices into thirds to form ¾-inch-wide strips.

5. Brush eight ½-cup ramekins with some of the melted butter. To assemble each charlotte, brush one side of a bread circle with melted butter and press it into a ramekin, buttered-side down. Brush one side of 3 bread strips with melted butter. Line the side of the ramekin with the buttered-side of the 3 strips, overlapping as necessary. Mound the cranberry-apricot filling in the ramekin and press a bread circle firmly on top. Brush the bread generously with melted butter.

6. Place the assembled charlottes on a baking sheet and bake on the bottom rack of the oven for 20 to 25 minutes, until the bread is crisp and browned. Remove from the oven and let cool for 10 minutes.

7. Run a thin knife around the sides of the ramekins to loosen the charlottes, then invert them in the center of large plates. Pour the Orange Muscat Crème Anglaise around the charlottes and garnish with the reserved orange segments and poached whole cranberries.

—Bob Chambers

• • •

CARAMELIZED BAKED APPLES WITH CINNAMON ICE CREAM

Cinnamon, brown sugar, caramelized baked apples are all favorite bistro flavors. This recipe comes from Bruno Gensdarmes, chef at Guy Savoy's restaurant Pont de Suresnes in Paris. Use any good baking apples, such as Rome Beauty, McIntosh or Cortland.

4 Servings

2¼ pounds baking apples (3 to 4)—
    peeled, quartered and cored

6 tablespoons unsalted butter,
    melted
¼ cup granulated sugar
¼ cup (packed) dark brown sugar
1 teaspoon freshly ground cinnamon
    (see Note)
Cinnamon Ice Cream (p. 248)

1. Preheat the oven to 375°. Layer the apples in a shallow baking dish. Pour the butter over the apples and sprinkle with the granulated sugar. Bake until soft and tender, about 30 minutes.

2. Preheat the broiler. Sprinkle the apples with the brown sugar and cinnamon. Broil 5 inches from the heat for 2 to 3 minutes, rotating the pan once or twice, until just caramelized. Serve immediately with Cinnamon Ice Cream.

NOTE: *Using a spice grinder to turn cinnamon sticks into powder will make a big difference.*

—Patricia Wells

• • •

NECTARINE-RASPBERRY COBBLER

Peach preserves sweeten and enhance the juicy nectarines and fragrant raspberries encased in this crumbly topping.

4 Servings

2 tablespoons unsalted butter
2 large nectarines, cut into ½-inch
    slices
⅓ cup peach preserves
2 teaspoons vanilla extract
½ pint raspberries
¾ cup all-purpose flour
¼ cup sugar
1 teaspoon baking powder
⅛ teaspoon salt

243

⅓ cup milk
1 tablespoon brown sugar
Whipped cream, for serving

1. Preheat the oven to 400°. In a small saucepan, melt the butter over low heat.

2. In an 8-by-8-by-2-inch square baking pan, toss the nectarines with the peach preserves and 1 teaspoon of the vanilla. Fold in the raspberries.

3. In a medium bowl, combine the flour, sugar, baking powder and salt. Make a well in the center of the mixture and pour in the milk, melted butter and the remaining 1 teaspoon vanilla. Stir with a fork until a thick batter forms. Using a tablespoon, drop the batter over the fruit. Sprinkle the brown sugar on top and bake for 25 to 30 minutes, or until the topping is golden brown. Serve warm or at room temperature with whipped cream.

—Jim Fobel

• • •

BAKED BANANA-PEAR CRUMBLE

6 Servings

4 bananas (about 1½ pounds), cut into 1-inch chunks
4 pears (about 2 pounds)—peeled, cored and cut into 1-inch chunks
3 tablespoons light brown sugar
1 tablespoon fresh lemon juice
4 tablespoons unsalted butter
20 amaretti cookies
Crème fraîche or whipped cream, for serving

1. Preheat the oven to 350°. Generously butter an 8-inch square baking dish.

2. In a large nonreactive bowl, combine the bananas, pears, brown sugar and lemon juice and toss to coat. Transfer the fruit to the prepared baking dish.

3. In a small saucepan, melt the butter over moderate heat. In a food processor, grind the amaretti cookies until they resemble coarse crumbs. Stir them into the butter. Sprinkle the crumbs evenly over the fruit. Bake the crumble for 20 minutes, or until golden brown. Serve hot or at room temperature with crème fraîche or whipped cream on the side.

—Lee Bailey

• • •

APPLE MUSH

When I was shooting an apple video with Pamela Cohen, a producer at ABC News, she started reminiscing about this recipe. To me, it is the epitome of what old-fashioned desserts are about: simple and satisfying dishes that have been passed down from generation to generation. Apple Mush is in the family of warm fruit desserts that also includes cobblers and crisps, but this recipe has an unusual topping that is baked until crisp and golden with sweet, softened apples underneath.

6 Servings

½ cup plus 3 tablespoons granulated sugar
½ cup all-purpose flour, preferably unbleached
1 teaspoon baking powder
1 egg, beaten

¼ cup (packed) dark brown sugar
1½ teaspoons cinnamon
4 large Granny Smith apples (2 pounds)
1 tablespoon fresh lemon juice
3 tablespoons unsalted butter, cut into small pieces
Vanilla ice cream or frozen yogurt, for serving

1. In a medium bowl, combine ½ cup of the granulated sugar with the flour and baking powder. Add the egg and stir until a smooth, stiff dough forms. Cover and set aside for 30 minutes.

2. Preheat the oven to 450°. Lightly butter a 9-inch pie plate and set aside. In a small bowl, combine the remaining 3 tablespoons granulated sugar with the brown sugar and cinnamon; set aside.

3. Meanwhile, peel, quarter and core the apples; slice them lengthwise ¼ inch thick and place in a large bowl. Add the lemon juice and toss well. Place one-third of the apples in the pie plate, sprinkle with one-third of the cinnamon sugar and dot with one-third of the butter. Make two more layers with the remaining apples, cinnamon sugar and butter, mounding the apples quite high in the center of the pan. Dot the apples with large pieces of the dough topping.

4. Set the pie plate on a baking sheet and bake for 10 minutes. Turn the oven down to 350° and bake for 45 minutes longer, or until the topping is nicely browned and the apples are soft. Let cool on a wire rack for about 30 minutes. Serve warm, topped with vanilla ice cream or frozen yogurt.

—Richard Sax

• • •

Exotic Fruit Soup (p. 249).

Nectarine-Raspberry Cobbler (p. 243).

Cranberry Pie (p. 207).

EXOTIC FRUIT SOUP

This clear, perfumed broth is wonderful with almost any fresh fruit—use whatever is ripe, plentiful and good. You'll need about three and a half cups of fruit for four servings.

4 Servings

1 orange
1 lime
⅔ cup sugar
½ vanilla bean, split lengthwise
Pinch of Chinese five-spice powder*
1 tablespoon plus 1½ teaspoons minced fresh ginger
2 stalks of fresh lemon grass, chopped, or 2 tablespoons dried lemon grass*
½ teaspoon coriander seeds, crushed
3 whole cloves
10 fresh mint leaves, plus more for garnish
2 passion fruits
1 cup ¾-inch cubes of fresh pineapple
1 mango or 2 peaches, peeled and cut into ½-inch chunks
½ papaya—peeled, seeded and sliced lengthwise ¼ inch thick
2 fresh lychees—peeled, halved and pitted
3 kiwis, peeled and sliced crosswise ¼ inch thick
1 banana, sliced crosswise ⅓ inch thick
½ cup raspberries or blackberries, or a combination
*Available at Asian markets

1. Using a sharp, swivel-edged vegetable peeler or very sharp paring knife, peel the zest from the orange and the lime in ½-inch-wide lengthwise strips.

2. In a large saucepan, combine the zest strips with 6 cups of water. Stir in the sugar, vanilla bean, five-spice powder, ginger, lemon grass, coriander seeds, cloves and mint leaves. Bring to a boil over high heat. Reduce the heat to low and simmer until very aromatic, about 30 minutes. Set aside to cool to room temperature, then cover and refrigerate until well chilled, at least 4 hours and up to 1 day.

3. Cut the passion fruits in half. With a teaspoon, scoop the pulp into a coarse strainer set over a small bowl. Push the pulp and juice through the sieve; set aside. Discard the seeds.

4. Strain the chilled broth through a fine sieve into a medium bowl. Arrange the fruit in 4 large, shallow soup bowls and spoon the passion fruit juice on top. Ladle the broth over the fruit and garnish with mint leaves. Serve cold.
—*Philippe Boulot, Mark's Restaurant, Mark Hotel, New York City*

• • •

PINEAPPLE-MANGO BISQUE

4 Servings

3 tablespoons sugar
2 tablespoons dark rum
One 3-pound pineapple—peeled, cored and cut into 1-inch pieces
2 mangoes—peeled, pitted, and cut into ½-inch pieces
3 cups cold milk
Pinch of cinnamon
½ cup chilled heavy cream, plus more for serving

1. In a small saucepan, combine the sugar, rum and 2 tablespoons of water. Bring just to a boil over high heat and boil until reduced slightly, 1 to 2 minutes. Remove from the heat and set aside to cool.

2. In a blender or food processor, combine the pineapple, mangoes and reserved rum syrup with ½ cup of the milk and puree until smooth. Strain the soup through a coarse strainer set over a large nonreactive bowl. Whisk in the remaining 2½ cups milk, the cinnamon and the cream. Cover and refrigerate until well chilled, at least 4 hours and up to 1 day.

3. To serve, ladle the soup into 4 soup bowls. Garnish with an additional swirl of cream if desired.
—*Fitzroy Mannix, Blue Waters Beach Hotel, Antigua*

• • •

ICED PASSION FRUIT SOUP WITH YOGURT AND VANILLA

Look for passion fruits that are large and heavy with dimpled skin.

2 Servings

10 passion fruits
¼ cup sugar
2-inch piece of vanilla bean, split lengthwise
1 teaspoon unflavored gelatin
¼ cup plain yogurt, whisked well
½ teaspoon freshly ground espresso coffee
Fresh mint leaves, for garnish

1. Place a coarse sieve over a medium nonreactive saucepan. Working over the sieve, cut each passion fruit in half. With a teaspoon, scoop out the pulp.

Cranberry-Apricot Charlottes with Orange Muscat Crème Anglaise (p. 242).

DESSERTS

Push the pulp and juice through the sieve; discard the seeds.

2. Add the sugar, vanilla bean and 1 cup of water to the saucepan and bring just to a simmer over low heat, stirring. Remove from the heat and sprinkle the gelatin evenly over the mixture. Set aside, undisturbed, to let the gelatin thicken on the surface of the juice, about 3 minutes. Then whisk the mixture well to incorporate the gelatin.

3. Set a fine sieve over a medium nonreactive bowl and strain the mixture. Let cool to room temperature, then place the bowl in a larger bowl filled with ice and water. Chill the mixture over the ice, stirring frequently, about 5 minutes. (*The recipe can be prepared ahead to this point; cover and refrigerate.*)

4. To serve, ladle the chilled soup into 2 shallow soup dishes. Top each serving with 2 tablespoons of the yogurt, sprinkle the ground espresso on top and garnish with mint leaves.

—*Robert Creasey*

• • •

WATERMELON GRANITE SOUP

For extra dazzle, substitute Champagne or sparkling wine for the water.

6 Servings

4 cups 1-inch cubes of seedless watermelon
3 tablespoons superfine sugar
1½ cups cold seltzer or sparkling mineral water

1. In a blender or food processor, puree the watermelon cubes with the sugar until smooth. Strain the puree

through a medium-fine sieve into a large, shallow dish. Cover and freeze until completely firm, at least 4 hours or overnight.

2. Using a large metal spoon, scrape the watermelon granité into 6 large, shallow soup bowls, mounding the shavings. (*The recipe can be prepared to this point up to 2 hours ahead. Place the bowls on a tray, cover and freeze.*)

3. To serve, pour ¼ cup sparkling water over the granité in each bowl and serve immediately.

—*Michel Richard, Citrus, Los Angeles*

• • •

CANTALOUPE SOUP WITH CINNAMON-PLUM STARBURST

Based on two fruit purees, this luscious soup couldn't be simpler.

6 Servings

1 cup Muscat de Beaumes de Venise or other dessert wine, such as late-harvest Riesling
1 cinnamon stick
1½ tablespoons light honey
1 ripe cantaloupe (about 2 pounds), cut into 2-inch cubes (about 4 cups)
1 pound Black Friar or Santa Rosa plums (about 7), pitted and cut into 1-inch cubes, plus 1 plum, for garnish

1. In a small nonreactive saucepan, combine the wine and cinnamon stick. Bring to a boil over high heat; boil until the wine has reduced to ¼ cup, 7 to 8 minutes. Stir in the honey and refrigerate until chilled.

2. In a food processor, puree the cantaloupe until very smooth. Pour into a bowl, cover and refrigerate until well chilled, at least 4 hours.

3. In a food processor, puree the cubed plums until smooth. Blend in the chilled wine syrup. Set a coarse sieve over a medium bowl and strain the plum puree. Cover and refrigerate until well chilled, at least 4 hours.

4. Cut the remaining plum into ¼-inch dice. To serve, stir the purees well. Pour about ½ cup of the cantaloupe puree into each of 6 small, shallow soup bowls. Pour about ¼ cup of the plum puree into the center of each bowl. With the tip of a small knife, make decorative swirls in the soup and garnish with the diced plum. Serve immediately.

—*Marcia Kiesel*

• • •

PEAR AND STRAWBERRY SORBETS WITH BLACKBERRY COULIS

When making the fruit purees for the sorbets, begin with the lesser amount of sugar and increase to taste.

8 Servings

Pear Sorbet:
2 pounds ripe pears
½ to ¾ cup sugar
¼ cup fresh lemon juice
3 tablespoons pear brandy (poire)

Strawberry Sorbet:
5 cups strawberries (about 2 pints)
½ to ¾ cup confectioners' sugar
2 tablespoons fresh lemon juice
1 tablespoon raspberry brandy (framboise)

Blackberry Coulis:
¼ cup sugar
1½ cups blackberries

Fresh mint sprigs, for garnish

1. Make the pear sorbet: Peel, core and cut the pears into medium chunks. In a food processor, puree the pears with the sugar, lemon juice and pear brandy until smooth. Pour the puree into an ice cream maker and freeze according to the manufacturer's instructions.

2. Make the strawberry sorbet: In a food processor, puree the strawberries in 2 batches until smooth. Press the puree through a fine strainer into a large bowl; discard the seeds.

3. Sift the confectioners' sugar over the strawberry puree and whisk to blend. Stir in the lemon juice and raspberry brandy. Pour the mixture into an ice cream maker and freeze according to the manufacturer's instructions.

4. Make the blackberry coulis: In a small nonreactive saucepan, combine the sugar and ¼ cup water and bring to a boil over high heat. Boil for 3 minutes. Let cool, then refrigerate until very cold.

5. In a food processor, puree the blackberries for 1 minute. Strain through a fine strainer and discard the seeds. Gradually stir the chilled sugar syrup into the blackberry puree, tasting as you go, until the coulis is as sweet as you like it. Cover and refrigerate. *(The recipe can be prepared to this point up to 1 day ahead. Let the sorbets soften in the refrigerator for about 1 hour before serving.)*

6. To assemble the dessert, swirl 2 tablespoons of the blackberry coulis on 8 cold plates. Top with small scoops of the pear and strawberry sorbets. Garnish with mint sprigs. Alternatively, fill 8 parfait glasses with scoops of the sorbets and drizzle the coulis on top.
—*Lydie Marshall*

• • •

CHOCOLATE-COFFEE SUNDAES

4 Servings

1½ cups pecans or walnuts
1 cup heavy cream
6 ounces semisweet imported chocolate, coarsely chopped
1 pint coffee ice cream

1. In a dry cast-iron skillet, toast the nuts over moderately high heat, stirring occasionally, until lightly browned, 6 to 8 minutes. Let cool, then coarsely chop.

2. Meanwhile, in a small heavy saucepan, bring ½ cup of the cream to a boil over moderate heat. Remove from the heat and add the chocolate. Set aside for 1 minute, then stir until smooth. Cover to keep warm.

3. In a medium bowl, beat the remaining ½ cup cream until stiff. Spoon the coffee ice cream into 4 dishes. Top each serving with the chocolate sauce, whipped cream and nuts and serve.
—*Jim Fobel*

• • •

HAZELNUT-COFFEE PARFAITS

6 Servings

1 tablespoon freeze-dried coffee granules
2 cups hazelnuts (½ pound)
2½ cups milk, plus more if necessary
1 envelope unflavored gelatin
½ cup plus 2 tablespoons sugar
5 egg yolks
1 cup chilled heavy cream
1 tablespoon hazelnut liqueur
1 ounce imported bittersweet chocolate, chopped

1. Preheat the oven to 375°. In a small saucepan, bring ¼ cup of water to a boil over high heat. Remove from the heat and stir in the coffee granules. Let cool to room temperature, then refrigerate the coffee in the saucepan until chilled.

2. Meanwhile, place the hazelnuts in a small baking pan and toast in the oven for about 10 minutes, until fragrant and browned. Wrap ¼ cup of the hot nuts in a kitchen towel and rub them together to remove their skins. Set the skinned nuts aside to cool.

3. When the remaining 1¾ cups toasted hazelnuts have cooled completely, place them in a food processor and finely chop. Transfer the chopped nuts to a medium nonreactive saucepan, add the 2½ cups of milk and bring to a boil over moderately high heat. Reduce the heat to moderately low and simmer gently for 3 minutes. Remove from the heat, cover and set aside for 1 hour to infuse.

DESSERTS

4. Meanwhile, finely chop the reserved skinned hazelnuts in the food processor and set aside for garnish.

5. Sprinkle the gelatin over the cold coffee and let soften for 5 minutes. Warm over moderately high heat to fully dissolve the gelatin, about 30 seconds. Set aside.

6. Pour the nut-steeped milk into a fine strainer lined with cheesecloth set over a small saucepan. Press on the solids to extract as much liquid as possible. Pour the milk into a 2-cup measure and add fresh milk, if necessary, to make a total of 2 cups. Return the nut milk to the pan and bring to a boil over moderately high heat.

7. Meanwhile, in a medium bowl, whisk the sugar and egg yolks until blended. Gradually whisk in the hot milk, then return the mixture to the saucepan. Cook over moderate heat, stirring constantly with a wooden spoon, until the custard coats the back of the spoon and the temperature reaches 165°, about 5 minutes. Immediately strain the custard into a medium bowl. Stir in the coffee and gelatin mixture.

8. Place the bowl in a larger bowl filled with ice and water and stir occasionally with a rubber spatula, scraping the bottom and sides of the bowl, until the mixture is thickened and chilled, about 45 minutes.

9. In a medium bowl, beat the heavy cream with an electric mixer at medium speed until very soft peaks form. Gently fold the cream and the hazelnut liqueur into the chilled custard mixture. Spoon the mousse into 6 goblets or parfait glasses. Cover and refrigerate until well chilled, at least 4 hours.

10. About 1 hour before serving, place the chocolate in a double boiler and melt over simmering water until

smooth. Using a fork, drizzle some of the chocolate over each parfait and sprinkle with the reserved chopped hazelnuts. Refrigerate until serving time.

—*Ann Chantal Altman*

• • •

CINNAMON ICE CREAM

This ice cream is a perfect accompaniment to any apple or pear dessert.

Makes About 6 Cups

---

1 cinnamon stick
3 cups milk
6 egg yolks
1 cup sugar
1 cup heavy cream

1. Break the cinnamon stick into small pieces and grind to a powder in a spice mill. In a medium saucepan, combine the milk and 1 teaspoon of the ground cinnamon. Bring just to a boil over high heat. Remove the milk from the heat, cover and set aside to infuse for 15 minutes.

2. In a large bowl, using an electric mixer, beat the egg yolks with the sugar at high speed until thick and lemon colored, about 2 minutes. Set aside.

3. Return the milk mixture to a boil and pour about one-third of it into the egg yolk mixture, beating constantly. Pour the milk and egg yolk mixture into the saucepan and cook over moderately low heat, stirring constantly with a wooden spoon, until the mixture thickens to a creamy consistency and coats the back of the spoon, about 5 minutes, or until it registers 175° on a candy thermometer. Do not let it boil.

4. Remove the custard from the heat

and immediately stir in the cream. Strain the mixture through a fine-mesh sieve into a medium bowl. Let cool completely, then transfer to an ice cream maker and freeze according to the manufacturer's instructions. (To speed the cooling, transfer the custard to a large, chilled bowl set inside a slightly larger bowl filled with ice and water. Stir occasionally until cold, about 30 minutes.) The ice cream can be frozen, tightly covered, for up to 1 week.

—*Patricia Wells*

• • •

TOASTED ALMOND FREEZE

This is a take-off on a toasted almond cocktail, which is a mixture of Kahlúa, amaretto and cream.

---

4 Servings

¼ cup sliced almonds
2 tablespoons coffee liqueur
2 tablespoons amaretto
1 pint low-fat vanilla frozen yogurt

1. Preheat the oven to 500°. In a small baking pan, toast the almonds until lightly browned, about 2 minutes.

2. In a small bowl, combine the coffee liqueur and the amaretto. Scoop the frozen yogurt into 4 small dessert bowls. Pour the liqueur mixture on top and sprinkle with the toasted almonds.

—*Susan Shapiro Jaslove*

• • •

VANILLA ICE CREAM SUNDAES WITH CARAMEL SAUCE

4 Servings

1 cup sugar
½ cup heavy cream
1 pint of vanilla ice cream
2 bananas, quartered

1. In a medium nonreactive saucepan, combine the sugar and ½ cup water. Cook, stirring, over low heat until the sugar is dissolved, 1 to 2 minutes. Increase the heat to moderate and let cook until the caramel is a dark amber, about 20 minutes.

2. Remove the caramel from the heat and immediately stir in the cream and 2 tablespoons water. Return the sauce to low heat and whisk until smooth. Remove from the heat and let cool slightly.

3. Scoop the ice cream into 4 bowls. Place 2 banana sections on either side of the ice cream and pour some caramel sauce (warm or at room temperature) on top. Serve immediately.

—Stephanie Lyness

• • •

ESPRESSO MOUSSE

This is my favorite easy dessert to make. The espresso must be of excellent quality and not bitter. If you like, serve a small pitcher of coffee liqueur with this mousse.

8 Servings

1 cup hot brewed espresso
1 envelope unflavored gelatin
¼ cup coffee liqueur, such as Kahlúa
2 cups chilled heavy cream
6 tablespoons sugar
8 chocolate coffee beans or chocolate-covered espresso beans, for garnish

1. In a small bowl, pour the hot espresso over the gelatin and whisk vigorously. Set aside until cool, whisking occasionally to thoroughly dissolve the gelatin. Whisk in the coffee liqueur and set aside.

2. In a medium bowl, beat 1 cup of the cream with a hand-held mixer, gradually adding 3 tablespoons of the sugar, until very firm. Transfer the whipped cream to a large bowl. Repeat with the remaining 1 cup cream and 3 tablespoons sugar.

3. Fold the cooled coffee into the whipped cream. Pour the mousse into 8 parfait glasses. Cover and refrigerate for at least 2 hours or overnight. Garnish each mousse with a chocolate coffee bean before serving.

—Lydie Marshall

• • •

HAZELNUT-CARDAMOM SOUFFLES

To serve, break into the center of each soufflé with a spoon and pour in some sauce.

4 Servings

⅓ cup hazelnuts (about 2 ounces)
5 cardamom seeds
⅓ cup sugar, plus more for dusting
3 tablespoons all-purpose flour
1 teaspoon unsweetened cocoa powder
Salt
1 whole egg
2 egg yolks
1 cup milk
½ teaspoon finely grated orange zest
3 egg whites
Coffee-Cardamom Sauce (p. 269)

1. Preheat the oven to 425°. Spread the hazelnuts on a baking sheet and toast in the middle of the oven until golden brown, about 8 minutes. Transfer the hot nuts to a kitchen towel and rub them together vigorously to remove the skins. Finely chop and set aside.

2. Using the flat side of a large knife, crush the cardamom seeds. In a medium bowl, combine the cardamom, ⅓ cup sugar, flour, cocoa and a pinch of salt. Whisk in the egg and egg yolks until smooth.

3. In a small heavy saucepan, heat the milk over moderate heat just until hot. Whisk a little bit of the hot milk into the egg mixture until blended, then whisk in the rest of the milk. Return the mixture to the saucepan and cook over moderately low heat, whisking constantly, until thickened and glossy, about

253

DESSERTS

4 minutes. Whisk in the orange zest and the reserved hazelnuts. Scrape the soufflé base into a bowl. Place a piece of wax paper directly on the surface and set aside to cool to room temperature, about 1 hour.

4. Preheat the oven to 425°. Lightly but thoroughly butter four ½-cup ramekins; dust with sugar.

5. In a large stainless steel or copper bowl, combine the 3 egg whites and a pinch of salt. Whisk just until soft peaks form. Stir the soufflé base thoroughly and, using a rubber spatula, fold in one-third of the egg whites until blended. Then fold in the remaining whites.

6. Pour the soufflé mixture into the prepared ramekins and tap them on a work surface. Bake the soufflés in the middle of the oven for about 15 minutes, until risen but still wobbly in the center. Serve at once with the Coffee-Cardamom Sauce.

—*Marcia Kiesel*

• • •

COCONUT-MACADAMIA PUDDING

6 Servings

¾ *cup shredded sweetened coconut*
½ *cup lightly salted macadamia nuts*
2½ *cups milk*
1½ *teaspoons vanilla extract*
¾ *cup sugar*
¼ *cup cornstarch*
¼ *teaspoon salt*
3 *egg yolks, at room temperature, lightly beaten*
1 *tablespoon unsalted butter*

1. Preheat the oven to 375°. Spread out the coconut in a cake pan or on a small baking sheet. Toast, stirring once or twice, until golden, about 5 minutes. Set aside to cool in a small bowl.

2. In a food processor, grind the macadamia nuts until fine but not pasty. Transfer to the cake pan or baking sheet and toast in the oven until lightly browned and fragrant, about 5 minutes. Add to the coconut and reserve.

3. In a medium saucepan, scald 2 cups of the milk over moderate heat. Stir in the vanilla.

4. In a bowl, stir together the sugar, cornstarch and salt. Add the remaining ½ cup milk and stir well. Gradually whisk the cornstarch mixture into the hot milk. Reduce the heat to moderate and cook, stirring, until the mixture boils and thickens, about 5 minutes.

5. Place the egg yolks in a medium bowl. Whisk in one-third of the hot milk mixture. Then pour this mixture into the saucepan of hot milk. Cook, stirring constantly, over moderately low heat until the temperature of the pudding reaches 165° on a candy thermometer, 2 to 3 minutes. Do not boil. Remove from the heat, add the butter and stir until thoroughly incorporated.

6. Pour the pudding into 6 custard cups or dessert dishes. Sprinkle the toasted coconut and macadamia nuts on top. Refrigerate until well chilled, about 2 hours.

—*Lee Bailey*

• • •

COCONUT RICE PUDDING

This rice pudding is wonderful with Satin Chocolate Sauce (p. 269).

4 Servings

1 *quart milk*
1 *cup shredded sweetened coconut*
½ *cup long-grain rice, preferably basmati*
¼ *cup sugar*
Pinch of salt
1 *vanilla bean, halved crosswise (optional)*
1 *teaspoon vanilla extract*

1. In a heavy medium saucepan, combine the milk, coconut, rice, sugar, salt and vanilla bean. Bring to a simmer over moderate heat. Reduce the heat to very low, setting the pan slightly off the burner if necessary to maintain a gentle simmer. Cook, stirring frequently to prevent a skin from forming, until the rice is very tender, the milk has reduced and the mixture is thick and creamy, about 1½ hours. Set aside to cool slightly.

2. Remove the vanilla bean and squeeze the seeds out of the open ends into the pudding; stir well. Save the vanilla bean for another use. Stir in the vanilla extract. Serve the pudding hot, warm or cold.

—*Marcia Kiesel*

• • •

DESSERTS

HONEY AND SAFFRON PETITS POTS

This is a delicate custard dessert baked in individual ramekins.

6 Servings

2 cups milk
¼ cup strong-flavored honey, such as thyme, heather or lavender
½ teaspoon saffron threads
⅛ teaspoon salt
3 egg yolks, at room temperature
1 whole egg, at room temperature
2 tablespoons (packed) brown sugar

1. Preheat the oven to 300°. In a heavy saucepan, scald the milk over moderately high heat. Stir in the honey, saffron and salt and set aside.

2. In a large bowl, whisk the egg yolks and whole egg until blended. Stir in the hot milk.

3. Place six ½-cup ramekins or custard cups in a baking pan, and pour in the custard mixture. Pour enough boiling water into the pan to reach 1 inch up the sides of the ramekins. Bake for about 30 minutes, until set but still slightly wobbly in the center. Let cool for 10 minutes in the water bath.

4. Preheat the broiler. Sprinkle each custard with 1 teaspoon of the brown sugar. Broil about 6 inches from the heat for about 1 minute, until caramelized. Serve warm or at room temperature.

—*Mireille Johnston*

• • •

COCONUT CREAM CUSTARD

This light, refreshing dessert, adapted from a recipe by Yuca co-owner Eleanor Levy, is a fine way to end a rich meal. It is served at the restaurant with a guava sauce flavored with rum, but here we use mangoes, which are easier to find.

6 Servings

3 eggs
2 tablespoons sugar
1 teaspoon unflavored gelatin
1 cup heavy cream
½ cup sweetened coconut cream, such as Coco Lopez
1½ tablespoons coconut-flavored or dark rum
Mango Sauce (p. 269)

1. Lightly brush six ½-cup ramekins with vegetable oil and set aside. In a large bowl, using a hand-held electric mixer, beat the eggs and sugar until light and fluffy. Sprinkle the gelatin on top and beat until incorporated.

2. In a heavy medium saucepan, combine ½ cup of the heavy cream with the coconut cream and bring to a boil over moderately high heat. Slowly pour the hot cream into the egg mixture, stirring constantly. Pour the mixture into the saucepan and cook over moderate heat, stirring, until it reaches 160° on a candy thermometer, about 2 minutes. Transfer the mixture to a large bowl set in a larger bowl of ice water and stir until cool. Stir in the rum.

3. In a small bowl, beat the remaining ½ cup heavy cream until stiff. Fold the cream into the custard. Divide the custard among the prepared ramekins and refrigerate for at least 6 hours.

4. Before serving, spoon an even layer of Mango Sauce on top of each custard.

—*Eleanor Levy, Yuca, Coral Gables, Florida*

• • •

WARM BITTERSWEET CHOCOLATE PUDDING

Emily Luchetti, executive pastry chef at Stars, thinks that women have a special way with desserts and pastry because of their delicate touch and sensitivity. She also believes that "desserts satisfy an emotional need." Whatever that need may be, it will certainly be gratified by this deeply flavored chocolate pudding.

6 Servings

1¾ cups all-purpose flour
½ teaspoon salt
1 teaspoon baking soda
½ cup plus 1½ tablespoons unsweetened cocoa powder
2 sticks (8 ounces) plus 1 tablespoon unsalted butter, softened
1¾ cups (firmly packed) brown sugar
4 eggs
1 teaspoon vanilla extract
1 tablespoon confectioners' sugar
½ cup heavy cream, lightly whipped, for serving

1. Preheat the oven to 350°. Into a medium bowl, sift the flour, salt, baking soda and ½ cup of the cocoa powder; set aside. Butter six 1-cup ramekins with the 1 tablespoon butter and set aside.

2. In a large bowl, beat the remaining 2 sticks butter with 1 cup of the brown

sugar at moderate speed until smooth and light. Add the eggs, 1 at a time, beating well after each addition. Beat in the vanilla. Stir in the dry ingredients until well combined; stir in ¼ cup of water. Spoon the batter into the ramekins; each one should be about half full.

3. In a small bowl, combine the remaining ¾ cup brown sugar and the 1½ tablespoons cocoa powder with ¾ cup of hot water. Spoon about 3 tablespoons of this mixture over the surface of each pudding. Place the ramekins in a baking dish or roasting pan and add enough hot water to the pan to reach halfway up the sides of the ramekins.

4. Bake until the puddings are barely set and have begun to shrink from the sides of the ramekins, about 25 to 30 minutes. A toothpick inserted halfway into a pudding 1 inch from the side of the ramekin should come out almost clean. The pudding will be cakey on the top and less set on the bottom. Sift some of the powdered sugar lightly over the top of each pudding and serve immediately with the whipped cream.

—Emily Luchetti, Stars, San Francisco

• • •

CHOCOLATE CUSTARD
WITH PECANS

This is for southern chocolate freaks, who seem to like their chocolate desserts milkier than others do. Allow enough time, since the custard needs a while to chill.

8 Servings

½ cup pecan halves (about 2 ounces)
¾ cup sugar
3 whole eggs

3 egg yolks
3 cups half-and-half or light cream
6 ounces semisweet chocolate, coarsely chopped
1½ teaspoons instant espresso powder
1½ teaspoons vanilla extract
Slightly sweetened whipped cream, for serving

1. Preheat the oven to 300°. On a small baking sheet, roast the pecans for 15 to 20 minutes, until toasted and fragrant. Let cool completely, then coarsely chop and set aside. (The nuts can be prepared up to 2 days ahead and kept in an airtight container.)

2. In a small saucepan, combine ½ cup of the sugar with 3 tablespoons of water and bring to a boil over moderate heat, stirring occasionally to dissolve the sugar. Boil without stirring until a dark golden caramel forms, about 10 minutes. Immediately pour the caramel into a 9-by-5-inch glass or ceramic loaf pan and quickly tilt the pan to coat the bottom; the caramel will harden within seconds.

3. In a large bowl, lightly beat the whole eggs with the egg yolks and set aside. In a heavy medium saucepan, combine the half-and-half with the remaining ¼ cup sugar and scald over moderately high heat. Remove from the heat and stir in the chocolate, espresso powder and vanilla until smooth. Whisk the chocolate mixture into the eggs until incorporated. Pour the custard through a strainer into the prepared loaf pan.

4. Set the pan in a small roasting pan and place in the middle of the oven. Pour about 1 inch of hot water into the roasting pan around the loaf pan. Bake for 1 hour, until the custard is set but still slightly wobbly in the center. Let cool in the water bath for 20 minutes, then remove the loaf pan and let cool to room temperature. Cover and refrigerate until well chilled, 6 hours or overnight.

5. To serve, loosen the sides of the custard with a thin knife and invert onto a serving platter. Sprinkle the reserved chopped nuts on top and pass the whipped cream alongside.

—Lee Bailey

• • •

INDIVIDUAL BAKED
CHOCOLATE CUSTARDS

4 Servings

1½ cups milk
2 tablespoons plus 1 teaspoon unsweetened cocoa powder
¼ cup (packed) dark brown sugar
Pinch of salt
2 eggs, at room temperature
½ teaspoon vanilla extract

1. Preheat the oven to 350°. Place four ¾-cup ramekins or custard cups in an 8-inch square baking pan.

2. In a small saucepan, whisk the milk and cocoa until combined. Bring to a boil over moderately high heat, stirring occasionally with a wooden spoon.

3. In a medium bowl, combine the brown sugar and salt. Whisk in the eggs and vanilla until thoroughly combined. Whisk about one-quarter of the hot chocolate milk into the egg mixture. Pour the remaining chocolate milk into the egg mixture in a steady stream, stirring gently with a rubber spatula until blended.

4. Pour the custard into the ramekins. Fill the baking pan with enough warm water to reach halfway up the sides of the ramekins. Bake for 20 to 25 minutes, or until the custards are just set but still slightly wobbly in the center. Remove the ramekins from the water and set aside to cool. Serve the custards at room temperature or refrigerate until chilled.

—*Susan Shapiro Jaslove*

• • •

LIGHT BREAD PUDDING

You can use Italian bread cut into one-inch pieces instead of a baguette.

6 Servings

4 tablespoons unsalted butter, softened
½ cup golden raisins
1 French baguette (about 10 ounces), cut into 1-inch-thick slices
½ cup plus 2 tablespoons sugar
4 large eggs
1 quart low-fat (2%) milk
1½ teaspoons vanilla extract
Maple syrup (optional)

1. Preheat the oven to 325°. Grease an 8-by-8-inch glass baking dish with 1 tablespoon of the butter. Sprinkle the raisins over the bottom in an even layer.

2. Spread the remaining 3 tablespoons butter on 1 side of each of the bread slices. Arrange the slices side by side in the prepared dish, alternating a buttered-side up with a buttered side down.

3. In a medium bowl, beat ½ cup of the sugar with the eggs, milk and vanilla. Pour the mixture evenly over the bread.

4. Place the baking dish in a larger pan. Add enough warm water to the pan to reach about halfway up the sides of the baking dish. Bake for 45 to 50 minutes, or until the custard is just set. Remove the baking dish from the water bath.

5. Preheat the broiler. Sprinkle the remaining 2 tablespoons sugar over the bread pudding and broil for about 1 minute, or until browned on the top. Let cool to room temperature. Serve on its own or with maple syrup drizzled on top.

—*Lee Bailey*

• • •

CHOCOLATE BREAD PUDDING

This dessert (also called *bodino nero*, literally, "black pudding") is a bread pudding, versions of which are found in several cultures. Many Italian bread puddings fall into a category called *torta di pane* and are flavored with anything from wine to saffron. This version was adapted from an old recipe in *Antichi Dolci di Casa* by Silvia Tocco Bonetti and was given to me by the cooking teacher and author Anna Teresa Callen. Halfway between a bread pudding and a cake, it is rich with chocolate and not too sweet. I like to serve it warm in a pool of cool Rum and Orange Custard Sauce.

8 Servings

1 tablespoon butter, softened
About 1½ tablespoons fine dry bread crumbs
6 ounces imported semisweet chocolate, coarsely chopped
2 cups milk
4 eggs
½ cup granulated sugar
8 ounces Italian or semolina bread, crusts removed, cut into ½-inch cubes (about 5 cups)
1 tablespoon confectioners' sugar, for dusting
Rum and Orange Custard Sauce (p. 268)

1. Preheat the oven to 350°. Butter an 8-inch springform pan with the softened butter and dust with the bread crumbs, shaking out the excess. Wrap the bottom and sides of the pan with aluminum foil to prevent seepage.

2. In a heavy medium saucepan, combine the chocolate and milk and warm over moderate heat, stirring occasionally, until the chocolate is partially melted, about 4 minutes. Remove from the heat and stir until smooth.

3. In a large bowl, whisk the eggs with the sugar until blended. Gradually whisk in the chocolate mixture. Fold in the bread cubes. If the bread was very dry, set aside to allow it to soften for 5 to 10 minutes.

4. Transfer the mixture to the prepared pan and cover with buttered foil. Place in a shallow baking pan filled with enough hot water to reach 1 inch up the sides of the springform pan. Bake in the middle of the oven for 45 minutes, or until the pudding is just set but still slightly wobbly in the center. Re-

move the pan from the water bath and let cool on a wire rack for 20 minutes. While still warm, carefully remove the foil collar and the sides of the spring-form pan.

5. Transfer the pudding to a serving plate, cool slightly and sift the confectioners' sugar over the top. Cut into wedges. Serve warm, in a little pool of the Rum and Orange Custard Sauce.

—Richard Sax

• • •

CHRISTMAS BREAD PUDDING

Easily made a day ahead of time, bread pudding is the ideal finale to Christmas dinner. If panettone is not available, substitute another similar, fruit-studded sweet bread. Just before serving, spread the Amaretto Sauce over the pudding and broil until golden brown and bubbly. ♟ The bread pudding, with its sugary glazed fruit is almost too sweet for a dessert wine. The best choice is an intensely aromatic one, such as a French Muscat de Beaumes de Venise from Paul Jaboulet Aîné or Prosper Maufoux.

12 Servings

1 panettone or other fruit-studded sweet bread (about 1 pound), cut into 1-inch slices
1 quart half-and-half or light cream
3 eggs
1 cup sugar
1 tablespoon plus 2 teaspoons vanilla extract
1 teaspoon almond extract
Amaretto Sauce (p. 268)

1. Preheat the broiler. Arrange the bread slices on 2 baking sheets and toast

2 inches from the heat for about 1 minute a side, or until lightly browned. Set aside for at least 1 hour.

2. Tear the toasted panettone into 1½-inch pieces and place in a large bowl. Pour the half-and-half over the bread, making sure all the pieces are moistened. Set aside for 1 hour until all the liquid has been absorbed.

3. Preheat the oven to 325°. Generously butter the bottom and sides of a 9-by-13-by-2-inch baking dish and set aside. In a medium bowl, whisk the eggs with the sugar, vanilla and almond extracts until blended. Stir into the soaked bread. Transfer the mixture to the prepared baking dish and bake in the middle of the oven for about 1 hour, or until the pudding is set and the top is golden brown. Let cool to room temperature. *(The pudding can be prepared 1 day ahead. Cover and set aside at room temperature.)*

4. Preheat the broiler. Just before serving, spoon the Amaretto Sauce over the pudding and broil 3 to 4 inches from the heat until bubbly and lightly browned, about 2 minutes. Cut the bread pudding into 12 rectangular pieces and serve immediately.

—Sheila Lukins

• • •

CANDIED PECANS

Toasted pecans are coated with molasses and roasted until crisp and brown. They can be kept in an airtight container for a week.

Makes 2 Cups

1 cup sugar
2 cups pecan halves
3 tablespoons dark molasses

1. Preheat the oven to 275°. In a medium saucepan, combine the sugar and pecans with 4 cups of water. Bring to a boil over high heat. Drain the pecans and spread them out on a baking sheet in an even layer. Bake for about 20 minutes, until dry but not browned. Transfer the nuts to a medium bowl, add the molasses and stir to coat.

2. Line a baking sheet with parchment paper. Using a slotted spoon, spread the pecans on the prepared baking sheet in an even layer. Return to the oven and bake for about 30 minutes, or until roasted and browned. Let cool completely. *(The pecans can be made ahead, then stored in an airtight container for up to 1 week.)*

—Richard Leach, Aureole New York City

• • •

258

CONDIMENTS, SAUCES & STOCKS

CONDIMENTS, SAUCES & STOCKS

GARAM MASALA

This spice mixture is usually added at the end of cooking. It is available pre-mixed, but in India every family makes its own blend.

Make About 3 Tablespoons

1 tablespoon cardamom seeds
1 cinnamon stick
⅓ of a whole nutmeg
1 teaspoon whole black peppercorns
1 teaspoon black or regular cumin
   seeds
1 teaspoon whole cloves

Put all the ingredients in a clean coffee grinder or spice mill and grind finely. Store in a lidded jar in a dark place.
—*Madhur Jaffrey*

• • •

FRESH CORIANDER CHUTNEY

Makes About ½ Cup

½ teaspoon cumin seeds
3 cups fresh coriander (cilantro)
   sprigs, chopped
½ cup fresh mint leaves, chopped
1 small green Thai chile, minced
1 garlic clove, minced
2 tablespoons fresh lime juice
¼ teaspoon salt
½ teaspoon freshly ground black
   pepper

1. In a small dry skillet, toast the cumin seeds over high heat until fragrant, about 30 seconds. In a mortar, pound the seeds to a coarse powder. Or, chop the seeds finely with a knife.

2. In a food processor, combine the cumin with all the remaining ingredients. Process to a paste, stopping to scrape down the sides of the bowl once or twice. Scrape the chutney into a bowl and press plastic wrap directly on the surface. Refrigerate for up to 1 day.
—*Madhur Jaffrey*

• • •

GINGERED CRANBERRY RELISH

Cranberries, which can be a bit predictable, are not when combined with tart and sweet dried Michigan cherries and crystallized ginger.

Makes About 2½ Cups

1½ cups dried cherries* (9 ounces)
1 cup fresh cranberries
1 cup sugar
¼ cup coarsely chopped crystallized
   ginger (about 1¼ ounces)
½ cup plus 2 tablespoons fresh
   orange juice
1 tablespoon finely grated lemon zest
*Available at specialty food stores

In a heavy, medium, nonreactive saucepan, combine all the ingredients with 6 tablespoons of water and bring to a boil over moderately high heat. Reduce the heat to moderate and cook, stirring occasionally and skimming as necessary, until the cranberries pop, about 8 minutes. Transfer to a small serving bowl and let cool. Cover and refrigerate for up to 3 days. Serve at room temperature.

—*Sheila Lukins*

• • •

GRANDMA JONES'S PEAR CHUTNEY

Serve this chutney with cured as well as fresh hams, or try it with game. Its flavor improves as it sits, so make a batch ahead.

Makes About 3 Cups

5 ripe Anjou pears, peeled and cored
One ¾-inch piece of peeled fresh
   ginger
2 tablespoons molasses
⅔ cup distilled white vinegar
2 small onions, finely chopped
1 medium garlic clove, minced
½ teaspoon minced Scotch Bonnet
   chile* or other fresh hot chile
   pepper
8 allspice berries, crushed
5 whole cloves, crushed
½ teaspoon cinnamon
¼ teaspoon ground cloves
*Available at Latin American or
   specialty produce markets

1. Cut 3 of the pears into 1-inch chunks. In a food processor, combine the pear chunks, ginger and molasses and puree, scraping down the bowl as necessary, until smooth. Scrape the puree into a medium nonreactive saucepan. Stir in the vinegar, onions, garlic, chile, allspice berries, whole cloves, cinnamon and ground cloves.

2. Cut the 2 remaining pears into ⅓-inch dice. Stir them into the pear puree and bring to a boil over moderately high heat. Reduce the heat to moderately low and simmer, uncovered, until the chutney is thick and jammy, about 45 minutes. Set aside to cool.

3. Spoon the chutney into a couple of small sterilized jars and refrigerate for up to 2 weeks. Let return to room temperature before serving.

—*Jessica B. Harris*

• • •

PEAR AND APPLE CHUTNEY

Makes About 1 Cup

2½ cups apple juice
2 tablespoons cider vinegar
2 tablespoons (packed) brown sugar
3 large shallots, chopped
1 tablespoon minced fresh ginger
½ teaspoon mustard seeds
½ teaspoon cumin
¼ teaspoon crushed red pepper
½ teaspoon salt
1 large Granny Smith apple, peeled and cut into ½-inch dice
1 large firm pear, preferably Bartlett, peeled and cut into ½-inch dice
1 teaspoon finely grated lemon zest
¼ cup dried cranberries or sour cherries*
*Available at specialty food stores

1. In a medium nonreactive saucepan, combine the apple juice, vinegar, brown sugar, shallots, ginger, mustard seeds, cumin, red pepper and salt. Bring to a boil over high heat and cook until the mixture has reduced to 1 cup, about 15 minutes.

2. Stir in the apple and pear. Reduce the heat to moderate and simmer until the fruit is tender, about 10 minutes. Remove from the heat. Stir in the lemon zest and dried cranberries. Let the chutney cool to room temperature, then cover and refrigerate overnight before serving.

—*Lee Bailey*

• • •

ROSY SALSA

Roasted red pepper, fresh herbs and lime juice add sprightliness to this chunky salsa.

Makes About 1 Cup

1 large red bell pepper
½ pound plum tomatoes—quartered, seeded and cut into ⅓-inch dice
1 tablespoon minced shallots
¼ cup minced fresh basil
2 tablespoons minced fresh coriander (cilantro)
1 teaspoon minced fresh thyme
2 tablespoons extra-virgin olive oil
1 tablespoon fresh lime juice
½ teaspoon salt
¼ teaspoon freshly ground black pepper

1. Roast the pepper directly over a gas flame or under the broiler, turning frequently with tongs, until the skin is charred all over. Transfer the pepper to a paper bag, close the bag and set aside for 10 minutes. Peel, core and seed the pepper and cut off the ribs. Cut the pepper into ¼-inch dice and place in a medium bowl. Add the tomatoes, shallots, basil, coriander and thyme.

2. In a small bowl, whisk together the olive oil, lime juice, salt and black pepper. Pour the dressing over the vegetables and stir to combine. Serve at room temperature or chilled.

—*Diana Sturgis*

• • •

PINEAPPLE-JALAPENO SALSA

For this salsa, use the best marmalade you can buy.

Makes About 1 Cup

1½ cups fresh pineapple chunks (about ¼ of a pineapple)
3 tablespoons orange marmalade
1 tablespoon pickled sliced jalapeño peppers, minced
1 tablespoon minced pimiento
2 teaspoons fresh lime juice
½ teaspoon coarse (kosher) salt
1 tablespoon chopped fresh coriander (cilantro)

In a food processor, pulse the pineapple chunks until finely chopped. Transfer to a medium bowl. Stir in the marmalade, jalapeños, pimiento, lime juice and salt. (*The salsa can be made to this point up to 2 days ahead; cover and refrigerate until 1 hour before serving.*) Stir in the coriander and serve.

—*Kathy Casey*

• • •

CONDIMENTS, SAUCES & STOCKS

TROPICAL FRUIT SALSA

This simple *salsa fresca* could be modified, depending on what fruit is available, although pineapple works particularly well with the salty Smithfield ham. Make sure you allow some time for the flavors to meld and ripen.

Makes About 3½ Cups

1 large ripe mango
¼ of a fresh pineapple—peeled, cored and cut into ½-inch cubes (about 1¼ cups)
1 papaya—peeled, seeded and cut into ½-inch cubes
1 medium red onion, finely chopped
2 serrano chiles, seeded and finely chopped
1 cup fresh mint leaves, coarsely chopped
¼ cup fresh lime juice (3 limes)
½ teaspoon salt
1 teaspoon freshly ground pepper
3 tablespoons peanut oil

1. Using a sharp knife, trim the skin off the mango, then cut the soft flesh from around the oblong seed. Cut the flesh into ½-inch cubes and place in a medium bowl. Add the pineapple, papaya, onion, chiles and mint. Toss well.
2. In a small bowl, whisk the lime juice with the salt and pepper. Gradually whisk in the oil until incorporated. Pour the dressing over the fruit and toss gently. Cover and refrigerate for at least 1 hour and up to 6 hours. Serve chilled or at room temperature.

—Susan Costner

• • •

LEMON-SESAME SAUCE

This sauce, which was designed for Sesame Chicken on a Bun (p. 88), can also be used as a dip for vegetables, or, thinned with more water, as a salad dressing.

Makes About 1 Cup

½ cup tahini (sesame paste)
¼ cup plus 2 tablespoons fresh lemon juice
½ teaspoon salt

In a small bowl, mix the tahini and lemon juice. Slowly mix in ¼ cup water until the sauce is smooth and creamy. Season with the salt.

—Susan Shapiro Jaslove

• • •

SESAME DIPPING SAUCE

This sauce can easily be doubled. Vary the taste by increasing the garlic, ginger or vinegar.

Makes About ⅓ Cup

1 tablespoon sesame seeds
2 tablespoons tamari*
1 tablespoon Oriental sesame oil
1½ teaspoons rice vinegar
1 small garlic clove, minced

1 tablespoon grated fresh ginger or 1 teaspoon dried ground ginger
½ teaspoon sugar
*Available at Asian markets

1. Place the sesame seeds in a small skillet and toast over moderate heat, shaking the pan occasionally, until lightly browned and fragrant, about 3 minutes. Set aside to cool.
2. In a small bowl, whisk the tamari with the sesame oil, vinegar, garlic, ginger and sugar. Stir in the sesame seeds. If desired, add water, 1 teaspoon at a time, until the flavor mellows.

—Mark Bittman

• • •

AMERASIAN DIPPING SAUCE

Makes About 2 Cups

1½ cups rice vinegar
¾ cup plus 2 tablespoons sugar
2 tablespoons minced garlic
1 tablespoon plus 1 teaspoon Vietnamese chile garlic sauce or red chile sauce (see Note)
Hot pepper sauce (optional)

1. Combine all of the ingredients in a medium bowl and whisk well to dissolve the sugar. Let stand at room temperature for at least 2 hours or overnight.
2. Strain the sauce into a jar and refrigerate for up to 1 week.

NOTE: *If you can't find this sauce, mix ¾ teaspoon crushed dried Asian chiles, 2 small minced serrano chiles and 1 teaspoon distilled white vinegar. Add to the vinegar-sugar-garlic mixture and let stand for at least 3 hours.*

—Linda Burum

• • •

ROUILLE

This fiery, spirited sauce can simply be a traditional mayonnaise flavored with garlic, saffron and hot red pepper. Or it can be prepared with pureed potatoes and olive oil. Here, it is made with cooked egg yolks. If the oil separates, puree the rouille in a blender.

Makes About 1 Cup

5 garlic cloves
1 tablespoon Dijon mustard
1 scant teaspoon cayenne pepper or hot pepper sauce to taste
½ teaspoon salt
½ teaspoon saffron threads, softened in 1 teaspoon warm water
2 hard-cooked egg yolks
¾ cup olive oil

1. In a large mortar, combine the garlic, mustard, cayenne, salt and the saffron threads and their liquid. Pound with a pestle until pasty. Add the egg yolks and mash until smooth. Transfer to a bowl.

2. Slowly drizzle in the oil, whisking constantly until the sauce is emulsified. Season with additional cayenne and salt to taste.

—*Mireille Johnston*

• • •

RED PEPPER MARMALADE

These peppers are great over pasta or as an accompaniment for many summer dishes.

8 Servings

6 large red bell peppers
2 tablespoons plus 1 teaspoon fruity extra-virgin olive oil
1 large garlic clove, minced
Salt

1. Preheat the oven to 450°. Line a broiler pan with aluminum foil. Rub the peppers with 1 teaspoon of the olive oil and place them on the foil. Roast in the upper part of the oven for 20 to 30 minutes, turning occasionally until soft. The pepper skins should be blistered and have a few charred spots but should not be charred completely. Put the peppers in a heavy plastic bag, close to seal and set aside until cooled.

2. Peel the peppers over a bowl and remove the cores, seeds and ribs; reserve the juices. Cut the peppers into 3½-by-1½-inch strips. Place the strips in a bowl and add the garlic, remaining 2 tablespoons olive oil, reserved pepper juices and 1½ teaspoons salt. Toss gently. Cover and refrigerate. (*The peppers can be made up to 5 days ahead. Let return to room temperature before serving.*)

—*Lydie Marshall*

• • •

CHUNKY MINTED YOGURT SAUCE

Makes About 2 Cups

1 pint plain yogurt
¼ cup finely diced cucumber
¼ cup thinly sliced radishes
2 medium scallions, minced
2 tablespoons minced fresh mint
1 tablespoon minced flat-leaf parsley
1 garlic clove, minced
½ teaspoon salt
¼ teaspoon freshly ground pepper

Combine all the ingredients in a medium bowl and mix well. Cover and refrigerate until serving time.

—*Linda Burum*

• • •

TARTAR SAUCE

Makes About 1 Cup

1 cup mayonnaise
1 tablespoon fresh lemon juice or white wine vinegar
2 tablespoons finely chopped cornichons
1 tablespoon chopped drained capers
1 tablespoon finely chopped flat-leaf parsley
1 tablespoon finely chopped chives

In a medium bowl, combine the mayonnaise and lemon juice. Stir in the cornichons, capers, parsley and chives. (*The sauce can be refrigerated, covered, for up to 2 days.*)

—*Diana Sturgis*

• • •

CONDIMENTS, SAUCES & STOCKS

TAHINI-GARLIC MAYONNAISE

Makes About ⅔ Cup

½ cup mayonnaise, at room
    temperature
2 tablespoons tahini (sesame paste),
    at room temperature
2 teaspoons chopped fresh coriander
    (cilantro)
½ teaspoon fresh lemon juice
½ teaspoon minced garlic
Salt and freshly ground white pepper

Whisk the mayonnaise with the tahini
until smooth. Mix in the coriander,
lemon juice and garlic. Season the mayonnaise to taste with salt and pepper.

—Linda Burum

• • •

SALSA MAYONNAISE

The quantities of ingredients added to
the mayonnaise can be altered to suit
your taste. It is important to drain the
chopped tomatoes well before adding
them.

Makes About 1¾ Cups

1 large tomato—peeled, seeded and
    coarsely chopped
1 small onion, minced
1 small garlic clove, minced
1 canned green chile, drained and
    chopped
1 tablespoon minced fresh coriander
    (cilantro)
2 teaspoons fresh lime juice

1 teaspoon minced fresh jalapeño
    pepper
⅔ cup mayonnaise

1. Place the chopped tomato on several sheets of paper towel and let drain.
2. In a medium bowl, stir together
the onion, garlic, green chile, coriander, lime juice and jalapeño. Stir in the
mayonnaise and drained tomato. Cover
and refrigerate for up to 4 hours.

—Lee Bailey

• • •

REMOULADE SAUCE

This is a tangy dipping sauce for steamed
or boiled shrimp.

Makes About 1¼ Cups

¼ cup vegetable oil
¼ cup Creole or Dijon mustard
¼ cup mayonnaise
2 tablespoons cider vinegar
1 tablespoon drained prepared white
    horseradish
1 tablespoon sweet paprika
2 medium celery ribs, minced
6 medium scallions, minced
¼ cup minced flat-leaf parsley
Salt and freshly ground black pepper
Hot pepper sauce

In a medium bowl, combine the oil,
mustard, mayonnaise, vinegar, horseradish and paprika. Whisk to blend. Stir
in the celery, scallions and parsley. Season with salt, pepper and hot pepper
sauce to taste. (*The sauce can be refrigerated, covered, for up to 2 days.*)

—Diana Sturgis

• • •

SHERRY AIOLI

Makes About 1¼ Cups

¾ cup mayonnaise
1 garlic clove, minced
1½ tablespoons fresh lemon juice
1½ teaspoons sherry vinegar
½ cup extra-virgin olive oil
½ teaspoon coarse (kosher) salt
⅛ teaspoon hot pepper sauce

In a medium bowl, whisk the mayonnaise, garlic, lemon juice and vinegar.
Gradually drizzle in the olive oil while
whisking vigorously until it is all incorporated. Season with the salt and hot
pepper sauce and stir well. Alternatively, blend all of the ingredients in a
food processor until smooth. (*The aioli
can be made up to 1 day ahead; cover and
refrigerate.*)

—Kathy Casey

• • •

TOMATO-CUMIN DRESSING

Makes About 1½ Cups

¼ cup fresh lemon juice (2 lemons)
¼ cup tomato juice
2 teaspoons cumin
1 garlic clove, minced
½ cup coarsely chopped fresh
    coriander (cilantro)
½ teaspoon salt
½ teaspoon freshly ground pepper
¾ cup olive oil

In a medium bowl, whisk together the
lemon juice, tomato juice, cumin, garlic
and coriander. Then whisk in the salt
and pepper and, if necessary, adjust the

seasoning. Gradually whisk in the olive oil until incorporated. *(The dressing can be made 1 to 2 days ahead and refrigerated, covered.)*

—Susan Costner

• • •

CREAMY ROASTED-GARLIC DRESSING

The sublime roasted-garlic flavor of this dressing would be a crowning touch on salads and sandwiches alike. Slather it on leftover meats or poultry, or mix it in with cold cooked sliced potatoes for another version of potato salad.

Makes About 1 Cup

1 medium head of garlic (3 ounces)
2 teaspoons mild olive oil
½ cup sour cream
¼ cup mayonnaise
1 medium scallion, thinly sliced
1 tablespoon white wine vinegar
¾ teaspoon freshly ground pepper
½ teaspoon salt

1. Preheat the oven to 375°. Cut approximately ½ inch off the top of the garlic head. Place the garlic on a 6-inch square of aluminum foil and drizzle the oil on top. Wrap the garlic in the foil to enclose completely. Roast for 45 minutes, or until soft. Set aside to cool.

2. In a medium bowl, stir together the sour cream and mayonnaise. Pinch the root end of the roasted garlic and squeeze the flesh into the bowl. Using a rubber spatula, mash the garlic against the side of the bowl and then stir it into

the sour cream and mayonnaise. Stir in the scallion, vinegar, pepper and salt. *(The dressing can be made up to 1 week ahead and refrigerated in a sealed jar.)*

—Tracey Seaman

• • •

BUTTERMILK-HERB DRESSING

Drizzle this dressing on salads of vegetables and greens arranged in pleasing color combinations. For instance, combine mixed crisp lettuce leaves, tomato wedges, roasted yellow bell pepper strips and thinly sliced carrots, cucumbers and red onion.

Makes About 2 Cups

¾ cup buttermilk
¾ cup mayonnaise
1 large shallot or 1 small onion, minced
2 medium garlic cloves, minced
½ teaspoon salt
½ teaspoon freshly ground pepper
⅛ teaspoon curry powder
1 tablespoon minced fresh basil
1 teaspoon minced fresh thyme

In a medium bowl, whisk together the buttermilk, mayonnaise, shallot and garlic. Whisk in the salt, pepper, curry powder, basil and thyme. *(The dressing can be made up to 3 days ahead and refrigerated in a sealed jar.)*

—Tracey Seaman

• • •

VIRGIN MARY VINAIGRETTE

Use this zesty dressing with a salad of grilled vegetables and meats. For example, poach and grill Italian sausage links; then cut them into chunks. Toss yellow and red bell pepper pieces, zucchini disks and halved mushrooms in the dressing, arrange on skewers and grill until charred. Combine with the sausages, add more dressing and toss well.

Makes About 1¼ Cups

1 garlic clove
¾ teaspoon salt
½ cup tomato juice or vegetable juice cocktail
3 tablespoons red wine vinegar
1 teaspoon Worcestershire sauce
1 teaspoon tomato paste
½ teaspoon freshly ground pepper
½ cup olive oil
¼ cup minced celery leaves
2 dashes of hot pepper sauce

1. On a work surface, coarsely chop the garlic. Using a fork, mash the garlic and salt together to form a paste. Transfer to a medium bowl.

2. Whisk in the tomato juice, vinegar, Worcestershire sauce, tomato paste and pepper until combined.

3. Whisk in the oil in a thin stream until incorporated. Stir in the celery leaves and hot pepper sauce. *(The dressing can be made up to 3 days ahead and refrigerated in a sealed jar.)*

—Tracey Seaman

• • •

CONDIMENTS, SAUCES & STOCKS

DIJON VINAIGRETTE

Serve this intense mustard dressing with a contemporary Niçoise salad. Use grilled fresh tuna, romaine lettuce, tomatoes, hard-cooked eggs, boiled potatoes and slender crisply cooked green beans; garnish with Niçoise olives.

Makes About 1 Cup

¼ *cup Dijon mustard*
¼ *cup red wine vinegar*
¼ *teaspoon freshly ground pepper*
½ *cup mild olive oil*

In a small bowl, stir together the mustard, vinegar and pepper. Whisk in the oil in a thin stream until incorporated. (*The dressing can be made up to 1 week ahead and refrigerated in a sealed jar.*)

—*Tracey Seaman*

• • •

CHUNKY-CREAMY BLUE CHEESE DRESSING

This dressing goes well with crudités or with a salad of red leaf lettuce, bite-sized chunks of Red Delicious apples, chopped toasted walnuts and pieces of cooked chicken.

Makes About 2 Cups

1 *cup mayonnaise*
½ *cup plain yogurt*
2 *teaspoons white wine vinegar*
¼ *teaspoon freshly ground pepper*
4 *ounces crumbled Danish blue cheese (about 1 cup)*
2 *medium scallions, minced*

In a medium bowl, whisk together the mayonnaise and yogurt until smooth. Whisk in the vinegar and the pepper. Fold in the cheese and scallions. Season to taste with more pepper. (*The dressing can be made up to 2 weeks ahead and refrigerated in a sealed jar. It will thicken slightly as it sits.*)

—*Tracey Seaman*

• • •

OIL AND EGG VINAIGRETTE

Try this dressing on a salad made with fresh spinach, homemade bacon bits, shiitake mushrooms sautéed in a dry skillet, cherry tomatoes and thinly sliced red onion. It is natural for this dressing to separate slightly.

Makes About 1¼ Cups

2 *tablespoons white wine vinegar*
2 *teaspoons Dijon mustard*
¾ *teaspoon salt*
½ *teaspoon fresh lemon juice*
¾ *cup mild olive oil*
4 *hard-cooked eggs, finely chopped*
¼ *cup minced fresh chives*
½ *teaspoon freshly ground pepper*

In a bowl, whisk together the vinegar, mustard, salt and lemon juice. Slowly whisk in the oil until incorporated. Stir in the eggs, chives and pepper.

—*Tracey Seaman*

• • •

NO-YOLK CAESAR DRESSING

For a simple salad, toss this dressing with torn romaine lettuce leaves. Sprinkle homemade croutons on top.

Makes About 1 Cup

2 *anchovy fillets, rinsed, or 2 teaspoons anchovy paste*
1 *large garlic clove, minced*
1 *tablespoon fresh lemon juice*
2 *teaspoons Dijon mustard*
3 *tablespoons red wine vinegar*
⅓ *cup olive oil*
Freshly grated Parmesan cheese
Freshly ground pepper

1. In a medium bowl, mash the anchovies to a paste with a fork. Whisk in the garlic, lemon juice and mustard until combined. Whisk in the vinegar.

2. Gradually add the oil in a thin stream, whisking vigorously until the dressing is thick and glossy. If the oil begins to separate out, stop pouring and keep whisking until it is thoroughly incorporated; then whisk in the remaining oil in a steady stream. (*The dressing can be made to this point up to 2 weeks ahead and refrigerated in a sealed jar. Shake before using.*)

3. When serving, add salad to the dressing in a bowl and toss. Season to taste with Parmesan cheese and pepper and toss again.

—*Tracey Seaman*

• • •

PEANUT DRESSING

You can make a quick slaw for this dressing in a food processor fitted with a shredding disk. Shred carrots, jicama and peeled broccoli stalks. Alternatively, grate the vegetables by hand. In a large bowl, combine the shredded vegetables with finely diced red bell pepper and bean sprouts. Toss the vegetables with the dressing just before serving. Peanut dressing also makes a tasty dip for grilled chicken, or mix it with leftover cooked noodles.

Makes About 1 Cup

¼ cup creamy peanut butter
2 tablespoons Oriental sesame oil
2 tablespoons fresh lemon juice
2 teaspoons minced fresh ginger
1 garlic clove, minced
½ teaspoon salt
¼ teaspoon cayenne pepper
1 tablespoon distilled white vinegar
1 tablespoon soy sauce
¼ cup olive oil
¼ cup peanut or corn oil

1. In a medium bowl, whisk together the peanut butter, sesame oil, lemon juice, ginger, garlic, salt and cayenne until well blended. Whisk in the vinegar and soy sauce.

2. Whisk in the olive and peanut oils in a thin stream until incorporated. *(The dressing can be made up to 5 days ahead and refrigerated in a sealed jar.)*

—*Tracey Seaman*

• • •

GREEN PEPPERCORN-TERIYAKI DRESSING

This Asian-inspired dressing marries well with a multitude of salad combinations. Mix with thinly sliced cooked flank steak—from last night's dinner perhaps—cut crosswise into strips, tossed with romaine lettuce, radicchio and endive and garnished with enoki mushrooms. You can substitute cooked shrimp or chicken for the steak.

Makes About 1¾ Cups

¼ cup soy sauce
¼ cup mirin (see Note)
¼ cup sake (see Note)
¼ cup plus 1 tablespoon rice vinegar
2 tablespoons drained green peppercorns, minced or lightly crushed
1 tablespoon minced fresh ginger
1 medium garlic clove, minced
½ cup plus 2 tablespoons vegetable oil

In a medium bowl, stir together the soy sauce, mirin, sake and rice vinegar. Whisk in the peppercorns, ginger and garlic, then whisk in the oil in a thin stream until incorporated. *(The dressing can be made up to 5 days ahead and refrigerated in a sealed jar.)*

NOTE: *Mirin, or sweet sake, is available at Asian markets. Sake can be purchased at most liquor stores.*

—*Tracey Seaman*

• • •

CREME FRAICHE

Makes About 2 Cups

1 pint heavy cream, preferably not ultrapasteurized
3 tablespoons cultured buttermilk

1. In a medium bowl, whisk together the cream and buttermilk. Cover the bowl with a towel and let stand in a warm place until thickened, about 12 hours.

2. When thickened, cover the bowl tightly and refrigerate until well chilled, 2 to 3 hours. *(The crème fraîche can be refrigerated, tightly covered, for up to 2 weeks.)*

—*Susan Herrmann Loomis*

• • •

TANGY YOGURT CREAM

A dollop of this light, glossy cream is a fine accompaniment for any crumb cake.

Makes About 3 Cups

1 cup heavy cream, chilled
2 tablespoons sugar
1 teaspoon lemon juice
⅓ cup plain yogurt

In a medium bowl, combine all the ingredients and beat until stiff. Transfer the cream to a serving bowl and refrigerate, covered, for at least 30 minutes before serving.

—*Diana Sturgis*

• • •

CONDIMENTS, SAUCES & STOCKS

VANILLA CUSTARD SAUCE

This sauce is a wonderful accompaniment to a variety of desserts including cakes, mousses and hot soufflés. It is also the base for most ice creams. Proportions of milk to yolks may vary. Be careful not to overcook the sauce; it may curdle.

Makes About 1½ Cups

1½ vanilla beans, split lengthwise
1⅓ cups milk
6 tablespoons sugar
4 egg yolks

1. Scrape the seeds from the vanilla beans into a medium saucepan. Add the vanilla beans, milk and 3 tablespoons of the sugar. Bring to a boil over moderate heat. Remove from the heat and set aside to steep for 20 minutes.

2. Meanwhile, in a medium bowl, whisk together the egg yolks and remaining 3 tablespoons sugar. Gradually whisk in all the warm milk. Pour the mixture into the saucepan and cook over moderate heat, stirring constantly with a wooden spoon, until the sauce reaches 165° on a thermometer, is slightly thickened and just coats the back of the spoon, about 8 minutes. Do not allow the mixture to boil or it will curdle. Immediately strain the custard into a metal bowl and set it inside a large bowl of ice water to cool, stir occasionally. (*The vanilla custard can be made 1 day in advance and kept covered in the refrigerator.*)
—*Richard Leach, Aureole, New York City*

• • •

ORANGE MUSCAT CREME ANGLAISE

Makes About 2½ Cups

1½ cups milk
3 egg yolks
Pinch of salt
¼ cup sugar
⅓ cup Essencia

1. In a medium saucepan, bring the milk to a boil over moderately high heat. Meanwhile, in a medium bowl, whisk the egg yolks with the salt and sugar until light and thickened. Gradually whisk the hot milk into the egg yolks.

2. Return the mixture to the saucepan and cook over moderately low heat, stirring constantly with a wooden spoon, until the custard coats the back of the spoon. Strain the custard through a fine sieve set over a bowl. Let cool, then cover and refrigerate until cold. (*The custard sauce can be prepared to this point up to 1 day ahead.*) Stir in the Essencia just before serving.
—*Bob Chambers*

• • •

AMARETTO SAUCE

Makes About 1 Cup

1 stick (4 ounces) unsalted butter, cut into pieces
1 cup confectioners' sugar
3 tablespoons Amaretto
2 egg yolks

In a medium bowl set over a small saucepan of simmering water or in the top of a double boiler, melt the butter.

Slowly whisk in the sugar until the mixture is creamy, about 30 seconds. Add the Amaretto and then the egg yolks, one at a time, whisking constantly. Cook, whisking constantly until the sauce is the consistency of honey and reaches 160°, about 4 minutes. Let cool to room temperature. (*The recipe can made up to 1 day ahead. Cover and refrigerate. Let return to room temperature before using.*)
—*Sheila Lukins*

• • •

RUM AND ORANGE CUSTARD SAUCE

Makes About 2 Cups

2 cups milk
1 vanilla bean, split lengthwise
2 wide strips of orange zest
⅓ cup sugar
5 egg yolks
1½ tablespoons dark rum, or more to taste

1. In a medium saucepan, combine the milk, vanilla bean, orange zest and 1 tablespoon of the sugar and bring to a boil over moderate heat. Remove from the heat, cover and set aside to steep for 20 minutes.

2. Meanwhile, in a medium bowl, whisk the egg yolks with the remaining sugar. Gradually whisk in half of the warm milk until blended, then whisk the mixture back into the remaining milk in the saucepan. Cook over moderate heat, stirring constantly with a wooden spoon, until the sauce reaches 165°, is slightly thickened and just coats the back of the spoon, about 8 minutes. Do not let the mixture boil or it will curdle. Immediately strain the custard into a medium bowl through a fine sieve. Add the rum. Let cool slightly, then cover and refrigerate until chilled. (*The custard can be made up to 1 day ahead.*)

—*Richard Sax*

• • •

SATIN CHOCOLATE SAUCE

The better the quality of the chocolate used, the better this sauce will be. Valrhona is the richest flavored chocolate I've ever tasted. Vanilla adds a subtle perfume to this luxurious sauce. Pour it over ice cream or any sweet treat that could use a touch of inspiration.

Makes About 1 Cup

¼ cup sugar
½ of a vanilla bean, split lengthwise
1½ teaspoons instant espresso powder
½ cup heavy cream
3 ounces bittersweet chocolate, such as Valrhona,* chopped
1 tablespoon unsalted butter
Available at specialty food shops

1. In a small heavy saucepan, combine the sugar with ⅓ cup of water. Using the tip of a small knife, scrape the seeds from the vanilla bean into the sugar water; add the bean. Bring to a boil over high heat and boil for 3 minutes. Whisk in the espresso powder, add the heavy cream and return to a boil, stirring frequently. Remove from the heat.
2. Add the chocolate and let stand until melted, about 2 minutes. Whisk the sauce until smooth. Then reheat over high heat, whisking, just until hot, about 30 seconds. Remove from the heat

and whisk in the butter. Serve hot, warm or at room temperature. (*The sauce can be refrigerated, covered, for up to 1 week. Reheat in a saucepan or in a microwave oven just until melted and warm.*)

—*Marcia Kiesel*

• • •

COFFEE-CARDAMOM SAUCE

Assemble this sauce a day before using to allow the flavors to fully infuse the cream.

Makes About ⅔ Cup

1 cup heavy cream
3 tablespoons espresso beans, lightly crushed
Seeds of 1 cardamom pod, crushed
3 tablespoons sugar
½ teaspoon vanilla extract

1. In a small saucepan, combine the cream, espresso beans, cardamom seeds and sugar. Bring to a simmer over moderate heat to dissolve the sugar. Pour the cream into a nonreactive container, let cool, then cover and refrigerate overnight.
2. In a small saucepan, warm the sauce over moderate heat. Strain through a fine sieve and return to the saucepan. Cook the sauce over low heat, whisking often and removing the pan from the heat if the sauce boils up, until reduced by one-third, about 3 minutes. Stir in the vanilla. Serve hot or warm.

—*Marcia Kiesel*

• • •

MANGO SAUCE

Serve this fruit sauce as an accompaniment to the Coconut Cream Custard (p. 255) or with vanilla ice cream, pound cake or other plain cake.

Makes About ¾ Cup

1 medium mango, peeled and seeded (about 1 cup pulp)
2 tablespoons sugar
2 tablespoons rum
2 teaspoons lime juice

Combine all the ingredients in a food processor and puree until smooth. Transfer to a bowl, cover and refrigerate until serving time.

—*Eleanor Levy, Yuca, Coral Gables, Florida*

• • •

PRESSURE-COOKER CHICKEN STOCK

It is best to make this stock a day ahead so that you can refrigerate it overnight and skim off the congealed fat. A young broiler chicken will produce a rich stock, but for optimum flavor use half of a five-pound stewing hen.

Makes About 2 Quarts

1 chicken or half of a stewing hen (about 2½ pounds), cut into 6 pieces and skinned
1 large onion, coarsely chopped
1 large leek, green part only, coarsely chopped
3 large celery ribs, each cut into 4 chunks

2 large carrots, each cut into 4
    chunks
1 large parsnip, cut into 4 chunks
6 parsley or dill sprigs
1 teaspoon thyme
2 bay leaves
½ of a lemon, thinly sliced
¼ teaspoon whole black peppercorns
Salt

1. Place all the ingredients in a pressure cooker. Add enough water to reach the maximum fill line indicated by the manufacturer. Lock the lid in place and bring to high (15 pounds) pressure over high heat. Reduce the heat to maintain high pressure and cook for 30 minutes.

2. If time permits, let the pressure drop naturally. Alternatively, quick-release the pressure according to the manufacturer's instructions, or set the pot under cold running water until all pressure is released. Remove the lid, tilting it away from you to allow any excess steam to escape .

3. Let the stock cool slightly before straining it, then refrigerate the stock overnight. Remove the congealed fat from the surface before using. (The stock can be refrigerated for up to 4 days or frozen for up to 4 months.)

—Lorna Sass

• • •

MICROWAVE BEEF BROTH

Makes About 1 Quart

2 pounds veal bones, cut into 2-inch
    pieces
½ pound beef stew meat, cut into
    2-inch cubes
1 carrot, diced
1 celery rib, peeled and diced
1 leek—cleaned, trimmed and diced

In a 5-quart microwaveable casserole or a large microwaveable mixing bowl, combine all the ingredients with 1 quart of water. Cover with microwave plastic wrap and cook on High, or full, power for 30 minutes. Prick the plastic to release the steam. Strain the stock through a fine-mesh sieve; discard the solids.

—Barbara Kafka

• • •

MICROWAVE COURT BOUILLON

Makes About 1 Quart

1 leek, green portion only, cut into
    1-inch pieces
¼ teaspoon thyme
¼ teaspoon tarragon
½ bay leaf
⅛ teaspoon sage
2 carrots, finely chopped
1 celery rib, peeled and finely
    chopped
1 small onion, finely chopped
2 shallots, finely chopped
1 garlic clove, smashed and peeled
¾ teaspoon salt

In a double layer of cheesecloth, combine the leek, thyme, tarragon, bay leaf and sage. Tie securely to form a bundle and place in a 2½-quart soufflé dish. Add the vegetables, garlic, salt and 4 cups of water. Cover tightly with microwave plastic wrap and cook on High, or full, power for 10 minutes. Prick the plastic to release the steam. Uncover and strain the broth through a fine-mesh sieve, pressing on the solids with a spoon; discard the solids.

—Barbara Kafka

• • •

MICROWAVE FISH STOCK

Makes About 1 Quart

2½ pounds fish bones and heads,
    such as cod, well rinsed
1½ cups dry white wine
1 large onion, cut into chunks
1 carrot, sliced

In a 4½-quart microwaveable casserole or a large microwaveable mixing bowl, combine the fish bones, wine, onion, carrot and 3½ cups water. Cover with microwave plastic wrap and cook on High, or full power for 30 minutes. Prick the plastic to release the steam. Strain the broth through a fine-mesh sieve; discard the bones and vegetables.

—Barbara Kafka

• • •

INDEX

CONTRIBUTORS

Ann Chantal Altman is a food writer, chef and cooking teacher.

Jean Anderson is a food/travel writer and the author of numerous cookbooks, including *The Food of Portugal* (Morrow), *The Doubleday Cookbook* (with Elaine Hanna) and *Jean Anderson's Sin-Free Desserts* (Doubleday). She is currently working on a cookbook of "new" German cooking.

Lee Bailey is a designer, the author of the "Entertaining with Lee Bailey" column in *Food & Wine*, and the author of numerous cookbooks, including the recent *Soup Meals* (Clarkson Potter).

Sandrino Benitez is executive chef at Il Tulipano in North Miami, Florida.

Mark Bittman is a food writer and teacher.

Philippe Boulot is chef at Mark's Restaurant in New York City.

Edward Brown is chef at Tropica in New York City.

Linda Burum is a food writer and the author of a number of cookbooks, including *Brownies* (Scribners), *Asian Pasta* (Aris), *Frozen Delights* (Scribners) and the forthcoming *Guide to Ethnic Restaurants and Food* (HarperCollins).

Kathy Casey is a food writer, chef and the owner of a restaurant consulting firm called Kazzy Creative Restaurant Concepts.

Bob Chambers is a New York-based chef and food stylist.

Susan Costner is the editor of *Tables* magazine (for Beringer Vineyard) and the author of *Susan Costner's Great Sandwiches* (Crown).

Peggy Cullen is a baker and food writer.

Ariane Daguin is the owner of D'Artagnan, manufacturers of duck and game charcuterie and foie gras.

Peter Deehan is chef at Mauna Lani hotel in Hawaii.

Robert Del Grande is chef/owner of Cafe Annie in Houston.

Linda Drachman is Cook-in-Residence at the Strawbridge & Clothier Food Hall in Philadelphia and the co-author of *Great Grains* (Simon and Schuster).

Todd English is chef/owner of Olives in Charlestown, Massachusetts.

Jim Fobel is an artist and food writer and the author of six books, including *Jim Fobel's Old-Fashioned Baking Book* (Ballantine), *Jim Fobel's Diet Feasts* (Doubleday) and *Beautiful Food* (Van Nostrand Reinhold).

Larry Forgione is chef/owner of An American Place in New York City and The Beekman 1766 Tavern in Rhinebeck, New York. He is currently at work on a cookbook, as yet untitled, to be published by Morrow in late 1992.

Annie Gilbar is the author of *Recipex* (Fireside).

Joyce Goldstein is chef/owner of Square One in San Francisco, a food writer and the author of *Mediterranean Kitchen* (Morrow) and a cookbook, as yet untitled, to be published in late 1992.

Christopher Gross is chef/owner of Christopher's in Phoenix, Arizona.

Jessica B. Harris is a food writer, culinary historian and the author of *Sky Juice and Flying Fish* (Fireside), *Iron Pots and Wooden Spoon* (Atheneum), *Hot Stuff* (Atheneum) and the forthcoming *Tasting Brazil* (Atheneum).

Andrea Hellrigl is chef/owner of Palio in New York City and the author of *Cuisine of the South Tyrol*, to be published in 1993.

Greg Higgins is executive chef at the Heathman Hotel in Portland, Oregon.

Josefina Howard is executive chef and co-owner of Rosa Mexicano in New York City. She is currently compiling a Rosa Mexicano cookbook to be published by Clarkson Potter.

Filippo Il Grande is owner of Il Tulipano in North Miami, Florida.

Madhur Jaffrey is an actress, illustrator, food writer, cooking teacher and the author of *Far Eastern Cookery* (HarperCollins), *A Taste of India* (Atheneum), *World-of-the-East Vegetarian Cooking* (Knopf), *Madhur Jaffrey's Cookbook* (HarperCollins), *An Invitation to Indian Cooking* (Knopf), *Indian Cookery* (Barron's) and *The Complete Vegetarian Cookbook* (to be published in 1994 by HarperCollins).

Susan Shapiro Jaslove is a food writer and recipe developer.

Nancy Harmon Jenkins is a food writer and culinary historian. She is currently working on a book on American ethnic groups and their foods, to be published in late 1992 by Bantam.

Mireille Johnston is a food writer and the author of *Cuisine of the Sun* and *Cuisine of the Rose* (both from Random House), *French Family Feast* (Simon and Schuster). She is currently working on a cookbook titled *On the Riviera* and on two books on French regional food for the BBC.

Barbara Kafka is a food writer and the author of *Food for Friends* (HarperCollins) and *Microwave Gourmet, Microwave Gourmet Healthstyle Cookbook* and *The Opinionated Palate* (all from Morrow). She is currently working on a book called *Party Food* for Morrow.

Marcia Kiesel is Associate Director of *Food & Wine*'s test kitchen.

Christer Larsson is executive chef at Aquavit in New York City.

Richard Leach is pastry chef at Aureole in New York City.

Eleanor Levy is co-owner of Yuca in Coral Gables, Florida. She is currently working on a cookbook of Cuban cuisine with Yuca's executive chef, Douglas Rodriguez.

Susan Herrmann Loomis is a food writer and the author of *Farmhouse Cooking* and *The Great American Seafood Cookbook* (both from Workman).

Emily Luchetti is executive pastry chef for Stars Restaurant, Stars Cafe and Star Mart in San Francisco. She is also the author of *Stars Desserts* (HarperCollins).

Wayne Ludvigsen is executive chef of Ray's Boathouse in Seattle, Washington.

Sheila Lukins is food editor of *Parade Magazine* the co-author of *The New Basics Cookbook, The Silver Palate Cookbook* and *The Silver Palate Good Times Cookbook* (all from Workman).

Stephanie Lyness is a food writer and cooking teacher.
Deborah Madison is a food writer, co-chef and part owner of Café Escalera in Santa Fe, and the author of *The Savory Way* and *The Greens Cookbook* (both from Bantam).
Fitzroy Mannix is chef at Blue Waters Beach Hotel in Antigua.
Joseph Manzare is chef at 44 restaurant in New York City.
Lydie Marshall is a cooking teacher (A La Bonne Cocotte, New York City) and the author of *Cooking with Lydie Marshall* (Knopf) and the forthcoming *A Passion for Potatoes* (HarperCollins).
Elin McCoy and John Frederick Walker are contributing wines and spirits editors for *Food & Wine* and the authors of *Thinking About Wine* (Simon and Schuster).
Mark Militello is chef/owner of Mark's Place in North Miami, Florida. He is currently working on a cookbook titled *The New World Cuisine: A Chef's Tour* to be published in early 1993.
David Outerbridge is a food, wine and travel writer.
Carl Parisi is a food writer, restaurant consultant, chef and cooking teacher.
Mark Peel is chef and co-owner of Campanile in Los Angeles.
Don Pintabona is chef at TriBeCa Grill in New York City.
W. Peter Prestcott is *Food & Wine's* Entertaining & Special Projects Editor.
Stephan Pyles is chef/owner of Routh Street Cafe and Baby Routh in Dallas, and Goodfellow's and Tejas in Minneapolis.
Kevin Rathbun is executive chef of Baby Routh in Dallas.
Seppi Renggli is chef at Sea Grill and American Festival Cafe in New York city.
Michel Richard is chef/owner of Citrus in Los Angeles. He is currently working on a cookbook titled *Cooking with Michel* scheduled for publication in late 1992.
Rick Rodgers is a cooking teacher and the author of *The Turkey Cookbook* (HarperCollins) and the tentatively titled *Best-Ever Chocolate Desserts* (Contemporary). He is currently working on a cookbook for Morrow called *Ready and Waiting*.
David Rosengarten is a cooking teacher, food writer, wine columnist and the author of *Food & Wine's* "Wine & Food" column, *Red Wine with Fish* (Simon and Schuster) and the forthcoming *Crashing the Borders: How to Create the New Global Cuisine*.
Debra Rosman is a freelance writer and consultant.
Julie Sahni is a chef, consultant, cooking teacher and the author of *Moghul Microwave* (Morrow).
Lorna Sass is a cooking teacher, food writer, culinary historian and the author of *Cooking Under Pressure* (Morrow), and *To the King's Taste: Richard II's Book of Feasts and Recipes* and *Christmas Feasts from History* (both from the Metropolitan Museum of Art). She is currently working on a book tentatively titled *Meals from an Ecological Kitchen* to be published by Morrow in late 1992.
Richard Sax is a food writer and cookbook author. He is currently working on *Old-Fashioned Desserts* to be published in late 1992.
Chris Schlesinger is chef/co-owner of East Coast Grill in Cambridge, Massachusetts, and co-author (with John Willoughby) of *The Thrill of the Grill* (Morrow).
Phillip Stephen Schulz is food writer and the author of *As American as Apple Pie* (Simon and Schuster), *Cooking with Fire and Smoke* (Fireside) and *American the Beautiful Cookbook* (Collins). He is currently working on a book on holidays to be published by Simon and Schuster in 1993.
Amaryll Schwertner is chef at Sol y Luna in San Francisco.
Tracey Seaman is Recipe Tester-Developer in *Food & Wine's* test kitchen.
Nancy Silverton is pastry chef and co-owner of Campanile in Los Angeles.
Diana Sturgis is *Food & Wine's* Test Kitchen Director.
Allen Susser is chef/owner of Chef Allen's in Aventura, Florida.
Jacques Torres is pastry chef at Le Cirque in New York City.
Barbara Tropp is chef/owner of China Moon Cafe in San Francisco and the author of *The Modern Art of Chinese Cooking* (Morrow) and the forthcoming *The China Moon Cookbook* (Workman).
Alice Waters is chef/owner of Chez Panisse in Berkeley, California.
Jonathan Waxman is chef at Table 29 in Napa, California.
Patricia Wells is the restaurant critic for *The International Herald Tribune* and the author of *Simply French* (Morrow), and *Bistro Cooking*, *The Food Lover's Guide to Paris* and *The Food Lover's Guide to France* (all from Workman). She is currently working on a book titled *Trattoria Cooking* for Morrow.
Brian Whitmer is executive chef at Highlands Inn, Carmel, California.
Elizabeth Woodson is *Food & Wine's* Art Director.
Eileen Yin-Fei Lo is a cooking teacher (China Institute in America, New York City), food writer and the author of *Eileen Yin-Fei Lo's New Cantonese Cooking* (Viking), *The Dim Sum Book* (Crown) and *The Chinese Banquet Cookbook* (Crown).

We would like to thank **Le Bernardin** (New York City), **Robert Creasey** and **Havana Clipper** (Coconut Grove, Florida) for their contributions to *Food & Wine* and to this cookbook:

PHOTO CREDITS

Cover: Jerry Simpson. **Page 17:** Jerry Simpson. **Page 18:** Susan Goldman. **Pages 18-19:** Mark Thomas. **Page 20:** Tim Turner. **Page 37:** William Abranowicz. **Page 38 top:** Mark Thomas. **Page 38 bottom:** David Bishop. **Page 39:** David Bishop. **Page 40:** Judd Pilossof. **Page 73:** Jerry Simpson. **Page 74:** Bob Jacobs. **Page 75 top:** Cynthia Brown. **Page 75 bottom:** Jerry Simpson. **Page 76:** Mark Thomas. **Page 93:** Jerry Simpson. **Page 94:** Jerry Simpson. **Pages 94-95:** Tim Turner. **Page 96:** Jerry Simpson. **Page 113:** Jerry Simpson. **Pages 114-115:** Tim Turner. **Page 115:** Jerry Simpson. **Page 116:** Jerry Simpson. **Page 149:** Jerry Simpson. **Pages 150-151:** Tim Turner. **Page 151:** Mark Thomas. **Page 152:** Jerry Simpson. **Page 169:** Jerry Simpson. **Page 170:** Mark Thomas. **Page 171 top:** Bob Jacobs. **Page 171 bottom:** Mark Thomas. **Page 172:** Maria Robledo. **Page 189:** Jerry Simpson. **Pages 190-191:** Jerry Simpson. **Page 191:** Maria Robledo. **Page 192:** Jerry Simpson. **Page 209:** Elizabeth Watt. **Page 210:** Mark Thomas. **Pages 210-211:** Jerry Simpson. **Page 212:** David Bishop. **Page 249:** Elizabeth Watt. **Page 250:** Ellen Silverman. **Page 251:** Jerry Simpson. **Page 252:** David Bishop.